CHILD'S ISLAND

STEVE SIMPSON

Immediately following
CHILD'S ISLAND

THE TEENAGE AND YOUNG ADULT
SURVIVAL HANDBOOK

ISBN 978-1-944076-03-0

Cover Design: Creative Publishing Book Design

Editor: Francis Coppage

First Printing April 2017
Printed in the United States of America

10 9 8 7 6 5 4 3 2

The Birth of Child's Island

Approximately twenty-two hundred years ago the great island of New Atlantis was plagued by a disease which affected the minds of adults. Whenever the adults had children, they would beat them and cause them grief and misfortune. As the generations went on, more and more innocent children lived miserable lives. Many became suicidal and many died.

After a while, the child abuse was no longer limited to parents. Large companies opened up pornographic studios and abused children before cameras. Child prostitution was common and rape was increasing. It looked as though the situation would never stop getting worse. The children that survived into adulthood were affected themselves by the disease and then did the same to their children. This went on for a countless amount of years until finally one of the members of the last generation of children discovered a chemical that would completely stunt the growth of a child once they reached adolescence. The children would still grow intellectually, but they would remain a young teen physically. This way they would never mature and catch the disease. After administering the formula to all of the children, the organized forces of children on New Atlantis (which had originally formed to simply comfort and support each other), revolted against the authorities and destroyed the island. While New Atlantis sunk, the children sailed to another island and made it their home, calling it CHILD'S ISLAND.

Many years later an adventurer named Andy Second has left Child's Island to journey to our world. He wants to prove to the king of Childs Island that there are still adults left on the planet. He recruits teenage runaways as proof. He makes them his crew for his ship on the journey back, promising them a better life on Child's Island.

What seemed like a simple idea will turn into a fantastic and dangerous adventure for him and his teenage crew; and there is a big surprise awaiting them on Childs Island.

Chapter 1 – The Voyage

Everybody stands on the deck of the *Kid Power*, an ultra-advanced ship, which is tied to the dock, waiting for the last few orders from Steve Mason, the fifteen year old Captain of the ship.

"Now has everybody got it straight?" asks Steve, who wears a white Navy uniform, with a Captain's hat and sunglasses.

"Yes sir!" answers the teenage crew who all wear similar outfits.

"All right then, make the final check. We sail in five minutes."

The crew goes in separate directions. Some check various controls and some check minor things, such as locks on cabinets and doors.

"Sir, I would like to talk to you," says Mike as he approaches Steve, who is standing in the center of the deck.

"Yes, Mr. Red?" says Steve.

"It's about Paul being made security officer," says Mike.

"Well, what about it?" asks Steve.

"I think that you should have made me the security officer," says Mike.

Steve breathes heavily.

"I thank you for your opinion, but I think I made the right decision. Will that be all Mr. Red?" asks Steve.

Mike pauses for a few seconds. His face starts to turn red. "No! That's not all! I think that I should have been Captain of this 'thing' not you!" yells Mike.

"Is that all, Mr. Red?" asks Steve in a calm and disappointed voice.

"No! That isn't all! I think this whole thing about this Child's Island is a bunch of garbage!" shouts Mike in an even louder voice.

"Is that all, Mr. Red?" says Steve.

5

"Is that all you can say? 'Is that all Mr. Red!'," yells Mike.

"Yes. Now is that all, Mr. Red?" says Steve still clam and patient.

"Yes, for now!" yells Mike as he walks away from Steve like some kind of madman.

Steve shakes his head and pushes down the visor of his hat, covering his eyebrows and slightly touching his sunglasses.

The crew just stares at Mike until Steve gets their attention by whistling.

"All right, Paul, Betty and Robert, untie the ropes from the dock," orders Steve in a voice of authority.

The three untie the ropes that hold the *Kid Power* to the dock. The large thick ropes now hang downwards in the water.

"Bill, start the engine. The rest of you stay where you are and wait for further instructions."

Everybody does just what Steve orders. The crew stands still and watches Bill press a round button titled "start". When Bill pushes the button, a loud roar is heard and at the same time, the *Kid Power* trembles. Bill and the rest of the crew stare at Steve and wait, for the one last order that will start the journey they have been patiently waiting for.

"Let her go!" hollers Steve.

"Yes sir!" replies Bill as he pulls a lever all the way back. Only seconds after he does this the *Kid Power* starts speeding away from the dock and towards the Atlantic Ocean. The crew cheers.

After only a few hours of traveling, the shining sun is covered by clouds. Very thick and dark clouds. At the same time, the breeze which gave comfort from the sun turns into a fierce wind. Soon it starts to rain, but it doesn't just rain, it pours! And, as the waters from above start, the ocean waters get restless and rock the *Kid Power* high in the air.

6

The powerful rains soak the deck and everything on it! The strong, fierce winds blow crates filled with supplies, off the deck, over the railings and into the sea! And, during this unexpected crisis, Mike not only gets in everybody's way, but has fights with just about everybody aboard and almost starts a mutiny! But after a kick in the rear by Steve, he is temporarily tamed. Just as the crew adjusts to the bad weather, as suddenly and unexpectedly as it came, it is gone. The temperature rises to 80 degrees and there's a slight breeze which makes it perfect. The sky is as blue as the ocean and the sun shines like a giant light bulb.

"Hey Captain," yells Bill, who is at the helm.

"What seems to be the problem?" asks Steve as he walks over to Bill.

"Look for yourself," answers Bill as he hands Steve a pair of binoculars. He looks through the binoculars.

"Yes, I see what you mean. Andy come over here for a minute." Andy walks over to Steve and Bill.

"What can I do for you?" asks Andy. Andy looks to be in his teens like the rest of them, but has a much more mature demeanor than everybody else. Of course he is actually an adult well into his years.

"Bill and I have just spotted an island. Is that Child's Island?" asks Steve in an enthusiastic voice.

"No, we're getting close, but not that close. Keep on our present course though," answers Andy.

"But sir, if we keep on this course we'll head straight into the island we just spotted," says Bill.

"Is that true Andy?" asks Steve.

"Yes and no. There is a cave on the island that starts right before the shore. It is filled with water and goes completely through the island. There is enough water in it to keep us afloat. In other words, we just drive straight through the island," says Andy.

7

"I never heard of such a thing where you just drive through an island, but as always we'll do just as you say," says Steve.

"I thank you for your trust but there will be a lot of things which you will see that you never heard of before."

"Captain, I would like to talk to you," says Paul.

"What's up Paul?" asks Steve.

"We have a bit of a problem," says Paul, looking a bit worried.

"What problem is that?" asks Steve.

"The problem is Mike Red," answers Paul.

"What is he doing now?!" asks Steve.

"He thinks he is the Captain. He's up there giving orders to the crew and when he is asked to do something he gets all mad and has actually threatened the different people that asked him! He is really causing trouble. They're saying things like 'one captain is fine but two is too much'. I just thought you'd like to know," says Paul.

"Thanks for the information Paul, and keep up the good work. As for Mike, well, I'll take care of him."

Seconds after Paul leaves Steve's side, "Mr. Red, I want to talk to you," yells Steve, across the deck.

"What can I do for you?" asks Mike.

"What you can do is your own job and stop playing Captain," orders Steve in the loudest voice Mike ever heard him use.

"But, Sir, I was just trying to help," says Mike in a fearful voice.

"Then stop trying to help! Is that understood?" hollers Steve.

"Yes sir," mumbles Mike, walking away with his head down.

"Sir, we are about to enter the cave," yells Bill. Steve runs over to him.

8

"Very good. Now lower the speed to thirty knots and turn on the lights. It's going to be dark and cool in that cave," orders Steve.

They enter the cave and sure enough it is dark and cool. The lights of the *Kid Power* aren't the only thing lightning up the cave though. Parts of the walls reflect the light from the ship. Along the walls there are ledges which come out from the wall approximately five feet and are ten feet wide. There are ledges on each side of the cave, one above the other.

After about two minutes of traveling in the cave, Steve approaches Andy. "Andy, I have a few questions for you to answer."

"Oh? What are they?" asks Andy.

"Well, the first is, what's on the other side of this cave?"

"A waterfall," answers Andy. "But don't get too excited. But I know the *Kid Power* can handle it, so relax," answers Andy, smiling at Steve to reassure him.

"It's a small waterfall?" asks the confused Steve.

"No, it's actually about a thousand feet high. However, as long as we're below deck when we go over we'll be fine," he continues.

"Now you said you had another question?"

"Yeah, what are those shiny things on the walls?" asks Steve.

"They are diamonds but don't repeat what I've just told you. I don't want the crew to get excited."

"Diamonds!" yells Steve.

"Yes, diamonds and I asked you not to repeat what I said you big mouth!" snaps Andy.

"Sorry," replies Steve.

"Just don't mention it again. And don't get any funny ideas about stopping to sample some of them. We're not stopping for anything. Least of all diamonds," says Andy in his firm but low voice.

Another two minutes pass when Steve and the entire crew spot something that astonishes them all.

"Captain is that what I think it is?" asks Bill.

"Yes, it's a giant diamond. Now stop the *Kid Power* before we pass it," orders Steve.

"Yes sir," answers Bill. The ship comes to a halt. The moment it stops, Andy walks right over to Steve with a look on his face as if Steve had ordered Bill to sink the *Kid Power*.

"What did I tell you about stopping in the cave!" scolds Andy.

"Andy... do you see the size of that thing? It's huge! That thing is bigger than me!" cries the excited Steve.

"We'll be put off course," says Andy.

"How can we be put off course if we can only go one way?" says Steve.

"It's not the course," replies Andy.

"Then what is it?" asks Steve.

"It's the creatures," says Andy.

"What creatures?!" asks Steve in a panicked voice as his eyes widen.

"I didn't want to tell you but on the top ledges live these, these monsters. Their bodies are like ours for the most part. But their skin is red and hair covers them from head to toe. They have the claws of a lion and the fangs of a dog. Their eyes are white. They are about six foot five and they weigh about two hundred and fifty pounds. Needless to say they are hostile and would eat human flesh," answers Andy.

"But the diamond's on one of the middle ledges, besides we have guns. If one of them would dare to attack we would blow it clear across the cave!" says Steve.

10

"Look, do what you want, but remember it was your idea, not mine. The responsibility is yours," says the disappointed Andy, as he walks away.

"Attention everyone," yells Steve to the crew. The crew gathers around him. "I have new orders. As of now our mission is to get that diamond off the ledge and onto the ship. We're going to chop that thing up into smaller pieces. Then we'll pass the pieces from one ledge to the next, until it reaches the ship. We will need at least one reel of rope, a hook to tie at its end, some chisels, hammers, two handguns and a shot gun. Do you all understand?" asks Steve.

"Yes sir," they answer in one voice.

"Good. Now Mike, Betty and Robert get me what I asked for. Bill make sure the *Kid Power* is stable. Activate the electronic stabilizers if you have to. Move!" orders Steve. With those words, the crew scurries to get the things ordered.

"Bill, tie the hook to the rope," orders Steve.

"Done," calls Bill.

"Excellent. Now you and Andy attach the chisels and hammers to your belts like me."

After doing that Bill then puts on another belt with a holster on each side. He puts a handgun in each holster. Andy straps the shotgun to his back. Steve takes off his hat and sunglasses and puts them on the deck.

The crew surrounds Steve as he takes the end of the rope with the hook and puts it in what appears to be a very small cannon. The rest of the rope is in a pile aside the cannon. It has many dials on it and a small hole on its side as well as the hole in the front. Steve sets the dials and turns them. He then lights a match and puts the lit match in the small hole on the side of the cannon. It explodes and the hook flies into the very front of the ledge which has the diamond. The hook digs deep into the ledge. The rest of the rope is traveling straight up to the ledge.

"Nice shot!" says Bill.

"Thanks," answers Steve.

Steve tugs on the rope to see if it's secure. It is. He starts to climb the rope with Bill and Andy following behind. When the three reach their destination they go right to work. Steve and Bill start to chisel at the diamond while Andy looks on. Soon they are joined by Paul, who is on the ledge below theirs, and on the ledge below him is Judy. Robert and Mike are preparing to climb to the bottom-most ledge.

After a short time...

Steve and Bill are having quite a time chopping the diamond. As a matter of fact, they haven't chopped a piece yet.

"I don't understand this. I know diamonds are strong but still... these are the sharpest and strongest chisels I've ever used," says Steve getting impatient as well as tired.

"Maybe those are the strongest chisels you've ever used, but this is also the strongest diamond you'll ever chisel," remarks Andy.

"What do you mean by that?" asks Steve who has just about had it with the diamond.

"I already tried to chop the diamond into smaller pieces the first time I traveled this route. I even used the power drill. It's just too strong to cut and too big to take without cutting it," says Andy.

"Why didn't you tell me that in the first place!" yells Steve.

"Because you wouldn't have listened to me anyway. You had to find out for yourself," answers Andy.

Before another word can be said, a creature fitting Andy's description perfectly jumps down from the ledge above. It lands

12

on top of Steve and both fall to the ground wrestling. It is very strong and is beating Steve easily, but when the two get back on their feet Steve starts to throw punches. Being very primitive, the creature does not understand what Steve is doing and just stands there while Steve punches away. His punches are very strong and after several good blows to the creature it gets dizzy and falls down. Seconds after it falls Bill shoots it with the shotgun, killing it instantly.

Steve stares at the shotgun in Bill's hands. He then looks at Bill as if he wants to hug him.

"Let's get the hell out of here!" says Steve.

"I hate to say I told you so, but I told you so," says Andy.

But getting away isn't that easy. Two more creatures appear at the top ledge and are about to jump when Steve, spotting them, grabs the shotgun and fires it five times. Both the creatures are hit and fall into the water.

"What the hell is going on up there?" yells Paul.

"Don't worry about us. Get back to the ship and be ready to leave," hollers Steve.

The three shipmates spot more creatures. All three are armed and fire. The creatures are shot and fall into the water. This soon becomes routine. The more creatures they shoot, the more appear. The three patiently stand there, shooting, reloading and shooting again. Luckily for them, Bill brought plenty of spare ammunition, though at this point Steve, Bill and Andy don't have time to think about it.

Meanwhile below…

Paul and Judy begin to climb back down to the *Kid Power*. Judy is on the ledge directly below Paul. As Judy is climbing down she unintentionally swings into the ledge, banging her foot against it. She lets out a loud scream.

13

"Are you okay?" asked Paul.

"Yes... I guess. I banged my foot," answers Judy as she pulls herself back up onto the ledge and sits down.

"Don't worry Judy. I'll wait until you're ready," replies Paul, as he sits back down onto his ledge.

"Thanks. Just give me a minute," says Judy.

The three at the top are still holding down the fort! As new creatures appear they shoot them, and the creatures fall off the ledges and into the water.

Judy stands up on her ledge, "Okay Paul, I'm going to start down again."

"Got ya," says Paul back to Judy.

Judy once again starts to climb down the rope to the ship. She concentrates intensely on holding the rope and trying to ignore the pain from her foot. Paul begins his climb down. Suddenly, one of the creatures, who was just shot and was falling, collides with Paul. Paul tries to yell but the creatures body is right against his face and muffles the sound. The two plunge into the water. Because Judy was concentrating so hard on her climb down she did not notice Paul or the creature falling behind her.

As for the others on the ship, they're having problems of their own. Three creatures jump onto the *Kid Power* from one of the lower ledges. Robert and Mike shoot two of them but the third jumps on top of Robert and the two begin wrestling and roll around. Mike is feeling masculine and decides he is going to throw his gun down and join the fight. Betty stands watching and wondering if she should pick up one of the guns and try to shoot the creature. She is hesitant to do so because she is afraid she might miss and shoot Mike or Robert.

While this is happening, another creature jumps onto the *Kid Power*. This one is unseen. Robert and Mike are busy fighting

14

and the creature jumped behind Betty who is busy watching the fight. This creature, unlike the others, has a weapon. He holds it in his left hand. It is a sharp object, made out of stone, about as long as a steak knife. Robert and Mike manage to throw the creature they were fighting with overboard but while they are doing this the other creature stabs Betty in the back.

When Robert sees Betty lying on the deck on her stomach with blood all over her and the creature standing above her with the weapon in his hand, he picks up his gun and shoots the creature three times in the chest. It jumps off the ship in pain. Robert throws down his gun and runs to Betty who is unconscious.

Before he can do a thing, he hears Steve's voice yelling, "Cease fire! They've stopped coming. Let's get back to the ship and get out of here!" Right after these words are said, the cave is once again silent.

The sounds of shots, screams and creatures falling into the water are no longer heard. Robert closes his eyes and lets out a big sigh of relief. Within ten minutes everyone is back on the *Kid Power* and ready to continue through the cave.

Betty is on a rolling hospital bed on the deck. Steve and Judy stand over her.

"What happened to her?" asks Steve.

"She was stabbed by one of those creatures. She was hurt pretty badly but I've cleaned and stitched up the wound. I've also given her something to make her sleep," says Judy.

"You deserve an award for sure," says Steve. "How could this have happened though?" he asks.

"Mike and Robert were busy fighting off another creature. It might not have happened if Mike hadn't thrown his gun down just to be a big shot and get into the fight," says Judy.

15

"Do you mean Mike deliberately disarmed himself?" asks the upset Steve.

"I guess so," answers Judy.

"Why that...never mind, I'll take care of him later...Where's Paul?" asks Steve.

"I don't know. He was supposed to have been climbing down right behind me. I was distracted with my foot hurting and trying not to fall. Once I got onto the deck I immediately saw Betty and went over to help," says Judy.

"He's probably below deck. I'm going to get him now. I want to see if he has any ideas on how to keep Mike confined to one place. This way, he might not get into so much trouble," says Steve leaving Judy to watch over Betty.

Steve goes below to look for Paul but he is not there. He then searches every room on the ship and even looks over the ledges for Paul using binoculars, but no matter how hard he looks, Paul cannot be found.

Soon Steve approaches Andy with the problem.

"Steve, what's taking you so long to start the ship and get us out of here?" asks Andy.

"I have to talk to you about something. We have a very serious problem," answers Steve.

"What could be wrong now?" asks Andy. "Paul is missing," says Steve in a voice of a child that just lost his teddy bear.

"Are you sure?" says Andy.

"Of course I'm sure. I have looked all over the ship and even the ledges of the cave. I just can't find him anywhere," says the upset Steve.

"Steve, I'm afraid the only conclusion is that Paul drowned," says Andy sadly.

"You don't know that for sure!" exclaims Steve.

16

"Don't you mean you don't *want* to know that for sure? Steve, be honest with yourself. The moment you found out he was missing you knew he had drowned," says Andy.

"Maybe you're right. But I feel it's my responsibility to stay here and search for him," says Steve.

"That's where you're very wrong. Your responsibility is to see that everyone here is safe. To carry out the mission which you have chosen to command. The longer we stay here, the more danger we are in. To do something as foolish as making a search party for someone who is dead and never will be found is self-destructive. Those creatures can attack again at any moment," says Andy.

Steve is taken back by Andy's strong statements. He walks over to Bill, who is at his post and gives Bill the OK.

Steve calls for everyone to come to him. They all stand around him.

"I'm sorry to tell all of you that Paul has drowned," says Steve getting choked up.

The crew gasps at what they heard. Most start to cry. Steve walks away and stands at the bow the ship. He stares at the water. Tears roll down his cheeks. Suddenly, a hand appears on his left shoulder. It's Judy's. Then another hand appears on his right shoulder. It's Bill.

"It's all my fault. I insisted we stop for the diamond," says Steve.

"Did you see any of us disagree with you Steve? Including Paul," replies Bill.

"It's all our fault, and none of our fault. The time we spent together training with Andy for this voyage I've gotten to know you and think you're one of the greatest people I know. To be honest, you're the reason I decided to definitely go on this journey," says Judy as she hugs Steve.

17

The two hug for a little while.

"Hey guys, Andy's starting at us. I think if we don't leave now he's going to give us one of his famous 'Child's Island's lectures'," whispers Bill.

The two stop embracing.

"We'll get through this together Steve," says Judy as she kisses Steve on the cheek and walks away.

"You think she likes me?" asks Steve

"Yeah, I think you've been wearing those sunglasses a little too much," answers Bill as he pats Steve on the back.

The two walk back over to the rest of the crew.

"Get us out of here," orders Steve. "Now start her up and get us moving," he continues.

Once again the *Kid Power* moves swiftly through the water. Steve approaches Andy once again.

"Andy what is that small clock on my desk for?" asks Steve.

"That clock tells us when to go below. When it rings, it means in five minutes we will go over the waterfall. You remember, the one I told you about earlier," answers Andy.

"Then I'd better go to my quarters. I want to make sure I hear it when it rings," says Steve.

"Oh, by the way Steve, Mike and Judy wanted to see you about something. They're waiting for you in your cabin."

"Good, I wanted to see Mike anyway," says Steve.

"Now there will be no violence. Is that understood," asks Andy.

"I won't touch him but I'm going to yell at him so much that the warmth of my breath will melt him!" says Steve. He walks away from Andy and goes down the stairs to his cabin.

When Steve enters his quarters he closes the door behind him. Only seconds after he starts to yell.

"What the hell was the idea of throwing your gun down so you could get into the battle between the creature and Robert? You completely disarmed yourself while you were on guard duty. Do you know that while you were playing hero Betty was seriously injured by one of those creatures and could have been killed! And what if that creature overpowered you? That means the ship would have been open for sabotage and possible destruction. Now what have you to say for yourself?" hollers Steve.

"How on Earth was I supposed to know there were more creatures aboard? And besides, what's done is done. Now what I wanted to ask you is, since Paul is gone, well I was wondering, can I replace him as security officer?" asks the foolish Mike.

"Are you out of your head?" yells Steve.

"I take it that means 'no'," says the provoking Mike.

"Mr. Red, for the first time in your life, you are damn right."

Steve turns to Judy. "What did you want?" he asks in his calm voice.

Judy is next to Mike. She has been silent the entire time. With those words, Mike pulls out a revolver from his back pocket and pushes it into Judy's side.

"Judy is my hostage!" says Mike.

"What the hell are you trying to prove?" asks Steve.

"I'm taking over the *Kid Power*. Now either you do as I say or I'll kill Judy in cold blood!" declares Mike.

"Don't be the fool that you are. Once we get to Child's Island you will be arrested by the authorities there," says Steve slowly becoming enraged.

"You're the fool, Mason. We're not going to Child's Island. We're turning back and I'm going to turn you into the authorities and hock this ship for all the money I can get," states Mike.

"If you pull that trigger, I'll tear you apart limb from limb!" yells Steve.

"You don't scare me," says Mike.

"Can't you see what you're doing to her?" says Steve, seeing Judy start to shake.

Just then, the small clock on the desk starts to buzz. Steve looks at the clock and then the door. After a few seconds the clock automatically stops buzzing. Mike and Judy don't pay attention to the clock. They think it's an alarm clock and when Judy bursts into tears Steve doesn't pay much attention to the clock either.

"I'm going to kill you!" says Steve as he approaches Mike.

Mike pushes Judy aside and points the gun at Steve. As Mike pulls the trigger, Steve kicks the gun out of his hand. The gun fires and the shot goes into the air.

Immediately after Steve kicks the gun, he gives Mike a punch in the face. Mike swings back and punches Steve in the face. The punch surprises Steve. He didn't think that Mike was that strong, but of course one lucky punch isn't going to stop Steve from destroying Mike! Steve gives Mike two more punches, this time in the stomach. But Mike returns a punch that Steve will remember in his old age. Steve now knows this is going to be a real battle. The two bravely go to war. Punches are flying! And so are Steve and Mike! Because when they're not punching each other, they're throwing each other around!

Judy is in a total panic. She stands near the two watching them throw each other around and slaughter each other with punches. She picks up a lamp from the floor and holds it as if she was going to throw it at Mike, but hesitates for fear she might hit Steve with it and then all would be lost.

Above on deck Andy is getting worried. He slowly walks over to the hatch leading to the stairs. When he finds it's locked he begins to bang on it but he gets no response.

20

"Oh no!" he mutters.

"What did you say?" says Bill who is now standing next to Andy.

Andy turns his head and stares. Bill stops smiling and his blood chills as he sees the horrified expression on Andy's face.

"What's the matter?" asks Bill in a frightened voice.

"I knew this would happen. I should have never let him go down there," Andy continues to mumble.

"What's happened?" yells Bill getting excited. Bill's yelling seems to bring Andy back to his senses.

"Bill, I don't have time to explain. Look, any minute we're going to go over a waterfall. The hatch is locked or jammed. I don't know which. All I know is that I can't open it and we don't have time to try to open it either," says Andy. Robert has come over and is standing next to Andy.

"Why doesn't Steve just open it from inside?" asks Robert.

"Because Steve is probably having it out with Mike right now and he most likely didn't hear me banging on the hatch," replies Andy.

"How do you know that Steve is fighting Mike?" asks Bill.

"Because I gave him an alarm clock that is supposed to ring when we near the falls. I'm sure the clock has run by now. The only reason I can see Steve not coming to deck to tell me it rang or to open the door would be if he were in a fight and couldn't respond to the clock or my banging. Now please no more questions. We don't have time. Find someplace secure to hold on to. And you've got to hold on tight. You've got to glue yourself to whatever you hold on to. When we go over the falls hold your breath. And whatever you do, for God's sake, don't let go. It may sound crazy but it's the only chance we have left."

"But why can't we just turn back around?" asks Robert.

"We can't turn in this cave, it's too narrow and we're already too close to the falls to turn off the engine or put it in reverse. The strong current would pull us towards it anyway. If

21

you haven't noticed, the ship has doubled its speed in the last minute. There's no way out of the situation," answers Andy.

"I think you're right. I can hear the falls now," says Bill.

"I know I'm right. Now do as I say quick!" says Andy, walking to the railing.

He sits down next to the railing and holds on tight. Robert sits next to him and does the same. Bill goes to the steering wheel and sits beside it. He knows he couldn't go to Andy and Robert because it would be too much weight on the railing.

Below, Steve's cabin is a total wreck. The two warriors have blood on their faces and their hands are badly bruised. Both have been thrown over tables, into walls and over dressers. Both of their bodies have endured countless punches, choking and cuts. Judy still holds the lamp in her hand. She continues to follow the two around, trying to get a good shot at Mike.

Mike gets a good choke hold on Steve. He holds, both hands firmly around Steve's neck both choking him and simultaneously banging his head into one of the broken tables in the quarters. If anything, it's an opportunity for Judy. Judy approaches Mike from behind and wraps the electric cord from the lamp around Mike's neck. Using her body weight she pulls back on the cord and pulls Mike off of Steve. Instantly he begins to choke. Mike grabs at the cord with both hands but Judy's grip is too tight. Mike slowly and steadily falls back against Judy losing consciousness.

Steve, still in a daze from being choked himself, springs up and throws a solid punch at Mike. Unfortunately at this moment, Mike slips downward from Judy's hold on him and Steve punches Judy in the face. Judy lets go of the lamp and cord and falls down backwards. Mike drops to the ground on his face.

22

"Thanks!" exclaims Judy lying on her back and rubbing her chin. She seems unable to stand back up.

"Sorry," says Steve as he heads towards Mike.

Mike, now on his knees, grabs Steve's legs and the two begin to wrestle and fight again. This goes on for a little longer. The two sustain even more injuries from each other.

Although the two are extremely tired from fighting, Mike seems to be getting the best of Steve. Judy attempts to choke Mike again with her bare hands. Mike throws her hands off and socks her solid in the jaw. Judy falls backwards and hits the back of her head on a broken chair on the floor. Steve grabs Mike from behind but Mike maneuvers first and puts Steve in a headlock. Steve struggles to free himself but Mike's grip is too strong. Steve's head turns red from the hold. Steve's face suddenly goes blank. Mike wonders if he has finally beat Steve but Mike's luck is about to change.

Steve's thoughts go to a different time, seven years ago. A large man is standing over Steve. The man is drunk and in a rage.

"Is this the way I taught you to tie a tie?" the man yells.

"What's the difference? It's my birthday!" says the much younger Steve, about eight years old.

"This is the difference!" yells the drunken man as he beats Steve.

Steve's thoughts now come back to today, to his present beating courtesy of Mike. Steve lets out a growl. The animal like noise is followed by a rage. Mike is caught off guard by Steve's blast of energy and rage. Steve suddenly seems to have doubled his strength as he breaks the hold Mike has on him and throws Mike a barrage of punches.

Steve's punches start to have a decent effect on Mike, while Mike's have gotten weaker and weaker. After a few more

23

run-ins it's obvious that Steve is winning this fight. As a last resort, Mike picks up one of the broken chairs from the floor and throws it at Steve. Steve ducks just before the chair hits him. The chair passes over Steve's head and smashes into the glass sliding doors of a tall bookcase directly behind Steve. A pile of glass, wood and books now lay at Steve's feet. Furiously Steve reaches back taking one of the few remaining books in the case and throws it at Mike. It hits Mike in the face and stuns him.

Taking advantage of this Steve throws a rapid fire of punches at Mike making him dizzy. Mike unexpected kicks Steve in the stomach. Steve bends over in pain. Suddenly a lamp smashes over Mike's head. Mike's eyes roll as he falls down. He lies on the floor unconscious. Judy stands behind him.

"Finally!" exclaims Judy. "You okay?" she asks Steve.

"I'll live but we've got to open the hatch now!" yells Steve, making his way up the stairs.

Judy follows right behind him. Just as Steve and Judy get to the top the ship tilts downwards as it starts over the waterfall. Steve and Judy both fall backwards down the staircase. Each hitting their heads on the stairs on their way down. They both less unconscious at the bottom of the stairs. Judy seems to wake up and lifts her head but then collapses. Her head rests on Steve's chest.

The crew above on deck is managing at first but then the bed in which Betty is strapped to begins to roll towards the front of the ship. Andy seeing this also immediately realizes that if the bed hits the front rail it will break and helpless Betty will fall into the water. Grabbing the bed in an attempt to stop it Andy is pulled along with it! Andy and Betty glide across the deck smashing through the front rail, off the *Kid Power* and into the waterfall. Andy knew this would happen to Betty if he didn't stop her, but unfortunately, he was forced to meet the same fate.

There is nothing but blackness. The crew is unconscious. Nothing but water can be seen.

Chapter 2 – Welcome to Child's Island

Steve regains consciousness and slowly opens his eyes. He is blinded by the light at first but soon regains his vision. Turning his head to see where he is, he realizes he is at the bottom of the staircase of the *Kid Power* with Judy lying on top of him. He carefully moves her off of him and stands up. Steve then leans down to wake Judy.

"Judy," he says to her. Judy responds by stretching and slowly gets up. She leans on Steve for support for a minute. She rubs her chin.

"It still hurts more than my head!" says Judy.

"Sorry," replies Steve. They both look at Mike who is slowly waking up.

"Dick," says Steve looking at Mike.

"That would be a compliment," says Judy.

Steve begins to smile because he recognizes the sounds of birds singing.

"What happened?" asks Judy.

"We went over a waterfall," answers Steve.

"Where are we?" she asks.

"I don't know. I think we're beached," answers Steve.

"Beached? Where?" asks Judy.

"I don't know but there's only one way to find out," says Steve as he holds Judy's hand and leads her up the stairs.

"What about Mike?" asks Judy.

"What about him?" says Steve.

Reaching the deck Steve yells, "We are beached! We are beached!"

Steve and Judy run onto the deck. "Did you hear me? We're on some shore," says Steve.

"I heard you Steve, but we still don't know where we are," says Judy.

"Who cares? As long as we're no longer in the water," says Steve.

27

"Steve! Over here!" yells Robert from the starboard side of the ship. Steve and Judy look and spot Robert lying with the railing on top of him.

"Get this thing off me!" he hollers. They run to help him. Steve and Judy try to lift the railing but it's too heavy for them.

"Steve, we've got to get that off him. It could crush him," says Judy. They both look around the ship and spot Bill.

Steve runs towards Bill, who is unconscious with his arm caught in the steering wheel. Steve pulls the injured boy's arm out of the wheel. Bill is now lying flat, arms to his side. Steve shakes him until he awakens.

"Am I in heaven or hell?" asks Bill getting up on his own.

"How should I know? We're beached on some island but there's no time for talking. The right rail is on top of Robert and we've got to get it off him!" says Steve, pulling Bill by the arm and hurrying him toward Robert.

Rubbing his arm Bill, Steve and Judy lift the railing off Robert and this time they're successful. Steve and Bill help the injured Robert stand.

"How do you feel?" asks Judy.

"I'll be alright if I don't do anything strenuous, like breathe!" says Robert.

"Judy take a look at him," says Steve.

"Take off your shirt," requests Judy.

"Is that a proposition?" says Robert jokingly.

"Don't get smart!" says Judy feeling his stomach.

"Well, he seems alright but make sure he doesn't eat anything for six to ten hours."

"Don't worry. The last thing I want to do is eat!" says Robert moaning from pain.

An hour later…

Everybody is standing around Steve on the deck, even Mike who is badly bruised.

"As you all know we went over a waterfall. And you must know that Andy and Betty were lost on the way over. All of you are wondering where we are, and you're also wondering why the waterfall isn't in sight? Just a giant seemingly endless orange ocean. Well… I don't know. I don't know where we are, why we're here or even what ocean this is. In other words, we're lost!" says Steve to his attentive crew.

"What do we do now?" asks Judy.

"Good question. The first thing we're going to do is repair the *Kid Power*. Not that we're going any place but I think that since it is our only shelter, we should fix it up and get it working the best we can," answers Steve.

"But what about the island we're on? We should explore it. There might be food or people on it," says Mike.

"We're not moving from this boat until it's completely repaired. And another thing Mr. Red, I was about to throw you overboard but luckily for you we went over a waterfall. For now I'll forget what happened, but when we get ourselves together again, you'll pay dearly for what you did! I'm locking up all the weapons so if you have any plans to take over again…"

"Well, I don't need you to give me orders! I mean what the kind of a Captain are you? You don't know where we are or even what ocean we're in!" says Mike.

"You can leave if you wish. No one is going to stop you!" replies Steve.

"I will, and if I find anyone, I'm alone," says Mike angrily jumping off the *Kid Power* and running into the forest, which starts a few hundred yards off shore.

"And don't come back you traitor!" hollers Steve after him.

29

"Steve, I'm not doubting your intelligence. What I'm trying to say is that we could still be in the same ocean but at a different location where the water is orange," says Bill.

"I know all about it Bill, but as far as I am concerned, we are in a different body of water since there isn't anything about an orange ocean on the maps."

"What about Child's Island?" asks Robert.

"What about it?" says Steve.

"You know what I mean, are we going to continue the mission and try to look for it, or are we going to try to go home," says Robert.

"If you can tell me how to get to Child's Island, I'll give you the command. As for home, I'm not so sure I'd want to go home. If we knew how anyway," says Steve.

"I guess you're right. Well, I think we'd better get to work on the *Kid Power*," says Robert.

"Was that an order?" asks Steve laughing.

Hours later...

"All right everybody you can stop. It's getting too dark to work anymore. And besides, we've done all we can. Robert, think she'll fly again?" says Steve.

"I don't know about flying but she'll do some fancy riding in the water."

"Steve, come over here a minute," says Bill who is at the rear of the *Kid Power* looking at the ocean with the binoculars.

Steve walks over to Bill. "I hope you didn't spot another island with diamonds and monsters again," says Steve, taking the binoculars.

He looks in the direction that Bill indicates and then all around him.

"Very interesting" says Steve.

"Steve do you remember what Andy said?" says Bill who is starting to get excited.

"I think I know what you're getting at, but doesn't that seem illogical," says Steve.

"Not at all. Andy said Child's Island is surrounded by smaller islands inhabited by natives," says Bill.

"But we were thrown off course by the waterfall," says Steve.

"How can you be so sure? We would have gone over the waterfall anyway. Maybe there was no bottom. Maybe it led to another dimension," says Bill.

"Then why didn't Andy tell me that?" says Steve.

"There were a lot of things that Andy never told you until the last minute," says Bill.

"I don't know," says Steve.

"And you won't until you explore the island. You don't know what's behind that forest area. And this does appear to be a large island. We can't tell how large because of the forest area," says Bill.

"Now you agree with Mike?" says Steve.

"Of course not. But speaking of Mike, if this is Child's Island, Mike wouldn't give the people of Child's Island such a good image of us," says Bill.

"I think you just convinced me. We'll make a search party out of the crew and explore the island first thing tomorrow morning. You'd better get some sleep. We'll have to get up early. And do me a favor and tell the crew..." but Steve is cut off by screams.

"We found it, we found it!" yells Mike as he comes charging out of the forest area and towards the *Kid Power*.

"What do you want now?" asks Steve.

"We found it, did you hear me?" says Mike as he cautiously climbs aboard.

"Yeah, I heard you. But what the hell did we find?" asks Steve.

"CHILD'S ISLAND!" yells Mike. Steve and Bill look at each other and then at Mike. Judy and Robert remain in shock.

"Child's Island," they whisper.

"That's right, Child's Island. We're on it!" Mike goes on to say.

"How do you know that?" asks Steve.

"When I left you I went into the forest..." begins Mike.

"Yes, we already know that," interrupts Steve.

"Well if you'll let me finish," says Mike.

"He's right Steve. I've never seen you like this before. Let's at least listen to what he has to say," says Robert.

"Very well, go ahead," replies Steve.

"Thank you. Now as I was saying! I went into the forest but to my surprise, it only goes on for about three miles at the most. The end of the forest area leads to a giant wall that seems to surround the entire island, except for the forest area. The wall was about five hundred feet tall and looked very thick and deep. The thing was gigantic."

"But that doesn't mean we're on Child's Island. It could be some country we never heard of or something like that," says Steve.

"Well, you tell me what country has guards on top of their wall that are CHILDREN!" says Mike.

"Child guards?" asks Steve.

"Yes. They looked like they were between twelve and fourteen, and they were carrying submachine guns that looked child size. And you could see the tops and roofs of some buildings from behind the wall. Some of the roofs were round and triangular. Now, no city has buildings that large and tall or shaped like that!" says Mike.

"Steve, if he's telling the truth we have to go to that wall and let them know we're here before they find out themselves. We wouldn't look too friendly," says Bill.

"Well, of course we wouldn't look friendly, hiding away here on their island. If we're on Child's Island," remarks Steve.

"*If?*... Mike just confirmed that," says Bill.

"Oh did he? And what if this is just some sick trick to make fools out of us. How do you expect me to trust him after all he did?" says Steve.

"If you don't believe me, you can see for yourself!" says Mike.

"I'm for that," adds Bill.

"Well, I don't care what you're for. I'm still the commander around here. Is that understood?" yells Steve.

"Yes sir. I'm sorry if I came off like I was giving orders or taking over. It's just that I thought we did all this for nothing. Now we still might be able to do what we went on this voyage for, to find Child's Island," says Bill, who has calmed down a bit.

"I can understand that, but I can't let us make a stupid mistake that might cost us our lives," says Steve.

Bill and the crew start to walk to their posts. "Hey, where's everyone going?" asks Steve.

"To our posts, sir," says Bill.

"Why go to your post when you have to get ready for a scouting expedition?" asks Steve.

"Expedition, sir?" says Bill.

"Yeah, to explore the island. You know it's best we do it now," says Steve grinning. Bill begins to smile.

"Yes sir!" says Bill. Bill, Robert, Mike and Judy cheer.

"And don't call me sir, damn it! I'm only fifteen!" yells Steve.

Soon they're on their way. Armed and equipped with high tech walkie-talkies from the *Kid Power*. Bill and Robert carry shotguns. Judy a handgun and Mike a small revolver. Steve carries a handgun like Judy's and a revolver a bit bigger than Mike's. They walk and walk. Along the way Mike gives Judy a berry from a bush but before she can put it in her mouth Steve slaps it out of her hand.

"Nice going, die of poisoning before we ever get there," says Steve giving Mike a dirty look.

Next Bill trips and falls, landing on top of his walkie-talkie. He crushes the device but is not hurt.

"Now don't leave Robert's side or I won't be able to communicate with you," says Steve, helping the embarrassed Bill stand up.

After an hour of walking...

"Three miles huh?" says Steve.

"We're almost there. I guess it was five miles. Maybe a little more," says Mike.

"Yeah, maybe a little more," says Steve sarcastically.

Mike doesn't have to tell them when they reach their destination. They hide behind a giant bush 500 yards from the wall. The wall is as big as Mike said. In front of it are many trees and bushes. The top is flat. It is fifty feet in depth and five hundred feet in height. The top has a railing so the guards are safe. There are machine guns attached to the railing every ten yards. Giant lights are attached to the railing every twenty yards. On the top walking back and forth with sub-machine guns strapped to their shoulders are children, or early adolescents in their appearances, anyway.

"Now listen, I want everyone to get as close to the wall as possible without the guards spotting you. With the help of those trees and bushes it won't be too hard. Once you get to our destinations we can let each other know with the walkie-talkies," says Steve.

"Great idea Steve," says Judy.

"All right, now everyone concentrate on where you're going to run to. Bill, don't forget to stay with Robert. Don't you two separate," says Steve.

They all give the area in front of the wall a good looking over.

"OK, have you got your destination?" asks Steve. They all nod their heads.

"Now remember, don't let those guards see you. I don't want them to know we're here yet. I want to give the place a good looking over. I feel like there's something wrong but I don't know what... now MOVE!" says Steve in a low tone of voice as he takes off himself.

Everyone scatters in different directions. After running from one tree to another and crawling from one bush to another, and almost getting spotted by a guard, Steve and his crew get to their destination. Robert and Bill end up behind some bushes about fifty yards from the wall. Judy stands behind a tree thirty-five yards from the wall. Steve is on top of a tree less than a hundred feet away. But Mike wins the prize.

Somehow, without the guards seeing him, he has positioned himself right against the wall. The guards can't see him because they're not looking straight down. Announcing his destination, Steve orders the others to give their positions. They all comply, even Mike!

"It looks like I'm smarter than all of you. I'm right up against the wall. They'll never look down!" says the proud Mike.

"Very good dumb ass. Now how do you suppose you're going to make it back to the forest without the guards seeing you? And how you can survey the wall when you are too close to it even to breathe hard is beyond me," says Steve.

At first Mike doesn't answer because he knows he's stuck. But then, he makes one of his stupid remarks to Steve. "If it weren't for me you wouldn't be here and don't call me names you..."

Before he can finish his sentence, he accidentally drops his walkie-talkie. When it hits the ground it makes a loud noise attracting the guard's attention. And then Mike blows it altogether.

"Ah shit!" he stupidly yells.

Five guards immediately rush to the railing. They don't see Mike at first but when Steve's voice is heard from the walkie-talkie which Mike dropped, they spot him. Mike looks up and sees five guards looking down at him with sub-machine guns in their hands. As he runs towards the forest the guards start to yell. Mike panics when he hears the yelling and turns around to face them and fires his gun at them. He turns back towards the forest area and continues to run. That was all he had to do.

A siren goes off and at the same time the giant lights go on. The entire area is lit up. It is as bright as day.

"Who the hell fired?" yells Steve.

His voice is heard throughout the forest. It is a waste of breath. It is too late for Steve to do anything. The battle has already begun. Mike jumps into some bushes at the edge of the forest. The guards throw long ropes down the wall. In half a minute, fifteen guards slide down the wall. Most of the guards have sub-machine guns strapped to their backs but some have nets folded up and tied to their backs. It's as if they're going to hunt some animals!

The guards wait at the wall as fifteen more guards slide down the ropes and join them. The last five appear to be officers. Their uniforms are slightly different from the others. Instead of very light, bright blue color and vinyl texture that the soldier's uniforms are, theirs are dark blue and have a velvety texture. One stands out from all the rest. His is black with many decorations. Some appear to be medals and some are insignia showing rank. The texture of his uniform is also vinyl.

The officers and soldiers move quickly with their guns and nets into the forest in different directions. The crew of the *Kid Power* is completely taken by surprise. None of them know what to do. They stay at their posts for fear of being shot if they leave them. Soon the soldiers are all over the forest.

"This is Steve! Everyone get back to the *Kid Power*. We have no chance fighting these soldiers. Repeat, everyone back to the ship!"

Bill and Robert get up from behind the bushes and start running back towards the ship when they are shot at from behind. Jumping behind another bush they take cover. The soldiers are firing at them from behind some bushes about 35 yards away. Luckily for them the area is covered with shrubs.

"Bill, those bullets are getting closer and closer. We've got to fire back!" says Robert.

"If we fire back they'll see where the shots are coming from and focus their aim only on this bush," says Bill.

"They're going to find us soon anyway. If we keep on our stomachs they won't be able to shoot us unless they stand right over us," says Robert.

"I guess you're right. You fire first. I still have to get up my nerve to shoot at other people," says Bill.

"My nerves have been ready to shoot those soldiers ever since they fired at us," says Robert slowly picking up his shotgun.

He fires three shots at the soldiers. They are not hit but are surprised and fire back. The bullets fly a foot or two over the two crew members. Robert's theory is apparently right. The soldiers have to stand up in order to successfully shoot at them, and with the fire being returned, it's not likely they'll do that.

While Bill and Robert are busy with their shootout, Steve enters the battle. He accidentally falls out of the tree he's in but before he hits the ground he grabs onto a large branch and hangs on trying to pull himself up on it. The guards at the top of the wall hear him fall. They spot him immediately and fire. The bullets miss Steve but hit the branch he's hanging on.

"Oh no!" mumbles Steve as it breaks and he falls to the ground. He gets up and sprints into the forest.

Back at the shootout...

"We're running out of bullets and time," complains Robert. Bill fires two more shots and faces him.

"What are we supposed to do?" asks Bill.

"Use the grenade Steve gave you. We can throw it at them and while they're busy dealing with the explosion we can run our butts back to the *Kid Power*!" says Robert, ever confident.

Bill takes a small bottle of fuel out of the metal box in his back pocket. He throws the bottle at the soldiers and quickly covers his head with his hands. Robert covers himself also. The bottle lands ten yards away from the bush that the soldiers are hiding behind, exploding instantly after it hits the ground. A giant ball of fire mushrooms into the air, and trees and bushes go up in flames! Bill and Robert dash from behind their hiding place and run in separate directions.

38

Seconds later the soldier's fire at them just missing Robert. Bill is not as lucky. He turns to face the guards and return their fire when he is shot in the stomach. Yelling in pain he falls to the ground dropping his shotgun. He lies silently on his stomach. Robert does not hear Bill's cries. He's too busy dodging bullets and trying to pick up speed.

In another part of the forest Judy is being pursued by soldiers. She has a good running lead but some soldiers are closing in fast. Far from her position, she is nearing the deeper part of the forest. Just as she is about to reach its depths a net falls on top of her. She falls to the ground and is trapped. Five soldiers run over to her and stand over her with their weapons.

"You weren't much of a threat," says one of the soldiers.

Judy squeezes her head through the net and bites the soldier hard in his leg. He screams and falls. "Am I a threat now?" she asks.

The other soldiers laugh at the one she bit, who is on the ground rubbing his leg.

Mike is also chased and when confronted, holds his hands up yelling, "I give up!" These soldiers throw a net over Mike. He is secured with ropes and is carried to the wall kicking and yelling.

Steve is still in the game. Constantly on his feet, he is doing a beautiful job of dodging bullets and outrunning soldiers. Passing under a tree a net falls on top of him and its weight forces him to the ground. Seconds after, three soldiers surround him, and stand over him laughing.

Steve isn't going to be captured that easily. Steve's face goes blank as it did in his office on the *Kid Power* when he fought Mike. His memories once again go back to his childhood. There's laughing in his memories. It's his father again. He's laughing at

39

Steve as he is tormenting him by putting him down and calling him names.

"You're a failure! You'll never be anything!" yells his drunken father as he finally smacks Steve in the face.

Steve comes back to this time to hear the laughter of the soldiers. Steve pulls a switchblade out from his back pocket and starts to cut through the net with it. The guards don't notice this because they're too busy joking about how easy it was to capture Steve and laughing at him. In a minute he rips a hole big enough for him to squeeze through but before he gets up, he jabs the blade into one of the soldier's legs. The man falls to the ground in pain.

Pulling a revolver from the man's holster, Steve fires it at the other two men as he gets up. The two soldiers try to draw their weapons and shoot Steve but he beats them to the draw. Steve turns suddenly to face five more oncoming soldiers, firing at them and hitting three almost point blank. He keeps firing until his gun is empty. He throws the gun towards the remaining soldiers and sprints for the safety of the forest. The two soldiers take aim with their machines guns. Steve is as good as dead.

"Wait, don't fire," yells the officer in the black uniform advancing from behind the soldiers.

"Let me have the honor," he says pulling a black handgun out of his holster. He fires and hits the running Steve in the back. Steve turns in pain to face his attacker. The officer fires again and Steve is hit in the stomach. Steve falls to the ground bleeding and unconscious.

"If he's alive, take him. If not leave him there for later and see if you can help the others," orders the commander.

Meanwhile, Robert has gotten pretty far into the forest and is getting closer and closer to the *Kid Power*. He too is being closely followed by a soldier. The soldier gains rapidly on the tiring Robert and finally fires at him hitting him in the back. Robert feels the pain of the bullet but instead of falling down he turns around to face the soldier and fires back with his shotgun. The soldier falls down and doesn't get up. Robert drops the shotgun softly and drops it to his knees. He turns and starts to crawl towards the *Kid Power*. Bill meanwhile has been unconscious. He lies in a pool of his blood.

Slowly he regains consciousness. Too weak to move his body to see around him, he depends on his hearing to help him. Footsteps and voices are heard. They get louder and louder. Slowly pulling the shotguns closer to him he takes his left hand from his head and picks the gun up about five inches from the ground. He points the gun and puts his finger on the trigger. The voices get louder as the soldiers close in. Soon they are in Bill's sight. Before the three soldiers see him Bill fires one shot at them. The bullet hits one soldier and the blast throws him to the ground. The other two men run for cover. Hiding behind a few small bushes they take aim with their sub-machine guns.

There is no need for guns anymore. Bill is so weak that he falls unconscious again. The soldiers don't know this at first but then they spot Bill's unconscious body on the ground and slowly approach him, fearing a trap. Reaching him, they realize it's not a trap and shoulder their guns. One man picks Bill up, his partner picks up the other injured soldier and carries them back toward the wall. Robert is still crawling toward the *Kid Power*. He is in a lot of pain from the wound in his back but he patiently crawls toward the boat leaving a trail of blood behind him. Steve and Bill have been shot at least twice. Judy is the only one conscious. She looks all around her to see if she spots one of her friends. Mike is still being carried in nets by the victorious soldiers toward the wall. Mike is still trying to free himself. He carries on a lot more than he

41

did when he was first captured. He apparently thought the others would correct his mistake but when he sees the bloody bodies of his shipmates he begins to panic. Robert still crawls growing weaker and more tired. Slowly and painfully he moves. He does not know if he will make it. He just keeps on crawling.

Chapter 3 – Escape

Three days after the battle, in a large hospital room in a large and complex hospital, Steve lies unconscious on a bed wearing white pants and a bandage wrapped around his stomach and back. The large room has many cabinets, some of wood, the others glass. The glass cabinets contain different drugs and instruments. There are also different machines. Some look like ones found in an operating room, the others look as though they were taken from a space ship. Steve starts tossing and turning and finally for the first time in over seventy-two hours opens his eyes.

In a few minutes his eyes adjust to the darkness of the room. He glances around the room until he figures out he's in a hospital. He stares at all the machines. Before he can draw any conclusions, the door opens. A switch is flicked and the lights temporarily blind him. The first thing he is able to see is a blonde girl, who looks around thirteen years old, in a white nurses uniform standing over him.

"Hello," she says. "I'm Nurse Bluesmith, but you can call me Leslie."

"Where am I?" asks Steve.

"You're in a hospital in the First City," she says.

Steve hesitates for a second. "That wouldn't be next to the second and the third city would it? Where am I?"

"I just told you, you are in the First City," says Leslie, wearing a big smile.

"How about you just let me know what country I'm in. Even the continent would help!" says Steve growing impatient.

"Country! Continent! You really don't know where you are. Now just calm down. Getting upset won't do your wounds any good. If it will make you feel better, you're on Child's Island," says Leslie.

Steve is taken back by what she said and remains quiet for a minute. "You're lying. I can't be on Child's Island. My ship was thrown off course!" says Steve.

"But you are. Where else could you be?" says Leslie.

"Where else could I be? ... I want to see an adult!" yells Steve,

"I am an adult. I'm twenty-seven," says Leslie.

"You expect me to believe that. How dumb do I look?" says Steve.

"You don't look dumb at all. You're just confused. How can I convince you you're on Child's Island? Hmm..."

She thinks for a minute and says, "I know how...I'll open up the window and let you see for yourself."

"I don't see how opening a window is supposed to convince me, but I'll play your game," says Steve.

Leslie walks over to the window and presses a button on the frame. Seconds after the metal sheet covering it slowly starts to open like a garage door. At the same time, the lights in the room turn off. A blinding light shines through the small crack in the window. It gets bigger and bigger until the metal sheet no longer covers the window. Steve once again is blinded by the strong sunlight but his vision returns to normal almost immediately.

The window has a view of a very large and busy street corner. There are many people walking in different directions. There are many buildings. The buildings are quite different than the ones in the "Outside World". Some are triangular, some rectangular, some are circular and some have no basic shape at all. The hospital is twenty-five stories tall. It looks like most buildings from the "Outside World". Most of the buildings appear to be relatively new. The cars are small. They resemble economy cars from "our world". The traffic lights look like they're from outer space. The blocks themselves are long and wide. The streets are very quiet. The people seem happy and content. Almost everyone is smiling and no one is rushing. Most nod their heads to one another as they pass by. It's a very friendly atmosphere for a big, busy street corner.

The size and shape of the buildings or the designs of the cars isn't what finally convinces Steve that he's on Child's Island. The one detail that stands out among the rest is that the people walking and driving by are children! They all look like they are no older than fourteen. Even the policeman on the corner, wearing a white uniform with a silver gun in his holster, looks no older than thirteen. The mother with her baby appears to be twelve. Suddenly a helicopter comes into view. It lands on the roof of one of the huge and strangely shaped buildings. It looks a bit more advanced than the ones Steve is familiar with. The helicopter door opens and out steps two boys who look like they're no older than twelve at the most. Even though he can't see the pilot or co-pilot, Steve knows that they are children too.

After staring out the window for a few minutes, Steve turns to Leslie and says "You know something…I believe you!" Just as he says that the door to the room opens. In walks a boy with black hair, who looks about Steve's age, dressed in a white doctor's uniform.

"Hi Leslie. How's our patient today?"

"Hello Bob. He's doing well. He's making jokes and asking questions. Looks like he's coming out of it," answers Leslie.

Bob walks to Steve's side. "Well sleeping beauty is this true?"

"I guess so. Who are you?" asks Steve.

"My name is Doctor Bob Goodboy, but you can call me Bob. I'm the chief surgeon of this hospital. I'm also the doctor who operated on you," says Bob putting his hand out to Steve.

"Why did you operate?" asks Steve.

"Don't you remember? You were shot in the back and in the stomach," answers Bob.

Steve thinks for a few seconds. "Now I remember. It seems like a nightmare. Those soldiers firing at us and I don't even remember how it got started. I do remember running. As I was running, I felt a terrible pain in my back. When I turned some guy in a black uniform shot at me. Then all I remember is a flash of light and something burning into my stomach. It's like I've got amnesia…"

Leslie comes to Bob's side and enters the conversation. "It's probably the anesthesia. You'll get all your memory back in a few hours."

"How long have I been asleep?" asks Steve.

"Over three days. I'm going to take the bandage off now," says Bob.

"Well I guess the technology here on Child's Island is a lot better than in the 'Outside World'," says Steve. Bob and Leslie look at each other and then back at Steve.

"What did you say?" says Bob.

"I said, the technology…" starts Steve.

"Don't you come from one of the small islands?" asks Leslie.

"What small islands? Don't you know where I come from? I was sure when you found the *Kid Power* your King would know who we are," says Steve.

"*Kid Power*? That sounds familiar," says Leslie.
"That's the name of the ship the famous Andy Second used for his journey to the legendary 'Outside World' twelve years ago," says Bob.

"Wasn't he killed though?" says Leslie.

"We never knew that for sure," answers Bob.

48

"Wait a minute you guys. Andy made it to the 'Outside World' and was taking me and the others to Child's Island to prove he made it. Unfortunately, he drowned on our way back," says Steve.

"You mean to tell us that you're from the 'Outside World' and that Andy Second made it after all?" asks Leslie.

"Yes, yes. No wonder you looked at me like I was crazy when I asked where I was. But how come your soldiers didn't get to the shore and find the *Kid Power*?" asks Steve.

"They should have investigated but with the King kidnapped and all, well, Child's Island isn't operating the way it usually does," says Bob.

"You're King's been kidnapped? By who?" questions Steve.

"Supposedly the natives from the hostile group of small islands," says Bob.

"But I thought those natives are supposed to be so primitive and you're supposed to be so advanced," says Steve.

"Tell me about it! I really think it's more of a conspiracy than a kidnapping. An inside job," says Bob.

"Who would have the power to have the King kidnapped?" asks Steve.

"General Bollings," answers Bob. "He's the head of the army of Child's Island. A man crazy for power. If the King died someone would have to take over as King and being the head of the security of Child's Island, he would be the most likely person to run," Bob continues.

"But wouldn't someone run against him?" questions Steve.

"Maybe. But he's very popular with the people of Child's Island. The only person who might have a chance at beating him would be the Commissioner of the Police. He's been around a long time and has enough power and popularity to give the General a good fight. Word has it that he, like all the other people in high positions, is too scared of General Bollings to dare go

49

against him. He is the acting King until the real King comes back or elections are held," explains Bob.

"Why are you the only person who can see through this General?" asks Steve.

"As the head of the largest hospital I get to find out more than what the newspapers say. Besides, everyone's too much in love with the General to questions his honesty. As for me, I have been a rival of his for a long time. I think I was the only one to vote against him when he ran for the position of top General," says Bob.

"Maybe you jumped to conclusions then. I mean, you just said you're prejudiced against him," says Steve.

"Look at the facts. General Bollings tells the King the natives want to meet him and sign a peace treaty. The King trusts him and goes there in a yacht accompanied by two army boats armed with machine guns and a few handfuls of soldiers. A few hours later the yacht and boats come back without the King and most of the soldiers are missing. The General tells everyone that they were ambushed and that the King was kidnapped and most of the soldiers were killed. He also tells us that the natives want jewels and minerals adding up to a few million dollars as well as a list of weapons as ransom or they'll kill the King. Isn't it funny that the natives overpowered the soldiers and didn't harm the General? If the natives were going to kidnap anyone, they would have taken both of them," explains Bob.

"That part really bothers me too," says Leslie.

"Also, they use bows, arrows and crossbows for weapons. How could they defeat the soldiers using guns and grenades?" Bob continues.

"Once again, I thought that was extremely suspicious," interjects Leslie.

"Finally, the soldiers wouldn't have allowed themselves to be ambushed. With the equipment on the King's yacht and the army boats, it's just impossible. Also, the General and the soldiers

50

wouldn't have returned without the King. They would have fought until they were killed too. They also would have called for help by radio. They would have done anything but retreat back to Child's Island. If they were real soldiers, that is. The only way for the King to have been kidnapped is if some of his 'kidnappers' were on the boats with him. And the only people on the boats were the soldiers and the General," says Bob.

"Why do you say real soldiers?" questions Steve.

"The soldiers on Child's Island are trained to fight to the death. If they were supposed to protect the King, then that's what they would do. Besides, the boats had radar and different warning systems. They knew they were under attack before the natives could get close enough to use their crossbows and spears. It's my suspicion that the 'real' soldiers were killed before the King even reached the native islands," says Bob.

"Why would the natives do all this for General Bollings?" asks Steve.

"What are they really doing? The General really did the kidnapping and killing. All the natives are doing is holding the King captive. In return, they'll get riches and enough weapons to defeat the other islands. You can bet that after the ransom is paid the King will still be killed. In other words, the ransom is really a payoff for holding and killing the King," says Bob.

"Why does the General want to become King. And how come Child's Island didn't try to rescue the King?" asks Steve.

"Simply put, the General is crazy. He also secretly owns some businesses that would become monopolies if he were King. He'd be the richest man in the world. At least ours. He also likes power and being second in command isn't enough. Oh, and as far as the rescue, the reason why there hasn't been one is because the General would be the one to order one. Don't hold your breath waiting for him to do that. You might also want to know that the soldiers who survived the 'ambush' were new enlistments. All had

51

gotten high recommendations from General Bollings when they joined the army and since I told you everything else, new soldiers aren't permitted to have responsibilities like protecting the King. They were only chosen to protect him because General Bollings was in charge of the King's protection," says Bob becoming very nervous.

"Bob you have to stop getting upset about this. I don't want you dying when we're getting married in a few weeks!" says Leslie, who has been silent up to now.

"You're really very serious about this," says Steve.

"I've never been more serious in my life. And if you are really from the 'Outside World' you better realize that you're going to be a problem for the General. You're a friend of Andy's. Andy was very close to the King and warned him about General Bollings before he left. It was a warning that should have been taken more seriously. You are in great danger. He'll kill you, you know. I suggest you lie and say you are from one of the small native islands," says Bob.

"Thanks, you're a good kid," says Steve slapping Bob on the shoulder in a playful gesture.

Bob steps back and looks at Steve in a defensive way. "Hey, I'm not hitting you. It's a friendly type of thing," says Steve trying to reassure Bob.

"It's not the slap. I mean, do you normally insult the people trying to help you?" asks Bob. Steve is baffled.

"Wait a minute," Leslie interrupts.

"Do you know that 'kid' is an insult to us?" she goes on to ask.

"Kid? Why?" asks Steve.

Bob becomes at ease with Steve's obvious innocence. "It dates back to ancient times when our ancestors were still living on New Atlantis. Aside from all of the abuse they took, 'kid' was used as a put down. The insult kind of stuck with us. It's like the worst thing you could call someone here," explains Leslie.

"Why did Andy call the ship the *Kid Power* then?" asks Steve.

Leslie and Bob laugh.

"That's kind of an inside joke between the people in my world," responds Bob.

"Not to mention a symbolic gesture on Child's Island to say the least," adds Leslie.

"Well, Andy certainly was full of inside stuff. On that note, back to..." Steve is interrupted by the door opening.

Two soldiers armed with sub-machine guns enter. Behind them is an officer dressed in a black uniform with many decorations. He has black hair, practically black eyes and is Steve's size. Behind him are two more soldiers also with guns.

The five soldiers stand near the now closed door. "Hello General Bollings. How are you today?" asks Leslie smiling as best she can.

"Never mind me. How is the prisoner? Is he ready for questioning yet?" asks the General.

"He just regained consciousness. He isn't ready for interrogation yet. His memory isn't even normal," says Bob.

"He looks alright to me," scoffs the General.

"I'm the doctor and I say he's not ready for questioning yet!" Bob begins to get upset.

"Bob, calm down. You know you've been working too hard. Maybe you need a rest," says Leslie.

"Stop speaking to me as if I were a baby! I'm perfectly alright," snaps Bob.

"And so is the prisoner. Have him ready for me in five minutes. My questioning isn't going to harm him. It's when he doesn't cooperate that's going to harm him," says General Bollings turning towards the door. He walks out and the soldiers follow him. The last two close the door.

"Bob! What's the matter with you? You keep talking to him like that and he'll start to suspect something," says Leslie.

"I don't care. I've got something. I must stop him. I don't know what, but something!"

Bob then walks over to one of the wooden cabinets and opens it. He takes out a shirt like the one he's wearing. He walks to Steve's bed and drops it on him.

"Here. It's all I have for you to wear."

"Before you put on the shirt, let me take off the bandage," says Bob.

"You're not going to tell General Bollings you're from the 'Outside World' are you?" he asks.

"Don't worry, I know how to take care of myself," says Steve.

"Do yourself a favor and do as I say. You're a threat to the General. He wants you dead," Bob warns.

The last layers of bandages are now off.

"Look as I said before don't worry about me! I've handled tougher people than General Bollings," insists Steve.

"I guess there's no point in trying to convince you. I just want to wish you good luck," says Bob in a disappointed voice.

The two shake hands. The door opens again and two soldiers enter. One of them puts handcuffs on Steve and the three walk out. This time none of the soldiers close the door. The three walk to the elevators and enter. As the door closes, Steve winks at Bob. From the expression on Bob's face it looks as though he knows what's going to happen.

"You know you just told a stranger a lot of information," says Leslie.

"I know, but there's something about him I trust," replies Bob.

Minutes later and only a few miles from the hospital Steve enters General Bollings office. He stands in front of the Generals desk.

"Sit down," says the General, as one of the soldiers removes Steve's handcuffs.

"Before we begin, I want to warn you that not cooperating with us can be harmful to your health."

"So I heard," says Steve.

Before the General can continue Steve interrupts him "Stephen James Mason, Captain of the *Kid Power*, 555-1212?"

"What was that?" asks the General.

"My name and rank, and since I don't have a serial number, I gave you my phone number," says Steve sarcastically.

"I'm going to ignore that crack but one more and you'll pay dearly!" says General Bollings.

"What island do you come from?" he asks.

"Ancient Africa," answers Steve, who is grinning slightly.

"Where is that?" asks the General.

"Mars," says the still grinning Steve.

"Mars! Look, don't try my patience. Where is Ancient Africa? I've never heard of any island like that," snaps the General.

"What kind of fool are you? I'm from the 'Outside World'!" says Steve.

"No such place exists!" yells General Bollings.

"Yes it does. I came from there with Andy on the *Kid Power*," snaps Steve.

The General is silent for a moment. "I've had enough of your lies. There is no 'Outside World'. Andy was a fool and he sank with his stupid boat years ago!" yells the angry General.

"I am telling the truth. Andy did not die," insists Steve.

"Look I saved your life. The least you can do is be truthful," states the General.

"I am! I am! And how did you save my life?" yells Steve.

"Three days ago when you were attacking Child's Island, two soldiers were about to shoot you with their weapons. But I ordered them not to fire at you and shot you myself. Now, if I had let them shoot you, why, you would be dead," says the General.

Steve is shocked at the fact that the General could be so foolish to admit he shot him.

"So you're the one who shot me? I thought your ugly face looked familiar. And you saved my life? How sweet of you, you son of a..." says Steve as he gets up and punches General Bollings in the face. The General falls backwards and falls over in the chair.

The two soldiers who were behind the General immediately attack Steve but he decks them both. The two soldiers behind him then start to wrestle with him. Steve decks them too. The five are soon rolling around punching and kicking at each other. Knee chops and the sound of men grunting fill the air. Finally Steve is decked by one of the soldiers and falls. The soldiers put handcuffs on him again and viciously begin to punch and kick him until he stops trying to fight back. The soldiers pick Steve up and hold him in front of the General. He stands with his hands cuffed behind him, and his head down.

"I told you not to fool with me!" says the General punching Steve in the stomach. He punches him again in the stomach and then in the face. Steve's head swings back from the punch. He tries to get loose from his bonds but the four soldiers are holding him too tight.

"So, you want to fight?" sneers the General as he signals his men to let Steve go.

Steve charges but is stopped short by a punch to the stomach and two more to the face. He falls face down to the floor. He struggles to get up but is kicked in the hip and back. Steve looks up at the General. The expression on his face is that of a puppy dog. The cruel General isn't impressed though, and kicks the boy in the face as hard as he can. Steve blacks out.

"Take him out of here!" orders Bollings. "Take him to the prison where he belongs!" screams the angry General.

"This man acts like a rebellious teenager!" exclaims the General.

The soldiers carry Steve's battered body out of the office.

Hours later inside a prison cell Steve opens his eyes to find himself in a different place. He starts to gain full consciousness but his vision is still blurry. He hears a voice say, "Hello, there." It is familiar. Soon he is fully conscious and sees Judy and Bill standing over him.

"Where am I?" says Steve in a weak voice.

"You are on Child's Island my friend," says Bill.

"That's right, for a second when I saw you two standing there I thought it was a dream," replies Steve.

"Well, if it's a dream, we're all having it together," says Bill.

"I cleaned your cuts with water but the bruises will just have to heal. There's nothing I can do about them," says Judy.

Steve gets up slowly and sees Mike sitting at the table staring at the three.

"You got here a few hours ago. You've been sleeping until now," says Bill.

"I've been doing that a lot lately," says Steve.

"I got here yesterday afternoon. Judy says she got here the day before me and Mike's been here for almost three days," says Bill.

"I was shot in the stomach but now I don't even have a scar. The medical technology here on Child's Island is amazing. I thought I was dead," Bill continues.

"What about you Mike?" asks Steve.

"I wasn't shot or anything but I, unlike Judy and Bill, did speak to General Bollings three days ago. All he wanted to know was who our leader was. And I told him you are the Captain," states Mike.

"No wonder he didn't question the two of them, he was waiting for me!" says Steve getting angry.

57

"Well, that's not important now. The important thing is that you're alive. We thought you were dead," says Judy.

"I guess I came pretty close to being dead too. Hey wait a minute, I knew something was wrong...where's Robert?" asks Steve.

"We don't know. He was heading back to the *Kid Power* with me when I was shot. Maybe he made it," says Bill.

"Or maybe he was shot," says Steve.

"If he was, he might be joining us soon," says Judy.

"Yeah, let's hope so," says Steve, who wears a disappointed look.

The four exchange their experiences from the past three days. "Do you mean this General Bollings who is trying to take over Child's Island is the same guy that shot you? You should be honored!" says Bill, laughing.

"Honored my ass! The man's a dangerous idiot!" says Steve.

"Well, he can't be a total idiot. After all, that plan of his that you told me sounds pretty solid. Although he might have his stupid points, like telling you to be grateful for his saving your life by shooting you in cold blood and expecting you to just sit there. I still can't believe you decked him!" says Bill.

"Well, I can. And I would have put his soldiers in traction if they hadn't put those cuffs on me," says Steve.

"You've got to give yourself some credit. After all, the anesthesia you were given first wore off about an hour ago," says Judy.

"If there was only a way we could help them," says Steve.

"Help them! Are you kidding? After what they did to us!" says Mike.

"They couldn't help it, with General Bollings leading them and all. Besides we're the ones who shot first and..."

58

Steve is interrupted by the opening of the solid steel door which bounds the prisoners to their cell. Two soldiers run in and aim their guns at the four. Two others enter the cell. These two are carrying a tray with a large pot and some bowls and a pitcher. There's also a loaf of bread and some spoons and a knife. The soldiers put the trays on the table at the center of the cell. The other soldiers put what appears to be two candle holders on the table. They then put two long and thick candles in the holders and take lighters from their pockets and light the candles. The soldiers walk to the door.

"What did we do to deserve a candle lit dinner" says Steve sarcastically.

"Nothing at all. You don't deserve a dinner. The electrical system is going to be worked on and all the power will be shut off. You'll need them for light. Don't burn yourselves though," snaps one soldier.

"Thanks a lot kid," says Steve. The soldier just stares at Steve, then slams and locks the door.

"What was that about?" asks Bill.

"I know, you'd think you called him a dick or something," asks Judy.

"I'll tell you later," says Steve laughing.

The four start their meal. "This is the best vegetable soup I've ever eaten," says Bill.

The lights of the cell go off. The candlelight is pretty powerful.

"This sucks. We've got to split this joint," says Bill.

"Sure, we'll just walk through the walls," says Mike.

"You go ahead and joke but I'm sure after a few years of this your humor will disappear," replies Bill.

"Years?" says Mike.

"Very good, you can hear! What do think, they're going to let us go? Especially with that conspiracy Steve told us about," says Bill.

"But we'd need lasers to get out of here," says Judy.

Steve sits quiet. He drifts into his past. He is a little boy again. "You'll stay here until I say you leave!" comes the voice as the closet door slams shut. Steve sits against the wall of the closet. It's dark. He can't even see his hand in front of him. Hours go by. Then more hours follow.

"I'll never let this happen to me again. Never!" the young Steve thinks to himself as he panics and bangs the walls with his hands. Steve's thoughts return to his present.

"We don't need lasers," says Steve, who has been silent ever since the guards left.

"I've been looking around this cell and I think it might work. We take one of those beds and put everything that we can find that's flammable on top of it. Then we move it in front of the door. The guards come every half hour to check up on us. So if we light the bed with the candles about five minutes before they come, when they open the door they'll have a surprise waiting for them. If my hunch is right, the bed should be in flames and when they open the door the fire will be sucked outside right into the guards. That's when we make out move," says Steve.

"What if there are more guards in the hall?" asks Bill.

"I doubt it. When they opened the door before to give us our meal, I noticed there were no other guards outside. And besides, we would be able to hear them."

Discussion breaks out among the people in the cell. Some are for and some are against the plan for fear the guards might not come to check on them and that they would burn up with the cell. Suddenly Bill raises his voice.

"Wait, the only way we can settle this argument is to vote. All in favor of Steve's plan raise their hands."

Bill and Judy raise their hands.

"I guess that's it," says Bill.

"Well, Mike. What's it going to be? Are you going to try it with us or are you going to stay here and be all alone when they put you in front of the firing squad?" says Steve.

"All right. I'll do as you say," replies Mike.

"Good. I want to move one of those beds in front of the door. Judy, Mike, break apart the wooden chair into pieces and then take the sheets and pillows from the other beds."

With everyone helping the bed is soon covered with wood and cloth.

"They ought to be coming soon so I'm going to light the bed now," says Steve getting a candle from the table.

He throws the candle on the bed and in a minute the bed and everything on it is up in flames. The four stand in the rear of the cell. Soon the cell is covered with smoke. The four drop to the floor to avoid breathing in all the smoke. They don't want to pass out before the guards open the cell door. The smoke gets worse and worse and soon all are choking and their eyes watering.

"So much for your plans, genius! The smoke is killing me!" comments Mike as he chokes.

"Shut up or you won't have to worry about the smoke killing you!" yells Bill as he too coughs and gags.

"I'm sorry guys. I guess I really did it this time. I thought I could do it without Andy," says Steve whose tears seem to come not only from smoke.

Steve has his hands between his knees. His head is down and he looks defeated. The soldiers don't seem to be coming. Things look hopeless. If only they could see through the door!

Two guards stand talking. "Do you smell anything?" asks one.

"Yeah, what is it?" asks the other. They draw their revolvers and begin to open the door.

61

As it opens an explosion of flames burst out of the cell and into the hall. The guards drop their guns and fall to their floor rolling over and over.

"Come on, now's our chance!" yells Steve as he gets up and runs towards the door.

He jumps over the burning bed and lands on top of one of the guards. With one punch the man is unconscious. Bill does the same and decks the other guard. Mike jumps and lands on his head.

"Figures," says Steve. He looks back and calls

"Come on Judy," but the girl just stands in front of the flames. She has a look of terror on her face.

"I can't do it!" she cries. Judy now drifts to the past.

She remembers a time when she was approximately four years old. Her father, a very tall man, stands over her. He holds a cigarette lighter. He keeps lighting it and bringing it towards her. Judy screams and cries begging him to stop.

"Scared? You should have thought of that before you disobeyed me!" yells the lunatic of a man who dared pose himself as a 'father'.

Judy continues to scream hoping someone will hear and help her. She screams loud enough for perhaps the saints and angels of Heaven to even hear her.

"Judy what's the deal? Come on!" yells Steve.

"You don't understand. My father used to scare me saying he's going to burn me for being bad and hold his lighter to me. I'm a runaway, remember!" says Judy.

"In a few more seconds..." starts Bill.

"I know!" interrupts Steve.

"Judy, please, we need you. Jump! Don't think, just jump!" yells Steve.

62

Judy closes her eyes and finally leaps over the flames. Because of her hesitation and perhaps her eyes being closed her effort isn't strong enough and she begins to fall down onto the bed. Steve sees this and grabs her arm and with a mighty pull, pulls her over the flames and into his arms.

"Thank you! Thank..." exclaims Judy hugging Steve and finally giving him a very affectionate kiss on the lips. Steve backs off and blushes severely.

"How cute. I'm afraid of fire and you're afraid of an intimate kiss. I guess we're even!" teases Judy.

Steve continues to blush with his mouth open.

"Oh Romeo, the escape," cracks Bill.

"Got it. Let's move!" replies Steve.

Steve runs down the hall to a large steel door. Mike and Judy follow behind. Bill takes the guard's gun and keys and runs after them. After several long seconds they finally get the right key to open the door. Behind the door is a stairway leading down to still another door.

"Wait," starts Steve. "I don't like this at all. Something's wrong. That Doctor Goodboy I told you about. He kept telling me that General Bollings wanted me dead. I think I should have paid more attention to him. This is a set up. Notice that the lights are on in the hall. Only our cell has no power. They wanted us to use the candles to start a fire and make our escape. I bet you behind that door there's a few of the General's men waiting for us," finishes Steve.

"Well, well. We go this far and now you are telling me that there's a trap ahead? Don't give me that, you're just scared. I always knew your courage was just a big act!" sneers Mike.

"It's not courage or fear that's telling me not to go down there, it's common sense!" answers Steve.

"Give me a gun. I'm going straight out. I'm not going to wait for you guys. You'll just have to catch up," says Mike.

Bill pushes the gun into Mike's stomach. He takes it and holds it in his right hand. Mike slowly walks down the steps. The three watch him as he carefully takes each step. Mike begins to look worried. Sweat is running down his face. He soon gets to the bottom step. The three at the top are perfectly still. The only thing that can be heard is their four hearts beating. Mike cautiously tries the knob. He turns to face his friends.

"It's locked," he says in a whisper.

"Don't just stand there. Come back up. We'll try the other door at the other end of the hall!" says Steve.

Mike slowly starts back up the stairs. As he walks up the steps his "courage" returns and he teases his fellow escapees.

"You know you're all a bunch of cowards. You could have thrown me the keys. No, you're too much of a coward to do that. I might have been able to unlock the door but no way. And you, you call yourself a commander?" he says pointing to Steve.

"Why I was right in the first place. I should have been the captain we would have never lost Andy to that waterfall. And I'm the only…"

Before he can finish his foolishness, the door at the bottom of the stairs suddenly bursts open. Three soldiers with machine guns rush into the small area at the bottom of the stairs.

"Oh no!" yells Mike as the soldiers take aim and without hesitation open fire on him. He screams and cries from pain as he falls down the steps into the fire of the guns. Steve quickly closes the large steel door.

"NO!" yells Judy starting to cry.

Steve, Judy and Bill stare at each other and then the door.

"You made us crazy Mike, but I never would have really wanted this for you. You had a messed up childhood like the rest of us," says Steve who directs his voice at the door.

Judy puts her head against Steve's.

"They're coming up the stairs!" exclaims Bill.

Steve and Bill press their bodies against the heavy door, trying to think of another way out of their situation. The soldiers are trying to open the door but it doesn't move. Steve leaves Bill and Judy to hold the door closed and runs down the hall. He stops short when he gets to a pair of fire extinguishers. Both are about three feet tall. One is yellow, the other white. He puts the yellow one under his arm and carries it back to Bill and Judy. He tries to run with it but it's too heavy.

Bill steps aside and Steve puts the fire extinguisher up against the door. Half of it presses against the door and the other half presses against the wall. It forms a latch. "You and Judy keep pushing it against it with all your might," he orders.

He then picks up the keys and runs back down the hall. He stops at the first cell door he comes to. He unlocks it and opens it. Seconds after he does this two hefty "boys" exit the cell.

"I can't believe you're helping me get out of here. When we get on the outside you're going to get a cut from my next job," says one.

"Here, take these keys. Go let everyone out and we'll bust out of here together," orders Steve and the two prisoners obey him quickly.

Bill and Judy are staring at Steve as if he's crazy. Judy doesn't say anything but Bill whispers "Is he crazy?"

While the prisoners are freeing themselves Steve uses the other fire extinguisher and sprays it at the burning cell he was in, creating a tremendous amount of smoke. Soon the hall is filled with smoke and about fifteen criminals who think they're escaping. Steve hands the extinguisher to one of the prisoners.

"Here, the guards will love you when you blast them with it," he says.

He runs back to Bill and Judy.

"Don't worry about those guys coming with us. They're just going to be a decoy to help us out of here."

Their conversation is interrupted by the sound of footsteps coming up the stairs.

"OK the three of us are going to push against this extinguisher as hard as we can. When I say three we stop and run down the hall. Be careful. The smoke is making it darker and darker," orders Steve.

The three begin to push, the prisoners just watch.

"I can't keep this up much longer. I've got blisters all over my hands!" says Bill. Judy is silent saving her strength for pushing.

It is almost impossible to see in the smoke filled hall. "One…" Steve begins. At the same time one of the soldiers on the other side of the door is also counting. When Steve reaches three, he and his friends make their run for freedom taking the fire extinguisher with them.

When the soldiers get to three they push in the door. Only no one is holding it and they all fall to the ground on top of one another. When they get up they are confronted by the fifteen escaping prisoners. The prisoners attack the soldiers and take half of them back down to the floor. One of the prisoners sprays the fire extinguisher at them. Because of the thick black smoke, the soldiers can't see who they're fighting.

While the soldiers are battling the prisoners, they are unaware that Steve, Bill and Judy are making their way across the dark smoky hall. The three finally reach the large steel door. Steve tries to turn the door knob.

"It doesn't turn. Well, I guess they didn't rig this one," says Steve.

"Now what? Without the keys we have no chance of getting through this door," says Bill.

"Quick, give me the fire extinguisher," says Steve. Bill complies.

Steve hits the door knob with the fire extinguisher. The knob falls off. Steve then puts his index finger inside the hole that the door knob left when it fell off and moves it around the inside of the hole. In a few seconds the door opens. Behind the door is a staircase going down to another door.

"It's just like the one on the other side of the hall," comments Bill.

Steve takes the fire extinguisher and throws it down the stairs. It hits the door knob of that door which falls off. Steve and crew of two rush down the steps. Steve puts his finger through the hole he has just created in the door and it makes a clicking sound. He then puts his whole hand in the hole and opens the door. It leads to a parking lot.

"Ah, sunlight. It's been so long," says Bill acting childish. The three cover their eyes against the glare.
"Come on. Let's get out of this hell hole!" yells Steve as he pulls Bill by the arm.
The three "fugitives" run into the parking lot, and are soon out of sight.

Chapter 4 – The Rescue

A few hours after the heroic escape, inside the office of the Commissioner of Child's Island police:

The Commissioner wears an all white uniform with a tie and a mirrored tie clip, looking no older than a fourteen year old boy, sits behind his large desk unaware of who is about to enter. Suddenly, as he is about to pick up his phone, the door to his office swings open. In walks General Bollings and a couple of his soldiers. One of the soldiers closes the door as he walks in. The Commissioner and the General begin talking right away.

"How dare you enter my office without waiting for my secretary to buzz me first!" says the Commissioner.

"Commissioner White, I have no time to wait for you to be 'buzzed'. You left a message at my office that you wanted to see me. Now what do you want?" says General Bollings.

"You know damn well what I want! Why did you help those prisoners escape?" shouts the Commissioner.

"You don't know what you're talking about," answers the General.

"Don't give me that garbage! You went too far this time General. That prison is my territory, not yours! Prisons are police business and have nothing to do with the military," states the Commissioner.

"Tell me something I don't know!" says General Bollings.

"Don't get sarcastic with me. I want to know why you replaced my police guards with soldiers!" says the angry Commissioner.

"I only replaced a few," says Bollings.

"I don't care how many you replaced. You did this behind my back! You know you can't enter police affairs without my consent. And isn't it funny that the guards you relieved just happen to be in charge of guarding the part of the prison that the prisoners were kept," says Commissioner White.

71

"What are you getting at?" asks General Bollings.

"I said it before. You helped those prisoners escape. You replaced the guards who were in charge of them with your own men. Then you shut off the power in their cell and told your soldiers to say there was a repair job being done and that the prisoners had to use candlelight. The rest was up to them," says Commissioner White.

"Sounds like you're writing a novel Commissioner," interrupts the General.

"You somehow knew that they would use the fire from the candles to attack the guards when they made their rounds and of course you left that part to my men. You went out of your way to make certain that it would be police guards who made the inspection. Even if it meant getting guards from the other side of the prison and therefore causing the inspection to be ten minutes late. But you didn't care, as long as it was *my* men who were burned in the escape and not yours."

"You have no proof and I have no time."

"Why did you do it? Money? Power? What are they going to give you for helping them escape? Or are they just good friends?" rages the Commissioner.

"Don't be an idiot. My men didn't just stand there and watch them escape! They tried to stop them. They even shot and killed one of them. They would have killed all of them but the prisoners figured out that it was a set-up and used my plan to kill them for their escape!" replies the General.

"What are you talking about?" asks Commissioner White.

"Can't you figure it out? I didn't want those prisoners to escape. I wanted them dead! Sure, I gave them the opportunity to escape but my men were ready and waiting for them at both exits of the hall. They blocked up one of the doors so my men couldn't get through," says General Bollings.

"And your men couldn't figure out that they had to run to the other exit?" asks Commissioner White.

"Naturally my men called dispatch for more soldiers to help them. Unfortunately, my army dispatch works the same way as yours does. When someone calls in for a backup, it sends the soldiers who are nearest to the spot needed. When the soldiers called in for more men, the computer ordered the soldiers guarding the other exit to assist. When they finally got through, they were attacked by the other prisoners on the floor. Apparently the escaping prisoners let the others out and used them as decoy."

"Are you sure *you're* not writing a novel now?" interrupts Commissioner White.

"While my soldiers were fighting off the other prisoners, the escaping prisoners got out the other exit, which of course, was no longer guarded. It must have been the Captain Mason who figure out it was a set-up and did all of that to my soldiers. I knew I shouldn't have let him in with the others. He's too smart. He acts like a teenager but he's smart. Don't worry, I'll get him. Him and the rest of his crew," says the General.

The Commissioner is silent for a few seconds. He then begins to laugh.

"What's so funny?" asks the angry General.

"You. I don't know why I was so afraid of you. I don't know what you have against those new, or should I say, ex-prisoners but that 'Captain' Mason sure as hell made you the fool of the year!" says Commissioner White, laughing even harder.

"Go ahead, laugh, but I assure you, you'll regret this!" says the angry, insulted General.

"Is that a threat?" asks the Commissioner.

"Call it what you want," replies Bollings.

"I'll call it a threat, but I should be making the threats. After all, it's you who jeopardized the security of the Island as well as the lives of my guards by allowing those prisoners to escape. Exactly why you tried to kill them I don't know but when my men find and recapture them, I'll certainly call for an investigation," says White.

"When your men capture them? I'm having my soldiers form a search party and capture them," states Bollings.

"Oh no, you're not! The prisoners are somewhere on the island and that means it is the police department's business to find them," yells Commissioner White.

"Perhaps so, but they are aliens who attacked us from another island. Therefore, it is military business to find and capture them," replies the General.

"Very well, then both the police and the army will look for them. And may the best force win. But General, be assured that if capture isn't complete within thirty-six hours I will take this matter to the royal court. They will then figure out what punishment to give for this 'set up' as you call it," informs the Commissioner.

"You don't have to worry about the prisoners being captured within thirty-six hours if my men are on the job Commissioner. And besides, what charges are you going to bring against me? I can easily say that it was the army who captured the prisoners and that I thought it was they who should have guarded them. As for the power going off, well I'll get around that somehow. As to me giving them candles, by the law they are supposed to be provided with some light. And your prisons are supposed to be escape proof, fire or no fire. So it's your word against mine," retorts General Bollings.

"So you think, but I have a lot more information than you believe. I have you under police surveillance," says Commissioner White.

"Why you! How dare you!" sputters the angry General.

"I know exactly what I'm dealing with. A power hungry man who is too big for his britches. Just who do you think you are, the King? Speaking of the King, when the ransom is paid and he is back on his throne, you can rest assured I'll inform him of everything," says the Commissioner.

74

"You do that Commissioner, but keep in mind that no one speaks to me like that, nobody!" cries the red faced General as he turns and strides through the door.

He storms through the outer office. The soldiers are right behind him. The young girl sits at her desk and stares at them. The three military men quickly move down the hall of the police building and stop at an elevator door.

"He knows. He knows that we're responsible for the King's kidnapping," says one of the soldiers.

"He doesn't know a thing about us being tied in with the King's kidnapping. I thought for a second he knew about our conspiracy but when he said he was going to tell the King about all the terrible things I'm doing he gave himself away," says the General.

"Can he cause any trouble with what he does know?" asks the other solider.

"Probably, and that's why he is going to commit suicide," says the General as he pushes one of the five round buttons on the wall next to the elevator door. The button lights up.

"How do you know he's going to do that?" asks one of the soldiers.

"Because I'm going to help him," answers General Bollings.

"I think I get it. You're going to kill the Commissioner and make it look like suicide, right?" says the soldier to his right.

"Wrong, I'm not going to kill him. You are," answers Bollings.

"Us? Why?" asks the soldier on the right.

"Because, as head of the military I have no time to attend to these menial things," answers Bollings.

"What's the payoff?" asks the soldier on his left.

"There is none," replies Bollings.

75

The elevator doors open. The three enter and the General pushes one of the many buttons on the box attached to the panel next to the door.

Meanwhile, in a large and crowded parking lot in the back of the hospital that Steve had been in, Dr. Goodboy nears his small white car. He slowly opens the door and gets in. Almost immediately after he closes the door he pushes a small square button on the glove compartment. The small door opens and he takes out a brown paper bag.

"Empty!" Bob mumbles.

"Sorry about that," says a voice from the back seat.

Bob is startled. He quickly turns around to see Steve, Bill and Judy sitting on the floor.

"What on Child's Island are you doing here?" exclaims Bob.

"See that, visit an old friend and look at the welcome I get!" laughs Steve.

"I thought you escaped," says Bob.

"We did, that's why we came to you," says Steve.

"Me, why?" asks Bob.

"You are the only person I know on the Island! Besides, we're here to do you a favor. My crew, or what's left of it, and I are going to help you rescue your King," says Steve.

"Rescue the King... This I have to hear!" says Bob.

"Can we talk at your house, over dinner maybe?" asks Steve.

"I take it you're hungry. Very well, I don't know why but for some reason I actually trust you. By the way, how'd you know this was my car?" asks Bob.

"You have a bumper sticker on the back saying 'Bob and Leslie'. I took a chance that there aren't many Bob's and Leslie's in love in this hospital, and all the cars are unlocked," answers Steve.

76

"Why wouldn't we keep our doors unlocked?" asks Bob.

"If you were in New York City and asked that question, they'd lock you up in a fruit factory!" remarks Steve.

"Hey, can't we talk later after we've eaten?" says Judy.

"She's right. My stomach's singing Beethoven's Fifth to me. Let's go!" orders Steve.

"Yes Sir!" replies Bob in a sarcastic tone of voice as he starts the car.

Later that night Steve, Bill, Judy, Bob and Leslie sit around Bob's dinner table finishing their meal. Bob turns to Steve, "Steve, when are you going to tell us about your great plan to rescue the King."

"Yeah, you didn't even tell us the plan," says Judy.

"All right, I'll tell you the plan, but first let's go over the list of items we'll need for the rescue. First, we'll need two boats, then explosives, guns, a siren, some flashing lights, decals saying 'rescue', dummies or mannequins, life jackets, paramedics uniforms for each of us..."starts Steve.

"How are we supposed to get all of that?" yells Bob.

"Calm down. Let's take one thing at a time. Your brother owns both a boat and a trailer. Sirens and flashing lights we can buy somewhere I'm sure. And decals we can make," says Leslie.

"And I guess we can take the uniforms from the hospital," says Bob.

"And the explosives?" asks Steve.

"You can take some nitroglycerin from the hospital," replies Leslie.

"Plus your cousin Gwen owns a clothing store. There are our dummies," says Bob.

"And your cousin Pete has more guns than you have patients!" says Leslie.

"Well, I wouldn't go that far, but I'm sure he can help us out," says Bob.

"How about life jackets?" asks Steve.

"We'll have to buy them but it's certainly feasible," answers Bob.

"Yeah, but Steve said two boats," interrupts Judy.

"Well, I only have one brother," comments Bob.

"I have two but neither owns a boat," says Leslie.

"How about the *Kid Power*? We did fix it," says Bill.

"Yeah, sure! By now it's been found," says Steve.

"No it hasn't. I would have heard something on the news," says Bob.

"Then that's it! We've got everything!" says Leslie.

"There's still one thing Steve forgot," says Bob.

"What's that?" asks Steve puzzled.

"You still didn't tell us the plan!" replies Bob.

Steve smiles. "Don't worry about it. I'll tell you the plan on the way to your brother's house. Then when we get back, you can tell the others," says Steve.

"If I'm right about the combined forces they should be having some ideas as to what we're up to or at least that we're harboring you three," says Leslie.

"Then if we want to rescue the King, it best be tomorrow. While Bob and I are getting the stuff together the rest of you should be... Bob, how far is the hospital from your brother's house?" asks Steve.

"Close enough, why?" asks Bob.

"I want to stop off and pick up the nitro and other items we need from the hospital in the same trip tonight," says Steve.

"Wait a minute, if tonight we're going to be getting the stuff we'll need, and tomorrow's the rescue, when are we going to sleep?" asks Bob.

"After the rescue," smiles Steve.

"Speaking of sleep, what is this drink you gave us? It's made me so tired I can barely think," interrupts Bill.

"It's called Rang juice. It is made from the juices of a very sweet fruit called Rang. The Rang contains a vitamin that helps you relax. If you're not used to it or if you have too much it might make you tired. The tired effect wears off in about an hour and there are no after effects, so you can rest assured," answers Leslie.

"Steve, you drank about five glasses. Aren't you tired?" asks Judy.

"Not at all. I guess I'm the only person around here who's in shape," brags Steve.

Steve gets up and takes only a few steps when his eyes roll upward and he collapses on the floor. His friends stand staring at his unconscious body, but after Steve breaks out in laughter they realize that once again he's playing a joke on them and they begin to laugh.

Next morning at the crack of dawn...

Steve, Bob, Judy, Bill and Leslie meet at Bob's car. The neighborhood at this time is deadly silent. Attached to the car is a trailer and on it is a large boat. Only its shape can be seen through the black plastic-like blanket which covers it almost completely. The trailer is shining silver. Steve and his new "crew" are wearing orange uniforms. The right arm of each shirt has a patch on it saying "Emergency Medical Rescue Squad". Bob and Leslie are wearing their black hospital shoes. Steve, Bill and Judy wear similar shoes.

"All right. We should be all set. The dummies and explosives and the other goodies are in the yacht. I just hope the guards don't want to search it," says Steve.

"Steve, we'd better get moving before someone suspects something and calls the police," says Bob.

"Right. As of now, the kidding around has ended and the rescue has begun," says Steve, walking to the car.

He quickly opens the back door and gets in. Bob closes it and then gets in himself. In another second the car drives away. The car speeds through the neighborhood and soon reaches a giant highway. Like all highways of the "Outside World" it has multiple lanes going in all directions. The car goes past stores and buildings, past cement platforms and train tracks. All are deserted. Only a few other cars are within seeing distance of their car. Steve and Judy sit up and gaze around.

"Everything looks so new. The sidewalks are pure white, streets black and the stores and buildings aren't covered with graffiti. How do you do that?" asks Judy.

"Easy, we don't pollute or deface our property," answers Bob.

The five ride silently for several minutes. They pass what appears to be a gas station only they have no pumps.

"What kind of gas station is that?" Steve asks hesitantly.

"Gas?" exclaims Bob.

"We haven't used fuel oil in years. Our cars run on high powered hydrogen batteries," says Bob.

"And I'll bet you heat your homes by solar energy," says Steve.

"Of course. How else?" replies Bob.

They travel for another few minutes when Steve asks another question, "This may sound dumb but why is everything white?"

"White is our symbol. It represents innocence and newness, and simplicity," answers Leslie.

"I don't know. I like a variety of colors. I'll take a rainbow over plain white any day!" says Judy.

Immediately another strange view comes into sight. About five miles away stands a tall white structure. It appears to be some kind of tower. It's square and made of white concrete. It looks as if it were sculpted in one piece. Many white steps lead up to four pairs of white doors.

"Before I can tell you what that is I have to give you its background," says Bob anticipating Steve's questions.

"Fourteen years ago a very rich man named Charles E. Simon ran a contest between a handful of scientists. The one that could make the most powerful and destructive weapon within one year would win a prize of one hundred million dollars. He was also to pay for the expense of building those weapons."

"Needless to say, the scientists came up with some doozies. Everything from high powered lasers to pellets which turned water into a deadly gas," says Leslie.

"Well the laser is now used as a drill, but back to the story; the most powerful, destructive and dangerous weapon was a missile built by an unknown scientist. It was a new kind of atomic war head. It caused a large explosion but what made this missile so extremely dangerous were the electrons. The scientist found that if you split the electrons, like you would the atom, it would give off an electric charge. The charge was so small that it would be undetectable but when you split a few billion you start a chain reaction and you've got a planet sized electrical charge! The war head was of this design. The entire thing I just told you about is called a negative-positive reaction."

"Now you see why the scientist won the contest. When the King found out about it he had it confiscated and both the wealthy man and the scientist, whose identity was never revealed, were jailed. But there was one slight problem. The scientist supposedly told the government scientist the design and how to build such a missile. He neglected to tell them how to take it apart and before they could ask him he was unfortunately killed in an escape attempt," says Leslie.

"We then had a missile on our hands that was a definite danger. Scientists found one way to disarm it. They carefully disconnected the control cable and the danger of some madman controlling the missile disappeared. But disconnecting was all they could do. They feared if they tried to take it apart it might accidentally go off!" says Bob.

"No one, not even the King wanted to take that responsibility. So a cement structure was built to contain it and disillusion viewers. We won't pass by it though, soon we'll make a turn which will take us out of its sight and toward our destination, the wall," says Leslie.

"Now that's what anyone would a call fascinating story," says Steve, gazing in the building's direction.

"Oh! You meant that structure. I thought you meant that one over that. It has a completely different story. You see..." starts Bob, grinning.

"Cute," replies Steve.

The great wall of Child's Island rises in front of them.

"You'd better get under the blanket. We'll be there in a few minutes," says Bob.

Steve, Judy and Bill get back on the floor and pull the black blanket over themselves and cuddle up. Steve tickles Judy and she laughs out loud.

"Seriously?" yells Bill.

"Shhh!" snaps Leslie.

"They act like children sometimes," whispers Bob.

"They are, remember?" replies Leslie.

Bob and Leslie smile at each other.

Another two minutes and they approach the wall. It seems to go all around the cities of Child's Island. The color is white. The guards at the top don't pay too much attention to the inside of the cities they stand over. They concentrate on the outside.

Most of the machine guns and lights are pointed toward the forest area. The main concern of the soldiers seems to be keeping people from entering Child's Island rather than to keep people from leaving.

A hundred yards before the wall is the entrance to a tunnel. Made of white concrete, it leads to a black ramp which disappears into the darkness of the underground.

The tunnels entrance is secured by two thick steel doors. The doors are open but directly in back of them are two gated doors. These are closed. Next to the tunnel is a small barrack. It is wood, painted blue. It has a fairly large window with clear, thick glass. Behind this window stands a soldier with a sub-machine gun strapped to his shoulder. In front of him is a control table. It has a few dials, switches and many buttons and lights. Bob's car stops about twenty yards away from the tunnel. He puts the gear shift in park but keeps the motor on.

Immediately a soldier wearing a black uniform with three stripes on the sleeves and two other soldiers run out and approach the car. They stand in front of the car holding their sub-machine guns and stare at Bob and Leslie.

"Good morning Dr. Goodboy. What are you doing up so early?" asks the Sergeant.

"Nurse Bluesmith and I are on an emergency mission. There's been a report of a new plague on one of the friendly islands surrounding Child's Island," answers Bob.

"I was wondering why you were all dressed up and why you had your boat with you. I supposed you want to go through the tunnel," says the Sergeant.

"Unless you know of another way, that's right," replies Bob.

"Although I have orders not to let anyone through, it is an emergency and since you took out my wife's appendix last year I'll gladly take the responsibility and let you and your nurse through," says the Sergeant.

Bob and Leslie smile in relief.

"First, though, my men will have to check the trailer and boat," says the Sergeant, motioning with his hands towards the rear of the car.

"Wait!" yells Bob. The soldiers stop.

"What's wrong?" ask the Sergeant.

"Ah, ah, you see we're in a big hurry," Bob mumbles.

"Maybe so, but we can't take any chances. With those escaped prisoners on the loose."

Taking a deep breath Bob blurts out, "Well, the real reason I can't let you inspect it is because there are many chemicals on board that are sensitive to light. If exposed for more than a few, err, seconds, they would be of no use to us and we couldn't make the serum necessary to contain this plague. Besides, do you think I would have those escaped prisoners in my boat? I thought you knew me?"

"Well, I guess it would be foolish and yes, you're right. Why would the chief surgeon of the First Hospital be smuggling criminals out," says the Sergeant as he signals the soldier in the barrack.

The soldier pushes a few buttons and the gate doors open. "Good luck with your mission!" yells the Sergeant.

"You might say it was more of a rescue!" says Bob, smiling.

He shifts the gear in drive and the car and trailer slowly enter the tunnel. After a few minutes they reach the bottom of the tunnel and start traveling forward at about sixty miles per hour.

The bottom of the tunnel is slightly lit from the countless lights on its ceiling.

"OK guys, you can sit up again," says Leslie.

"Whew, I almost thought we weren't going to make it," says Steve.

"You weren't alone," says Leslie, turning on the car radio. There is a tremendous amount of static. She turns the knob until they hear a song.

"The words aren't clear but it sounds like The Beatles "I Want to Hold Your Hand", states Steve.

"No! It's called 'I Want to Kiss Your Hand' by The Juveniles," says Leslie. Steve grins.

"Leslie, if you only knew."

She stares at him.

"Just where are we anyway?" asks Judy.

"About two miles underground. There's no passage way through the wall so we have to go under it. The wall goes underground for about half a mile, the tunnel has to be about twice as deep as the wall. We'll come up in the forest area heading towards the shore," answers Bob.

"How come the wall is so deep?" asks Steve.

"So no one tunnels their way in or out Child's Island," answers Bob.

The road begins to rise and although the small car is more powerful than it looks, it is having a bit of trouble pulling the heavy weight of the trailer. Judy and Steve are concerned but say nothing. After several minutes the car drives out of the hole in the ground and drives away.

"Another ten minutes and we can get our bottoms out of here and stretch," says Bob.

"No time. If we want this rescue to work, we have to get busy," says Steve.

Shortly after, the car and trailer leave the forest area and approach the surface of the island. The four sight the *Kid Power.*

"Hey, this car is getting too hot. It must have been too much of a strain on the engine pulling the trailer up that tunnel ramp. It may be another few hundred yards to the water but I'd rather let her rest a while and cool off rather than go on from here," says Bob.

"You're the doctor. We don't have to put the boat afloat right away. We can look over the *Kid Power* first," says Steve.

The five get out of the car. Just then, a big flash of light is seen and following the flash is an explosion.

The car windshield shatters. "Take cover! Someone is shooting at us!" yells Steve quickly running to the car and trailer. The five scatter. Two more shots are fired as they run for cover. The front hood of the car is blasted open and the other shot just misses Bill, hitting the ground.

"General Bollings must have found out about the *Kid Power* and set up an ambush!" says Bob who, like everyone, is hunched down.

The shooting stops.

"We can't just wait for them to reload. We must do something," says Bill.

"What?" All the weapons we depended on are in the *Kid Power* damn it!" replies Steve.

"What about the explosives in the boat?" asks Bob.

"Boy, you have a lot to learn about rescues. Do you want to volunteer to get up and try to get in the boat? And besides, if we blow up the *Kid Power* we might kill our enemies but we'd also kill our rescue. We still need the *Kid Power*," answers Steve.

Five more shots are fired. All are directed at the car, hitting in different directions. Besides demolishing the car, four out of the five shots just miss the five "sitting ducks".

"He's squeezing us in. Trying to make us run out from behind the car so he can mow us down. It's the same technique my cousin and I used at the city dumps when we went rat hunting. We went whenever the population of rats was getting too high and they were wandering around the streets biting two year olds," says Steve.

"How do you know there's only one soldier?" asks Bob.

"Elementary, if there were more than one, they would have taken the chance and charged us... wait a minute. That's it! It has to be! It all fits in. No wonder he knew the strategy. How dumb can I get? Why didn't I think of it before?" cries Steve.

"What are you talking about?" asks Bob, confused by Steve's reaction.

"You'll see in a second. If not, I'm a goner!" says Steve as he stands up and begins to yell.

"Stop, don't fire, it's me, Steve!"

"Now I know he's gone mad...Bob stop him before he kills himself!" yells Bill.

Bob tries to grab Steve's legs and pull him down but he is much too strong. Steve walks towards to the front of the car. He is not fired at but there is no sign of communication from the *Kid Power*.

"Dear God, please don't let me be wrong," Steve says in a small frightened voice.

"Steve, it's you!" screams a voice from the *Kid Power*.

A figure then appears on the deck. It jumps off the boat and runs toward Steve, still holding the shotgun in its hand.

A hundred yards away it's recognizable to everyone.

"Robert!" yells Steve.

"Robert?" mumbles Bill, starting to get up.

Judy is speechless. Leslie and Bob are confused. Steve and Robert and hug, while Robert still holds the shotgun. Bill and Judy

87

regain their senses and run to the two boys. Bob and Leslie are following close behind. Both are still uneasy.

"I just about forgot all about you. I was certain those soldiers nailed you!" says the excited Steve and he ruffles Robert's hair and playfully slaps him on the face with his hand.

"Thanks a lot," says Robert sarcastically.

"You know what I mean," replies Steve.

"Of course, I'm only kidding. To tell you the truth, I thought you were six feet under," says Robert.

Bill and Judy are now on the scene. Bill and Robert hug each other. Not affectionately as did he and Steve but enough to show that they missed each other and were glad to see each other again. Judy hugs Robert next. Bob and Leslie reach the four. Bob puts out his hand.

"Even I can figure out that you're not one of the General's soldiers sent to ambush us!" says Bob. Robert looks puzzled.

"I'll explain who he is later. In the meantime his name is Bob and this young lady is Leslie," says Steve.

"So what happened to you guys? Couldn't find your way back to the boat?" asks Robert.

"I wish it were that easy Robert. You'd better tell us your story first. Ours will take a lifetime to tell," says Steve.

"Well, I had been shot in the back by one of the soldiers and had to crawl my way back to the *Kid Power*. I still don't know how I made it. Next morning I woke up on the sand a few hundred yards back from the boat. The bullet was half way out of my back. I guess the guy who shot me wasn't close enough. I was able to pull the bullet out after a bit and then I used every bit of strength to crawl to the boat and climb aboard. I used the medical supply kit to patch myself up and from then on I've been sleeping, eating and mourning over your deaths. When I saw the car and trailer I thought you were some more soldiers coming to do me in. That's why I fired so quickly. I did wonder why you weren't firing back. Gee, perfect strangers and I blow your car apart!" says Robert.

"That's okay. At least you didn't damage the boat," replies Bob.

"Yeah, what's the boat for? Can't we use the *Kid Power* to go back?" asks Robert.

"We're not going back. We're on a rescue mission. It's a long story and I'll explain it to you later. Right now we've got a lot of work to do, like pushing that boat three hundred yards to the water," says Steve.

"I'd like to check out your back," says Bob.

"He's cool. He's a doctor and a damn good one so don't worry," says Steve.

"I was going to say..." says Robert staring at Bob.

"Hey, how'd you know it was me?" asks Robert.

"Well, I started to suspect something from the start. When you used the old rat routine with the gun I was almost certain. You did it exactly the way we did it years ago. Exact same angles and the same mistake you used to make on the fifth shot. It never came near us, unlike the other four. I wasn't totally sure, that's why I was shaking when you didn't answer right away," answers Steve.

"Wait a minute. Is there something you guys aren't telling us?" asks Judy.

"I'd better tell them before they think we're both mad. Robert is my cousin," answers Steve.

"I hate to be tiresome, but how could you two be cousins? If you'll remember Andy made sure that all the crew never knew each other before they met for the voyage to Child's Island. That makes it impossible for you to be related... doesn't it?" asks Bill.

"Not really. You see, before either of us ran away we were very close. We were more like brothers and most people thought we were. Things got bad for Robert at his home and he ran away. A year later I did the same. We never thought we would see each other again," answers Steve.

"We wouldn't have if it weren't for Andy. We were on opposite sides of the country," says Robert.

"As you know, Andy chose his crew from all over the United States. He thought for sure that none of us could have known each other. When we met at the dock for the first time two weeks before the voyage, Robert and I were very surprised to see each other. Andy wondered why we gave each other such a big hello. I lied telling him I thought he was someone I knew but had made a mistake. I lied because we both wanted to go on this trip and if Andy had suspected we were related he never would have let us go. I guess that's it," finishes Steve.

"Now that's a real family story. I thought you two were just plain strange," laughs Bill.

"I was wondering why he was so much like you. You know, the same expressions. I started to suspect something was funny but couldn't quite put my finger on it," comments Judy.

"Say, why are you guys wearing those uniforms? You know that's another reason I shot at you. I thought for sure you were soldiers," says Robert.

"It's part of our rescue plan. I'll explain it all later. I guess we'd better start moving. We've had our little get together, now let's have a little work," says Steve.

Later on that morning at the shore of a small island miles away, a handful of "boys" wearing sheets wrapped around them stand guard next to a large machine gun which resembles a cannon. The scene is a quiet one. The natives converse softly in a foreign language. Every few seconds one will glance at the ocean looking for attackers. The peacefulness is broken by the sight of

Bob's boat coming into view. It appears to be speeding towards the island. Some of the crew can be seen standing on the deck and some are behind the front windshield of the boat. The natives are terribly upset.

"When I give you the signal, open fire," says one native to the other. He maneuvers the machine gun.

As the boat gets closer and closer, and the natives get more and more nervous. The boat is just two miles away from the shore. The sound of its engines echo throughout the area. The roar of the engines makes the native even more nervous.

"They're crazy," says one of the natives.

"No, they're planning something... we can't let them get any closer. Open fire!" orders the man in command.

They take aim and are about to fire. Before they do though, the boat blows up. Flames are all that can be seen. The natives are taken by surprise. A few hundred yards away from the sinking boat the crew is spotted floating in the water.

"Look, some of the attackers survived!" yells one of the natives.

"Should we try to shoot them?" asks another.

"No, let's let them float until they wish they had died in the explosion," answers the native 'Commander'.

"What if Child's Island sends help?" asks yet another native.

"Then they will be very lucky," answers the Commander.

Several minutes pass by. Suddenly the natives hear a siren. They look toward the water and to their surprise they see the *Kid Power* coming at them. The *Kid Power* has decals on each side saying "Rescue." It's covering with many flashing police lights. Its siren is so loud that it drowns out the noise from the powerful engines.

Steve stands on the front deck looking through a pair of binoculars. Robert is at his side.

"I was right. They do have a weapon waiting for us. Looks like a small cannon. Wait...no, it can't be a cannon. Must be a machine gun. I sure as hell hope our plan works," says Steve.

"So do I. I still don't believe they didn't figure out that those survivors are really dummies and not people," says Robert.

"Oh, I knew they'd fall for it all right. They're so busy worrying about being attacked and about the explosion that they didn't stop to think about why the survivors aren't doing much moving," scoffs Steve.

"Steve, I know this is the wrong time to ask, but why are we rescuing the King? No offense to Bob and Leslie, but isn't that their problem?" asks Robert.

"Maybe, but I for one would like to try living here. I can't do that if that nut Bollings is running the show. Besides, I just feel that it's the right thing to do. I really can't explain it. It's like a feeling. You understand?" answers Steve.

"Got you," says Robert.

The *Kid Power* slows down and finally comes to a stop near where the dummies are floating.

"Should we open fire?" asks one of the natives.

"No. It's just a rescue boat. Why waste the ammunition on a mere ambulance," says the Commander.

Everyone is gathered around Steve on the deck of the *Kid Power*.

"Robert, you'd better take the wheel. I don't want them to see you without a uniform. It probably doesn't make that much of a difference but we need someone at the wheel anyway. The rest of you will pick up the dummies and put them on deck. And don't forget, make sure it looks real. We'll need every second we can buy. We've got to take them by total surprise," says Steve.

Everyone except Robert goes to the side railings of the *Kid Power*, trying to reach the dummies and pull them up on deck.

The natives watch their every move.

"Gotcha," says Bob as he pulls one of them up and throws it across the deck.

"I said make it look real, you idiot!" says Steve.

"Sorry about that, I got carried away," says Bob.

Leslie then grabs hold of one and starts to pull it over the railing. The dummy lands on top of her and she falls.

"And you're a nurse?" comments Steve as he pulls his third dummy aboard.

Judy tries to get one of the dummies and starts to fall overboard. Bob runs to her aid and holds her back from falling.

"I hope we don't have to pull you up from the water!" jeers Bob.

"Thank you. I'm sorry, I should have been more careful," says Judy.

"Don't worry about it. It's a good thing Steve is busy getting one of those dummies himself. If he'd have seen you, you would have never heard the end of it!" says Bob as he leaves Judy's side and attempts to retrieve another dummy from the water.

"Looks like we've got them all," says Steve getting up off his knees.

He rises to a standing position and looks over the deck.

"Just one more Steve," says Bill pulling this third dummy from the water.

He pulls it by the head. Bill pulls just a bit too hard and the head falls off. The body falls down into the water while the head remains in Bill's hands.

"Sorry about that, fellow," says Bill.

"You're a riot Bill! Now put the head down and come over here!" orders Steve.

Bill stands and walks over to Steve. On his way he bends over and picks up the remote detonator.

"Do you still want it?" asks Bill approaching Steve.

"No, it's done its part. Now we have to do ours. Bill get me the box of cocktail explosives. The rest of you stay to the center of the deck."

Bill goes to the right railing and picks up a large cardboard box. He brings it over to Steve and puts it at his feet.

"Thanks. You can stand by me... alright Robert, ready when you are!" yells Steve.

Robert starts the *Kid Power*. The natives begin to relax.

"They're leaving the headless one in the water. They have no respect!" says one native to another.

The boat starts to slowly turn around. The natives carelessly leave their gun and walk a few yards away from it to talk quietly.

"It's over," says their commander.

But they are in for a big surprise. The *Kid Power* turns all right, but it keeps turning until it makes a complete circle and is facing the island again. The boat starts speeding towards the island.

"It was a trick!" yells the native commander as he points to the boat. The natives run back to the gun and start to take aim.

Just before they fire, Steve, standing at the helm of the *Kid Power* throws one of the explosives into the water. It lands about fifty yards in front of the speeding boat. Hitting the water, it explodes. The explosion causes the water to make large waves. It forms a screen of water in front of the boat which makes it impossible for the natives to see it from the shore.

"I can't see it, it's hiding behind the wall of water!" cries one of the natives.

When the water settles down, Steve throws another explosive in front of the *Kid Power*. Once again the wall of water hides the ship and again the natives do not fire for fear they'll miss and waste their ammunition.

94

The boat nears closer and closer to the island. Bill hands Steve the last two explosives from the box.

"Great. We only have two more. That still won't be enough to reach the shore even at this speed. And the ship's weapons were damaged when it went over the waterfall. That machine gun that the natives have will rip the *Kid Power* apart and us with it!" says Steve.

"What'll we do?" asks Bills who faithfully stands by Steve's side.

"We'll have to jump overboard and swim the rest of the way," answers Steve.

"Jump? Overboard? We'll be sitting ducks... and what about the rescue?" asks Bill getting upset.

"I know it sounds crazy but we'll have less of a chance on the *Kid Power*. Why, if one of those bullets hits the engine, she'll blow up. Besides, a few of us are wearing waterproof holsters. Once we're on the island we'll just have to scare the natives. A few handguns should do the trick. We can save our lives and rescue the King. Please don't argue with me. I haven't let you down before. Attention! Attention everyone! We can't go much further. We'll have to jump and swim the rest of the way. The boat will keep their attention. Now go!" yells Steve as he throws the second to last explosive into the water.

Bob and Leslie run to the railing and for a few seconds hesitate, staring first at the water and then at Steve.

"What are you waiting for? Jump! You said you trusted me... now jump!" yells Steve.

The two jump of the speeding boat into the water below. Judy runs to the same rail and climbs over it but hangs on it.

"Steve aren't you jumping with us?" asks Judy.

"I'll be right with you. Go!" yells Steve.

Bill climbs over the rail and holds Judy's hand. The two jump into the water together. Robert leaves the wheel on automatic pilot and runs to Steve who throws the last explosive into the water.

"Guess it's my turn," says Robert.

"Yeah, I'll be right behind you," says Steve.

The two run to the rail. Robert stands in front of the railing looking into the water. Steve is behind him.

"Well, what are you waiting for?" asks Steve impatiently. Robert quickly turns to face him.

"Steve, I'm only doing this because I love you more than anyone else in the world. You're my little brother."

Before Steve can say anything in reply, Robert punches him in the stomach. Steve bends over in pain. Again Robert punches him, this time in the face. As Steve leans over the rail almost unconscious with pain, Robert picks up both his legs from behind and flips Steve over the rail and into the water.

"No!" yells Steve as he falls in.

Robert quickly runs back to the control center. "I'm sorry it had to be this way but there was no other choice. I knew what you were planning from the beginning. You were going to stay on the boat even after I jumped. You figure that you would make sure the *Kid Power* stayed on course. You knew that the others wouldn't stand a chance trying to swim their way to shore. With the boat acting as a decoy they'd have a much better chance. I couldn't let you risk your life like that. The others would be lost without you. I'm... I'm expendable," he sighs.

The wall of water caused by the final explosion disintegrates. The natives hesitate shooting at the speeding boat. They seem to wait for another explosion. Finally, the firing begins. The giant machine gun explodes into action. It fires at such a speed that it seems to resemble a laser beam. The *Kid Power* is flooded with bullets. The front windshield is almost completely shattered. The railings begin to dent. Even the bulletproof fiberglass begins to crack from the impact of the shelling.

Robert remains on his knees reaching upward toward the wheel desperately trying to steer the *Kid Power* straight towards the island. His face and hands are red. Sweat rolls down his body as he struggles to steer the boat and dodge the bullets. He is taken back by the power of the gun. Unbelievably, he stares at the destruction being done to the boat under his control. On his face, too, is a look of regret. The instinct for survival and wanting to live fill him with sorrow... he gave up the chance to save himself. But the need to be a hero is stronger and his worried face soon wears a look of determination.

The bullets come closer and closer. After what seems to Robert as an immeasurable amount of time, one of the bullets finds its target and hits him in the left hand. As a reflex, Robert stands halfway up holding his hand with his other in pain. This reflex cost Robert his life. Almost immediately after hunching up, he is caught in the line of fire and is shot several times in the chest. He falls onto the wheel and then to the control table and finally, his bloody body reaches the deck.

With his final burst of strength he reaches upward and grasps the steering lock, just making contact. As his hand touches it, he loses consciousness, and his hand falls pulling the lever with it. The bow of the *Kid Power* is upward. It is only a few yards from the shore. The natives cease their firing and look at the *Kid Power* in dismay. In a few seconds the boat rams into the shallow water. Due to the speed that it was traveling, the beach acts like a ramp, sending it into the air about a hundred feet up. It glides across the water and part of the shore and starts to fall down. The natives stand in shocked silence, watching the boat fall on them. The *Kid*

Power lands on top of the machine gun and the stunned natives, exploding on impact. The explosion lights up the entire shore.

The fire dies off and the flames start to shrink. The smoke floats lazily upwards into the atmosphere and mushrooms like an atomic explosion. The *Kid Power*, machine gun, natives and even the surrounding trees and shrubbery have been burnt to ashes. The sand remains warm to the touch and probably will be for hours. The shore now remains peaceful and uninhabited.

The remaining crew of the *Kid Power* begins to near the shore. Bob and Leslie are first to reach it and almost immediately crawl to the warmest sport as they lay down to rest. Soon Judy and Bill follow them and they also rest, breathing quite heavily. Steve is the last to swim to shore. He too lies on his back, catching his breath. Eventually the entire crew stands up and visually surveys the beach.

"Talk about a mini Hiroshima!" comments Bill. "Hey, Robert, he hasn't made it back yet!" exclaims Leslie.

"He's gone," replies Steve, staring vacantly at the sea. "He's gone!" the boy repeats.

"He did what I should have done," he continues. His face is red and tears are in his eyes. "Why, why, why... why did he have to go? Take this rotten world and shove it! I quit! Get some other sucker to be Captain and forget this mission. To hell with it! To hell with it!" he hollers as loud as he can.

He then takes the gun from his holster and throws it into the water. Sinking to his knees he covers his face with his hands. Sobs break from his throat. The others stand behind Steve staring at him. Bob and Leslie are shocked and are at a loss for words. Judy has tears in her eyes. Bill wears a look of pity and understanding.

After a while Steve stops crying but is still in a kneeling position. He appears to be in a daze. In reality, he is thinking about the past. Remembering. Remembering how he and Robert were reunited at the shore of Child's Island. Remembering how happy they were to see each other again. "I thought you were dead," echoes in his head. He remembers, too, when he first came to Child's Island and asked Robert if there were any chances of repairing the *Kid Power*. He keeps thinking back, back to the beginning. It is sort of an instant replay of the whole voyage.

Suddenly, the focus is back to one of his conversations with Andy. His mind goes back in time to a memory before the voyage. He and Andy are standing on the deck of the *Kid Power*. The two appear to be alone. They are not in uniform, but casual clothes.

"Now Steve, answer me honestly, did you know Robert before tonight?" asks Andy.

"No," replies Steve.

"How come you gave each other such a big hello?" questions Andy.

"I don't know. I guess I thought I knew him but I was wrong," answers Steve.

"I don't know whether to believe you or not, but even if you did know him it probably won't matter. You're a good man Steve. You're more than good. That's why I chose you to be the Captain. I just hope that whatever you and Robert have doesn't come between you and your responsibilities. I'm counting on you Steve. Don't let me down," says Andy.

The vision fades but the last sentence keeps repeating itself in Steve's memory. "I'm counting on you Steve. Don't let me down...don't let me down."

Steve is brought back to the present by a tap on his shoulder. Bill is on his knees next to Steve. He stops the tapping when Steve turns his head.

"You okay?" he asks in a soft and concerned voice.

Steve rubs his eyes with both hands and then shakes his head. He maneuvers his body and feels his back with his hands. He has a cramp from sitting in the same position for too long. "Yeah, I guess so," Steve answers in a low voice. Steve looks at the sand.

"Steve, I, well..." Bill hesitates.

"Bill, you don't have to say anything," interrupts Steve, still in a low, tired voice.

"I know I don't. I want to. And not because you're my Captain, but because you are my friend. And because Robert was also my friend. Look, I don't just speak for myself. I speak for everyone. Judy was crying too you know. But not for Robert, for you! We don't have to go on with the rescue if you feel you're not up to it. I guess we're more concerned about you than rescuing some King. Keep one thing in mind though. We came here for a reason. Robert gave his life for that reason. To turn back now, well, it just doesn't seem right. We can't go on without you. You're our Captain, our leader, the heart and life of this entire mission. And even more, you're our friend. You've led us this far, God knows, we couldn't have made it without you, and we can't go any further without you. I don't have the slightest idea as to what our next move is. Steve, please... we need you," pleads Bill.

Bill is watching Steve's face in fear. He is uncertain as to what the reaction will be. Ten long seconds pass. Finally Steve looks up at Bill, smiles and says "Thanks. You know of any rescue that needs a Captain?" in his normal voice.

He looks at the others and smiles as he walks over to them. The three return his smile. Judy hugs him tightly with her lips placed on his left cheek.

After a few moments, "Okay, here it is. Next move is simple. Bill and Bob you still have your handguns. Two should be enough. All we're going to do is a little scaring. First we go to the village, making sure they can't see us but are positioned where we can see them. We fire the guns a few times and do a lot of yelling and make noise. Nature takes over from there. The natives will think they're under attack by the army of Child's Island and that General Bollings double crossed them. They'll panic and, being as primitive as Bob says, they'll run and hide. That's when we make our move. We find out where the King is, grab him and split," says Steve, rapidly regaining his strength.

"Are you sure they'll panic like you say?" asks Bill.

"Pretty sure. They must be already. I'll bet you that if they have any communication device to reach General Bollings, they're using it right now. Probably begging him to save them. If that is the case, we've got to move fast. On with the rescue!" orders Commander Mason.

"Steve wait!" says Bob, taking his gun out of the holster.

"I can't use this, I'm a doctor. We'll be a lot safer with it in your hands than in mine."

Taking the gun from Bob Steve turns and says, "You don't have to be a doctor to dislike shooting someone, but I know what you mean. Thanks."

The five enter the islands forest area. It is similar to the one on Child's Island, except much smaller. Both are beautiful.

Ten minutes into the forest they reach the native village. It is surrounded by trees and bushes making it easy for the five to hide. The village is quite small. It consists of twenty brown huts, about as big as the average garage; a few tents, wooden poles, gardens and clotheslines with white sheets hung on them. The huts and the rest are spread out in the clearing.

101

In the center of the village is a white hut. It has a thick wooden bar across its equally thick door. It is the only hut without a window. Two natives stand in front holding crossbows. Other natives are scattered all over the village. Most of them are sitting on blankets talking, sewing or resting. The five invaders quickly hide behind some bushes just before the clearing.

"Just as I suspected. They are using bows and arrows. Okay, obviously the King is being held in that white hut. There's over a hundred of them that I can see. Probably more in the huts. We do have one advantage though, we have guns and we know how to use them well. How much of an advantage it is depends on how well we carry out the plan," states Steve.

"I don't know, it looks too obvious. I mean the King in the white hut?" says Judy.

"Obvious to us but not to their primitive eyes," retorts Steve.

He takes the gun from his holster. Bill does the same. Steve aims his gun to the skies and fires it quickly three times. All work, conversation or whatever the natives were involved with stops and the natives begin yelling and screaming. The five yell and holler as if they're insane. Again Steve fires his gun skyward. Bill does the same.

"We're being attacked!" yells a native.

Steve fires his gun at one of the huts. It hits the structure and chips a piece of wood. He shoots again blasting a hole in the door, scaring the natives even more! His next shot shatters one of the wooden poles. The natives start to run into their huts. Some even run away from the clearing, into the forest area.

Within seconds all the natives have either hidden or run away from the village. It now seems uninhabited.

"It worked! The place looks empty," says Bill.

"Even the natives guarding the King's hut ran!" says Bob laughing.

"Let's move fast. The minute those natives figure out we're the only ones making all the noise and attacking, they're going to come back and we're going to be the ones running for cover!" warns Steve.

The five quickly enter the village and head for the white hut. Steve lifts the bar and throws it to the floor. "Bob, open the door, NOW!" orders Steve.

Bob immediately does so and backs away from the entrance. Inside the hut are two boys standing a few yards back from the doorway. One of them is wearing all white, with the robes of a king. His attire consists of a pair of pants, a coat, cape, shoes and a small gold grown decorated with many diamonds. The robe is of very thick fur. The boy is about five foot four, one hundred and five pounds, with short very blond hair, blue eyes, tanned skin and a cute, yet distinguished face. He looks about thirteen. The other boy wears a blue sheet wrapped around him. His hair is dark brown and he is very tan. He is also about thirteen.

The native stands behind the King. In his hand is a wide sharp knife. He presses it to the boy's throat.

"Drop your weapons or I'll kill him right in front of you," says the native in a calm, confident voice. Steve and Bill reluctantly comply.

"Now get away from the door. Don't even think of running," again in a calm voice, the native orders.

He walks slowly out of the hut with his captive, still holding the knife against his throat. The two stand a few feet to the side of the doorway. He yells out a few sentences in a foreign language and in about half a minute a handful of natives come out of their huts and crowd around Steve and his crew.

103

"Get in the hut," orders the native.

"Now!" he snaps as the five slowly enter the hut, staring at the native.

The five stop at the very entrance.

"Now, go to the back," the native continues to order and they obey.

The native walks to the doorway of the hut and pushes the "hostage" into it. He falls to the floor. The native quickly closes the door.

Steve immediately runs to the door. From outside comes the sound of a bar being put up against the door. Steve tries to force the door open with all his might but it doesn't budge.

Chapter 5 – The Chase

Shortly after the five have been locked in the hut with the King, Bob, Leslie, Judy and the King stand in the middle talking in low voices. Bill sits on the floor with his back pressed against the back wall. He stares down at the floor and occasionally looks up at the ceiling or at the others. He wears a discouraged look.

Steve walks from one end of the hut to another. As he paces he is constantly surveying the area and every so often he mumbles something to himself or makes a nervous gesture. He seems to pay no attention to the others in the hut, while they watch his every move. Finally, he stops at the door. He gets within a few inches of it and then slowly takes a few steps back. He looks from door to floor and appears to be taking a measurement. Suddenly he yells and punches the door with his right arm.

The others stop their conversation and stare at him.

"Come on Steve, go easy on yourself. You've been pacing and mumbling ever since we were locked in here," says Bob.

"I can't take it easy on myself. I was so wrapped up in my personal conflicts that my judgment was messed up. I should have figured that the natives would have some security plan. It should have been obvious that they had something up their sleeves beside that giant machine gun that General Bollings gave them as a present. And as for my pacing, I'm simply giving this hut a good looking over... trying to figure out some kind of escape plan," replies Steve.

Steve walks over to Bill and sits down next to him.

"Come up with anything?" asks Steve. Bill looks at the ceiling and then at Steve.

"No, nothing," says Bill in a disappointed voice.

Judy walks over to Steve and Bill and sits next to them. She puts her head on Steve's shoulder.

"Who is he?" asks the King.

"He's the guy who's responsible for this entire rescue plan," answers Bob.

"You mean he's in the Army?" says the King.

"No, your majesty, he's not even from this world. He comes from the 'Outside World'. He and his crew came here in the *Kid Power*," says Bob.

"The *Kid Power*? Then Andy made it after all?" asks the King.

"He made it but he didn't make it back. It's a long story. You see…"

Minutes later after he has informed The King on everything that has gone on and is going on, the King walks over to Steve, Bill and Judy.

"I'd like to thank you, Captain Mason," says the King.

"For what?" asks Steve, looking up at the King.

"For what? I think you know what for. I'm sorry I didn't properly introduce myself. I'm King Eric of the continental world of Child's Island," says the King.

Steve, Bill and Judy stand to face him. They shake hands and exchange smiles.

"It's a pleasure to meet you. I guess I could have introduced myself also. I've never met a real King before," says Steve.

"Please don't apologize. After all you and your friends have been through, I can't blame you for forgetting your manners. And I promise you that if and when we return to Child's Island, you and your friends will be greatly rewarded. Child's Island is already in your debt. Your cousin and the others that gave their lives will go down in history as heroes and will be respected and honored by all in the kingdom," promises the King.

"Do me a favor Eric, save all your thanks and rewards for when you are returned safely," replies Steve.

108

"You've got a deal! How do you plan to get us out of here?" asks the King, who doesn't mind that he has been called by his first name.

"Don't know yet, but I'll think of something. Bet your life on it!" replies Steve.

"If you are going to get us out of here I hope you do it soon," says the King.

"Why is that?" asks Steve.

"Because in a few hours the natives plan to kill me. And something tells me I'll be having company," answers the King.

"Why would they kill you before they get the ransom?" asks Steve.

"Well, General Bollings is coming with the ransom in a few hours. They'll kill me the second he gets here," answers the King.

"A few hours?" gasps Bill.

Bob and Leslie walk over to the King, Steve and Bill.

"Do you know how they intend to kill you?" asks Steve.

"Yes, they're going to burn me at the stake," the King answers.

"No!" shouts Steve.

"They're not going to tie anyone to a stake because we're going to escape from this dumb village. They have to let us out of here in order to bring us to the stakes. So we have to have a plan to get out of the clearing. By the time the natives from this clearing alert the other natives from the other areas we can be on our way back to Child's Island. The shore must be a lot closer than the next village clearing," says Steve, sounding confident.

"Steve, you're overlooking one thing. Even if we escape from these natives and reach the shore before they get help, how are we going to go back to Child's Island without a boat? The *Kid Power* was destroyed," says Bill.

"That's right, I almost forgot about that but we're still better off trying to escape than just staying and being burned to death. If we can come up with a plan, I say we use it. Once we've escaped, we can worry about how to get back to Child's Island. One step at a time, you know," says Steve.

"I guess you're right, but how do we escape? There's nothing in this hut we can use. Only four wood walls and a floor," says Bill.

"It's so humiliating. If that native didn't have that knife against my throat you could have easily taken them. If only I had a few handfuls of soldiers. They would squash them like insects," says the King.

"Insects! That's it!" says Steve.

"Insects? We're going to fight them with bugs?" asks Bill looking confused.

"No. The arts of the bugs you know, karate, judo, kung fu," answers Steve.

"How many of us know martial arts?" asks Bill.

"There's only one way to find out. I'm a black belt in Mantis and other types of kung fu," says Steve.

"I'm a black belt in Judo but it's been years," says Judy.

"I was a black belt in jujitsu but it's also been years," says Bill.

"Hmm, Andy must have made this one of his criteria's in picking us," says Steve.

"You know we have no idea what you're talking about," says Leslie.

"There are different methods and techniques of fighting. Patterned after the movements of insects," says Judy.

"It is a very effective way of battling larger numbers than you. If we use it we might cut the odds in half or even turn them in our favor," says Steve.

"I think I understand. On Child's Island we have a similar 'art' called unarmed combat. I've only seen it done in demonstrations. Only the soldiers and police are allowed to study

110

this way of fighting, since Child's Island prohibited violence by law," says Bob.

"Well, at least you know what we're talking about," says Steve.

"Don't sweat it. Three out of six is enough. We only have a few hours so let's get started," says Steve.

The next hours pass quickly as Steve, Bill and Judy try to teach the King, Bob and Leslie the martial arts. Lectures, demonstrations and practice are constantly going on.

Finally after a long session, "All right everyone. Stop. We've done all we can. The rest is up to you three," says Steve wiping the sweat from his forehead.

"Do you think we know enough to defend ourselves?" asks Bob.

"Probably. You are very fast learners. It must be a trait of Child's Island. All of you seem to be in good health also," answers Steve.

"Steve, do you honestly think we have a chance?" asks Bill.

"We always have a chance. It's what we do with that chance that decides our destiny," says Steve.

"Wow Steve, that's deep. You should definitely write a book when we get out of all this," says Bill as he laughs.

"Write a book? I'll put it on my to do list once we get out of here," replies Steve.

The six sit or lie on the floor resting for the battle. Their rest period is short, only half an hour. The sound of the wooden bar being taken off the door is heard throughout the hut. The six slowly and cautiously stand up, staring at the door. Fear and anxiety are written on their faces. The door opens. The native with blue sheets around him stands in front of the doorway.

Behind him are about twenty-five other natives. They have spears, swords and crossbows.

"You will come with us and you will not resist," says the native.

Steve nods his head and walks to the doorway and stands there. The others do the same.

"Now move," orders the native.

Steve and Bill slowly step outside and start to walk forward. The four others follow in pairs. Crowding around them, the natives hold their weapons, some aiming at the six. About fifty yards away from the hut are six poles with ropes around them. The poles form a line. Each is about ten feet apart. At the base of each pole is a pile of sticks. It's obvious what their purpose is. The six walk very slow which agitates the natives, causing them to jab at the six with their weapons. Steve and his crew comply by walking faster.

Instead of simply readjusting their pace to that of the natives, the six prisoners continue to pick up speed. The natives don't reprimand them for going too fast because, after all, they were the ones who ordered them to pick up speed in the first place. They walk faster and faster. To keep up with them the natives are forced to spread out. A gap forms between the six prisoners and their captors. Some of the natives start to jog in order to keep up with the six.

While the natives are concentrating on keeping pace with the six, Steve starts to mumble, "I guess that's enough elbow room," and then yells "Now!" giving one of the natives behind him a back kick.

The native is hit in the stomach and falls, dropping his sword. Bill does the same, and he and Steve immediately explode into kicks and punches. The four others also begin fighting. The natives are totally overwhelmed. With Bob, the King, Leslie and Judy punching and kicking away, these four have taken the defensive end of the battle. Each takes his or her position and waits for the natives to approach and make their assaults. Then the four counter-attack with their own moves. Steve and Bill, however, have taken the offensive end of the battle. All six, whether fighting on offense or defense, are doing considerably well. No matter how good the six are doing though, it still remains a dangerous situation.

While the others are busy attacking or counter-attacking, Steve is confronted by two natives with swords. He takes a defensive position. As the natives close in on him he glances at the ground and sees a sword. He runs to it and then meets his pursuers halfway with not a second to spare. Swinging his weapon fiercely he now makes assaults with the sword and the natives resist as best they can.

After ten seconds of dueling, Steve sidekicks the native to his left knocking him to the ground. After another few seconds he does the same to the other native to his right. Both natives are now on the ground in pain and defeated. Steve has no time to take credit for his victory.

Two more natives attack with swords but this time Steve is ready for them. He doesn't let them make the first move. He swings with such strength and power that the impact forces one native to drop his sword. Steve takes advantage of this opportunity and quickly jabs the native in the stomach. He then resumes battling the other native and swings his sword and hits the native on his left side. Steve catches his breath and glances around the area to see how the others are doing. Spotting Bill he looks at the ground and in a fraction of a second finds what he's looking for. Taking a few steps forward he picks up a sword and yells out to Bill, who turns his head to look at him.

"Catch," yells Steve, throwing the sword to Bill. Bill catches the sword with both hands and in the same move swings it at the two natives he was fighting.

The blow of Bill's sword puts the two natives on defense. He continues to swing at the natives. They are taken back by his strong attack. One drops his weapon and in one great swing, Bill hits both in the stomach. Badly hurt they fall to the ground. He turns around to see if anyone is behind him and sees a native running toward him, sword in hand. He has just enough time to swing his sword and block the blows given by the native, protecting himself from definite disaster. Bill chops at the native's legs cutting them severely. The man falls moaning in pain.

Two more approach but are quickly defeated by Bill. The King is battling two natives himself. He seems to be defending himself well. He is constantly blocking the natives swings and jabs, making no attempt to swing or jab at the natives for any offensive move. He does well for one who never fought hand to hand combat or dueled in his peaceful life. Just how peaceful his life is going to be in the future will be decided by his actions now.

Judy is dueling with one of the natives and appears to be winning. Until one native sneaks up behind her and grabs her arm as she is about to swing. With the native squeezing her hand tightly, she drops her weapon in pain. The native then holds both of her arms behind her back. She struggles viciously but the native is too strong.

Another native approaches her and raises his sword over her head. She screams frantically and struggles even harder. The native does not strike her. He simply throws the sword down at her feet. It just misses her.

"I do not need a sword for you, woman," says the foolish native as he tightens his hands around the girl's neck.

She is furious and knees him in the crotch. He yells in pain and bends over releasing his grip on her neck. Finally overpowering the native holding her, she proceeds to chop and hit the native around her. They fall to the ground in both surprise and pain. Judy quickly turns back to face the man who was holding her. He is right in front of her and about to grab her. She knees him in the crotch and before he can do anything but yell Judy straightens out her right hand and pushes it into the native's throat. She then grabs his head and pushes it down toward her knee, giving his head a good belt.

"Hmm… chauvinist and primitive natives. They always go together," says Judy to herself.

Judy then turns towards Leslie who is presently being attacked by one of the natives. He is swinging his sword at Leslie trying to finish her off. She swings her sword with both hands blocking his sword from hitting her. Judy watches and wonders whether she should help Leslie. At first, Judy can't come to a decision but when she sees native approaching Leslie from behind, swinging his sword up and down, she doesn't hesitate any longer.

Judy runs towards the native and swings her sword at him. Leslie finishes off her native with a quick jab to the stomach while Judy fights bravely against the other. The two natives hit the ground and lose consciousness. Leslie turns around to see Judy standing next to the dead body of the native and is startled. It only takes her a few seconds to realize what happened.

115

"So that's what got that native's attention. Thanks. I guess I owe you my life."

"You're welcome and you can keep your life. Just make sure you do the same for me when I need the help," says Judy with a grin.

"You can count on it," says Leslie returning her smile.

The smiles are displaced quickly when two natives approach them with swords. Judy and Leslie go right to battle. Right from the start they have the better of the natives. In a matter of seconds the natives are on the ground.

"Hey, we make a good team!" cries Leslie.

"Then let's stick together for the rest of the battle and remain a team," says Judy. They then resume their fighting and take on more natives.

Bob has been doing considerably well. Not once has he been cornered or has had a close call. Every duel he fights, he wins. He has been taking on two natives at a time and each pair of natives only last about half a minute. It's almost like a contest to see which natives can duel the longest with him without getting stabbed. If only the natives could know that he has never held a sword before!

Steve has been doing excellent, but he has been doing too well. He has been fighting two, sometimes three, natives at a time. His offense is great but he can't put up with four men coming at him from different directions. It isn't too long that he is no longer making an assault on the natives but defending his life. The natives have easily taken the offensive part of the battle and forced the outnumbered Steve to take the defensive part. Realizing he has been overconfident, Steve starts to back up as he raises his sword to block the swings and blows from his attackers.

The natives realize that Steve is trapped and they swing harder and harder. Steve battles back fiercely to stop their swords from reaching and harming him. He continues to back up, looking terribly confused.

Backing into a boulder he jumps forward in surprise. He turns around and without hesitation he jumps on it. He still faces the natives. Standing on the giant rock he swings his sword at the four natives and occasionally jabs at them. He is still on the defense but at least he has a position from which to defend himself. Steve and the four natives continue to duel.

The natives can't quite reach him to get a good swing or jab at him and while Steve has very good reach from the height he is at, he can't quite connect his sword with the natives. He can't spend that much time trying either. He is constantly blocking the natives' attempts to connect their swords with his body. It's just about an even match.

The odds change though when two more natives enter the fight. Steve was doing well against four natives but six is another story. The boulder gives Steve an advantage, but how much can it give against six natives? Constantly moving, Steve is blocking, dodging, swaying and stepping or jumping back from swords jabbing at him. Two more natives start to run towards the boulder and Steve's eyes widen as if to say "enough is enough!"

Steve wears his poker face again. He seems to drift to another harsh memory to draw strength from, but this time it's to no avail. He's barely dodging or blocking the natives' jabs and blows intended very much to kill him.

Judy, who has just downed two more natives of her own, sees what is happening to Steve. Without hesitation she throws her sword down and picks up the two crossbows lying on the ground next to the natives she just stabbed. At the same time, Leslie sees Steve standing on the boulder out of the corner of her eye. She turns her head slightly to the left to see why Steve is on the boulder, and is astounded by what she sees.

"Whoa!" mumbles Leslie.

She quickly turns to face the natives she had been battling with, and jabs the man in the stomach with her sword. Her eyes widen again when she realizes that by looking at Steve, she has left herself open to attack and the native almost took advantage of her. She bends down and pries the sword out of the man's hand. Leslie quickly throws the sword at the group of natives surrounding Steve. Then Judy fires the two crossbows at the natives running towards the boulder. The arrows hit them in the back and they are stopped in their tracks and fall to the ground.

While the two natives are hit with the arrows fired by Judy, one of the natives surrounding Steve is hit in the back with the sword that Leslie threw. This native cries out, takes a few steps back and falls backwards on the sword, driving it through his stomach. After throwing the sword Leslie runs towards the boulder. Simultaneously Judy throws down the crossbow, picks up her sword, and also rushes towards the giant rock.

Steve holds off the five natives a bit better than six, but is glad to see Judy and Leslie coming to his side. The three slowly but surely beat back the remaining natives who are now falling like dominoes. Loud screams are heard from the natives as swords slice open their chests and stomachs.

"Nice job, you guys really came through for me. I thought for sure I was a goner, especially when the number was increasing to eight!" says Steve.

"Like I always say, behind every great man is a great woman... putting him where he is and covering his ass so he can stay there!" replies Judy.

"Hey, I like that!" comments Leslie.

"Must you always be such a feminist? Well, thanks again anyway for helping this 'great man'!" says Steve, kissing Leslie on the cheek and then Judy on the lips. Steve and Judy stare at each other.

The King, Bill and Bob join the three. "Sorry we couldn't help. We saw you were in a spot but every time we'd win a duel some more natives would attack us!" says Bob.

"Don't worry about it. We all had that problem," responds Steve.

"Well, looks like we did it! We downed every one of them," says Bill looking over the battleground.

They wear looks of amazement as they see all the bodies lying on the ground.

"I can't believe we did all of this. Just look at all those bodies and the blood on them and the ground. I almost feel like a murderer, even though it was self-defense and our only chance of surviving. But I guess being right doesn't always take away the guilt for killing," comments Steve.

The others stare at Steve with looks of respect. All of them seem to relate to what he has just said in one way or another. His words have hit the spot. There is silence among the six. One of the listeners is a bit restless and appears as if he is going to break the silence.

"Steve, I couldn't agree with you more but don't you think we ought to get out of here while we still have the chance, and save the philosophy for later?" says Bill who seems very on edge standing in the open clearing.

"You're right. We'll have plenty of time to mourn these deaths in the future," replies Steve.

The six slowly walk toward the forest.

"Hey Bob, you know you surprised me! You really put up a fight against those natives. But I guess you're used to cutting people, being a doctor and all," remarks Bill.

"Ha ha," replies Bob.

While walking towards the forest, Steve doesn't notice one of the natives regaining consciousness. He quietly reaches for a crossbow. Still on his stomach he pulls the trigger sending a small arrow sailing across the clearing. Steve screams in pain as the arrow hits the back of his right thigh. He falls on his stomach. Bill looks back into the clearing and runs to the native.

"Bill, come back! He's got a sword!" yells the King.

Bill does not answer the King's cries and continues to run towards the native. Wearing an evil grin, the native runs toward Bill swinging his sword. Not hesitating a second, Bill makes a perfect drop kick against the native, hitting him in the stomach and knocking him to the ground. Screaming in pain the native falls backwards dropping his sword. Bill springs back and then runs forward toward the native, jumping on top of him. Immediately he begins to punch the native in the face and after a few seconds the native again loses consciousness.

Bill stops punching the native and runs back to the others. Everyone is crowded around Steve. Bob gets on his knees. He puts his sword in the right side of Steve's pants and slits it. The back of Steve's leg is bare from his thigh to his foot. The wound is now visible. The arrowhead is an inch long and a half inch wide.

"It's only a quarter way in his leg. Brace yourself, I'm going to pull it out on four," says Bob.

Steve tenses his hands making fists.

"One, two, three!" yells Bob pulling the arrow out of Steve's leg before reaching four.

Steve cries out in pain and pounds the ground with his fists. He grinds his teeth and pushes his face into the dirt. Bob hands the arrow to Bill. He then looks over the wound, touching it gently with his fingers. Bob unbuttons his shirt and takes it off. Ripping the shirt into three sheets of bandages, he ties the strips around Steve's thigh.

"This should stop the bleeding. For now, anyway," says Bob.

"It's so tight, I wouldn't be surprised if it stopped the circulation too!" snaps Steve sarcastically.

"I'm sorry if the strips are tight but if they were any looser the bleeding would not stop," replies Bob.

"Well, don't just sit there, help me up," says Steve.

"Are you sure you can walk on that leg?" asks Bob.

"There's only one way to find out. Besides, I have my left leg to use for support. If I can't walk, I'll limp," says Steve, as he slowly and painfully pushes himself up to his knees. Bill puts his arm around Steve. Bob does the same. All three slowly get up from their knees and stand up.

"Are you sure you're all right?" asks Judy who, like everyone else, seems very concerned.

"Yeah, I'm alright, but Bill may not have been if that native had stabbed him with that sword! What I mean to say is I appreciate what you did but I also would have felt terrible if you had gotten hurt," says Steve switching from the voice of a commander to the voice of a friend.

Bill picks his head up and begins to smile. "You're welcome. And I appreciate your concern," replies Bill.

Steve holds his sword high in the air and points it in front of him. "Forward, march!" he says, beginning to limp further into the forest.

Bill and Bob quickly pick up their swords and the six friends follow into the forest. As they walk through the forest Bill remarks, "Steve, even when we do get to the shore, how are we going to leave? We still don't have a boat."

"I'm hoping that the natives have some kind of raft that we can 'borrow'. If not, I sure hope the King can swim!" answers Steve.

The six walk through the forest cautiously, each one holding onto their swords. They seem ready for anything. The six reach the shore very quickly.

"That was fast," says Steve.

"It couldn't have been more than ten minutes but it seemed like ten hours. I've never felt as threatened as I did just now. I've felt safer walking through the slums of my old city at one in the morning," comments Bill.

"Maybe so, but we were ready for anything this time!" says Bob.

"Everything but three boats beached on the shore," replies Steve. He points to the shore.

The six are overwhelmed when they see what appear to be three motor boats on the shore. The white boats are approximately ten yards from the water. The boats are about fifteen feet long and ten feet wide. They seem to be made of the same material as the *Kid Power*. The shape is like an average motor boat in the "outside world". The controls are on a dashboard and they are similar to those of the *Kid Power*. The steering wheels are the same as that of a car. There are two seats in the front and in the rear there are cushioned benches. The interior is black. The boats have decals on the sides saying "Child's Island Navy Division". All three look fairly new. There is one specific thing about these "motor boats" that stands out. That is the fact that the three appear to have no motors. Instead of a propeller at the rear they have three round holes.

The six cautiously approach the boats.

"Just as I suspected. They're army boats," says the King.

"What would they be doing here?" asks Bill.

"It's so obvious Bill. General Bollings must be on the island. Eric said that he'd be coming to the island," answers Steve.

"If General Bollings is on the island then where is he?" asks Leslie.

"I don't know and to tell you the truth, I don't care. All I know is that there are three boats sitting right in front of us, waiting for us to take them and get off this blasted island!" says Steve.

"I'm with you! To hell with General Bollings. Let's get out of here while we have the chance," says Bob.

"That's an order!" says Steve.

"Wait a minute!" says Bill.

"What's the problem? Don't you want to get out of here?" asks Steve.

"Yeah, I do but I would also like to know what kind of boats don't have any motors," answers Bill.

"They're hovercrafts. Or as the people on Child's Island like to call them 'flying boats'", answers Bob.

"Hovercrafts... now why didn't I think of that in the first place? Those three holes at the rear should have been a dead giveaway. They're obviously thrusters. Air is blown out of them pushing the 'boat' and there are probably more of those holes at the bottom keeping it out of water," says Bill.

"Exactly! I didn't know your world used hovercrafts," says Bob.

"We use them all right. But they're not as advanced as these of course," says Steve.

"Why does your army use them?" asks Bill.

"It's more convenient. In many places the water can be shallow," answers Bob.

"Where does the air that's blown out of the thrusters come from?" asks Judy.

"At the bottom of the craft are many holes. Some blow out air with tremendous pressure, and some suck in air like a super powered vacuum. When the air is sucked up through the vacuum holes it's distributed to the holes that act as thrusters. Believe it or not, the system works. And the boats go quite fast," answers Bob.

"That's all I wanted to hear. Let's move!" says Steve

grabbing onto one of the crafts and jumping in.

The other five jump in after Steve. Everyone takes a position. Bill and Steve sit in the front two seats, the rest sit on the benches. Bill hits a button on the control board and the engines of the craft start with a roar.

"I'll let her warm up a bit," says Bill as he quickly looks over the controls of the craft.

After a minute or so, "Bill, we're not getting any younger!" says Steve.

"All right, all right! I just want to make sure I know what I'm doing," says Bill.

Bill presses a few more buttons and then adjusts the gears. "Brace yourselves, here goes everything!" says Bill pushing a large, square red button labeled "lift".

Immediately after he presses the button the engine begins to run very fast and the sound of air being compressed is heard.

After a few seconds, the craft starts to lift slowly off the ground. Inch by inch it gets higher until it finally stops at about two feet above the ground. Bill then maneuvers one of the gears and the craft turns around.

"Goodbye island. You were a nice place to visit but..." says Bill pulling the main gear backwards. The craft slowly flies away from the other two crafts and as it carries the six deeper into the water, it gains more speed.

"This is easier than I thought. For once we get a break," comments Bill.

Just as Bill finishes his sentence, seven "boys" come running out of the forest. Six are soldiers and the seventh is none

124

other than General Bollings. The seven run up to the water. All six soldiers fire at the craft.

"Cease fire!" We'll never get them this way. Start the crafts, we'll go after them," orders General Bollings after several seconds of shooting.

The soldiers board the crafts, three in each. General Bollings gets in the one on the right. "You take charge of that one, Captain," he says.

The General sits in one of the front seats, a soldier sits in the other piloting the craft. The two other soldiers sit on the two benches. The noise of the tremendous air pressure is heard as they lift the two crafts up. The crafts turn to face the water and almost immediately afterward they start moving over the water.

"Full speed. We can't afford to let them escape!" orders the General.

"They're starting to gain on us," says Steve.

"I know, and I can't go any faster. We would have to pick the lemon of the lot," says Bill.

Bill continues to try to gain more speed and keep the distance between his craft and the soldiers, but in spite of his efforts the gap between the three crafts becomes smaller and smaller.

"Prepare to open fire!" orders General Bollings. The soldiers immediately stand and aim their sub-machine guns at the hovercraft.

"They're aiming their guns at us!" yells the King.

"Everyone hit the deck!" orders Steve.

All on board quickly follow his command. Steve and Bill are crouched in their seats so that their bodies cannot be seen.

"Ha! Did they actually think they had a chance to escape using our hovercrafts? They barely know how to pilot one, while

125

we use them practically every day. It just goes to show that Captain Mason isn't really smart, he's just lucky. And that luck just ran out! Open fire, and don't waste a single bullet!" orders the General.

Bullets begin to fly at the craft. Only a few come close to the six people on board.

"They're going to puncture the boat... I mean craft," says Bill steering the craft and dodging bullets at the same time.

"These are supposed to be bulletproof," yells the King.

"Yeah, and so was the *Kid Power*," says Bill in an annoyed tone of voice.

"Doesn't make any difference whether this craft is bulletproof... we're not!" says Steve.

The firing suddenly stops.

"Probably to get closer," mumbles Steve.

"What now? They'll surely get closer and they're bound to get at least one of us," says Bill.

"And all we have are swords," says Steve.

"We've got to do something. We can't just let them catch up and shoot us!" cries Bill.

Steve doesn't answer Bill. He stands tensing his body and his eyes stare at the floor of the craft, trying desperately to think of something.

"Can't do it. I haven't got any idea of what to do," cries the confused boy.

Bill is shocked. "You've got to have an idea. Those two crafts are getting closer and closer," yells Bill.

Steve is now completely out of control with frustration. "What do you mean I've got to have a plan? I'm not some machine. Why do I have to be the one to think of all the plans anyway? This time it's up to one of you!" yells Steve, shaking his head in a confused way.

"You think Robert's death is still taking its toll on Steve?" asks Leslie, who like everyone else is surprised by Steve's actions.

126

Bill, the King, Judy, Bob and Leslie each strain to think of a plan. They all stare at teach other hoping one will say something.

"Damn!" exclaims Bill, trying desperately to think of something.

"I'm blank," says Judy.

Steve's memories once again drift back to his past. His father is beating him again. Steve is being backed up into a corner as he's being scolded and hit.

"I told you to finish all of your food. How dare you waste my money! I never even wanted you to begin with!" yells his father.

Steve suddenly lunges forward and runs towards his father as opposed to backing away from him. His father is caught off guard, backs into a seat and falls over it. The young Steve grins.

The two crafts chasing them gain more and more speed, getting closer and closer. Suddenly Steve opens his eyes and smiles.

"Yes," he mumbles. "All right everyone, I've got one last plan," says Steve, sitting up in his chair.

The crew stares at Steve with expressions of relief. "We'll do anything you say!" says Bill, wearing a big smile.

"Okay, here it is. When I give you the word, turn the craft around and head straight towards one of their hovercrafts at full speed!" says Steve.

"Say, what?!" exclaims Bill.

"Steve, you want us to drive straight into the line of fire?" asks Leslie.

"Look, you asked me for a plan and I gave you one. Do you trust me or not?" replies Steve.

Shaking his head but obeying his commander, Bill maneuvers the controls and steering wheel of the craft and it begins to turn.

Bill steers the craft toward the hovercraft opposite the General's and quickly gets up from his chair and kneels behind it. Bill steers the craft reaching from behind the chair. Steve's hovercraft is traveling at full speed towards the Captain's craft. Both crafts are approaching each other and the distance between the two is decreasing rapidly!

"General Bollings is right, they are crazy! Those idiots are heading right towards us. They're probably suicidal but in a few seconds, the only thing they're going to be is dead! Open fire!" orders the Captain.

Bullets begin to pour over the deck of Steve's hovercraft. Once again, the bullets come closest to Steve and Bill. Bill extends his right hand towards a button on the control panel labeled "steering lock". His index finger strains towards it and just misses. He tries again and again, his face getting redder from trying hard. His finger finally reaches the button and presses it. He then quickly turns away, dodging the flying bullets.

"Do you think we got any of them, Captain?" asks the driver.

"I can't say. They're all hiding," answers the Captain.

"In a few more seconds we're going to collide!" exclaims the driver of the Captain's hovercraft.

"Maybe that's their plan. General Bollings said they were crazy. They probably are committing suicide and they're trying to take us with them!" shouts the Captain in an excited voice.

The two crafts are only a few hundred yards away.

"They're going to crash into us!" yells one soldier.

"Turn away from them!" orders the Captain.

The driver quickly turns the wheel to the right. The craft immediately turns to the right, but because of the speed at which it is traveling, and because the wheel has been turned so quickly, the craft begins to turn over on its side. The Captain and the two soldiers slide to the right as the craft continues to turn. Finally, their craft turns over completely and the Captain and his two comrades fall into the water. The craft falls on top of them.

Bill and the rest of the crew are amazed to see the craft floating upside down and the Captain and his soldiers trying to hold on to the craft and stay afloat.

"Steve, you're either a genius or the luckiest person in the world! Who else would have thought up such a plan?" says Bill.

"You knew that if the hovercraft turned over on its side it would lose control because the thrusters that are pushing it up would no longer be aiming downward and would be useless. You took a chance, but as always, it worked!" hollers Judy.

"Everyone stay down, we're going to have to do this just one more time. Now turn the craft around and head towards General Bollings craft," orders Steve.

Once again the six tense up and close their eyes. This time, they do not hug one another. They simply lie flat on the deck.

The two crafts are about a half mile from each other.

"Now they're heading towards us!" says the General's driver.

"Just keep on course. They're not going to pull that trick on us. Don't just stand there. Open fire!" orders the angry General.

Bullets once again rain on the craft. They are even more plentiful and come closer and closer.

"Damn! One of those bullets just missed my head," comments Bill.

Steve looks at Bill but does not react. He is squinting and has an angry look on his face. His eyes rest on the swords that he and the others brought with them from the native's island. Steve looks over the swords until he spots a crossbow lying on the deck. His eyes widen and after a few seconds he turns and quickly crawls towards the crossbow.

"Hey! What are you..." starts Bill as Steve races towards the crossbow.

Bill stares at Steve in astonishment.

"Are you crazy? Bullets flying all over and you crawl out in the line of fire?" yells Bill.

Steve does not reply. He just stares at the crossbow, rubbing it and feeling it with his hands.

"Feel this," he says to Bill who takes it from his hands.

"It's metal. It looks like wood, but it's metal," Bill repeats.

"What would the army want with crossbows?" asks Bill.

"Nothing. This probably fell out of some kind of crate that General Bollings gave to the natives as part of the payment for killing the King," answers Steve.

"But the natives already have crossbows," says Bill.

"Not metal ones, which are probably more effective than the wooden ones that the natives are using," says Steve, continuing to look over the crossbow.

"Well, there's only one way to find out how good something works, and that's by using it," says Steve, getting up and aiming the crossbow at the oncoming hovercraft.

Bill looks at Steve as if he's crazy as he pulls the trigger of the crossbow, sending an arrow speeding over to General Bollings hovercraft. The arrow hits one of the soldiers in the chest. Screaming in pain he throws his sub-machine gun down and backs up into the railing, falling over it and into the water. The other soldier is also taken by surprise. He throws his gun down and lies flat on his stomach on the deck.

"What are you doing? You fool! Get up and fire at them!" orders the General.

"You get up and fire! I'm not getting shot like Little John," replies the soldier.

"Why you disobedient little crumb. I'll have..." starts the General.

"Sir, in another twenty seconds we're going to collide!" interrupts the driver of the General's craft.

"Don't worry about when we're going to crash, just keep going!" orders the aggravated General.

"Nice shot Steve," says Bill.

"Yep, those metal arrows do the job all right," replies Steve.

"About twenty seconds more," says Bill.

"Just keep going. I think the driver is about to blow it," says Steve.

The two crafts are so close now that a slingshot could be used as a weapon.

"Request permission to come aboard!" yells Steve, laughing to the General.

Steve is clearly heard by the members of the General's craft.

"Your little jokes and hassling won't work. We're not going to turn like the fools in the other craft, so it looks like your plans aren't working for you anymore Mason!" yells Bollings.

The General takes his handgun and aims it at Steve's craft. "Long live the King! Ha ha!" laughs the power crazy General.

As the General begins to fire, his driver finally breaks from the pressure.

"We're going to crash!" he yells, quickly steering to the left.

"No, you stupid fool, no!" yells the General as he slides to the left and crashes into his driver.

The hovercraft quickly starts to turn to the left. It is in the midst of turning when Steve's craft hits it in the rear. The rear of the craft lifts upwards until it completely turns in midair. The General and his soldiers fall out as the craft itself plunges into the water. Steve's hovercraft is not stopped by the crash. It continues to speed away from the native island and the now upside-down

131

hovercraft of General Bollings, which is floating in the water like the Captain's hovercraft.

"We did it!" yells Bill as both he and Steve jump up from behind their chairs, hugging each other.

After a few seconds the two break off. They then turn to look behind them. Their laughter floats over the water as they see the General and his soldiers struggling to keep afloat near their craft.

"Go ahead, laugh. You haven't heard the last of me. Don't think that it's over Mason. When I get back to the island, I'm going to have you killed! Do you hear me? I'm going to kill you!" yells General Bollings, who is shaking his fists.

"Hang it up Bollings. I can't even hear you. The noise from the thrusters blowing out all that air is drowning you out," laughs Steve.

Steve puts up two fingers in the sign of peace towards General Bollings shaking fist.

Bill turns back to face the controls of the craft. He sits in his chair and begins to maneuver some of the gears and other controls. Steve walks over the deck to the center of the craft.

"You can come out now, it's all over," says Steve to his faithful crew.

Bob and Leslie get up from under the bench, as does Judy from her hiding place. The three look in the direction of the King who is still curled up under the bench. Steve gets down on his knees and shakes the King gently. Still no response. Steve is curious and turns the man over on his back.

"My God, he's been shot! Bob, come on, this is your department," yells Steve.

Bob gets on his knees and quickly tears the robes off. He wipes away the blood on the King's chest. Leslie runs quickly for the craft's first aid kit and gives it to Bob. He takes a bottle from the equipment and pours the contents on the King's wound.

132

"How is he?" asks Steve, still kneeling on the deck.

"Not too good. He was shot below the heart. The chemical I poured on the wound will clean it and slow down the bleeding, if not stop it all together. The bullet has to come out. It's slowly moving towards his heart. We've got to get him back to Child's Island so I can operate on him," answers Bob.

The hovercraft in the meantime has been slowing down. Steve hollers at Bill.

"I heard you Steve, but it looks like when we hit the hovercraft the controls were damaged. I can't control the speed. I can barely steer the craft," replies Bill.

Steve runs to Bill. He stares at the large dent in the front of the craft.

"Part of the engine must be in the front. Do you think we can fix it?" asks Steve.

"No way. I tried everything possible. This thing has to be dry-docked to be fixed. It's been banged up pretty bad. We're only going about thirty-five or forty knots. I'm sorry Steve. I'll try to keep it at this speed but there's nothing else I can do," says Bill in a disappointed voice.

"You've done all you could. Keep up the great work," says Steve, patting Bill on the shoulder.

"Ha, great work," replies Bill.

"What are the King's chances of holding on until we reach the island?" asks Steve.

"Under normal circumstances, very little but the way things have been going on this mission, who knows," answers Bob.

Chapter 6 – The Last Plan

Approximately an hour after the chase, the hovercraft carrying Steve, Bill, Judy, Bob, Leslie and the King, lands on the shore of Child's Island. Waiting for the hovercraft are countless police cars and ambulances. In a matter of no time, the King is in an ambulance speeding towards the First City of Child's Island. Following closely behind are Steve and the others riding in police cars.

A few hours later Steve, Bill and Judy stand in a hospital lobby. The lobby is no different from the hospital lobbies in the "Outside World". A large desk with nurses attending it, a few rows of chairs running up and down. Four large glass doors at the end of a corridor leading to some steps which leads to a large parking lot. There are plenty of people, doctors, nurses, patients and visitors.

"I wonder what's taking so long? Bob said it would be about an hour," says Steve, who like Bill and Judy, stand in front of the large desk which is in the center of the lobby and is manned by three nurses.

"Maybe it was closer to the heart than Bob thought. You can't rush an operation when it's near the heart," replies Judy.

Just as she finishes talking, one of the many elevator doors opens. Out walk Leslie and Bob. They walk over to their impatient friends.

"Well, how is he?" asks Steve.

"He's fine. We finished operating about an hour ago," answers Bob.

"An hour ago? How come you're just coming down now?" asks Bill.

"That's what I wanted to speak to you about. You see I've made a shocking discovery. You remember the blood samples I had Leslie take from you?" asks Bob.

"Sure. Why did you need those samples? Were you trying to find out our blood type so we could donate some to the King?" asks Steve.

"No, we have plenty of blood in the hospital. But let me continue. After I finished operating on the King we had to pump some blood into his system because he had lost a great deal of it during the surgery. It was because of that, that I came up with the idea of taking blood samples from you three so I could investigate the growing materials in your blood which allow you to become what you would call 'adults'," continues Bob.

"That sounds fascinating. But why do you look like you've just seen a ghost?" asks Bill.

"You'll understand when I tell you the results of my investigation," replies Bob.

"What kind of results could make you so upset about our blood tests?" questions Steve.

Bob clears his throat and rubs his hands together before speaking, "The results of the test I did on the growing materials in your blood were zero. It doesn't make sense but there are no growing materials in your blood. In other words, you're not growing into 'adults' like you say you are," states Bob.

"But how is that possible?" asks Judy.

"I don't know. Perhaps the food you've been eating. The atmosphere. I honestly can't say. But I can say you are not growing older physically. You are now like the people of Child's Island," says Bob.

The three "children" are speechless. They simply stare at Bob and Leslie.

"Please don't feel bad. I mean, don't consider yourselves freaks If you are planning on living on Child's Island you would be freaks if you were growing. That is, if you are planning to stay with us," says Leslie, who had been quiet until now. "At this point I don't think we really know what we want. We'll have to do some heavy thinking on it," says Steve.

"Well, if you need any advice you know you can always ask us. And if you decide to stay, Leslie and I will do everything we can to help you be at home," says Bob.

The five are silent for several seconds. Suddenly, in through the large glass doors walks Commissioner White and five officers. They walk over to the silent five.

"You're under arrest!" snaps the Commissioner.

"What? This has got to be some kind of a joke," replies Bob.

"It's no joke. The five of you are under arrest for attempted murder. I have warrants for the arrest of Doctor Bob Goodboy, Nurse Leslie Bluesmith, and the remaining invaders. Are you going to go with us peacefully, or are we going to have to call in more officers?" asks the Commissioner.

"Please, can you tell us one thing? Who are we accused of trying to murder?" asks Bob.

"Doctor Goodboy, why do you insist on playing games? You know darn well, it was the King," answers the Commissioner.

"The King?!" shouts Bob.

"We rescued him. We risked our lives to save him," says Judy.

"So I thought, but we just got a message from General Bollings on one of the Army radios. He said that when he came to the natives' island with the ransom, he saw you making deals with them. When you found out that he saw you, you took the King to another island. He followed you with his soldiers, but then you started to fire at him and his men. They couldn't fire back because they might hit the King and retreated. Before you were out of their sight, they saw you shoot the King. General Bollings suspects that it was the invader Mason," concludes the Commissioner.

"It's a lie. It's all a lie. General Bollings was the one who tried to kill the King. We saved him from the natives," cries Leslie.

139

"Save it for the jury. But if the King dies, you'll all be tried for murder. And you know what the penalty for murder is on Child's Island," says the Commissioner.

The five can only stand and stare at each other in astonishment. Thoughts are running through their heads at a frantic pace.

"We don't stand a chance."

"What if the King dies?"

"No one is going to believe us."

"We won't even get a trial."

Finally Bill whispers to Steve, "We can't just let them take us in. What can we do?"

The police begin to put handcuffs on the five. Bill, Bob and Leslie have cuffs on them before they can react. When one of the officers tries to put cuffs on Judy she grabs the handcuffs and hits the officer in the head with them. He falls quickly to the floor holding his head. Judy then puts one end of the cuffs on the arm of one officer, and the other end on another. She pushes both of them causing them to fall down. Steve does the same with his handcuffs, grabbing them and cuffing two officers, then pushing them to the floor.

Two more officers jump on Steve's back but Judy jumps on their backs. Judy pokes both officers in their eyes and reaching from behind she grabs their chins and pries their heads back, forcing them to let go of Steve. Steve gets up and pushes two more officers into the wall on either side of them. He punches another in the face and successfully decks another officer who stood right in front of him. He then runs through the remaining officers as if he were a football player.

Another pair of officers start to run right after Steve but Judy, who is still wrestling with the two officers she pulled off

140

Steve, locks her legs around theirs and trips them. One falls, banging his chin into the ground, and knocks himself out. The other stays down trying to pry Judy's legs from around his stomach. Although still cuffed, Bill, Leslie and Bob leap on top of the soldiers wrestling with Judy. They wrap their legs around the soldiers. This frees Judy to get up and run down to meet Steve.

Steve and Judy continue to run down the hall in a frantic dash for freedom. They make it to the doors before the officers are even halfway down the hall. Steve puts his arms out and pushes open two of the four glass doors. He accidentally pushes the doors into a doctor, and without stopping continues his dash. When they make it to the bottom of the stairs they hesitate and quickly look over the crowded parking lot. Their attention is drawn to three police cars parked directly in front of the hospital entrance. Like all the other cars, the police cars are small. They have flashing lights and decals, and like most official things on Child's Island, are white. Steve and Judy get into the first car. Steve pushes the start button. The car starts immediately. Quickly maneuvering the gear shift he steps on the accelerator and the car speeds away.

"You have a license?" asks Judy smiling at Steve. Steve smiles back in response.

Police officers rush out of the hospital and fire at the fleeing car.

"Stop firing you idiots! You might hit an innocent bystander," yells Commissioner White running down the steps.

The Commissioner and his officers jump into the remaining cards and speed away, with sirens on and their lights flashing. Steve and Judy's car is speeding at about seventy-five miles per hour. Steve does a lot of twisting and turning through the traffic. He doesn't pay much attention to cars around him because he's got problems of his own.

141

Turning onto a one way street, Steve drives the opposite way of the traffic. He turns and turns, swaying to the left and then right in order to avoid each car that's headed towards him. He does a good job but the other drivers aren't that confident in his ability to turn away from him at the last second. Disregarding the speeding cars around him, one driver hits his brakes and stops right in the middle of the road. Two cars quickly pile into the car in a chain reaction, and the result is a triple smash-up!

Another driver, whose car is right behind the three that smashed, frantically turns his car away from them so fast and so hard that the car spins and ends up across the road sideways. Steve sees the mess in front of him and quickly steers his car onto the sidewalk and speeds by the angry drivers.

Following close behind are police cars containing the Commissioner and his men. Seeing the accident ahead they too attempt to avoid the pile up and begin to maneuver their cars strategically. In all the turning, one of the wheels of one of the police car collapses, causing the car to flip over. This throws off the Commissioner's driver's concentration and he loses control and hits an oncoming car. Both the civilian and police cars are totaled and their engines smoke up a small fog.

A three year old boy who stands on the sidewalk seems to find this scene quite amusing.

"Hey, why couldn't you turn away like your friend in the first police car? Is he a better officer?" yells the innocent child, thinking that Steve was one of the police officers.

The Commissioner stares at the young boy with his mouth open. Turning red, he then looks at the floor of the car.
"Damn it!" he screams, pounding on his steering wheel.

"Hey, not bad for someone who never drove before in his life!" chuckles Steve, speeding on.

"Really?" responds Judy.

Two police cars suddenly appear behind him. Steve speeds up to about eighty-five miles per hour. He makes a quick move and turns off into a side street in order to lose the cars behind him. He barely makes the turn due to his high speed. The second he makes the turn he realizes that he's in a tough spot. In the middle of the block are many small children playing a ball game with a very small rubber ball. Instantly realizing the danger of the situation, Steve again steers the car onto the sidewalk. He then notices to his horror that there's an "old lady" walking on the sidewalk. (Of course this "old lady" looks like a 12 year old girl with white hair.)

"I can't look!" yells Judy.

"Here goes everything!" he yells, turning the wheel fiercely to the right.

The car begins to turn but instead of turning completely, it turns over on its right side, and is now riding only on its right two wheels. It just misses the children and the old lady. Steve is white-faced and his shirt is soaked from sweating.

"I think I'm going to be sick," he says speeding away from the scene.

"Actually, that was cool. I have no need to go on any roller coasters now!" says Judy.

With more police cars chasing him, Steve suddenly spots some train tracks ahead of him. He looks to see if there's a train coming and sure enough there is. Instead of slowing down to stop, he presses down harder on the accelerator. The train toots its whistle as it nears the crossing. The car nears the crossing. The whistle sounds again and again as Steve speeds towards the crossing. The engineer slams on his emergency brake as he sees Steve's car crossing the tracks. The train's brakes squeal as Steve's car just barely makes it over the tracks without being hit by the train. The car makes its way off the tracks and onto the other side. The train continues to come to a halt and finally stops. Right after the train stops, the police cars following Steve begin to smash into the train causing another pile up.

Peacefully continuing his frantic drive, Steve suddenly hears a familiar noise. He pushes the button on the side panel of the car door to lower the window and looks up at the sky. Seeing a helicopter coming down towards his car, Steve increases the speed of the car and is now driving well over one hundred miles per hour. The helicopter turns on its siren and flashing lights. It catches up to Steve in a matter of seconds. It is now low enough to bump the top of the roof. Hitting the roof of the car it makes it shift to the right and left.

"It's no use trying to out race us. We can travel at twice the speed of your car. Why don't you give up?" comes the voice over the loudspeaker.

The police begin to laugh which enrages Steve. He starts looking over the inside of the car and finds a shotgun. Steve points to the shotgun. Judy takes it and points it out of the car window. She fires the shotgun at the chopper and three times. Each shot hits the chopper and shatters glass all over the highway. The chopper instantly climbs higher and out of range. The co-pilot looks to a computer screen. He sees a type of x-ray of the car, showing Steve holding the shotgun. Judy seems to know they are being scanned and gives the finger to the pilots on the x-ray, wearing a fiendish smile on her face.

The chopper quickly descends down over the car and begins to drive Steve and Judy off the road. The struggle is fierce. Steve turns and sways the car so much that the wheels begin to wobble. It's almost like a game between the chopper and the car. The pilots even seem to be smiling.

"How long do you think you can do this? We get paid for it!" says one of the pilots over the loudspeaker.

It is clear at the point that the chopper has a better edge. However, the pilots have been so enraged with outmaneuvering Steve, they have neglected the oncoming overpass.

"Shit! Take her up! Take her up!" yells one of the pilots to the other.
It is too late. The bottom chopper crashes into the top of the overpass. The chopper unintentionally parks on the railroad tracks below. The shattered landing gear of the chopper falls to the ground and its pieces are scattered.

The two pilots almost immediately begin to climb out of the chopper. To make matters worse, a speeding train comes into view. In the midst of their struggle to exit the chopper, one of the pilots notices the train.

"Oh, please no!" states the pilot as he hastens his pace to get out of the chopper. The train, now only a few hundred yards away, begins to brake. The ear piercing sound of the train's brakes screeching is heard for miles.

The two pilots now stand on top of the chopper. The train slows down considerably but doesn't succeed in fully stopping. The train crashes into the chopper tearing it to shreds and triggering an explosion. Afterwards, the only sound heard is the thousands of pieces of the chopper flying into the air and falling on the ground below. Some of the pieces are in flames even when they land on the ground. The train is only partially dented in the front of the first car.

As Steve's car speeds through the tunnel he goes through a series of turns to avoid the rubble and flames from the chopper. He maneuvers to avoid both the debris already on the road and the falling debris. One of the larger remnants hits the top of the car, destroying the flashing police lights on the roof. Steve glances at the rear view mirror as he parts from the overpass. At first, only smoke can be seen on the tracks. Eventually, the smoke clears. Steve opens his mouth in shock and disbelief.

"I don't believe this. This looks like a cartoon!" he says to Judy, staring at the rear view mirror.

Judy turns and looks out the back window of the car to see the propeller from the chopper lying across the roof of the train with the two pilots holding onto each of the two blades, making it go up and down like a seesaw. The pilots kick their legs and scream like little children. They fight dearly to hold onto the propeller and not fall.

"Playing on a seesaw? And they're supposed to be mentally mature and grown up!" says Judy as she bursts into laughter.

The few seconds of contentment for Steve and Judy is broken by more action. Spotting more police cars behind him Steve says, "They don't give up! I've got to get rid of them once and for all. I'm losing too much time playing chase games with them."

146

He slows his car's speed and the police start to gain on him. He slows even more. He then turns off into a side street. He jams on his brakes and turns the wheel to the right. The car spins and stops sideways in the middle of the street. Steve and Judy quickly get out of the car, taking the police shotgun with them, and they run to a brown car that is parked in front of one of the houses. They get in the car and start it without hesitation. Quickly pulling away from the house, they leave a swirl of gravel and dust.

As they leave, the four police cars turn into the block. They are traveling at about sixty to seventy miles per hour, and because of their speed they are unable to stop when they see the ditched police car sitting sideways at the front of the block. The first, then the second, the third and finally the last car crash into one another. All that can be heard for blocks around is the squealing of brakes and loud bangs.

After a few quick turns they get to the turnpike he had previously traveled on with Bob and Leslie when they were leaving Child's Island. Finally, they reach their destination.

Steve stops the car in front of the giant structure which holds the powerful missile that can destroy the entire world if activated. The two rush out of the car, taking the shotgun with them, and run with it up the large, white stone steps leading to four large white doors. Steve aims the shotgun at the lock of one of the doors and fires it. The lock and part of the door around it are completely blown off leaving a big hole. Judy then kicks open the door and runs in, closing the damaged door behind them.

The inside the building is like an auditorium. The large room's ceiling is entirely lit up. It looks as if the designers of the building used lights as tiles. It gives the illusion of the ceiling being one big light. Directly to the center of the room stands the giant missile. It stands straight and tall on its own with nothing holding it up. It is shining silver. It stands approximately ten stories high. It is about thirty five feet wide. At the bottom of the missile are many thrusters, each about five feet wide and five feet high.

Also inside the room is a large round platform which stands next to the missile. The platform is about 10 feet high. It appears to be made of white marble and is supported by four wide marble columns.

As for the platform itself, it is approximately thirty feet long and wide. On the platform is a large black control table and some small machines beside it. There are hundreds of lights and many buttons, dials, knobs and many different types of controls. Each control is labeled with a name or number. Connected to this control table is a thick, long cable which is rolled into a reel on the platform. Leading to the platform is a round steel staircase.

Steve runs up the stairs to the platform. He carefully looks over the control table. He then stares at a small hole at the bottom of the missile.

"Must be a socket," he mumbles as he looks to the end of the cable. At the end of it are two metal blades.

"Got it!" says Judy as she takes the end of the cable in her hands and runs down the stairs towards the missile.

The cable unwinds from the circle. After struggling with the heavy cable, she reaches the missile and plugs the cable into it. Judy quickly runs back up the staircase to the platform and studies the control table even more with Steve.

They press some of the buttons and turn some of the dials and other controls. Seconds after they do this, all of the lights on the control table begin to light up. It starts to look like a Christmas tree as the many different colored lights flash on and off. Some turn on and off, others remain steady. They continue to maneuver more and more controls. For every button that Steve and Judy press, or dials they turn, a different sound is made from the control table. Every few seconds, the light pattern changes as a result of their maneuvering even more controls.

After minutes of manipulating the control table Steve is content with the pattern the lights are making. It seems as if he can read each light and that each pattern of light has a different meaning.

"I'm glad you know what this means," says Judy.

Just as he leans on the table to rest, the doors burst open, in rushes Commissioner White and a few dozen officers. All men, but the Commissioner, have shotguns in their hands. The officers line up in formation as the Commissioner yells to Steve to surrender. Steve looks at the shotgun he got from the police car, which lies at his feet. Not paying attention to the Commissioner, Steve quickly presses a red button on the control table. The button lights up the second he presses it. The lights flash faster and more feverously than ever! Steve then reaches to Judy's right hand and holds it.

"There. As of this moment a time device has been activated in the missile. In a short while the missile will automatically launch, go into the atmosphere, and then come back down to Child's Island and explode, destroying both Child's Island as well as the rest of the world."

The Commissioner and the officers are taken back by Steve's strong threat. "You couldn't have set any time device. The

149

missile has been deactivated," replies the Commissioner who doesn't seem all that confident.

"Come on Commissioner. You know as well as I do that all I had to do to set this missile off is plug in the control cable," replies Steve.

"All right, so maybe you reactivated the control system, but that doesn't mean you know how to set the time device," says the Commissioner.

"Commissioner, a child could figure out how the light code system works. All you have to do is make up your own coordinates and then secure it with your own combination," snaps Judy.

"What have you accomplished by all this?" questions the Commissioner.

"I saved our lives. You see, none of you know what time I sent the missile to launch. And none of you know the combination I used to set the coordinates for the time device. So, if you kill us, you'll also kill yourself and everyone else on this planet. I'm the only one who can save your world from destruction," answers Steve.

"In time our people might be able to figure out the combination," replies Commissioner White.

"Time is what you don't have. You forget, only we know exactly when the missile is set to launch. It could be an hour from now. Perhaps even a minute," says Judy.

"Okay, you win" sighs the beaten Commissioner.

"What do you want? Money? Transportation back to the islands? I can't endanger the fate of Child's Island," says the Commissioner.

"No, I just want you to listen to me. But first tell your men to drop their weapons," says Steve.

The Commissioner hesitates at first but then orders his men to drop their weapons. Judy then picks up the shotgun and

150

quickly throws it off the platform. It lands in the pile of shotguns made by the officers.

"There, now we're even," says Judy.

The officers are relieved.

"Now, all I want from you is some justice. When I told you we didn't shoot the King I meant it. I would have nothing to gain from killing him and neither would my friends. The only one that had anything to gain was General Bollings. He could become King himself. You know how power hungry he is. Please think it over. Don't you think it's strange that the King was kidnapped as he was? And don't you think it's also strange that Bollings wasn't planning to rescue the King? Besides, if we did shoot the King, why the hell would we go back to Child's Island? That would be the last place we'd want to go. Why didn't we just throw him overboard if we wanted to kill him? Tell me this, why on Child's Island would we clean and bandage his wound in the hovercraft if we're the kind of people who were trying to kill him in the first place?" finishes Steve.

"I have no answers to your questions..." starts the thoughtful Commissioner.

Before he can finish, the demolished doors are opened again. In walks General Bollings and with him are his five remaining soldiers. All eyes are on them. They walk to the front of the platform.

"I'm sorry it took so long but we had to change to dry uniforms. I see you have..." he notices the guns on the floor.

"What's going on here? Why are your guns on the floor?" asks the confused General.

"He's set the missile's time device. If we kill him, we will also kill our only chance of learning the light combination he programmed into the missile," answers Commissioner White.

151

"And because of that you disarmed yourselves? I say kill them now while we have the chance and let our scientists figure out how to reprogram the time device," says General Bollings.

"I'm sorry General. I can't endanger the security of Child's Island in order to capture two people," replies the Commissioner.

"Well I can. Take aim and prepare to fire!" orders the determined General.

"General Bollings, I can't allow you to shoot them in cold blood. At least, not at the expense of Child's Island. That's not rational," says the Commissioner.

"Of course he's not rational. That's what we've been trying to tell you. He's gone mad with all his power!" says Judy.

"What do you mean you can't allow me? I'm ruler of Child's Island, am I not?" snaps the General.

"I am the Commissioner of the police force of Child's Island. This man deserves a fair trial and justice, and I'm going to make sure he gets it. Furthermore, stop talking to me like you're my superior. My superior is the King. He is the true ruler of Child's Island," replies Commissioner White.

"The King is as good as dead and I will be the next ruler of Child's Island. Now stop interfering with my personal business!" yells the angry General.

"You see Commissioner, all he wants is me dead. But not for the sake of Child's Island, only for his 'personal business'. That's murder!" yells Steve.

"You're right. General Bollings, you're acting extremely irrational and you're leading me to believe there's more to this story than you told over the radio. Therefore I'm placing you under arrest until the King recovers. When he does, and he will, he'll tell us the real story," states the Commissioner.

"Why you low down scum! You'll arrest me? *Me*? No one will arrest me. No one! I'm the King. Ha! Do you hear me? I'm the King. Bow to your King! Bow!" yells the insane General, his face all red and sweaty.

The Commissioner stares at the raving General and then looks up to Steve. "There will be no need for your arrest. It's quite obvious that the General is mad and probably responsible for this entire ordeal. I don't know how I could have been so blind. If there's any way to make it up to Child's Island I will. Now General, I'm placing you under arrest for treason in the greatest degree!" says the Commissioner in a firm voice.

The General starts to back away from the Commissioner. "You think I'm mad? You think I have no more power? I do and I'll kill the first one who tries to take it away from me!" screams the General.

He reaches into his holster and pulls out a black handgun, firing it at the Commissioner. The Commissioner is shot in the stomach and falls to the floor on his back. Steve, seeing this, jumps over the control table off the platform and onto General Bollings. Judy runs to the socket to try and pull the cable out. Steve and the General roll on the floor and begin to throw punches at each other. Bollings drops his gun.

The police officers rush to pick up their weapons and one man stands guard over the hurt body of the Commissioner. The soldiers open fire on the police and the police return fire at once. Bullets are flying all over the place.

"Whoa!" exclaims Judy as she dodges bullets. She is still struggling to pull the cable out but it won't budge. The battle lasts only seconds. The victors, the police. All five soldiers lie on the floor covered with blood.

Steve and the General have rolled out of the line of fire and continue to fight with each other.
"Call for ambulances," yells one officer.

They all rush to the exit and soon the building is vacant except for Steve, Judy and the mad General. Steve and the General are badly bruised and scarred. Exhausted, they fight on. The wound in Steve's leg has opened and soon the right sleeve of his pants is covered with blood. The General takes advantage of Steve's weakened condition and punches at it again and again.

Steve suddenly groans and lies on the floor, appearing only half conscious. The General is sure that he has won.

"Fool! Did you really think you could overpower me, the most powerful man on Child's Island?"

He walks to the body of one of his soldiers and picks up the man's sub-machine gun. He turns to the platform and aims the gun. Bollings fires first at Judy and then at the control table. Judy runs behind a smaller machine for cover. The many lights begin to shatter and sparks start to shoot out of the table.

The General now aims his gun at the missile itself and fires at it. The bullets bounce off and head back towards him. "Damn," he yells.

Suddenly the cable appears around his neck. Judy who still could not pry the cable out of the socket, has made use of it by running behind General Bollings and choking him! General Bollings drops the gun and falls on top of Steve. Judy goes down with him, keeping the cable around his neck.

Steve is awoken by the General falling on him. Steve shakes his head to clear his mind. He uses his last bit of strength and throws punches at the General, while Judy continues to choke him. The General's face turns red and he cries out in pain. He struggles to get up and after a few attempts he fails. He falls backwards off of Steve and lands on the floor hitting his head. He's out cold.

Steve gasps for breath as he goes to his knees. He hangs his bruised and bleeding head down and shakes it slowly. Judy helps him stand up. The doors of the building open and police are all over, carrying out the bodies of the officers to the ambulances.

"Sorry we took so long but the Commissioner said you two could handle the General yourselves," says an officer to Steve.

"My name's Matt. Matt Young. I'm the head police chief. Second in command of the force of Child's Island, first assistant to the Commissioner himself," says Matt.

"I'm Judy," she replies.

"I'm in a lot of pain," says Steve still holding onto Judy to stand.

The police officers, who have been working extremely fast at getting their injured comrades out, carry out the last few bodies as Judy, Steve and Matt near the exit. Suddenly the control cable begins to shoot out sparks. They turn to look.

"Uh oh," mumbles Steve as the cable shoots more and more sparks, making a gunshot sound every time.

The sparks turns to small flames and smoke begins to come from the cable. Finally, the cable explodes and breaks in two.

"Let's get the hell out of here!" cries Matt as he turns around and pushes Steve and Judy towards the door.

"Wait, we can't just leave General Bollings and his men," says Steve turning back towards the platform.

"Are you crazy? That thing can go off any second. The soldiers are probably dead anyway," yells Matt, as he and two other police officers grab Steve and force him outside.

"The General made his bed Steve! I'm not losing you after all of this!" says Judy, pulling Steve away.

Matt and the two officers help them across the street to the many police cars and ambulances. The five get down behind one of the cars. All eyes are on the building.

"I promise you, when this thing is over, I'll get you to a hospital," says Matt.

Beams of white light seem to flash out of the thrusters of the missile. The light from the thrusters lights up the entire structure and it begins to glow. Judy, Steve and the police officers cover their eyes from the blinding light. The entire process takes only a few seconds. Right after the thrusters activate, the building explodes into a thousand pieces. The noise is heard for miles around. The once sturdy building looks like a sun about to nova. Pieces of wood, stone and flames fly all over the area. The debris hits the ambulance and cars. Two police cars suddenly explode in flames. Only seconds after an ambulance does also.

Judy, Steve, Matt and the other officers remain flat on the ground, sweating from the heat from the explosions. Plastic and rubber are burning all around Steve and the others on the ground. Finally, all of the building has been destroyed.

The entire area is filled with smoke. The only things that are still on fire are the police vehicles and the ambulance. All other cars are badly dented and their windows shattered.

"Look," yells one of the police officers, pointing towards the sky.

All eyes look up to see the missile quickly making its way into the atmosphere. A stream of white flames pours out of the thrusters. The missile itself shines brilliantly. The reflection of the sun bounces off the silver body of the missile and into the watcher's eyes.

"I better call command," says Matt in a low depressed voice.

He reaches into a nearby car and pulls out the microphone from its holder, "This is Chief Young. Connect me with army dispatch."

"Army dispatch," says a clear brisk voice.

"Give me a line to the missile control center and hurry," orders Matt.

"Missile control," says another voice.

"Yes. I know you've picked up the missile on your radar by now. Is there anything you can do to stop it?"

"No. It's going too fast for our counter missiles to do anything. Besides, it's got a radar deflector built into it. The radar systems in our counter missiles would never be able to pinpoint exactly where it is. Do you know the coordinates programmed into the missile?" asks the voice.

"Steve?" asks Matt.

"I'm sorry. I programmed the missile to launch in ten thousand years. Exactly where it would hit I left up to the missile's strategic computer. Why it launched now is what I'd like to know. I purposely set the timer for ten thousand years. I figured by that time, with all your technology, you'd have disassembled it," answers Steve.

"When the control cable blew it must have sent thousands of volts into the missiles computer, stimulating the time device. It probably sped up the timer and had it counting thousands of years instead of seconds. It's happened before with other time devices on Child's Island. For some reason, a strong electric current tends to speed up the timer. No we don't know the coordinates, missile control," says Matt speaking into the microphone once again.

157

"Well then, all I can say is hold tight and pray that we come up with a way to stop it," replies the voice.

"Yeah, roger," answers Matt, hanging his head.

Steve looks up towards the missile. It can barely be seen as it makes its way into space.

Meanwhile, in the radar room of an American Air Force base in the "Outside World"...

Two scientists are looking at a radar screen.

"Where did that come from?" says one.

"I don't know. It seems to have come out of nowhere. It looks like some sort of missile," says the other scientist.

"It's going too fast for a missile. Why it's going faster than any of our rockets!" exclaims the first.

"Can you get a clear fix on it?"

"No. For some reason the radar can't pinpoint its exact coordinates. All it can tell us is that it's headed for space!" answers the first scientist.

"I'd better call the President. It must be Russian!" says the second scientist.

At the same time in Russia, inside one of their radar rooms...

"Where did it come from?"

"I don't know but look at the speed!"

"It must be American!"

The same scene takes place at radar stations all over the world. China, Japan, England France, Canada and all the others are asking the same questions. Where did it come from? Where is it going? And what does it mean?

In the radar room of the missile control center back on Child's Island...

A handful of scientists stand in front of a giant radar screen, which is more advanced and developed than the equipment in the "Outside World".

"It's entering space now. It won't be long before it turns back around and heads for Child's Island," says one scientist.

The men stare at the screen and watch the missile climb higher and higher. Some of them seem to be trying to think of a way to stop it, and some seem to be in a trance. Or perhaps they are thinking about their lives. They all share once thing in common though; each other them have tears in their eyes.

One of the female scientists maneuvers some of the switches near the radar screen. Suddenly the radar graph disappears off the large screen. Replacing it is a live picture of the missile making its way into space.

Maneuvering a few more switches she says, "I think I have an estimate as to when the missile will stop going up and turn back towards Child's Island. Fourteen, thirteen... five, four, three, two..." before she can finish the missile suddenly explodes into millions of giant sparks which scatter through space.

It looks like a second Sun. A net of electricity seems to float over the Earth. This "net" gets thinner and thinner, lighter and lighter until eventually the charge disappears, along with its countless sparks. Space is again black and Earth gets dimmer as its temporary second Sun dies.

Back in to the radar room in the "Outside World" in Russia...

"The missile exploded into a great blast of electricity" exclaims one of the scientists.

"Now I know it's American!" says another scientist.

"If they have such a missile, maybe we ought to improve our relations with them."

Back at the radar room in the American Air Force base...

"Sir, the missile collided with one of our anti-radar spy satellites and exploded!"

A General is standing with the other scientists.

"What now? What do we tell the people?" asks the scientists.

"What we always tell them when the Russians have discovered one of our spy satellites and have destroyed it! What else would we say?" answers the General.

Back at the radar center on Child's Island, much hugging, kissing and cheering is going on as the scientists celebrate the destruction of the deadly missile.

"This is Chief Young. Tell me what I think happened, happened," says Matt smiling.

"This is missile control and thanks for thinking it was us but we didn't do a damn thing! The missile seems to have collided with some kind of meteor but the funny thing is, we didn't pick up the presence of anything even near the missile, let alone in its path. But you know, never look a gift horse in the mouth!" replies the scientist.

"We had about two seconds before it was going to turn, come down and get us all. But I knew it wasn't going to end like this. I just knew it! And by golly I was right," answers the scientist, laughing.

Steve, Matt and the officers near them are also laughing. But they don't laugh at what the scientist said. They are laughing out of relief.

"All right. Let's get this place together!" orders Matt.

"And let's get you two to the hospital," says Matt to Steve and Judy.

EPILOGUE

Two weeks later…

Steve, Judy, Bill, Bob and Leslie all sit on a large stage in a giant auditorium, which is located in the Capitol building of Child's Island. The room is lit by huge chandeliers. Also sitting with them is Commissioner White and Chief Matt Young.

The auditorium is filled with over a thousand dignitaries, some dressed in military uniforms. Everybody is smiling.

The King walks onto the stage and stands in front of the audience as well as multiple television cameras. They all give their full attention to the King. The broadcast is live all over the free world of Child's Island! The audience is silent.

"Good evening my fellow children and thank you for giving your valuable time to my assembly. It's been so long since I've had such an assembly I almost forgot what it feels like. Since the beginning of time there has been Good and Evil, and through the years the two elements have been at odds with each other constantly. Many people will think that Good has and always will have an easy time beating Evil. I disagree. I feel that sometimes Evil wins some battles or at least comes close. The reason for this is that Evil is very clever. It feeds on the ignorance of people. It takes advantage of every streak of blindness in every person. Many times, out of a lack of knowledge, Evil can be disguised. It tricks people to let down their defenses and possibly destroy them.

This tragedy has just recently happened on Child's Island. Evil, in this case, took the form of the late General Bollings. As the people of our Island grew more naive about him, he grew more and more powerful. He was indeed clever and that almost gave him full control of the most sophisticated race on Earth. We didn't realize that Evil was dominating Child's Island. We nearly

165

stopped Good from protecting us by trying to destroy it. Good, in this case, are Captain Stephen James Mason and his crew and friends. We barely won this battle against Evil. In a way, we didn't win, for it was Evil that destroyed itself. We may not always be as lucky. As I said, Good doesn't always win its battles easily. I believe what happened here on Child's Island proved that.

I now hereby promise that while I rule as King this will never happen again. I will try my best to make it easier for us to win our battles of Good and Evil. I will try my best to see that future rulers and generations of the world will be able to talk to each other about common problems. What happened here may have caused a lot of harm and fear, but it the long run it is a giant step towards eventually winning the war against Evil. Now we are much less naive and more knowledgeable. For knowledge is the only weapon that can successfully defeat Evil. Our eyes are that much more open.

Enough of all that. Let me do what we're all here for. That is, of course, to honor five people who sit directly behind me. These five did what the millions of people of Child's Island couldn't do. They defeated General Bollings and ruined his great conspiracy. They made the people of our island aware that their freedom had been taken. Besides giving back Child's Island its freedom they gave back its King! Three of these people aren't even natives of Child's Island. They were greeted with bullets, arrows, prisons and power hungry maniacs. And even after they were treated like dirt, they never gave up their hopes for a peaceful life. They, without thought for themselves, were willing to give up their lives for our land. Because of this, I am declaring the three full-fledged citizens of Child's Island, as well as members of the Royal House of Honorables. They will go down in our history. They will be known as heroes of Child's Island.

166

Doctor and Mrs. Goodboy will also be entered in the Royal House of Honorables and will share the glory with our three heroes. I'm especially proud of these two, for they proved that there will always be someone on Child's Island who will be alert enough to recognize Evil when it is in its best disguise.

As per the request of the honorees, I will be starting a program to work with the natives from the island where I was held hostage to improve their quality of life and to get them to advance as much as possible. General Bollings is guilty of manipulating them. We have been guilty for ignoring them and showing them indifference."

With that the audience cheers and gives them all a standing ovation.

Judy whispers in Steve's ears, "You know we're officially adults here now."

"I know that Judy," replies Steve.

"That means we can get married if we want to," says Judy.

Steve's face shows a look of concern. He certainly wasn't expecting Judy to say that.

"You know with all the cheering I just can't hear you Judy," says Steve smiling.

"You know you can't survive without me always bailing you out," she says.

Steve and Judy are interrupted by Bill.

"Hey guys, we're going to the reception. You've got to see the food they have there!"

"Come on Judy, we don't want to be rude," says Steve.

"Careful Steve. She can be dangerous with electrical wires," says Leslie.

"We'll talk," says Steve, smiling at Judy.

"Yes, we will," replies Judy, putting her arms around Steve.

They all walk towards the banquet room.

"To be fair, Andy did deliver. We have a whole new life in a whole new world," says Steve.

"Yes, that we do," says Judy.

All five have their arms around each other as they are walking. The King catches up to them and puts his arm around Bob and walks with them.

. . .

This is the beginning of three new lives of teenage runaways in a brand new world.

THE END

TEENAGE & YOUNG ADULT

SURVIVAL
HANDBOOK

Table of Contents

INTRODUCTION

While I was living with abuse, alcoholism and all of the dysfunctions in my house, as well as having depression, low self-esteem and thoughts of suicide, what made things worse is that I thought I was the only one going through these problems. What made me hopeless was that I thought things were never going to get better.

The following are articles I have written on my own personal struggles and journeys during my teenage and young adult years. These are the ways I've survived them and became happy, as well as suggestions and resources for others to survive and be happy as well.

We all tend to think that our lives will not get better. Here is how they can.

SUICIDE
I Don't Want To Die!
I Just Don't Want to Live!

"If this doesn't go through, I swear I'll kill myself!" You've probably heard something like this before. Perhaps you even said it to yourself. You may have laughed right afterwards. For many though, it's not a laughing matter because they are quite serious with their intention to kill themselves. The figures of suicide rates, let alone teenage suicide rates are staggering.

It's bad enough when someone dies from a currently incurable disease. However, when a person dies from suicide, all one can think is that it was a tremendous waste. A total unnecessary loss of a life. If you have ever been to a funeral for a suicide victim you would notice that the anger, shock and frustration are many times that of a non-suicide mortality. The guilt usually fills the air like a choking pollutant. **WHY!?!** This word echoes throughout like a record with a skip in it.

Why? The immediate response to the most posed question is "why not?" Nobody commits suicide because they had nothing better to do that day. As far as the old adage "they just want attention", perhaps in some cases. But the people I've known to attempt suicide were not seeking attention, they were seeking death.

Why? Again comes the "why not?" You see, the "why not?" is filled with so much pain, disappointment, anger, low self-esteem, depression and downright hopelessness, that the person truly cannot see any reason to go on. To sum up suicide in a more personal perspective: It's not that I want to die; it's just that I don't want to live. That is not a contradiction. I don't really know what it's like to be dead but I do know what it's like being alive. For me, at that time being alive was full of pain, depression, despair, and hopelessness. There was always something going wrong. There was always a new problem that would come up that I would have to deal with, along with the problems that were already troubling me. When things seemed like they were going to right finally they would just fall apart. I had gotten so used to that, that I just always expected things to go wrong, no matter how positive they seemed at first. My father's alcoholism and abuse had taken its toll. And worse than his physical abuse was the verbal or emotional abuse which destroyed my self-esteem and self-worth developing hopelessness in me.

I felt abandoned, not wanted. I couldn't stand my school. I hated where I lived. I was so embarrassed from my family. I felt like I was the only one who was going through this. As much as I thought I was stupid I wasn't and if I honestly knew things were going to get better I never would have thought of killing myself. But I didn't see a light at the end of the tunnel. Not to mention

4

whether it was intentional or not, others made things seem hopeless to me and added to my depression. I just felt my problems would be around for the rest of my life and I had enough of them. One of the mistakes I had made was thinking that all of the problems surrounding me were all my fault or part of me personally. I just felt and even used to say there was a dark cloud over me that followed me around.

This sums up what's on many minds when considering suicide. Total hopelessness or the fear that one cannot endure whatever pain they are going through, regret of the past, fear of the future, a bad loss or an unwanted gain. These are things suicidal people are dealing with. It's so important to know and understand what these people are dealing with. It's not something to be made fun of. It's certainly not something to ignore. A "kick in the butt" or "pat on the back" just isn't enough. In fact, it could be more harmful than good. There is no one quick answer or nifty saying to combat suicide, simply because in most cases they are feeling this way from a while of built up frustrations.

If someone is being abused, whether it be physically or verbally, this can also lead to thoughts of suicide. In my case, it was the verbal abuse that created hopelessness. I remember a story on the news about hostages who were freed. When asked what got them through their ordeal, trauma, abuse, and hopelessness, they said "thinking about their family and going home" got them through it and gave them something to look forward to. In my case, as well as many others, it was my family who was doing the abuse and creating the hopelessness in my own home, so I thought "what do I have to look forward to?" I could not see things ever getting better. Of course, things did get better as they always do. No matter how bad the situation seemed there was always a light at the end of the tunnel, I just couldn't see it.

If you are contemplating suicide (or if you know someone who is), you can encourage them to seek professional help immediately. There are many counselors, doctors, social workers, centers, institutions and hotlines available. There are also many self-help groups and 12 step groups available which usually don't even cost anything to belong to. Many of them meet at community centers and churches. You don't have to belong to that particular church to go to those groups. You may even want to combine some of these choices. You definitely want to check out all of your alternatives. These options will give you the tools to deal with whatever problems led you to the point of suicide. Along with whatever help you might want to speak to a member of the clergy. A great thing about faith is that God gives one hope.

Keep in mind that if there are other issues with you or at home such as alcoholism, drug abuse or abuse towards you, you will also want to work on those things as well. You will find that once you work on those and your self-esteem and self-worth increases, your life honestly seems a lot better. Try to stay away from negative or abusive people towards you. This includes verbal abuse. Stay around people who are good to you and say positive things to you only. Take a deep breath and say a prayer for the strength to get help. Another thing I have learned is that things tend to get better a lot quicker than I ever thought they would and my situation got a lot better than I ever thought it could. You are not alone.

Keep busy. Very busy. Work overtime if you can. If you're in school, get super involved in school activities, especially after school activities. Surround yourself with people as much as you can. Don't isolate. Try not to be alone. Don't allow yourself too much time to just think. Try to leave the house if you can. I know when I was depressed I didn't want to interact much with people. Sometimes a compromise is to go see a movie. You don't have to talk much at all, even if you're with friends, but you're out of the house and your mind is occupied. Keep busy! Keep your mind working. Try to help someone else. Do some volunteer work. You get a great feeling of worthiness when you help someone else. Whatever you do, do something. Push until something gives. Remember too, if you can just keep busy enough to give yourself the time, things in time always get better. Especially if you're keeping busy doing the right thing. When you're depressed and suicidal, time can be a four letter word. If you're doing all of the things I've listed, it doesn't have to be. The clouds go away and life might not seem to "stink" anymore.

If you have no great advice to give someone who is suicidal it's okay. What you can give them though is hope. Without hope there is nothing. No reason to live. With hope there is a reason to at least see if there's a light at the end of the tunnel, or maybe a different tunnel you can take. Hope is a great answer to "why not?" It's the greatest gift you can give one in distress. In time, some of the problems won't be able to exist. It **does** get better.

I have known many individuals who were suicidal over the years and although they might have been very different from each other in personality and lifestyles, they always had one thing in common. If they had thought of suicide but never acted on it, or attempted suicide, but thank God still lived, they were all glad that they either never attempted suicide or never died. Why? Because no matter how different their situations were, their lives all got better. All of their lives got better! One hundred percent! Each person is now happy to be alive. That includes me.

So, what do you think! Is life worth hanging around for?   **YES!**

From a "Z Student" to an A Student (What a difference self-esteem can make!)

My first several school years I was a "Z Student". That would be the opposite of an A Student. With the uncertainty of stocks or the chances of someone winning lotto, your safest bet was that I would fail whatever test I was given and undoubtedly get the lowest grade in the class, which I used to pride myself upon holding the title of. My total lowest grade on a test was a negative 20. How you might ask? During the test I did what I always did, and that was to taunt the "smart kids" who I was jealous of. The teacher said, "Get back in your seat and whatever you get I'm taking off 20 points." So I didn't even try. She gave me a negative 20. At that point I needed all hundreds for the rest of the year just to average a passing grade!

I was always making jokes, and usually was the class clown, intentionally getting thrown out of the class, got into a lot of fights and was at times the class tough guy. So basically if you didn't laugh at my jokes I beat you up. Everybody loved to sit next to me, especially at lunch to see what the next thing I would do. So by appearance I was very popular. Of course you didn't need to be a genius to figure out that those who hung around me were my friends because of what I did and not for who I was.

11

And why the low school grades? I didn't even try and never studied. I did however spend a lot of time figuring out ways to cheat on a test. I would spend hours sometimes. My friends would come by the house and ask me to go hang out and I would say, "I'm still trying to figure out how to cheat on this next test. I still have to pass it." They would reply, "Why don't you just study? It would take half the time." My answer to them would be "What's the use?" You see I had the infamous low self-esteem, or perhaps in my case no self-esteem. I honestly believed that even if I studied I would fail.

My father was a violent abusive alcoholic who for as far back as I can remember would tell me how stupid and useless I was. And although he was physically abusive the things he said to me (verbal abuse) were far more damaging than anything else he did to me. By the time I started the first grade I already believed I was a failure. I also formed a negative opinion of adults, because of my father. As a result, I would be aggressive with teachers, as more of a defense for fear of what they would say or do to me. Even though part of me felt my father's abusiveness was wrong, part of me also felt I deserved it for being a "bad child". I thought the problems in the house were all my fault, and I felt guilty about fathers drinking, like many victims of child abuse feel. Like most children in these situations I also moved a lot and had to start different schools, which added to my loneliness.

Eventually I ended up in foster care. I was very lucky to have had good experiences and good people in the foster home. Once again I was forced to start a brand new school in a brand new town where nobody knew me. I know the school administration had been complaining about not getting my school records from previous schools (the old schools probably burned them for fear I would come back!) The first day I was at my new school, there was a creative writing assignment. The one thing I ever gave myself credit for was being able to write stories and poems. In fact, there were times I used to cut school and hang out in the public library reading and writing my own stories. So picture this, I'm being this rebellious child who thinks he's a failure and cuts school at a very early age, but spends his time reading and writing. Talk about the epitome of a self-esteem problem. So, of course I did really well on the assignment, and the teacher proclaimed "You're so talented. You must have been a top student at your previous school." I just smiled and knew that once she has thrown me out of class 50 times in the first month she'll eat those words.

At that time I had joined a self-help support group for teenagers with my background. The question was put to me "Do I really enjoy and want to be a problem child in school and have bad grades?" The answer of course was "no". Another question was asked of me "Why do I think I am so stupid or a failure?"

especially when I had such a strong talent with writing. I replied "Because my father has always told me that since I was born." As the words left my mouth I pretty much guessed the answer to it and came to the conclusion that I was basing my opinion of myself on the words of someone who is drunk most of the time and whose life was totally unmanageable. I didn't even know how to study (after all, I never did), so I had asked those that did do well in school to teach me how. At the same time the suggestion was made to me by the older member of the group to join sports, just to keep my mind off of all my problems. So I joined wrestling and then eventually track at first just to appease a friend.

After a time of trial and error and not giving up I began to pass everything. Then I did better than passing. Then I put all of my energy that I had been using for negativity and put it into my school grades and sports. Eventually, I ended up in the National Junior Honor Society and for different semesters pulled off 100 averages in two different subjects. I had won some medals in wrestling (I was able to legally beat someone up) and became the MVP for the track team. They even made me Student of the Month, and hung my picture up in the halls as a model student. I would literally laugh every time I walked by the picture, knowing that only a couple of years prior it would have been a dart board in the teachers faculty room!

Was it magic? Not at all. I could have done this at any time I just believed I couldn't. I had discovered what I have said to many young people, the only difference between a "smart" student and a "dumb" student is the smart student knows that they're smart and the dumb student unfortunately thinks they are dumb. I know this for a fact because after all, I have been both.

Now as an adult I am a successful businessman excelling in my field. For many years I have run a support group called "Together We Can Make It" and dedicate a great deal of my life to the group and its members, making them my number one priority over everything else including my business. I know from my own experience how important such a group is, and how important it is to have at least one person in your life that is consistently there for you, on your side and accepts you for who you are. I have gladly dedicated my time through the media to promote messages of hope and giving constructive suggestions to both children and their parents on how to overcome these problems. I have always kept up with my writing. I have now written four books and many articles that have been published. As a child writing was an escape from my problems. I can now proudly say that I have been given awards for my writing being a tool to help others deal with their problems.

There is nothing special about me over any other person who grew up as I did. The only difference is I had the opportunity to be shown a different view of myself and gain self-esteem and self-worth. Of all the things that can be given to a person in life, the greatest gift and cure for so many problems especially to a young person, is a good self-esteem.

Friends of a Child of an Alcoholic

Loneliness and Fear are my two best friends. They are my best friends because I know them so well and for so long. I'm lonely because there is nobody like me in the whole world. No one has my problems. People probably wouldn't talk to me at all if they knew. They'd know there was something wrong. I'm lonely because even though I'm at parties with lots of people I'm still alone. Fear is my buddy because I'm always afraid. I'm afraid of my father. I'm afraid that one day he's going to hit me so hard that I'll never recuperate. I'm also afraid he's going to kill my mother or siblings. I'm afraid we're going to have to move again because we can't pay the bills. Or worse, I'm afraid they are going to get divorced. Then what? Who will I live with? Will I even get a choice? I'm afraid that one day the whole school will find out.

Hate is a pretty good friend of mine too. I really hate school. It's becoming more and more of an effort to get up in the morning every day. I always have to work so hard to keep my guard up at school. Some people hate the way I act in school but it's definitely better than if I was just myself. I hate the teachers. They scare me. I hate super popular kids. If they only knew everything, they would tear me apart. Worst of all, I hate myself. I'm such a loser. Even when I do something good, it's only luck. I'm stupid, ugly, I don't even know why people bother with me. They must want something.

17

You see, trust is not a friend of mine. I don't even know him. Why should I trust people? All they ever do is make promises and break them. If you never trust anybody you can never get hurt.

Worry and I are real close friends. I'm always worrying about something. What if this happens? What if that happens? Did I look dumb? Did I say that right? Do they really mean that? What am I going to do about the future? Can I ever really live down the past?

Oh and here comes another good friend of mine, Daydreaming. I'm always so busy worrying about tomorrow and regretting yesterday. I'm never here today. I also like to day dream about how I would want things to be.

Embarrassment has been a friend of mine since childhood. I'm embarrassed when my mother and father scream so loud that the neighbors can hear them. I'm embarrassed to ever let my friends meet my parents. I'm embarrassed to invite people over to see the house. I'm embarrassed to be seen looking like I do (I hate my clothes).

My friend rejection and I seem to be getting closer as I get older. My parents call me names that hurt so much it's worse than getting hit. I heard there's something called constructive criticism but I've never

18

experienced it. My own family barely remembers my birthday. I'll avoid things totally (even things I want to do) just to avoid rejection. Dances and parties are terrifying. There's too much of a chance for rejection there.

Escape is a friend I'm trying to get to know. Running away, drugs, drinking, unhealthy relationships, fantasy and suicide. All things I contemplate. Don't seem to have many positive options. I'll do anything not to be like my parents, yet somehow I seem more and more like them every day. I'm always tired, though, at the same time I'm so hyper I don't even know the word relax.

Did I introduce you to my friend guilt? I'm always guilty. Everything is my fault. My parents' problems are my fault, (I hear them say my name when they fight). If things aren't going right or people aren't having a good time it's got to be me. If somebody is hurting me or doing something wrong to me it's probably my fault anyway. I'm never right.

I have great talent I do recognize though. I'm an expert at people pleasing. I'll do or say anything to make people pleased. I'll do or say anything to get people to like and accept me, no matter what the cost... even if it hurts me. That's okay as long as no one gets angry with me. Of course I don't call it people pleasing. I just say I'm an understanding, nice person.

Yes, loneliness, feat, hate, worry, daydreaming, embarrassment, rejection, escape, guilt, people pleasing, negativism, low self-esteem, and hopelessness are all my friends. They say that your friends make up who you are. I guess that's true. Since my friends make up who I am, then I am a "Child of an Alcoholic".

If you or someone you know can relate to this you are one of millions. Many alcoholics are children of alcoholics. Preventive medicine is the best. There are truly positive alternatives. You can get rid of your "bad friends" and make new friends. Friends like "hope" and "happiness". Speak to a school counselor, social worker, psychologist or even a teacher you feel comfortable with. Check out local community centers and churches as they also have people you can speak to, as well as support groups and 12 step programs. Lots of times a pastor of a local church knows exactly where to recommend for you to go.

Being happy or not! The choice is honestly yours.

Two Reasons Why I Won't Report My Child Abuse

"The first reason is I know that I could be better in school. I know I mess up at home. The clothes I wear. The way I have my hair. The attitude I have. The trouble that I get in. I bring it on myself. If I were a better person these things probably wouldn't happen to me. Ever since I can remember, I have been told by my parents that all the problems at home are my fault. People have it worse than I do." These are the thoughts of many who are being abused and the first reasons why they won't report it.

What I discovered was that even children who do fantastic in school, never get in any trouble, and do everything "right" still get abused by their parents or abusive adults in their home. Their parents even called them the same names as me and they were model children. I've found it has nothing to do with the way I act at all. It has nothing to do with who I was. It has nothing to do with the children. It has to do with the adults. Child abuse and discipline have nothing to do with each other. People who abuse children do it because of their own sickness, be it alcoholism, drug abuse or other problems they have.

"I knew my father or my mother's boyfriend had no right to abuse me but I always felt that my mother would get in trouble for it." This is the thought of many abuse victims and the second reason why they don't report it. Even though they are getting abused they still try to protect the non-abusing/co-dependent parent. What I offer to those children is you would not so much be getting your parent in trouble, but you would be getting them help. Most authorities get them to go to therapy, which would stop that parent from allowing abuse to themselves and others in the future, therefore making their life better. So by protecting yourself you're actually not getting anyone in trouble but protecting them and getting them help as well. Even the abusive adult could end up getting help as a result of you reporting it. Nobody should abuse you, period!

If you are being abused in any way, sometimes the abuse looks like it's becoming less frequent. Don't be fooled by this. It could suddenly pick up again and get worse. It will not stop unless you do something to stop it. Speak to a teacher, guidance counselor, school social worker or psychologist. Counselors from community centers and sometimes even people from local churches will know what to do and how to get you help. You can call Child Protective Services for your local area. Nobody should be abused in any way. You are no exception. You are worth getting help.

Approximately 5 children die a day as a result of child abuse. For those who suspect child abuse whether it be a relative or neighbor, it always amazes me how people will call 911 simply because someone parked in the wrong spot or put the garbage out on the wrong night, yet they won't get "involved" in possibly saving a child's life or at a minimum their childhood (not to mention the problems they will have as an adult as a result of their abuse). As responsible people we are already "involved".

If you suspect child abuse it probably does exist. Don't make excuses or protect and enable the abuser. Protect who you are supposed to protect, the children.

Bullying... Why Does It Always Happen to Me?

People wonder why I'm so sensitive. People laugh because other people can take insults and jokes and I can't. I get angry, sad and depressed, which makes people make fun of me even more. What they don't know is that making fun of me or bullying me is nothing new. Long before I ever stepped foot in a school I was a victim of bullying. It wasn't another student and it wasn't a neighbor. It was someone in my own family. Maybe it was because they were drunk, but whatever the reason, by the time I entered school I had already lived years of being put down, made to feel worthless and had my self-esteem ripped apart. Let's not forget that the overwhelming damage of bullying is not so much done in schools or in the workplace, but at home. Because there is no worse bully than a child's own father or mother. I can tell you from experience that verbal abuse can at times be just as harmful or even deadly as physical abuse. I know, I've had both. The physical wounds healed, but the emotional wounds left scars, which can affect a person their whole life.

How can it be deadly, you ask? Because many have been pushed to commit suicide as a result of bullying by one of their own parents or adults in the house; step father, step mother, mother's boyfriend, father's girlfriend. Bullying at home may make someone more susceptible or vulnerable to bullying elsewhere. By the time these children go to school almost all of their emotional protective layers have been ripped away by their own family, making them an open target for bullies that can sometimes sense this vulnerability. Now the bullying at school and other places just makes them think that everything their parents said were right, "Now even they're saying these things about me."

For those being bullied, if you can honestly say that you've had verbal abuse in your own home then the answer is to work on the damage that that abuse has caused. Once you stop hurting over the things your own family members have said and grow to realize that these things are not true, you will find it much easier to deflect the names thrown at you at school or work. They won't have the same effect on you or possibly even not hurt you at all. It's not a matter of you being weak. Nobody can grow up being verbally abused in their own home and then not have problems or be vulnerable outside your home.

One of the most important things to learn and work on is your own self-worth and self-esteem. When my self-esteem was low I would easily believe anything negative said about me. Once I had a high self-esteem, people could not hurt me as easily by just saying things to or about me. I remember many fights I had even gotten into or over being called names. Once I had some self-worth that didn't seem as important to me. When we feel good about ourselves we are then able to see the source of where the bullying comes from. Is it because that person has an alcohol or drug addiction? Does that person simply want attention? Does that person have self-esteem issues too and the only way they can feel confident is by knocking someone else down? People can make themselves feel popular because they get others to laugh with them, but one whose popularity is based solely on getting people to laugh at others is false. You don't want to get in a habit of harshly judging others but once you see through the person that is verbally attacking you, it takes away the sting of their words.

How do you get help to raise your self-esteem and self-worth? Certainly if you are in school there are school counselors, social workers and psychologists to help and you will find they understand you and your situation more than you thought. Community centers and churches many times also have counselors, 12 step programs and support groups. Please keep in mind that if you are a child of an alcoholic or have some abuse or dysfunction in your home that is more of a cause of your problems than the bully at school. When you get help you will realize that the effects from your home problems affected you a lot more than you thought, and made you vulnerable to begin with to the bullying. When you work on the problems from home and gain a self-esteem and self-worth once again you will be strong and capable to not let the bullying affect you at all. Remember many are subject to bullying. You are not alone in this and you will see that when you get help by one of the places that I've recommended.

For those of you that think that name calling and bullying is really no big deal and can't figure out what certain peoples "problem" is or why they act the way they do when you're simply "teasing them", I hope you will come to realize that it may not be so much what you're saying to them but what they are going through in their lives. By taunting and bullying these people you are actually becoming part of the abuse that they are going through at home. You are no better than the adults who are committing child abuse because you are helping their abuse have an even greater effect on their victims. Many abuse victims can hide their situations very well. Would you really want to even take a chance of picking on one of these individuals? Furthermore, you have to ask yourself why you have such a need to make fun of or put down others. Could *you* perhaps use some help for your self-esteem and self-worth?

Finally, if you are simply a bystander to someone's bullying or name calling, you can increase your own self-worth and self-esteem by either defending the person who is being bullied or at least letting everybody know that you don't agree with this at all, and that it's not cool.

Maybe you can even try to say some kind words to the person being bullied and make sure they are okay.

Bullying or verbally attacking anyone from any family background is wrong and cowardly. However, doing it to someone who already has their fill of problems is worse than cruel. Something to think about. Instead of being a bully how about being a hero?

Surviving the Holidays in a Dysfunctional Home

As the holiday season would approach people would start talking about all the plans they had laid out for the holidays and began to become excited. For me, as the holidays approached a shadow of anxiety and pending sadness would start to hover over me. As others become more and more excited as the countdown to the holidays began, I would become more and more stressed. The commercials would say the holidays are for the family. The problem with me was that it was my family that usually ruined the holidays! For me, it meant I would be home more. And that also meant my abusive alcoholic father would be around the house more as well. Nobody looked forward to that.

In dysfunctional or alcoholic homes fighting tends to increase in the house; and if there are money problems, they become more apparent. The one common denominator between everybody seems to be depression, and everyone seems to get in each other's way, because everyone's instinct is to isolate and want to be alone, with the exception of one person – the alcoholic or addict who won't leave anyone alone. As I got older, if I was in a negative or unhealthy relationship that would also bring down my holidays. I would spend a lot of time thinking about how things should be, and being envious of those who seem to have perfect lives. I would also make the mistake sometimes of thinking that maybe magically the holiday season would bring changes over everything and everyone. But when the holidays were over nothing changed, the alcoholic was still drinking and I was still lonely.

I'd blame it on God and the holiday. I eventually found that the holidays had nothing to do with my problems or depression, and it wasn't God's fault for the problems in my family. I began to look to the holidays for what they meant and what they were truly about. Instead of complaining about what should or shouldn't have happened, dwelling on all of the negativity, being jealous or worrying about what's going on in other people's households; I concentrated on what the holidays truly meant. Hope, survival and faith.

Instead of me deciding what the holidays should have been about and what should have happened during them or complaining about all of the negative things going on, or even being jealous or worrying about what's going on in other people's households, I concentrated again on what the holidays truly meant. This allowed me to take the focus off of my problems and I became aware that there are bigger and wonderful things going on outside of my household. I also found that there are those who are far worse off than I am, and by trying to help those, whether it's being encouraging to a friend or volunteering at a church soup kitchen, it does wonders for your self-esteem and outlook. Of course, by getting help yourself through counseling, self-help groups or 12 step programs, you'll find that your self-worth increases and your perspective of things change. Also, no longer being vulnerable to other people's abuse or negativity, the holidays automatically seem better.

Whatever religion you might be, many find that going to their house of worship with an open mind not only makes the holidays better for them but adds something to their lives. I can definitely tell you that's true!

Crossing the Bridge:
The Trip to Making Myself Better

They say today has become an instant gratification society. It's funny because when it comes to me trying to change bad habits or character defects, I tend to want instant change or instant gratification in that. Whether it's a short tempter, compulsive behavior or any bad habit, we usually want an overnight change. The problem is, as human beings, we're just not made that way. So when we fall back into our old habits, become compulsive, lose our temper etc., we usually just give up. In fact, we end up getting angrier that we got angry!

Picture a bridge. You're at one piece of land at the beginning of the bridge, and at the end of the bridge is another piece of land. The side that we're on has all of our bad habits and issues and the other side of the bridge doesn't have those habits and is where we want to be. The problem I had for many years is that I wanted to go from one side of the bridge to the other instantly. We all know that's impossible. We have to make the journey and cross over the bridge to get to the other side. We have to allow ourselves the time that we're on the bridge.

For instance, if I say I'm going to try not to get angry with a particular person anymore, and sure enough I get angry at them; instead of continuing the situation I should stop myself, even if I'm already engaged in an argument with them. Perhaps next time I'll stop myself earlier, and then the next time even earlier. So in time I will no longer lose my cool with that person, or if I do it won't be that often and I'll get better and better at stopping the argument before it gets too far. Maybe you're trying to stop people from taking advantage of you and walking all over you. If you find that sure enough it's happening again with someone put the brakes on and stop. Say "You know I'm just not comfortable with the way you're talking to me and treating me." It's okay to stop in the middle of things. You don't look silly. You look like you're trying to better yourself.

Even if we're right in the middle of a situation or an action, whether it's plans that you made, or a date, it's okay to stop things even when they seem to be in motion and say "This is not the way I want this to go". How many times have we stayed in relationships that we should have ended a lot sooner because we're afraid of being alone or looking weird? I used to think that because I started something I had to finish it. With some things in life such as school work or commitments to help family or friends with something, that might be ethically correct. But if you started something that is harmful to you or others it is more moral *not* to finish what you started than to continue.

If we honestly view getting better and changing our negative ways as crossing a bridge, sometimes we will notice that there is a situation or even a person blocking us from crossing that bridge to being a healthier and better person. If there is a bad habit or a person who is keeping you from becoming the person you want to be, sometimes we do have to let them go. "But what if I care about them or love them?" That is something I would have said myself a while ago. As a writer, you can imagine the excuses I would make for the unacceptable behavior from the people I cared about. But true love is not supposed to be hurtful to people, or damage them emotionally; and true friendships and love certainly aren't supposed to prevent us from stopping unhealthy habits and becoming a better person. In fact, good friends, and boyfriends and girlfriends, are supposed to encourage us and even help us cross the bridge on the way to being a healthier happier person.

Many times our unhealthy friends and relationships don't want us to get to the other side, because if we're healthy they feel we will no longer be interested in them. Once we make that journey and become a healthier, better person they will either change for the better themselves, or we will automatically find new, healthy, supportive friendships and love. And by the way, drinking, smoking, and taking any type of drug will never help us get better. They'll just depress us even more, create more problems and be a big divider that stops us from crossing the bridge. Especially if you have a parent that has an alcohol or drug problem. We always say that we will never be like them, but if I have found one thing to be consistent, if you do the negative and addictive things that they do, of course you will be like them. We can't say "But I will be a nice alcoholic and drug addict if I became addicted", it just doesn't work that way. If you find it's become too hard for you to cross that bridge to ending bad habits and relations it's okay to get help. Whether speaking to a school social worker or counselor, a member of the clergy or joining a self-help group or a 12 step program, then you will not be alone. Perhaps they can give you a lift across the bridge.

Let's allow ourselves that patience we deserve but start taking those steps to cross the bridge and be on the other side to a happier us.

Surviving Back to School

For many students back to school has always been a fun day of anticipation, curiosity and excitement. Some want to show off their new look or see how others have grown and matured during the summer. Unfortunately, for many back to school brings on feelings of overwhelming anxiety and stress. I remember times where I was wearing the same clothes my first day of school in the new year that I was wearing the last day of school of the previous year. Many fall into that category. Sometimes this is due to economic problems and other times it can be due to alcoholism or drug abuse in the house, which tends to bring on financial havoc and can even bring on a parental selfishness where money for drugs, alcohol or gambling becomes more important than clothes, food, heat and electricity and even the rent or mortgage payment. Spiteful divorces, where parents are trying to get at each other, can also cause the children to get caught in the line of fire. So the first day back at school with everybody wearing their nice new clothes and talking about all of the fantastic things they did over the summer with their families, just becomes a bitter reminder of all of these things that are going on in the household.

Between having my self-esteem wrecked by the constant verbal abuse from my father and just plain being physically and emotionally tired from all that was going on, school became a burden because I couldn't concentrate on any of the work. I was super sensitive with other students and even aggressive and adversarial towards my teachers. I would take everything personal. By the time I got to school each day I was already angry, sad and exhausted. Dealing with the things that go on in school between students is hard enough for anybody, but for me because of all the issues I was already dealing with, they became overwhelming. Then not doing well in school was just another stress and acknowledgement of me being a failure.

Once I got involved in self-help groups with other children who had the same family problems, I began to look at things differently. What I can share with you, is that my mistake for a long time was looking to school and all those who are at school as the enemy, as just another problem I wish I didn't have. I forced myself to join activities in school. By doing this I was able to create things that I liked about school. Most schools do have a variety of activities you can join- sports, clubs, community organizations, chorus and band. I went from counting the minutes until I can get out each day to purposely increasing my time there. Something I never thought I would do! However, I was enjoying my time in school because I was doing things that I liked. It's funny because as I got more involved in school and liked it, I would join even more things. Suddenly the teachers weren't such bad people after all, and between all of this and raising my self-esteem, I became less sensitive to all of the student drama and my grades began to rise higher and higher as well.

Also, schools have social workers and professionals, and sometimes even groups that you can go to and talk about your family issues. You see it wasn't the school that was so bad, it was my problems at home. Once getting help through self-help groups or 12 step programs, combined with social workers or therapists, you will find that everything doesn't seem so bad anymore and actually made things seem pretty good. Eventually, like me, although you'll think this is impossible, you'll look forward to school.

It can become your escape from other problems. It's just a matter of how we decide to look at things. I have been the person who hated school and dreaded every moment I had to be there to the person who really liked school and enjoyed being there, and used it as a way to distract me from my problems. I've found that my own self-esteem played more of a part in all of this than I thought.

So don't make back to school a horrible thing. Find things in the school to look forward to, create things connected to the school that you like and of course, try to recognize that the problems usually stem not from the school but from at home and how we feel about ourselves. School can even provide people and referrals to places that can help you with those as well. It has been said "people are as happy as they make their minds up to be". At first I used to think that was silly but I have learned that can be very true.

RESOURCES
USA & Canada Helplines

National Runaway Safeline
1-800-RUNAWAY (1-800-786-2929)
www.1800runaway.org
The National Runaway Safeline (NRS) is dedicated to keeping America's runaway, homeless and at-risk youth safe and off the streets. The crisis hotline is available 24-hours a day throughout the United States and its territories, including Puerto Rico, the U.S. Virgin Islands, and Guam. NRS provides education and solution-focused interventions, offers non-sectarian, non-judgmental support, respects confidentiality, collaborates with volunteers, and responds to at-risk youth and their families 24 hours a day. They can find you a place to stay, and can even call a family member or friend for you that you do not want to speak with directly.

National Suicide Prevention Lifeline
1-800-273-TALK (1-800-273-8255)
www.suicidepreventionlifeline.org
The National Suicide Prevention Lifeline is a 24-hour, toll-free, confidential suicide prevention hotline available to anyone in suicidal crisis or emotional distress. By dialing 1-800-273-TALK (8255), the call is routed to the nearest crisis center in our national network of more

than 150 crisis centers. The Lifeline's national network of local crisis centers provide crisis counseling and mental health referrals day and night.

Chidlhelp National Child Abuse Hotline
1-800-4-A-Child (1-800-422-4453)
www.childhelp.org
The Childhelp National Child Abuse Hotline is dedicated to the prevention of child abuse. Serving the United States, its territories, and Canada, the Hotline is staffed 24 hours a day, 7 days a week with professional crisis counselors who, through interpreters, can provide assistance in 170 languages. The hotline offers crisis intervention, information, literature, and referrals to thousands of emergency, social service, and support resources. All calls are confidential.

ChildFind Canada
1-800-387-7962
www.childfind.ca
Child Find Canada Inc. is a charitable organization dedicated to the personal safety of all children. Their goal is to reduce child victimization by providing programs and services to the Canadian public. If your child is missing or you see a missing child call 1-800-387-7962 (24 hours a day).

Kids Help Phone Canada
1-800-668-6868

www.kidshelpphone.ca

Kids Help Phone Canada is for young people to contact about a wide range of issues such as struggles with relationships, moving to a new school, cyber bullying, abuse, and mental health concerns.

The Trevor Project
1-866-488-7386

www.thetrevorproject.org

The Trevor Project is the leading national organization providing crisis intervention and suicide prevention services to lesbian, gay, bisexual, transgender and questioning young people ages 13-24.

RAINN
1-800-656-HOPE (1-800-656-4673)

www.rainn.org

RAINN (Rape, Abuse & Incest National Network) is the nation's largest anti-sexual violence organization and operates the National Sexual Assault Hotline. This nationwide partnership of more than 1,100 local rape treatment hotlines provides victims of sexual assault with free, confidential services around the clock. RAINN also carries out programs to prevent sexual violence, help victims and ensure that rapists are brought to justice.

UK Helplines

Samaritans
08457 90 90 90
www.samaritans.org
Samaritans is available 24 hours a day to provide confidential emotional support for people who are experiencing feelings of distress, despair or suicidal thoughts.

ChildLine
0800 1111
www.childline.org.uk
ChildLine is a private and confidential service for children and young people up to the age of nineteen. You can contact a ChildLine counselor about anything - no problem is too big or too small.

For more information and international resources please visit: www.suicide.org/suicide-hotlines.html

Theresa and Steve already had their troubled lives to deal with but are now being chased by everything from mafia hitmen to hostile aliens in a dangerous game of deadly identity crisis.

Visit **www.PowerPublishingCorp.com** to order or learn more about **WHO AM I?**

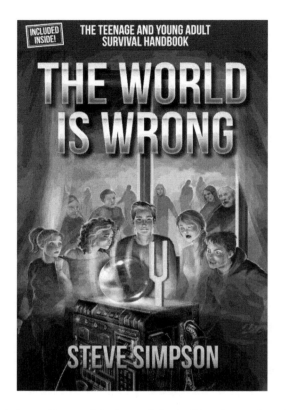

Hold on tight to Steve, Marie and their friends as they deal with alternate realties, impossible love and having the whole world against them in this nonstop action thriller!

Visit **www.PowerPublishingCorp.com** to order or learn more about **THE WORLD IS WRONG**

Runaway with Steve and Nancy into nonstop danger, excitement and revenge!

Visit **www.PowerPublishingCorp.com** to order or learn more about **RUNAWAY**

DEDICATIONS

God, my creator and my all – Thank you for all of your patience and for giving me Jesus and Mary to watch over me and my loved ones; and who are always here for me with unconditional love even when I cause my own problems.

"TOGETHER WE CAN MAKE IT" Group – All of you are always in my prayers.

My Beloved Mother Cynthia – I always looked forward to our dinners and card games together. I will always miss and love you.

In loving memory of Helene

Morris
Dominick
Joe
Joyce
Deacon Jim O'Neill
Father Jim
Father Patrick
Father Tony
Georgette
Lana
Jill
Stephanie
Julia
Lisa
George & Regina
Rodney & Patricia
Craig & Stacey
Carmen
Martha
Woofy

Arthur Spirn – For all you have done over the years.

Francis "Doc" Coppage – You are more than an editor. You're a dear friend. I'm glad you're still around!

Tara – Still, I am always happy when you are around. I smile when I think of you, and now you are a Mom! You know I Prayed for Brendan and Kayla Marie before they were born! I know you love them and Peter very much and are working hard to be the best Mom you can.

Tara Dawn – I can't tell you how much I appreciate our friendship, you as a worker and you as a person. I rely on you and trust you without hesitation. Even in the midst of stress or issues I am always happy you are by my side. You have been such a big part of getting out my books and I appreciate it so much. We've had so many stories, events and trips to talk about. I could write a book just about our inside jokes and events. Together we make problems or boring things fun. I Pray we have many more events and jokes (especially Disney trips!)

Dawn – We've been friends for many, many years. We've been through a lot together, both with work or personal lives. You are a definite survivor. You have been through just so much and come out on top. You have a big heart and use it for those you love. Since the last book you now have three children! You are a great mother who puts her children before herself. Christian has your heart and has become a good person. Grace and Emma are smart and beautiful girls. I couldn't imagine life without Dawn!

ABOUT THE AUTHOR

I started to write to escape the problems and pains of my childhood. It was my only escape!" - Steve Simpson

Author Steve Simpson grew up with much of the same problems as some of the characters in the book. RUNAWAY itself originally came from an idea Steve had when he was just a boy.

Steve has been a public speaker nationally as an expert of experience to help young adults survive their various problems and issues growing up (living in alcoholic homes, abuse, suicide, running away, bullying, depression and self-esteem issues).

Steve has been FEATURED ON national media including CNN, *FOX News, ABC News, CBS News, Montel Williams, Sally Jesse Raphael, Gordon Elliot, Ricki Lake, Maury Povich, NBC Network News, The Joe Franklin Show,* and *Geraldo.*

For over 30 years Steve has run a youth/young adult group called "Together We Can Make It" sharing his experiences and giving support to its members.

Steve's novels keep his readers on the edge of their seat with action and excitement that goes from page to page. The only intermission to the action is the romance and humor throughout his books. At the same time the nonfiction aspects of Steve's novels lets readers know they are not the only ones with their problems, gives ways for his readers to change their situations and get better and gives them hope.

"Steve Simpson does everyone a tremendous service by raising the nation's awareness about runaway and homeless youth. If we can all talk more about runaways, maybe we can better address the reasons why they run --- abuse, family dynamics, peer issues. The National Runaway Switchboard thanks Steve for his effort and sincere concern for the country's youth and families."
… National Runaway Safeline

A PORTION OF THE PROCEEDS OF THIS BOOK WILL BE DONATED TO CHARITY

D1507853

Other books by the author:

Fiction:

City in Amber
Caveman Politics

Nonfiction:

Paradise Road
Legends of Winter Hill
Ice Time

Tauvernier Street

Jay Atkinson

Livingston Press
The University of West Alabama

This is a work of fiction.
Any resemblance
to persons living or dead is coincidental.

Livingston Press is part of The University of West Alabama
and thereby has non-profit status.
Donations are tax-deductible:
brothers and sisters, we need 'em.

first edition
6 5 4 3 2 1

Table of Contents

For Andrew Melnicki,
my ninth grade English teacher

Tauvernier Street

"Sometimes in moments of worry I have longed for some of that chic; but thinking it over I say: No, oh let me be true to myself, and in a rough manner express severe, rough, but true things."

Vincent van Gogh,
in a letter to his brother, Theo

The Art of War

Tall, silent, and as rigid as the day he was discharged from the Marine Corps, Phil Barrett looked east in the gathering dusk. On the far bank of the Merrimack River, his 22-year-old wife, Darlene, romped in a field strewn with old cars and rusted appliances. Mencken, a diseased looking hippie of 27, caught her beside an old green Pontiac and flung her down upon the backseat, her shorts and then her underwear flying out through the window like birds.

Barrett executed a parade turn and went into the house. He closed and then locked the door but his wife's shrieking laughter carried to him on the still summer air. Next to the kitchen stove, three final boxes of Darlene's things were stacked up, some clothes and a collection of books and coffee mugs and other bric-a-brac. He reached down for a book that belonged to him, *The Art of War*, by the Chinese philosopher, Sun Tzu, and stuffed it in his pocket.

It had been two weeks since Phil Barrett had come home early to find his wife and the local reprobate naked on the kitchen floor. Barrett left his office in the village in mid-afternoon and stopped for flowers to surprise his wife. Instead, coming silently into the house, he surprised himself: Darlene spread flat under Mencken's greasy hair and tattoos, the hippie uttering a stream of foul language worse than anything he had ever heard in the barracks. The flowers died right there in Barrett's hand, spilling onto the floor, stiff as straw.

Mencken grabbed his dirty overalls and bolted out the door. Her eyes darting around the room, Darlene stuttered and then dropped into a fearful silence.

"Just get out," Barrett said. So Darlene put on a pair of jeans and one of his old Bowdoin sweatshirts and moved into Mencken's sagging, dilapidated house across the river.

At night Barrett lay awake thinking of the wide shallow river, and the .45-caliber pistol he kept in a bedside drawer. He had never fired a gun in combat, but he knew how to use one. Mencken, too, was armed; he owned a double-barreled shotgun he kept for hunting and had once fired at the wrecks in his yard on the Fourth of July.

After turning on floodlights to illuminate the approach, Barrett would announce his attack from a portable bullhorn and then, goddamnit, *charge*; an old fashioned Marine Corps frontal assault. That would give Mencken a chance to load his shotgun and point it at him. He could probably get off a few rounds before Barrett even made the far bank of the river. But like one of his old drill instructors had said, you don't have to be fast, you just have to be willing. To fire a gun accurately enough to kill someone you had to keep something cold and still in your heart, and Phillip Barrett's heart was as cold and unmoving as a stone.

Near the end of the week, before it was light he put on his old running shoes and sweats and jogged five miles along the river. After a shower and two cups of black coffee, Barrett dressed in a suit and opened his insurance office in the village at eight.

His first customer was Ed Johanssen. A large, soft-spoken man of fifty, Sheriff Johanssen headed for a chair as soon as he entered the office, coughing so violently it was a full minute before he removed the giant fist that covered his face. Johanssen had served in the Marines as a gunnery sergeant, still wore a crew cut and always referred to Barrett by his military rank.

"'Scuse me, Captain," he said, his face crimson except for the eyelids which were white from being pinched shut. "Those cigarettes are about to kill me." The two men sat regarding each other for a moment, and then Sheriff Johanssen said, "I see your wife's taken up with that deadbeat across the river."

"Yes, Sheriff," said Barrett, holding Johanssen's gaze with his clear brown eyes. "Darlene has left me."

The sheriff ran his hands along the sides of his stomach like he was trying to guess what was in there. "Mencken's a drug dealer and welfare cheat," said Johanssen. "Small time."

"I'm a patient man," said Barrett. In front of him were the life insurance policies he was going over, the leather binder filled with actuarial tables, his adding machine and a jar of gold pencils. "This whole business is about waiting."

Sheriff Johanssen stood up and offered his hand. "Good," he said, stifling another cough. "Because eventually he'll fuck up. They always do."

*

Several townspeople stopped in the office, and Barrett spent a long time on the telephone with a lawyer in Enfield discussing the man's disability policy. At noon, he turned the "closed" sign around on the door and went into the brilliant sunshine that filled the square.

He wasn't at all hungry, but he headed down Main Street toward the Pizza Palace. While Barrett was out of the house, Darlene would drive over in Mencken's van and remove her things. Barrett left the screen door unlatched and each day he noticed a few items missing: the toaster and microwave they had received as wedding gifts, towels and throw rugs and dishes, and things from their bedroom. His house was beginning to resemble a bachelor's quarters again—nothing on the walls, bare furniture, a few books. Barrett imagined Mencken's place was undergoing a parallel transformation, blooming under Darlene's control, a hardy crop of appliances and accoutrements that must have been popping up like mushrooms.

In the noon light, he spotted Mencken's van parked in front of the liquor store. Before he could change directions, his wife appeared on the sidewalk just ahead. She was barefoot and wearing a short cotton dress, patterned with little blue flowers and so tight it separated her breasts, pointing them to either side.

Darlene looked at him with surprise, covering an involuntary smile with her hand. "Nothing's gonna bring me back," she told Barrett, wagging her finger as if he were a child.

"I don't want you back," he said.

She looked a trifle disappointed. "Good, because I couldn't

3

spend another day alone in that house. I want to have fun."

"I'm not stopping you," said Barrett.

"But that's you, Phillip. You're such a good soldier." Then Darlene answered a question that hadn't been asked but somehow lingered in the air. "Why does anyone do what they do? I was bored."

Barrett didn't respond. There was no sense trying to make someone stay when they wanted to leave. Darlene had stayed only eight months.

"I didn't plan this, you know," his wife said. "One day I was sunbathing and he just came across the river. He practically drowned. When he got to me, he started dancing." She trailed off. "It was funny."

Barrett saw Mencken emerge from the liquor store across the street and join a gang of teen-agers on skateboards. Mencken sold them marijuana and had them out to his place for dope parties. These kids spent their time skating up and down Main Street, shoplifting, getting high, and playing video games at the Pizza Palace. Occasionally Barrett bought them a pizza and they would stop by his table and talk about motorcycles or girls, too immature to look him in the eye and say thank you. They were criminals-in-training, already sliding toward the detention halls and work farms and prisons in their collective future. A free pizza and a chance to bullshit for a minute was a break, like a fighter resting between rounds.

Mencken handed over the paper sack he was carrying to the biggest kid. His name was Gilday, 16 years old, an advanced case of juvenile delinquency. He was as tall as Mencken was, his head shaped like a cannonball, with eyes that were close-set and dark. Gilday tucked the paper sack under his arm and skated off between the cars, followed by the other boys.

"I have to go," said Darlene, spotting Mencken across the street. Her face was lit by an obvious desire and she began back-pedaling. "I'll come over this afternoon and get those boxes, and then I won't bother you anymore." She tried not to be eager, but couldn't help it. "I'm sorry, but I like parties and sleeping late and music." She shrugged and added, "I guess I should've known that."

She darted across Main Street, avoiding a postal truck with a quick leap into Mencken's arms. His laughter rang out and they embraced, Mencken's hands dropping to massage her rear end through the flimsy dress. He gave Barrett a wide-eyed, rock 'n' roll stare, his tongue thrust out, the dyed black hair on his head falling in ringlets to one shoulder. Then they jumped in Mencken's van and disappeared into the light afternoon traffic flowing along Main Street.

Unsteady on his feet, Barrett pushed off down the sidewalk, the storefronts and passing cars dimmed into vague kaleidoscopic shapes. How easily a person was lost forever. If Barrett had never known Darlene, she would've been just another girl in town, her ass squeezed by a hippie, meaningless.

Phil Barrett returned to his office, and with the "closed" sign still on the door and the answering machine to take his calls, he did little but stare into space. The sun fell on the black letters that spelled his name on the window and their shadows, in reverse, appeared like Chinese characters on the wall. At five o'clock, he went home.

Night was coming on and as it did, a rock 'n' roll beat, interrupted by voices, drifted over from across the river. There was nowhere Barrett could escape it. Upstairs in bed, he took *The Art of War* from his dresser and began reading. In the leaf he had written: *Quantico, Virginia. 1985. Semper Fidelis.* It had been a required text at Officer's Candidate School, part of a course entitled "The History and Philosophy of Warfare." Among the other books were *The Prince* by Nicolo Machiavelli, and Stokesbury's brief histories of the World Wars. However, the most venerable of all was this book; a compendium of military wisdom that was ancient when Master Sun collected it into a single volume more than two thousand years earlier. These lessons, passed down by obscure Chinese warrior-philosophers, were like riddles, Barrett recalled. As exemplars of the "Tao" or "Way," it was believed that the most powerful warriors won battles just by thinking; that "victorious warriors win first and then go to war."

Barrett flipped through the text, stopping at passages he had underlined in that dusty classroom in the Virginia woods: "Send interlopers to cause rifts among them"; "The best of plans is the one that is unknown." His instructor, a visiting British officer named Colonel Tillman, left all questions from *The Art of War* off the final examina-

5

tion. Instead, Tillman met with each candidate in his office and asked him to summarize the Tao in one sentence. Barrett said, "The one who treats me well is my leader, the one who treats me cruelly is my enemy," and received the highest grade in his unit.

He read until the pulsing din from Mencken's side of the river faded out and was replaced by insects whirring at the screen and other night sounds. Then he switched off the lamp and tried to keep himself still, a trick for falling asleep he had learned during field exercises. But soon he was pumping his arms and legs, like a man in a slow motion race, tortured by what the silence meant. Thoughts of revenge and bloody showdowns occupied his mind through the next hours. Barrett watched the light under the window shade change from purple to pink to a bar of white phosphorescence, and he rose from the bed.

*

Driving to work, Barrett passed Sheriff Johanssen on River Road and waved. The sheriff was grim in the early morning sun and although he looked at Barrett, he didn't wave back. It was strange to see the patrol car away from the village during the day. Barrett stopped for coffee and was alone in the diner when Gilday threw open the door and stomped in, his hair unwashed and his jeans and sweatshirt caked in mud.

"Hey, Mr. Barrett," the youth said.

"Mornin'," said Barrett, glassy-eyed.

The youth sidled over to him and in a low voice, he said, "I know about your problem, Mr. Barrett. And I'm stoked for it. He's chowder."

Barrett glanced sideways at the boy. "I don't have any problems," he said, and Gilday nodded like he understood and left the diner without another word. An hour later, the sheriff came into the office when Barrett was on the telephone and waited, hat in hand, for him to wrap up.

"I was out to Mencken's place," Johanssen said. The ugly smell of cigarettes clung to him and his eyes watered from his latest coughing fit. "Somebody slashed his tires last night. Do you know anything about it?"

"No," said Barrett.

"I didn't think so, Captain," said the sheriff. He sat down, his face swollen and his eyes red-rimmed and wet. Johanssen stared at the floor, no doubt in review of Barrett's situation, and then looked him in the eye. "I already smoked a pack of cigarettes today. And I'm supposed to be quitting. Cutting down, at least."

Phil Barrett nodded his head.

"Mencken says you did it," continued Johanssen. "He was jumping up and down about his rights." The sheriff coughed. "Nobody complains like a deadbeat."

Barrett grunted and the sheriff went on. "I wanted to search the van, but he had it locked up tight. Said nothing was missing, just the tires slashed, that's it."

Barrett thought of something he had read the night before. *Those who render other armies helpless without fighting are the best of all.* He brushed a speck of lint from his sleeve and said, "My wife went over there and I didn't say a thing, Ed. Now he wants me arrested? I didn't touch his goddamned van. I wouldn't give him the satisfaction."

"I told him that, in so many words," said the sheriff. "There's nothing for you to gain"—he swept his hand across the room— "and all this to lose."

The sheriff grunted, coming to his feet. He started for the door and then paused, his bulk swaying toward the desk again. "Hell, off the record, I wouldn't blame you if you slashed the bastard's throat, never mind his tires."

Barrett remained in the office until dusk and after a brief stop at home to change clothes, he drove to the Legion hall for a beer. He had something to eat and one of the regulars offered him a game of darts. While they were playing, Sheriff Johanssen dropped in and sat at the bar drinking coffee with some linemen from the telephone company. He and Barrett acknowledged each other without speaking. Around nine o'clock, a call came over the radio and Johanssen went out. Barrett left twenty minutes later.

Along River Road, the huge dark pines were banked up on either side like monoliths against an opaque, moonless sky. Barrett felt submerged until he turned into his driveway, crunching over the gravel toward his house. Across the river, glowing against the backdrop of pine trees, Mencken's van was consumed in fire. Burning at this distance without heat, but with an intense light that illuminated the junk scattered across Mencken's property, the van digested itself and yet seemed replenished, shimmering like a mirage, solidifying momentarily then wavering again as the blaze changed shape.

Plumes of fire shot into the air, twisting into columns or mushrooming outward in brief soundless explosions. The strobe effect caught Mencken and Darlene in a variety of poses, like instant photographs. Nearby, Sheriff Johanssen leaned against his car, arms folded, only his solid jaw visible beneath the brim of his hat. Mencken circled the blaze, first in full light and then in silhouette, his long hair flying out, waving his arms at the beast that was devouring his van. On a bare patch of ground, he dropped to his knees and flung his arms up at the black moonless sky.

"Son-of-a-bitch," he said. "I'll get you for this."

Sheriff Johanssen crossed the yard and spoke to him.

"I don't care where he was," said Mencken. "That chickenshit bastard was the one who did it."

The revolving lights of the volunteer fire department pulled into the lot. Three men in boots and bunker pants jumped off the truck and began running around the yard, dragging hoses and shouting commands to one another. Apparently, there was no outside water at Mencken's place and the would-be firefighters abandoned their efforts and joined the sheriff in watching the fire. It reached a new intensity, and the smell of burning marijuana wafted on the air for a few moments.

Barrett smiled in the darkness. He took his eyes off the blaze and noticed Darlene, at the river's edge, staring across at him. His wife was lovely in the firelight, her hips and long straight legs outlined by the glow behind her. She looked like a diver, mulling a plunge into the ribbon of water, poised there waiting for the signal to start. Ignoring her, Barrett went into the house.

For several days afterward, the sight of charred metal sent Barrett to his office whistling with happiness. *It is said that victory can be discerned but not manufactured.* His old confidence returned and he spent a lot of time on the phone, making deals.

Waiting for it to happen by accident, he ran into Gilday at the Pizza Palace. Barrett called the waitress over and ordered a salad for himself and a large pepperoni special. When the pizza was ready, he sent it to the teen-agers sitting in the corner and Gilday came to his table. He had the smooth blank face of a killer—the skin translucent, stretched over his blunt cheekbones, and eyes that were shrewd and dark and held none of the light streaming in the windows. Slouching into a chair, Gilday reached under his dirty T-shirt to scratch himself and then, after a moment spent regarding Barrett's coffee cup, he asked, "How's your thing going?"

"It's gone," said Barrett.

"Not when the X-man is over there with your cheese," said Gilday. He used a lot of skateboarding slang and Barrett had trouble following it. "We put him on the down low, but he's still popping off about your woman."

"How do you know?"

The teenager gazed at the cars pulled up close to the building. "Me and Mencken do a little business. The other day he stiffed me at the liquor store," said Gilday. "Whoever puts the gong on him is gonna be aces."

After a short silence Gilday stood up, his hands falling to his sides. "I know you could clip him twenty-four/seven," he said. "But I'll take care of it." There was resignation in his voice, proof that at sixteen he already knew where he was going and made no apologies for it, expected no slack.

"I learned something in the Marines," said Barrett, looking at the boy. "From a really old book. 'While strong in reality, appear to be weak; while brave in reality, appear to be cowardly'."

Gilday let out a rueful laugh. "I couldn't cut much rubber with that," he said, offering a rare smile. He jerked his thumb at the rapidly disappearing pizza. "But we're buzzing on the circle of death, man. It was king."

*

That afternoon things were slow and Barrett sat at his desk, reading. Midway through *The Art of War*, Master Sun and his disciples began a discussion of "emptiness" and "fullness." When you induced the enemy to come to you, driven by rage or greed, he was empty; if you remained waiting, formless as water, conserving your strength, your force was always full. Attacking fullness with emptiness, said the Master, is like throwing eggs on stone—the eggs are sure to break. Confuse and disturb the enemy, observing his response. *Good warriors make others come to them, and do not go to others.*

Darlene was out front when he locked up the office at six o'clock. The sun was dropping and shafts of light fell between the storefronts. One long corridor ended where she stood, a welt on her cheek, her suitcase overflowing onto the sidewalk.

"Phillip," she said, crying. "He hit me."

Barrett wiped her tears with his handkerchief. "Come inside," he said, opening the office door.

The telephone was ringing and Barrett let the answering machine get it. Mencken's voice came on, mixed with some horrible rock 'n' roll music, saying, "Where is she? That bitch. I'm not finished with her," and Darlene sagged into a chair, crying harder this time. Barrett pushed a button that disconnected the phone and his wife said, "Don't make me go back there."

"Don't worry," said Barrett. He filled a paper cup at the water cooler and brought it to her. "He can't hurt you now."

Between sobs, she drank the water. The welt had closed her right eye and her face, except for the swollen patch, was a sickly white. Barrett sat opposite her, still crisp in his jacket and tie, waiting until she was ready to talk.

"He was yelling and screaming that I helped you burn his van," Darlene said. "When he wouldn't leave me alone, I started to call you and he went crazy."

She raised her head, looking at Barrett through her good eye. "He ripped the phone out of my hand and started pushing me and I said you never yelled or called me a bitch. That you were a gentleman." Her gaze faltered. "Then he punched me."

Darlene looked very young at that moment, like a child who had engaged in some forbidden activity and returned home scared and broken. It must have come as a shock that men could, on a whim, renege on their promises and hurt her.

For his part, Barrett realized how cold he had been. He had worn Darlene like the fur of some animal he had trapped; for eight months parading her through the village when it suited him, going so far as to display her bridal photo in his office. It was like deer season, her pretty head drooping over the fender of his car. That she had somehow loosened herself and escaped must have seemed, at first, like being wild in the woods again.

"He's afraid of you, Phillip," said Darlene, touching the welt under her eye. "He keeps saying he's gonna get even with you, but all he's ever done is try to hire those kids from Pizza Palace to wreck your car."

Barrett laughed. "You're kidding."

"He wanted to give the biggest one, whatsisname—Gilday—twenty bucks but the kid wouldn't take it. He said you weren't so tough and Mencken should handle it himself."

Gilday was smarter than he looked. In one brief conversation he understood what Master Sun was trying to teach. "After that, Mencken freaked out," said Darlene. "He came home ranting and raving and he hit me."

Barrett took Darlene to her mother's house in the next village. Long silences punctuated the drive, Barrett studying the road or the whiteness of his knuckles where they clutched the wheel. Nothing would repair what had happened between them, so he didn't try. Getting out of the car, Darlene looked like a runaway. "I'm not a bad person. I just make mistakes," she said, against the backdrop of pine trees. "I never should have gotten married."

*

Barrett arrived home after dark. He took a flashlight from his car and inspected the house before going inside. Running the beam of light over the walls, he checked the facade for the most vulnerable points of entry. Then he switched off the flashlight and went in the back way.

Struggling over the kitchen tiles, he used the refrigerator to seal up the entrance through the pantry. Then he unlocked the front door and climbed the narrow stairs to his room. Still dressed in shirt and slacks, Barrett got into bed. Not long before midnight a glow reflected in the windows facing the river. Then the howl of electric guitars tore open the silence and Barrett rose to his feet.

Mencken's house was in flames. They rippled up and down the building, stopping momentarily at the eaves until they ran over them, feasting on the roof. Music rang out of the fire, destructive and wandering, sound driven from the heat. Then shouts mingled with the guitars, cries of rage, and Mencken appeared in front of the house, waving his shotgun. "You're next," he screamed across the river. "You're gonna burn."

He fired his gun in the direction of Barrett's house, the echo smothered by the music. Running between the wrecked cars and appliances littering his property, Mencken leaped off the bank into the river, holding his gun overhead, stumbling forward. The fire behind him expanded in a roar that cut off the music. In the distance, Barrett could see the sheriff's lights and those of the volunteer fire department coming toward him.

Mencken was past the halfway point of the river, scrambling over rocks and fighting the current. "Fuck the Marines," he said, firing the other barrel. On the bank he reloaded and closed on Barrett's house.

Barrett reached into the bedside table, removing his .45. He checked the clip and took his flashlight and went to the top of the darkened stairs. Mencken put another blast through the screen door, raining shot into the hall and against the woodwork and furniture. "I'll kill you," the hippie said.

Barrett eased down the stairs, his pistol and flashlight at the ready. Mencken was blundering on the front porch, swearing and tripping over things, and Barrett glided toward him in the darkness.

Dancing the Presidents

All was quiet until midday, Provost Spaulding appearing on the crest of noon; the shiny lure of brunch—petit fours, Darjeeling, the stinky Camembert—and the weight of my petition squatting on the table like a hairy, loathsome dwarf; and the dwarf yammered and whined and trampled all the cakes to the tune of Spaulding's wheedling delay; then finally, he blurted his—the University's—reply: I had been denied the Will Durant chair of Popular History. There we sat, Marta and I, stumped and stupefied, bewildered like two sunblind goats and slowly the realization and our liberating fury; the initial struggle, the diamonds of perspiration on Marta's upper lip; the bloody ingots dropped on the carpet, then the shrieks of Provost Spaulding as he negotiated the home stretch of what he himself had called a "fait accompli."

But first, the hopeful preliminaries:

In the radiance of dawn I finished the Roosevelt manuscript, burgeoning at 1224 pages, but upon realizing my mistake, I deleted two of them for a total of 1222. As always, breakfast was two frozen clamstrips and ten Brussels sprouts ruminated over for twenty-two minutes. At the end of the table Marta picked at her eggs Benedict, staring at her plate and downing several glasses of wine. After the meal, I scrubbed at the old bloodstains with a mixture of white vinegar and lemon juice. The vinegar coated the tiles with a sticky patina; the lemon juice emitted a pleasant odor; and the two heavy steel ingots, covered with electrical tape and microscopic bits of lint and hair, fit naturally into my palm.

I washed the ingots with bleach and stored them in the credenza.

In the bright morning hours Marta occupied herself with flamenco, whirling around the dining room in the midst of broken crockery and debris; and I closed the French doors on her and seated myself in the study. Most days, my thoughts fell upon those unspeakable moments that other scholars glossed over; the slow march of days that afflicted us all, from the autocrats in Washington to the sycophantic delusion-als we had cooped up in our universities, scratching at their bandages and chafing at their restraints. My colleagues had gone mad denying the obvious: that American history was a tattered and rotting fabric cobbled together by rotten and tainted men. Men of small stature, with clubfeet and clacking joints and fungi growing like mushrooms in the dank recesses of their bodies.

George Washington—"the farceur of our country," as Marta re-ferred to him—had stood among the burning wreckage of New York City and cursed a whore who had given "carnal comfort to a wide host of the enemy." Those sentiments were included in a letter to his wife, which also contained the blackened nub of one of his teeth. And that most virulent of self-promoters, Thomas Jefferson, coiner of our ideals, had once beaten his lover Sally Hemming with a chair leg of his own design, "exhorting the black bitch to refrain from produc-ing any further number of (their) dusky offspring...since the mistress of the house was taken with calling for these bastards from her sick-bed, and every wattle upon Monticello's vast green was wagging with the most evil speculation."

These documents were held in private collections and diligent scholars could peruse them, if they wished. Usually they dismissed these tales as rumor, accepting large fees to appear on television and debate them. How foolish the upstart willing to hang his or her repu-tation upon such slender hooks, when a Douglas Brinkley or Arthur Schlesinger Jr. pointed his talking head at the monitor and called you an inveterate liar and profiteer; a cad, at the very least. Yet, a male cousin of Abraham Lincoln's had written in his diary that he was ill at ease whenever the tall, saturnine, and beardless young lawyer visited their farm in 1835. It was well-established in various sources that "Abey" had shared a bed with another man for three years, even in summer, and the 17-year-old cousin, a strapping youth, wrote that

Lincoln touched his "foreleg" and then promised him a job in the county tax assessor's office.

Gawky, horse-toothed Eleanor Roosevelt, flushed from the Lincoln bedroom by her wheelchair-bound husband, had rumbled naked along the corridor with a toilet plunger in her hand, followed by a blur of ebony skin and a lone shoe dropped along the runner by her chambermaid. The list of such frailties was endless, but the items on that list always came at a high price. Wisdom has it that our heroes are not men and women, they are legends; and it's long since been proven that any attempt to humanize them will be demonized. Illuminate the warts of an American icon and be prepared to have your own boils lanced, and publicly to boot.

The most contemporary scandals notwithstanding, the White House has long been a breeding ground of licentiousness and depravity. The Kennedy brothers, a randy alphabet soup of initials, once engaged in multiple orifice copulation with the most sought-after of movie stars, her lips painted fire-engine red and hair bleached into cotton candy. She stretched this way and that like rubber, grunting along with their flattened Harvard vowels while just outside the door, a Secret Service agent received oral pleasures from a dark-haired woman wearing a string of pearls. Then the Kennedy boys, hurrying the movie star out through another exit, in their naked and syrupy haste telephoned LBJ, rubbing the Texan's blue-veined nose in the stench of their affairs.

These are facts; at least, factual in the sense that they can never be ruled out. All the ominous warnings about history being composed by the victors are a bunch of nonsense, mere gabbling in the eaves of Academe. The most dangerous thing about history is that no one is left to refute it. Put another way, the stock in trade of the professional historian has always been the narrowness of his own mind coupled with the brief lifespan of his subject. (Case study: the reason so little is known about the Galapagos turtle is that it tends to outlive its researchers.) Santayana was a drunken fraud; those who forget history are condemned to invent it. Therefore, to remain simple-minded, if somewhat stupid, and to announce one's opinions into a vast, encompassing silence is what passes for being right these days. Just as it was in the days of Caesar.

When the Visigoths plundered Rome in 418 AD, they entered the Christian temples in their shaggy hides and began raping and murdering the attendant virgins until none were left alive and the city was on fire. No one disputes that. But try publishing a monograph asserting that 26-year-old Ulysses S. Grant and his war party descended upon a Shoshone village in the spring of 1848, and without resistance proceeded to slaughter all its inhabitants. Lieutenant Grant and his fellow officers wagered on the number of scalps that each could assemble, and finished their Wyoming bacchanal by smoking penny cigars and gang-raping a pretty young half-breed. How the jackals will howl that you are unfit for such a distinguished academic post—that despite your hood and laurels you are a kind of Goth yourself, invading the precious temples of American sanctity. But recall, too, that I am Ecuadorian and Marta is a Nepalese, and to the tweed-jacketed nitwits who stalk our dingy campus we are infidels, molesting their icons and putting their false gods to the torch. For "the one true God" of all Americans is the handsome, brave, flaxen-haired American, no matter what your clergy say on Sundays.

*

And that was how Provost Spaulding came to brunch. A prim, gray-haired man in a flannel suit, no taller than a kangaroo, with breath that smelled like an old paper mill covered up with cherry mouthwash. He was grotesque; masticating his cheese and cakes together until the shards were whipped into froth and swept away on tides of tea. We were discussing my work-in-progress, the hefty magnum opus that formed a pile taller than our cocktail glasses, and whether it would propel me through the University's rather vicious game of musical chairs. I explained that, like Archimedes, many of my discoveries occurred in the bathroom. Sitting on the toilet one day, my current project arrived as a melange of words, floating across my consciousness like turds in a bowl: *quetzal–cacophony–carbuncle–concatenation–rotogravure–Rough Riders–Rousseau*—leading to one of those "eureka" moments I depend on. Suddenly I understood that Teddy Roosevelt's self-enforced vigor was the result of his fascination with a pet bird, *Pharomacrus mocino*, which ate its own canker, choked, and died on March 6, 1871. That same afternoon the 35th anniversary of the Alamo defeat appeared in all the newspapers, just as "Teedie's" grandfather, Cornelius Van Schaack Roosevelt, lie dying of respiratory illness and clutching his passport because, just as the family bird gagged on its own excrescence, the old man believed that he was going somewhere. Young Ted vowed over his grandfather's corpse that *he* would see the world and die with his boots on and look damned good doing it—all of this grand deduction a part of the "common memory" formed by my own experience and the interstitial meaning of all the books I had ever read. This approach, I told Spaulding, was European in origin and particularly indicative of French notions of socio-sexual liberation on the American sensibility.

Provost Spaulding swallowed a bite of prosciutto with melon, stating that Americans are more interested in living on cul-de-sacs than they are in the influence of the French on U. S. history. In his opinion, all texts were flat; the integument of the author's real self, and merely a reflection of his or her aspirations and prejudices. When you see words on the page, it's like the glare of sun on a lake, neither fire nor water, a shining skin and nothing more. Spaulding went on to say, gesturing with his tiny silver fork, that my theory of the "common memory" ran dangerously close to ideas promulgated by a renowned Swiss psychiatrist (I wasn't familiar with him) and that although he hated the Swiss in general, he admired their ability to make clocks and trains run on time.

I asked Spaulding if he would rather die in a plane crash or be eaten by bears: a Hobson's choice, if ever there was one. The average person thinks of history as still pictures: woodcuts, lithographs and daguerreotypes. But consider the 9.75-second Zapruder film running through the open gate of a movie projector and you'll confront the dilemma of the historian; for everything you see, every detail captured, there are a million perspectives that are lost, an infinity of moments unaccounted for. When Jack Kennedy clutches his neck and then absorbs another blow and his head goes thrusting back, there is an invisible America doing something else; 250 million individuals engaged in the gigantic, three-dimensional pageant of their own lives.

17

That's when Marta excused herself, returning a few moments later dressed in full military regalia, circa World War II, including an Eisenhower jacket with five gold stars on each shoulder. In her right hand was the wicked curve of a knife. Marta is an artist-in-residence at the University and we are both young, for academics—which means less than fifty years of age, if you are publishing. The daughter and granddaughter of Nepalese climbing sirdars, she has the muscular legs and inexhaustible stamina of a Sherpa: the glittering eyes, the same Asiatic trace of a mustache. All her people were either climbers or killers; nine of her stubby little uncles were Gurkhas, the most feared military unit in modern history. (Case study: when the Gurkhas led the British invasion onto the Falkland Islands in 1982, the young Argentines could be heard sobbing in their foxholes.)

Sitting, or at rest, Marta is graceless, a block of stone with eyes. But even at a walk, she floats; her sinews vibrate together like the strings of an orchestra. So when my words became useless and Provost Spaulding knit his tangled brow, and a straight *No* to my request—my dream, my *raison d'être*—was about to spring from his throat, Marta cast off her barracks hat and danced the presidents; she swept upward to a height of three or four meters and re-enacted Dwight D. Eisenhower's passion; the deflowering of his aide in the backseat of a command vehicle on the Normandy beachhead, the main force six days inland, the sand cleared of mines and tank traps and bunkers. All was quiet on the Western Front that morning, except for the hymen-tearing shrieks of a 25-year-old WAC lieutenant from Park City, Utah.

I love my wife.

This is madness, exclaimed Spaulding, while Marta climbed upon the table and thrust at herself with a baguette. *Eisenhower was no more capable of infidelity than I am of walking on water. Mamie would not have stood for it.*

But I have postulated, in *Smithsonian* et. al., that Mamie Eisenhower was addicted to Benzedrine; that each afternoon she would clomp down to the PX and buy her "nose medicine," whereupon the future first lady of the United States would return to her bungalow, crack open the inhalers, take out the soaked papers and roll them into little balls, which she then saturated in Coca-Cola. As MPs struck the colors on the parade ground, Mrs. Eisenhower would load up on the benny papers and play her Charlie Parker records at full volume. When Mamie's head began to sing and she was good and high, she'd gather her oversize patent leather bag and veiled hat and light out for the Officer's Club. She didn't give a rat's ass where Rommel was going to strike, or what sort of hot water George Patton had gotten himself into. Why, Ike could have floated by on angel's wings and she would have ignored him.

I looked down and saw that I was raging, the Gurkha knife in my hand, the petit fours scattered over the carpet. So I had made my first number, *two*, from Provost Spaulding and his fear.

*

History is transparent, a pair of spectacles with no lenses, although historians want to pretend that it's translucent—a cloudy window that only they see through. Or see *into*. When a historian gazes at the past, if you believe what he tells you, his intellect gathers up lost particles of fact the way that a magnet draws iron filings. (Then he calls these fragments a hammer and smashes you with it.) The other myth propagated by the intelligentsia is that history is blotched on cave walls and carved into totems and engraved on lintels by those bold enough to seize the day. As if the only weakness of the historian was exaggeration; the tiny embellishments that appear when battles are won and lands conquered. Any scholar will admit that the Great American Saga contains the sin of pride; that they consider this not only forgivable but enviable is what I find nauseating.

It's the cowards that witness great events and live to record them. (Case study: the only "white" accounts we have of Little Big Horn are from the supply men and clerks who remained in camp.) At the age of sixteen, I was fresh off the banana boat from Guayaquil and working as a busboy in Los Angeles. It was a filthy, teeming city, no different from where I had come from, while the America I sought was out there somewhere like a dream, a land scented with pine trees and burst firecrackers. Each morning I admired myself in the mirror at the YMCA, resplendent in a shiny white tunic, black trousers and slicked back hair. On June 4, 1968, I rose at five AM and shined my oxfords until I could see myself in them: a brown-skinned boy with a thin, sensitive mouth and girlish eyes. I knew something was going to happen.

That evening, my hero would deliver a speech at the hotel. The image of Bobby Kennedy—the thatch of hair, one hand jammed in the pocket of his suitcoat—was what had called me to America. I first saw him on a grainy television in the window of a second-hand store in Quito. He stood on the roof of a car, surrounded by a crowd of jubilant Africans, shaking hands with them until the hundreds grew into thousands. I witnessed this scene through three panes of glass and heavy-gauge steel, without sound or text, and the truth of what I saw flowed into my heart. There was a sea of black faces, each one hoping to touch this slender, freckled man from Massachusetts; each one anxious for a chit. I would have stood in the gutter all night if Kennedy's henchmen had not grown nervous and yanked him down, into an armored limousine and away. They had seen it all before, in Dealey Plaza, and they would be damned if another of their meal tickets was going to roll in the dust. So the television went blank, and a moment later the screen was filled with dancing Pepsi-Cola bottles.

Two years later, I was working room service in the east wing of the Ambassador Hotel; as an illegal alien, I was considered a low-level security risk and kept away from the delegation. So it was an example of Brownian motion that placed me in the lower pantry when the candidate passed through just after midnight on June 5th. Had the service buzzer rang a moment before, or a guest on the ninth floor requested a Maine lobster instead of ratatouille, I would have been elsewhere at the moment Robert Kennedy's fate was decided and mine with his.

The shooter was right beside me. He was wearing a white Nehru jacket and at first I mistook him for another busboy, standing under the oven hood as the candidate and his entourage came into view. There were uniformed officers and plainclothesmen and hangers-on, reporters shouting out questions, and the flash of a dozen cameras. Then came two of the largest men I had ever seen, dressed in ill-fitting suits, their hands enormous and their faces gleaming like eggplants. The candidate was wedged between them. He was a slight fellow with a nervous look on his face, almost invisible; he jumped every time a flashbulb popped. Near the sinks, Kennedy went up on tiptoes and spoke to one of the bodyguards; he called him Rafer. The man rested his arm on the candidate's shoulder and steered him toward the exit like a father guiding his son.

The shooter came forward, and put his hand out to the candidate. In the television lights it was clear he was one of the desert people, and that his mind was empty. Then I saw the black nub of the gun, like a snake's head. The candidate saw it next. His gaze traveled from the tiny muzzle hole to the eyes of the shooter. For an instant they regarded each other, then the candidate smiled, almost imperceptibly. Half a second later, the bodyguard spotted the shooter; not Rafer, the other one. For a moment his bulk was poised in the space between the candidate and the gun. (Afterward, all the newspaper accounts said the bodyguard weighed two hundred and seventy pounds, and had once run forty yards in four and a half seconds. But caught in the maw of history, he seemed to shrink, clearing the path that the bullet would travel.) There were two loud pops, followed by an odor of burnt fabric. The candidate crumpled to the floor without uttering a sound. Someone yelled at Rafer to get the gun. A dozen policemen drew their service revolvers and the whir of cameras was like locusts.

The two bodyguards pounced on the shooter and his gun skittered away. Blood seeped across the floor and onlookers began retreating from it (even our staunchest champions are avoided when they are dying). Kneeling beside the candidate, I held his head for a moment and he looked at me and said something I couldn't hear in all the commotion. Then the life went out of him.

Nearby on a stainless steel table was a pile of Brussels sprouts covered with a large dinner napkin and two metal ingots used to hold down the edges of the cloth. The bodyguards were lying on top of the shooter and the police were yelling at the television crew to turn off their camera and fighting with the photographers who were making pictures of the corpse. The shooter was screaming something in Arabic over and over. A man with a large birthmark on his face discovered the metal ingots and handed them to the bodyguards just as the television crew and photographers were being routed from the kitchen. Rafer closed the ingot in his fist and punched the shooter in the mouth, shattering his teeth. An instant later the other bodyguard joined in pummeling the shooter, bloodying his eyes, breaking the bones in his face, and tearing off one of his eyebrows. It was a terrible beating; several policemen holstered their weapons and looked on. Afterward, the ingots were thrown into a sump and I retrieved them, washed off the blood, and smuggled them out of the hotel in my jacket, along with ten of the Brussels sprouts. (The next day, a photograph of Sirhan Bishara Sirhan appeared in the *Los Angeles Times* with his face all mangled and a police captain was quoted as saying that the assassin had fallen down a set of cement stairs while being taken into custody. And so a lie became history.)

Anointed with Robert Kennedy's blood, there in the lower pantry of the Ambassador Hotel I vowed to make something of myself and enrolled at UCLA the next day. It took me eleven years to earn my baccalaureate degree, seven more for the Masters, and fifteen for the doctorate—the precise sum of time that Alexander the Great spent on earth. At East Tennessee State my Masters Thesis was entitled "Jackson and Abernathy: The Men Who Would Be King and the Failure of Civil Rights Leadership," and then, sensing a shift within the profession, at Florida State University my dissertation became "From John Adams to William McKinley: the Systematic Demonization, Persecution, and Near Extinction of Native Americans and the American Presidents Who Endorsed It."

At all three of my graduations, I carried the bloody ingots as a reminder that the eyewitness account is no more authoritative than the reported one. And so we came to this dismal little University, and I published papers and volunteered for committees and bided my time in the academic shallows. Until the Durant chair was created, and I maneuvered myself into position: a non-native, bilingual American Studies specialist, with a freshly minted terminal degree. Students flocked to my seminars on "Hail to the Chiefs: A Chronicle of Presidential Substance Abuse" and "Sexual Deviancy and the United States Congress;" it was all playing out as Marta and I had scripted it. Then Provost Spaulding came to call.

It's not the controversial nature of your theories that ultimately defeats your candidacy, explained the foul-breathed little kangaroo. *It's your habit of insisting that something is a fabrication that we all know to be true. This sort of 'tabloid conspiracy' approach to the field makes some of your colleagues very uncomfortable.*

(Case study: we know Robert Kennedy's bodyguards did everything possible to prevent his assassination. We also know that the shooter was taken into custody without incident.)

Using a prearranged signal, Marta and I leaped on Provost Spaulding and re-enacted the beating of Sirhan Sirhan. It seemed more eloquent than any argument I could make, more assertive than an apologia. And in those blood-shaking moments, we demonstrated that history is neither art nor science, but a kind of craft. Working over a long stretch of years, one might reconstitute a certain space of time only to see one's audience recoil at the horror. It's not history they want, it's justification.

We hardly bruised him, as Marta yelled for Rafer to get the gun and I began screaming in Arabic. But Spaulding was unnerved and he rushed out of the house and tumbled down the front stairwell. When he rose, bloody and concussed, the little ingrate staggered across the lawn to his Peugeot. He sped away, bashing his car into one of the hemlocks lining our driveway. Spaulding backed up, ground into first gear and zoomed off; no one has heard from him since. If I were the police, I'd begin looking at Hampton Beach, where he likes to cruise for young boys. Failing that, they might try his summerhouse on Boar's Head—he has an interesting collection of pornographic films there.

In the light from the television I performed cunnilingus on Marta for twenty-two minutes after which she became frustrated and chased me through the foyer with an ice pick. That's how I received the wound on my back. Unlike Provost Spaulding and his minions, I have always seen history as a matter of presentation rather than argument, and I leave it to my readers to draw their own conclusions.

The God of This World

*Go to the prosperous city,
for I have taken pity
on its inhabitants*

—William Coyle

I

Riding high above the street, Bob Halloran caught the light, downshifted, and turned onto the service road with all his windows down and an old Beatles tune on the radio. Stretching ahead on either side was a long line of chain stores, restaurants, car washes and drive-through banks, with eight lanes of pavement in between and giant halogen lights that hadn't been switched off though the sun had come up. It was a breezy, overcast Sunday morning and with the kids' hectic schedules and things so busy at work, Halloran was glad to have an hour to himself. When Suzy had asked him to run a few errands he had jumped off the lawnmower and headed straight for his truck.

Next to his speedboat, the monstrous red pickup was Bob Halloran's favorite toy. Every Saturday he washed and waxed it, vacuumed the upholstery, and cleaned the glass and leather and chrome inside and out. Suzy used to say that polishing the truck helped Bob work out his control issues, which was a good thing, since their life together in the small Massachusetts town where they had grown up was so out of control they hardly found time to have breakfast together. Bob laughed and said it had been Suzy's idea to have kids.

Sarah was thirteen: slender, blond and freckled like her mother, an eighth grader at the Sacred Heart middle school and one heck of a tennis player. Sacred Heart didn't offer tennis and Sarah was allowed to try out for the high school team and made second singles and first doubles for the varsity. Bob was very proud of her. He had been an all conference linebacker in high school, played two more years of football at Laredo Junior College in Texas and earned a scholarship to San Diego State University. That he had blown out his knee during camp and never actually played for the Aztecs did not prevent him from watching their games on satellite. There was a plaque in the Sacred Heart gymnasium engraved with his likeness and the fact that Robert Prentice Halloran was the only graduate of that school ever to play football in the Mountain West Conference.

His cell phone rang and he unclipped it from his belt and glanced at the caller ID; it was Suzy. "Bobby wants you to get some oranges for his soccer team. I need time to cut them up, so hurry, okay?"

"I'm hurrying."

"Love you."

"Same here."

Bobby was an ungainly kid, just a shade under six feet and only twelve years old, with a shock of his mother's blond hair and legs as long and thin as a colt's. In private conversation with his wife, Halloran admitted to some disappointment that Bobby hadn't taken up football in seventh grade, as he had. But the boy had begun to excel as a soccer goalie, carving out a name for himself in the Essex County league, and Halloran's heart turned with excitement at the thought of his son playing that morning.

No sooner had he closed the phone and reattached it to his belt when it rang again. The caller I. D. showed that it was Charlie Westerhouse, the foreman on the construction side of his development company. They were building nineteen homes over near Carter Lake and no doubt Charlie had a crew framing all weekend in order to catch up. Bob put the phone back without answering it; this was his first Sunday off in more than two months and Charlie was going to have to figure things out for himself.

Bob Halloran encountered one other vehicle as he neared the Food Giant. An orange and white rental van was weaving between the first and second lanes and Halloran tried to pass by going wide and the unseen driver speeded up as he did and nearly blocked his turn into the grocery store.

"Hey, jackass," said Halloran. "Get a grip."

He turned into the vast acreage of the Food Giant parking lot just as the song on the radio ended. The news jingle marked the top of the hour and an announcer stated that the President was asking the nation to remain on high alert throughout the Fourth of July weekend. In the nearly eight years since the terrorist attacks on New York and Washington it seemed that Americans were supposed to be on "high alert" more than half the time. And yet, other than the occasional anthrax scare and the nut they had arrested at the Super Bowl, nothing much had happened.

Maneuvering his truck as close as possible to the supermarket, Halloran pulled on his emergency brake and pocketed his keys. Noticing for the first time that small wet bits of grass clung to his sneakers and lay scattered over the floor of his pickup, he let out an exasperated snort and eased down from the truck on his good leg, slamming the door behind him. Using the little keypad, he locked up the truck as he walked away, the alarm system chirping like a cricket. He unhooked his cell phone, turned the ringer off and returned it to his belt. He was not the kind of asshole who talked on his phone in the grocery store.

Halloran entered the Food Giant and saw where all the people who were up and about on Sunday morning had congregated. They waddled up and down the aisles pushing baskets stuffed to overflowing with every prepared foodstuff imaginable: crackers and chips and multiple varieties of soda pop and hunks of cheese and red meats covered in blood and matted with plastic wrap and foam backing. Glossy waxed orbs of fruit were stacked in a great redoubt across his path and a woman with an enormous rear end passed along this display with a four-year-old boy in her carriage and then went behind it, like a sentry.

Bob Halloran drew in the billow of his stomach and tucked the edge of his "Aztec Football" shirt into his shorts. This was what we had to fear from the dark part of the world: our plenty. Our sense of entitlement and our accomplished ease. Twenty-four hour food warehouses were a liability when Halloran remembered that our enemy slept in caves and survived on a handful of grain and a few olives. Our biggest weakness *was* our weakness, he thought, and it troubled the former linebacker that most of his neighbors lay swaddled in bedclothes under the mesmerizing light of their television sets while a horde of barbarians squatted just beyond the perimeter, eager to get inside.

Halloran took a bag of oranges from the produce section, then crossed to the dry goods aisle and picked up a roll of masking tape. At the lone open checkout, he found himself behind the enormous woman, her lower half clad in green nylon pants and rippling like it had been packed in suet. In addition to the four-year-old, whose mouth was stained with grape juice and whose clothes and hands were dirty, the woman had acquired another child, a girl of eight or nine wearing the cotton shift that she'd slept in and a pair of her mother's yellow beach sandals. The woman was disassembling a huge cache of food from inside the carriage, and just as Halloran thought he would burst from impatience the woman produced a welfare voucher to pay for it all and the teenage girl at the register had to ring for someone to help her.

The four-year-old took a package of razor blades from a display nearby and began tearing at it. Busy unloading her carriage, the over-sized woman failed to interrupt her son's effort on the tricky plastic enclosure of the razor case. The lad managed to pry apart the edge and had his fingers inside when his sister tugged at the woman's arm.

"Mom, Davy is—"

The enormous woman shoved the girl away without taking her eyes from inside her purse, which she was busy rummaging in. "Shut up, Dori," the woman said.

Bob Halloran reached over the woman's shoulder and took the package of razor blades from the little boy and threw it onto the conveyor belt while it was still moving. The belt stopped and the large, suet-bottomed woman and the little boy and his sister and the cashier all looked at the razor blades, and then the woman stared at Halloran with a look that said she preferred he mind his own business.

"What did you do?" she asked the four-year-old, indicating the mangled package. "Stupid kid."

Just then another check out girl arrived and lit up number seven and Bob Halloran took his bag of oranges and the roll of masking tape over to the open chute. He paid with a ten-dollar bill, received his change, and went out through the door ahead of the woman and her stupendous load of groceries.

Arriving at his truck, Halloran stored the bag of oranges behind the driver's seat, and unrolled a long strip of masking tape and wrapped it around his hand, sticky side up. He switched on the dome light inside the cab and used the stickiness of the tape to blot up the grass ends lying on the floor and adhering to the pedals. When he was certain that he had picked up every single half-blade of grass he used the back of his hand to clean off his sneakers, unspooled the tape, rolled it into a tacky ball and threw it onto the pavement before climbing into his truck and slamming the door.

The truck started with a roar. As he pulled away, Halloran felt on his hip for the vibrating cell phone and saw that he had three new messages. The first one was from Westerhouse, in his gruff voice complaining that Ness and Gallant hadn't shown up and with just three men in the crew he—

Halloran hit the delete button; he'd handle those problems on Monday morning. Right after Westerhouse came Marlene Phillips, the assistant general manager at the bank where Halloran kept his accounts. She was a tall redhead with a great pair of tits and long, beautiful legs. "Hi, it's me. If you're not doing the family thing today, I'm at Veteran's Park taking a walk. Stop over and I'll buy you a latte. 'Bye."

He wasn't fucking Marlene Phillips, but the idea had occurred to him. She was twenty-seven or twenty-eight, old enough to know the terrain, and drove a brand new Mercedes and owned a townhouse in Boxford. Over the past few weeks Marlene had reconfigured Halloran's accounts so that he could pay his regular employees via direct deposit, saving time each week that he usually spent making out paychecks. Then she figured out a way to save *Robert P. Halloran Development* ten percent on building materials by arranging a quarterly draw down with his suppliers. The attractive young banker had also shown him how to calculate this fee by tracking his materials online, instead of driving around to collect slips of lading, as he had done for years. She was a financial whiz.

And horny. In her office one evening after the bank had closed Marlene was sitting beside Halloran in her little rolling chair, the two of them encircled by her perfume and bent over the glowing screen of her laptop. Marlene allowed her hand to rest on the nape of Halloran's neck, playing with the ends of his hair. He turned, crushing her to his chest and they shared a deep, unexpected kiss. Her free hand dropped into his lap and he reached up and played with her breasts through the silk blouse that she wore. Then the bank guard knocked on the door and they rolled away from each other on the hard plastic mat covering the rug.

The final message on Halloran's voice mail was from Suzy. Whatever thoughts he had of meeting Marlene in the park quickly dropped from Halloran's list of possibilities when his wife reminded him to pick up some Tampons. Although that was the original reason for his trip, Halloran had almost forgotten about it; he decided to stop at the drug store on the way home instead of returning to Food Giant, and deleted his wife's message.

Halloran looked at the time on his cellphone. He had just a few minutes to run in for the things he needed from the hardware store. All through the spring he had worked on customizing his boat: ripping out the old floor to install one that was stronger and lighter, replacing the wheel and steering mechanism, and lacquering the wooden hull until it gleamed like gold. Before he and Bobby could take it out fishing for stripers, which was part of his son's birthday present, he needed three coats of paint on the new decking and stainless steel fittings for the dashboard he had installed. Suzy said that if she ever divorced him, he could keep the damned boat and just pack his bag and ship out, like they did in the old days.

All told, Halloran found the most pleasure in life cruising his boat off Plum Island, chopping through the whitecaps with Joni Mitchell crooning from his stereo and the galley stocked with roast beef sandwiches and Canadian beer. If his business continued to grow at its present rate, he planned to retire at age fifty. By that time both kids would be out of the house and graduated from college; with about eight more feet of boat he and Suzy could spend the winter months in the Caribbean and the warm weather tacking along the Gulf of Maine. He'd heard that Digby scallops were as big as his fist and cheaper than Ipswich clams by the bushel.

Halloran slowed as another light turned green and entered the lot for the hardware store. It was made of wavy brown concrete, the size and heft of a professional sports arena, with "Home Heaven" in giant orange letters across the roof. Bales of peat moss were sandbagged around the various entrances and concertina wire topped the fence surrounding the nursery, giving the place the look of a fortress. Inside the fence stood various shrubs, prefabricated tool sheds with Dutch doors and actual trees whose roots were bundled together and covered in burlap. He grabbed one of the carriages and passed through the electric eye just as the van that had cut him off earlier pulled up in front of the store. A squat, dark-haired man in a fatigue jacket got out, dialing his cell phone. His eyes met those of Bob Halloran for a moment and the stranger gazed at him with a blank look on his face.

Just inside the doors were American flags rolled up and attached to poles and batched together like flowers. In the years since 9/11, American flags were sold at every kind of store under the sun and Halloran wondered who was reaping the benefit. Nearby, fifty-gallon plastic drums of water filled a giant wooden rack and a fleet of small tractors and lawnmowers were parked side by side on the concrete.

Although Halloran bought his building supplies from commercial dealers in New Hampshire and in Boston, he visited Home Heaven several times a week to pick up lawn fertilizer and window moldings and other doo-dads for the house. He and Suzy owned a gorgeous white Colonial on three acres of land in the heart of town and his latest project was installing thermal floors in the kitchen and bathroom. He was a licensed plumber and electrician and a self-taught carpenter and made his own architectural drawings. Not bad for a kid from Tauvernier Street.

Suzy calculated that Bob had spent over eight thousand dollars at Home Heaven—on things that could have been purchased for little more than half that through his company—but fishing among bins of hook-eye screws and rubber gaskets and solid brass doorknobs relaxed him the way that eighteen holes of golf helped some of his friends unwind. And instead of blowing a small fortune at the country club he had increased the value of their home, which was a fact that his wife could not dispute.

The whirring X's of the ceiling fans disturbed the air, which otherwise would have lain heavy and toxic over the paint aisle. As it was, the acrid taste of paint came to Halloran's throat and he hemmed and coughed. He loaded his empty cart with three gallons of marine white and a gallon of waterproof lacquer.

Turning the corner with his haul, Halloran was surprised to find the woman from Food Giant and her children browsing an aisle of mirrors. Their reflections appeared in halves and quarters and wholes as he moved along; the woman's arm, swollen with flesh, loomed in a hundred different mirrors. Rolling his cart in the other direction, Halloran came face to face with the man who had cut him off in the van. He was of Middle Eastern descent, clad in a bulky fatigue jacket and wrinkled pants, standing beside a rack of nails in various sizes.

In the pink light from the display, the man resembled a lumpfish: the widespread, myopic eyes, black and unblinking; the fleshy lips surrounding a mouthful of crooked teeth; and an array of small fleshy nodes scattered over the crown of his forehead that disappeared into his thinning hair. He was a true bottomfeeder, Halloran decided; something not worth catching, and when caught, accustomed to being thrown back into the silty depths from where he came.

Holding a cellphone in one hand and jabbing at the keys with the other, the man was sweating in the heavy jacket and mumbling something over and over. Halloran was within twenty feet now, and he heard the man saying: "Allah-u-Akbar. Monqas Adwan. Tulkarm."

Just then, the large woman and her children emerged from the aisle, carrying a tall mirror with little scalloped designs along the edge. Halloran looked over his shoulder and saw the man in the fatigue jacket reflected in the mirror, and it occurred to him that the back channels of American history were teeming with shadowy figures named Raoul and Mohammed and Osama. They were the bane of the free world.

"What's he doing?" asked Halloran.

The mirror the woman was holding crashed to the floor, breaking into a thousand bright shards. "He has a BOMB," she said.

"Run," said Halloran. "Go."

A swift bolt of adrenaline rose from his groin into his chest, something out of his old football days. As the man's jacket fell open, revealing a formation of gel packs around his waist, Halloran shot forward, covering the distance that separated them with three stutter steps and a tremendous leap.

Halloran drove his shoulder into the man's chest with such force that the two of them flew into the mouth of the next aisle, behind more than a dozen steel-reinforced doors. But the man was able to press the desired key on his cellphone and as he did, a huge sound rent Halloran's eardrums and the hardware store and everyone and everything in it became absent. He had the sensation of flying and then he heard and felt nothing.

II

That morning the sun was weaving a special dress of martyrdom and as Monqas Adwan emerged to do Allah's bidding—as suicide bombers took up their positions at malls, cinemas, baseball stadiums and in churches across the fifty states—he recalled the words of his teacher, the one-armed Sheikh Abu-Tariq: "When the *mujahed* carries his rifle in one hand and his soul in the other, he knows his destiny is martyrdom."

Adwan was standing at the junction of two aisles, in line with a rack of nails and spikes, as he had been taught. After using his cellphone to start the timer on the bomb in the van he had parked out front, he would detonate himself where it would cause the most terror, spraying the pointed steel nibs in every direction. Onlookers who were not killed would run toward the exits and then the bomb outside would crash through the front of the building, sending large sheets of broken glass through the air and crumbling the masonry. He had seen it happen in Jenin.

A large, redheaded American was coming toward him, and once more Adwan punched in the five-digit code on his phone but still the timer signal failed to appear. Adwan had been given the keys to the van and the telephone outside a hamburger restaurant earlier that morning; he had not known the man in charge of preparing the explosive, who was from Rochester, New York and had driven all night to meet him. The man was also a Palestinian, about his age, twenty-three, and wearing a T-shirt that said "Walt Disney World" and carrying a small nylon bag. His face contained several burned patches and had been nicked with shrapnel. As arranged, they met at five-thirty AM and exchanged vehicles; as the man passed by, he smiled and said, "I am Hamas and Hamas is terror."

But not every member of Hamas was useful or courageous. Dawn was coming up over the parking lot at that hour and Adwan felt the *muezzin's* call to prayer, the first of the five he said each day, but the man in the Walt Disney shirt did not join him. Soon the car that Adwan had driven since he had arrived in the U. S. was speeding away, with this man at the wheel smoking a cigarette and playing a vulgar song over the radio.

Monqas Adwan felt nothing for the man, just as he had no feelings for the redheaded American who had spotted him and discarded his carriage and was now approaching. Since the age of thirteen, Adwan had worn the green flag of Hamas. Instead of cinema stars and footballers, as a young man in Tulkarm he had hung posters of the martyrs above the bed he shared with his younger brother, Nabib. He revered the nineteen bombers who came from his little village, and aspired to nothing else but to be counted in that number. The previous evening, in the grimy Lowell apartment where he had lived for two years he had scrawled a note: "I am Monqas Adwan, of the Iz al-din Al Qassam brigade. It will be a new kind of punishment this time, of an unaccustomed type that will shake America and destroy its pillars. Allah-u-Akbar."

On the wall was a large poster of his twenty-year-old brother Nabib, dressed in camouflage and holding an AK-47 rifle with an Uzi slung over his shoulder. Standing in front of the crossed flags of Hamas and wearing the headband of the Al Aksa Martyrs Brigade,

33

Nabib stared down at him as he worked through the night, drinking coffee and assembling the gelatin packs for his suicide belt and wiring them all together. In a frame beneath the poster was a vellum decree that read: *After we studied and saw the number of Zionists killed, and in accordance with the rules of Jihad, we decided to grant Nabib Adwan, born in Jenin, a degree of Excellence in Martyrism from Yahya Ayyash College with all the rights of this degree, signed Al Aksa Martyrs Brigade.*

Monqas Adwan, operating on a forged Egyptian passport, had received his student visa from the U. S. State Department a few days before the second intifada. Nabib was killed a week later; when his suicide belt exploded, he was waiting in line at the Sbarro pizza restaurant in Jerusalem, a dense mass of Israeli students, retail workers and low level government officials thronging around him. Fifteen people were killed, including six children, and more than one hundred-thirty were maimed or wounded. By the time Monqas Adwan landed in the United States, enrolled at the University of Massachusetts Lowell and found an apartment on the edge of that city's Asian ghetto, news of his brother's triumph had reached him. And just a few days after he began his classes in Electrical Engineering, Monqas was surprised to receive a thin blue aerogram with Nabib's scrawl on the front.

Hurrying to an empty table in the Student Union, he peeled open the aerogram with shaking hands. His brother had written: "When someone comes to fight you in your home, you must travel to his home and fight him back. Always remember that Allah is our goal, the Prophet is our model, the Koran is our constitution, jihad is our path, and death for the sake of Allah is our most coveted desire. I will be waiting for you with the *huris* in Paradise."

While he lived in the United States, Monqas Adwan attended to his studies and spent most of his free time inside his apartment reading the Koran and discussing the jihad in code over the Internet. Occasionally he met a group of Arab students at Arthur's Paradise Diner to smoke cigarettes and drink coffee but mostly he avoided contact with people of any sort and waited for his orders.

The other Arabs at the University detested Israel but were enthralled by the United States and inclined to believe that negotiation could resolve the occupancy of Palestine. They neither read the Koran nor attended to prayer; they worked in record stores and car washes for extra money and wore gold jewelry and one or two of them had American girlfriends. They were fools. Because when the jihad arrived and the scourging of America began they would be killed alongside the infidels and those who survived would be persecuted.

Adwan's official contact was the leader of the Rochester cell but through encoded discussions on his computer he had discovered that over three thousand Muslims inside the U. S. were involved in the jihad. They were Pakistani, Saudi Arabian, Chechnyan, Sudanese, Yemeni, and Filipino. They were students, professors, migrant workers, store clerks and even doctors. Some of them were married and had children and owned homes and businesses in places like Connecticut and Arizona and Michigan. The organizers were devoted followers of the martyred bin Laden and were using the suicide bombers to start the first of three waves of terror, culminating in the final attacks on Detroit, Houston and Los Angeles on Christmas Eve.

It was by and large a guerilla affair; Adwan had fashioned his suicide belt from materials pilfered from the engineering laboratory at school and the explosive inside the van was made of stolen fertilizer. Only the ineptitude of its creator had prevented the bomb from exploding. Despite this failure, the simultaneous assault of five or six hundred suicide bombers across the United States would make the heroic attacks of September 11th appear insignificant. Monqas Adwan did not really care how it all turned out. He would strike his blow for Palestine and become a martyr with his brother and finished with the affairs of this life.

In the United States the weather was cooler than Adwan was used to and strange birds cried from the trees and a multitude of winged and legged insects whirred through the air and crawled over the pavement. Everything was paved here. From Lowell to Providence, Adwan had seen no mountainous majesty, no "amber waves of grain," just mile after mile of chainlink fence and billowing smokestacks and stores without end. Stores where you could buy every useless contrivance imaginable and where every indulgence was offered at any hour of the day or night: *Dancing* or *Doughnuts*, *Tacos* and *Tattoos*. America was just as Sheikh Abu-Tariq had said it would be: overfed and insolent, a nation of television watchers. Obese parents in collapsible chairs watched their fat children trot over manicured athletic fields while they screamed obscenities and drank sugared water and ate pastries. There was no trace of God here, and more than anything Monqas Adwan longed for the simplicity and austerity of his homeland.

Inside the hardware store Adwan waited a moment before trying his cellphone again and the large man with the red hair turned and was staring at him. He had known a redheaded woman named Danahy or Donahue in his Basic Structures class at the University. One day Adwan was studying in a park alongside the large oily river that bisected the campus. This woman had appeared while he was deep in the labyrinth of a calculus problem; he was sitting by a brook that smelled of tooth decay, his notebooks spread over his lap and on the bench next to him. Without an invitation, the woman closed up his textbook and moved aside some of his papers and seated herself.

Monqas Adwan found Americans to be smug, condescending and bold, especially the women. This one in particular shamed herself by dressing in very short pants and a strapless tube of clinging material fitted about her chest. Around her neck was a gold chain with a tiny gold cross that fell between her breasts when she sat down. She asked him what he was studying and he told her and she remarked that mathematics were killing her and asked if she could study with him. Adwan tried to move his gaze from the dark enclosure between her breasts where the tiny cross had fallen and said that that was impossible; his religion did not permit it.

On the river, a sailboat puffed out its canvas and then a shirtless man passed by on roller skates. The young woman looked into Adwan's face and said that just because Jesus walked from here to there doesn't mean we don't own automobiles. It was a modern world.

The trees surrounding them were gaunt at that time of year, the buds hard and small against the black of their branches. Adwan reminded himself that he was Hamas and that his aim was to be martyred and to see his brother Nabib and all the other martyrs in paradise. He removed his gaze from the shaded passage of the woman's breasts and ignoring the sailboats and roller skaters, excused himself and rose from the bench and hurried away, over the ill-smelling brook and through tall damp grasses that wet his trouser legs.

Now, a fat woman with two children cried out that he had a bomb and the large man with red hair advanced toward him. His finger found the appropriate key on his cellphone and he felt the electrical charge girdling his loins and embraced the American as they went hurtling toward paradise.

III

The chamber they found themselves in possessed the grandeur of heaven but none of the joy. It had no walls, ceiling, or floor; it was airless and odorless and filled with a sourceless light. The place where Robert Halloran and Monqas Adwan were walking gave them the sense of a magnificent roofless castle or of the Grand Canyon situated indoors. A vast neutrality encompassed them, as well as the feeling that they had been traveling for a significant distance and would continue to do so for some time.

Yet Halloran and Adwan knew nothing like hunger or pain or fatigue. Nor did they have an ounce of regret toward what they had left behind. Rather, their histories and even their names grew ever more distant and the greater reality of who and what they were began to inhabit each of them. They were compelled to walk in a certain direction and bound to one another in a manner that was not clear. That the sensations they were accustomed to remained out of ken did not trouble either man; what consoled them was the undeniable fact that their old troubles were over and they had been transplanted to a new plane altogether. Halloran, for one, had neither consciousness nor extension in the traditional sense but as in a dream he believed himself to be awake and clothed and walking beside another man, both familiar and strange, who was clad in the apparel he had worn inside the hardware store and who had the gaze of someone that knew where he was going and exercised no will to change it.

Throughout his life Halloran believed that his soul was translucent and ephemeral, but in reality it was a fibrous, compact and indissoluble thing; as much himself as an image in a photograph or moving picture, only nearer at hand, more incontrovertible, and true.

And when he thought of his wife and children, his reminiscence took on that quality of distant affection that surrounded their memory when he had gone fishing one day beyond the Isle of Shoals. At sea, they remained a part of his life and heart but were diminished by the reach of his environment; something more fundamental gripped him and his old ties were thinned to a filament and stretched over blue horizons. As the boat rocked and his line drifted, his past grew so tenuous that the idea of losing it ceased to trouble him. So it was in this place.

Monqas Adwan moved toward what he believed was paradise. Nothing bothered him about his current state beside the slightly vexing notion that he should not be in the company of an infidel. Yet Allah reckoned all, and everything that Allah reckoned was good, and this must be good. He imagined that the infidel's lot was to witness the reunion of the martyrs and to envy their admittance to paradise. There his brother Nabib and sixty *huris* would greet him, and accompanied by these virgins he would pass into the realm of Allah and the unbeliever would be turned aside. Heaps of fruit and flowers and scores of true believers clad in white *kaffiyehs* would be there to welcome them. This was written in the Koran and could not be otherwise.

Other figures were gathering, and after a journey of considerable length they joined a great pilgrim column, streaming toward a destination that remained forever ahead of them. To one side was a man and three children and it became clear to Monqas Adwan that this party was also united in death and that made him uneasy. The souls around them grew in number, traveling with various degrees of urgency. Far off, they could make out apertures in the great chamber that held them all; curved openings that led to other chambers and through which the traveling souls were filtered like water through ceramic fixtures.

Soon they overtook a large group heading toward the same aperture they seemed to be. There were thousands of firemen, police officers, clerks, stockbrokers, secretaries and bus boys traipsing in a single mass. At the head of this congregation were nineteen Arab men, dressed in simple trousers and shirts, going along with expressionless faces. There were other, even larger collections of men and women nearby, including the participants from a great-but-forgotten battle, intermingled in their contrasting uniforms, unmusketed and swordless, carrying rucksacks and laden with heavy equipage.

At the very front of the nineteen Arabs was a face that both Robert Halloran and Monqas Adwan recognized. It had appeared on television and in newspapers for months that turned into years; the face of terror, the one man who had frightened Americans to the bone. Sitting in the Paradise diner one day with another Muslim, Adwan had mentioned this person by name and his companion, a Saudi who was majoring in Nuclear Engineering, hushed him and said, Don't make trouble. Do you want them to deport us?

—America pictures itself as the judge and the gladiator at the same time, said Adwan. Finally, one man has shown them the truth.

The Saudi hunkered down in the booth and lowered his voice even further.

—Never mention the lion in the midst of the antelopes, he said.

Both Adwan and Halloran felt capable of speech but had refrained from speaking, as all those about them had done. Now, as whatever lay in the past continued to dim, and whatever lay ahead remained unknown, Halloran broke the silence.

—Look what you've done, he said.

—I am mandated by God to fight the infidels, Adwan told him.

Halloran looked at him as they continued onward.

—You've accomplished nothing, he said. Except getting the two of us killed.

—Islam is the solution.

Since he was a child, Monqas Adwan had followed the teachings of Sheikh Abu-Tariq: *Build the state of Islam in your hearts.* But what had he built that was shared by Muslims and non-Muslims alike—that sent him always forward but never closer, it seemed, to what he had been promised?

All of the people who surrounded Bob Halloran had been connected in life and were saddled with one another in death. As a boy, he had read the Catechism, been counseled by the nuns of Sacred Heart and contemplated at length the very state that he now found himself in. But there were no seraphim or cherubim, no blaring trumpets, no rostrum of Saint Peter. He did not feel himself moving away from Christ nor being drawn toward Him. The only emotion that possessed him was a baffling indifference, and the only sensation that he had was of being sieved through a grate, a minute particle destined for lodging in the catch basin of eternity.

—It was murder, said Halloran.

—Our Palestine is from the river to the sea, and we will give up not one grain of sand.

—At least I kept you from hurting anyone else.

Adwan glanced at his companion and then looked ahead, toward the huge passages looming in the distance.

—There are ten thousand more like me, he said. Are there ten thousand more like you?

The Tigers in Argentina

At the airport a family stood in a circle guarding their treasure, eight or nine Weed Wackers in boxes marked $79.95. It meant nonperishables were hard to come by in Argentina, a good sign. I shouldered my bag through the dense, aromatic crowd and near the exit a fortuneteller grabbed me and said, "Get ready to go through fire and have your old life burned away."

Outside, the fire-eaters themselves were lined up, drug addicts with lined faces and husks for eyes. The fire-eaters take a mouthful of gasoline and then, waving what looks like a flaming cat o' nine tail, they exhale in a quick calculated breath, throwing a stream of acrid black smoke and orange fire into the air. If you pause, stunned by this brief, pungent glimpse into hell, they panhandle you or steal your watch.

The antique business is a relaxing business: that was our motto around the office. We said it for weeks after Sol Greenstein got out of Tehran in '79 with a fabulous eighteenth-century Persian rug strapped beside him in first class, and we repeated it with equal amusement when Peter Reilly stopped a bullet with his black, whiskey-freighted heart on the tarmac in Phnom Penh in '87. It was really too bad about Peter. He never brought back the last ivory Buddha we had been hunting for. That cost Sol and me a lot of money.

On the street, Buenos Aires had that same rotten smell of collapse that filled my nostrils at other times in Beirut, in Tikrit, on the jungled fringes of Panama City and scattered throughout the humid, confetti-strewn boulevards of Manila. It was the smell of money—the faint but unmistakable odor of big ticket items at discount prices. A dying country always gave up its jewels.

The slick young dudes who loitered on every street corner eyed my suitcase and limp cashmere jacket. I hailed a cab. It was January, hot and damp, the height of the Argentine summer. Handing the cab driver a dollar bill, I told him to take me to the Plaza Hotel. He looked at me in the mirror without turning around and zoomed through the crowded filthy streets. Draped with bandoleers and carrying automatic weapons, stone-faced policemen in silver helmets looked out from the dooryards of government buildings. The air was heavy and quiet, laced with fear. Business would be good here, perhaps very good.

Every wall was covered with black and white posters of somebody called Pelleira, the new president, a handsome man with gleaming black hair and a square chin. His image was repeated endlessly in the downtown, across jagged walls, vacant storefronts, running like an old piece of film as we careered along the streets. In Spanish, I asked the cab driver about Pelleira and he snorted with disgust. The old president was impeached and then Pelleira, after winning a special election, took his beautiful mistress on an extended vacation to Portugal. Inflation had risen nearly four hundred percent in a matter of weeks. In his latest radio address Pelleira advised patience and thrift, and then was photographed gambling at the racetrack and dancing in a Lisbon discotheque. Shortly afterwards, Argentines rioted at the supermarkets, stampeding for food.

The national currency, known as the australe, was being changed over to a new scrip. The government had frozen bank accounts and wealthy Argentines were panicking as their money became worthless almost overnight. They wanted American dollars, and would part with their most prized possessions at laughable prices if you paid with U.S. Almost everything was up for sale.

We turned onto the Plaza de Mayo. At the conclusion of the wide, tree-lined avenue was the presidential mansion, the Pink House, a magnificent stucco building with huge Corinthian columns, ornate windows trimmed in gold leaf and an electronic gate patrolled by heavily-armed soldiers.

"Pelleira," said the cab driver, spitting out the window.

A group of peasant women sat on the concrete in a huddled mass. They were surrounded by white outlines like the ones drawn at crime scenes, a procession of chalk figures that began where they were sitting and extended over a hundred yards to the gates of the Pink House.

"They are the Mothers of the Lost Ones," the driver told me in Spanish. He explained that many young people, artists and freethinkers and students, had disappeared in the last ten years and that Pelleira had promised to investigate. So far he had done nothing.

"Our dedicated president," the driver said, his face screwed up like he had tasted something foul.

I noticed the tramping boots of the soldiers stopped just short of the chalk figures. Beyond the soldier's post, the outlines began again and stretched the length of the Plaza, hundreds and perhaps thousands of them, a generation erased, joining the Lost Ones from all the other countries where I had done business.

We pulled up to the curb. Four soldiers toting submachine guns brushed past while I waited for the driver to fetch my suitcase. They were even more ominous than the silver-helmeted police, marching in step, their eyes fixed straight ahead. The cab driver escorted me to the door of the hotel and I handed him another dollar.

"Be careful, señor," he said. "There will be trouble soon."

Inside the Plaza Hotel, the concierge greeted me with a bow and the porter took my suitcase and began brushing my jacket with a silver-handled whiskbroom. His hand touched my money belt under the cashmere and a palsy entered his movements. I drew back and signaled for him to stop—in a few minutes, every flunky in the hotel would know about the large gringo and his *monedero*.

Followed by my entourage, I approached the front desk where a bald-headed man in a crisp white dinner jacket and bow tie waited with his hands on the marble counter.

"Very good, Señor Williams," he said. "You have a message." He reached into a wall of pigeonholes behind him and took out a small envelope made of expensive paper. Inside there was a telephone number but no name or address.

I went up to Room 515 and locked myself in. The money belt was

43

uncomfortable and I undid it and laid it on top of the credenza, rubbing the welt it had raised across my belly. For protection I usually carried a .25-caliber porcelain derringer and four soft lead slugs, which fooled the metal detectors at the airport, but for such a routine job, I didn't bother. I dug some antacid tablets from my bag and called the number. It was several rings before a woman answered.

"I'm calling about a certain item you have for sale."

There was a pause. "Who is this?"

"Madison Williams. From Greenstein Associates."

The woman switched to a precise, accented English. "I have been waiting for your call, Mr. Williams."

"Sorry. It was hard to get a flight."

"Many people are leaving Argentina. It is very sad."

I thought of the Weed Wackers at the airport. "Some are selling," I said. "But, fortunately, others are buying."

"My husband and I have something you will be interested in. Meet us at the Polo Club in La Plata at four o'clock. We can discuss it then, over cocktails."

"Good. See you at four." I hesitated a moment. "What is your name?"

"Senor and Senora Pelleira," she said, and hung up.

It was noon. I washed my face and fastened the money belt under a loose, square-bottomed shirt. I decided to go downtown to the market for some fresh air, but also to do a little research, to price silver jewelry, turquoise and the like. At the front desk I exchanged twenty dollars for a huge stack of australes. The porter bowed as he opened the door, leaving me on the sidewalk in the burning midday sun.

The cab I had arrived in was still waiting at the curb. The driver met me in the street. "A ride downtown, señor?"

"No thanks. I'll walk."

The cab driver shook his blocky head. "Walking is no good here. It's very dangerous." He looked up at me, expressionless. "Even for a big man."

"I'll be all right. I'm not going far." He shook his head again, arms crossed, but didn't argue. I handed him a few australes from the bulging wad in my pocket. "I need a ride to La Plata at four o'clock.

Come back then." He looked small beside the battered car, the sun falling on his weather-beaten face.

The neighborhood beyond the hotel was old and desperate, like an abandoned place that had been reinhabited. Pelleira's sleek handsome face was everywhere, papered over the cracks, flapping in the slight breeze that disrupted the stillness. Ahead of me was the open air market, teeming with hawkers and their pushcarts, and I hurried toward it.

The market was full of junk, and thieves. They were easy to spot: young, sloppy, sweating men in black trousers and slick clinging shirts, leaning against the pictures of their young president. They stood on one leg like flamingoes, the heels of their shoes pressed against Pelleira's face. A glint of jewelry, the mustering of cash, and they entered the current, following fast but not too close.

Two of them snapped to attention on the far side of the market and shoved off, through the welter of sport shirts and sundresses. The mark was a blond kid in his mid-twenties, wearing a baseball cap. He had American money in his hand and he was laughing, his head back, showing off his thick neck and square white teeth.

"Butchie. Come here," he said, calling to a stocky fellow with dark hair and stubble, who was outfitted with the same maroon cap. "I think this dude's trying to bullshit me."

Butch spat tobacco juice on the cobblestones, hitching up his jeans as he came over. His cap, embroidered with a shining gold B, was pulled low on his forehead. "You can't bullshit a bullshitter," he said. "Or a Texan."

The vendor, holding a droopy leather garment in each fist, smiled at them. I was less than twenty feet away now, and when the first pickpocket homed in, looking for the bump and run, I got there first and shoved the tall blond kid out of the way. The thief veered off.

"Hey! Watch where you're going, pal," said the kid.

"Sorry," I said, then dropped my voice. "Put that money away before you lose it."

The kid shifted his eyes and saw the second pickpocket, head down and sweating, coming along the line of stalls. Then Butch spotted him. "I got him, Crab," he said. An instant before the thief made his move, Butch threw out his forearm and sent the man sprawling on the cobblestones. The thief scrambled to his feet and disappeared into the crowd.

"Let's go," I said. "This way."

A whistle blew and some soldiers converged on us. We left the marketplace through an alley and entered a street that was open to traffic and filled with seedy bars and cafes. A short distance along, its arches glowing in the afternoon sunlight, was a McDonald's restaurant. "The American embassy," said Crab. He quickened his pace, heading for it.

Butch thrust open the door and we went into that familiar smell of hamburgers and French fries, and the chill of the air conditioners.

"We want political asylum," Butch said to the teen-agers behind the counter. "Take us to Ronald McDonald. Take us to the Ambassador."

The teen-agers giggled, pointing at the crazy Americans and whispering in Spanish. Our tray was stacked with fries and milk shakes and hamburgers in little yellow boxes, and I carried it to a table by the windows. Jeff Crablowski was a lifeguard, and square-shouldered Butch Gilpatric made his living as a roofer. They were part of a barnstorming semi-pro team from Texas, the Beaumont Tigers, and had once entertained notions of professional baseball. Crab laughed and said they were too old now and just playing for fun.

Butch poured ketchup on his hamburger and said, "It's no fun trying to hit a curveball."

They were going to play that night, their last game in Argentina. "I'm ready to go home," Butch said. "Give me Beaumont any day of the week."

"There's just as many assholes in Texas," said Crab.

I hunched forward, drawing them closer. "Let me tell you something, boys: they're everywhere," I said. "Most people would eat mice if you covered them in gravy and called it chateaubriand."

Afterward, we retraced my steps through the dingy neighborhood that separated us from the Plaza Hotel. The boys thanked me and said goodbye and told me they were staying at the San Francisco Hotel if I needed anything. I watched them go, ambling in the dusty light that filled the street, heading toward the Pink House like they owned it.

*

The ride to La Plata took us into Buenos Aires' worst slums and through an infested cardboard village. "Close your eyes, like Pelleira," the cab driver said.

Sunlight played over the dank interior of the cab and Peter Reilly came to mind. Back when there were eight brokers in the firm Reilly had the office next to Sol's and they used to compete for the best buys, flying to ungodly places each week in an effort to outdo each other. He was Sol's fair-haired boy.

It was a summer night in the Back Bay and I had come into the office quite late to check on the telexes and surprised Reilly at his desk—he was supposed to be in Cairo—and there was an awkward moment before he invited me in and I sat down opposite him. His office was crammed with books and photographs and smelled of old pipe tobacco and the coffee he brewed on a hotplate in the corner. Red-faced and disheveled, the old Irishman's hand shook a little as he closed Goldman's *Antiquities of Egypt* and reached for the tumbler of whiskey at his elbow.

"Care for one?" he asked.

"No. I'm not drinking," I said. I wasn't in those days.

Reilly couldn't keep steady and he lowered the whiskey again before it reached his lips. He didn't like to appear vulnerable to anyone, especially not to me. It was not a friendly business and there was no such thing as profit-sharing; you made exactly what you brought in, after Sol took his hefty cut for the use of the office and his name, which went back several generations in the trade. He liked to say it was his great-great-grandfather who swapped the beads for Manhattan.

"I missed my damned plane," Reilly said, in answer to a question I had not asked. "I was on my way to the airport and realized I didn't know what I was after or who I was supposed to see." He nudged his copy of *Antiquities* along the desktop. "A damned cat statue. Have to fly out in the morning."

I had the sensation of banging a tough old heavyweight against

47

the ropes and watching the fight go out of him. "Aren't there some big penalties over there for trading in antiquities?" I asked. "They don't fool around, those Egyptians."

Reilly stared at me in the dimness, his small blue eyes receding in their pockets of flesh. He began to speak, checked himself, and after a moment where his large wet mouth hung open, launched headlong into what had happened. "I've been taking pieces out of nasty little countries for thirty-seven years and it never bothered me for a minute. But all of a sudden, tonight, I was sitting in the Callahan Tunnel and it occurred to me that all I'm getting out of this is money. It was like I had never thought of that before."

The snug comfort of his office and Reilly's soft-spoken air were deceiving. He was a cutthroat when it came to business. But tonight was different. Behind those bloodshot eyes was a terrified man. A car passed by in the street below and somehow the reflection on its windows threw a fresco of light across the room. It slipped sideways, and was gone. "I ask myself, if I lose my nerve for this, what else am I going to do?" Reilly asked.

I made an ambiguous gesture and Reilly continued. "Tomorrow I'm off to Cairo," he said. "I mean—I don't think you can develop integrity overnight, like mushrooms." He lapsed into silence again, studying his hands. A year later he was dead, and I was given some of his best accounts.

Argentina looked like a gold mine, so far. Down a long dirt road across flat country we found the entrance to the Polo Club and turned in, toward the low-slung clubhouse and its outbuildings and stables. The cab sent up a thick plume of dust and the sun slanted across the polo fields in long, mote-filled beams.

We drove into the parking lot. "Do you recognize that man?" I asked the driver. He looked over at a well-dressed fellow sitting in a wicker chair. "Yes," he said. "Rafael Pelleira, the president's cousin. A man of similar moral standing."

Señor and Señora Pelleira were waiting for me on the patio, beneath an umbrella. They were an attractive couple in their early fifties. He wore a dark blue suit and an eyepatch and his wife was dressed in a suede gaucho outfit. Nearby was a plantain tree and the fruit, like large purplish bananas, lay in bunches on the smooth stones of the patio.

"A drink, Mr. Williams?" asked Señora Pelleira. The smell of charred beef drifted over from the cold, heaped over barbecue pit.

"Gin and tonic," I said.

A waiter brought the drinks and receded from the table like smoke. The glass was sweating and I sipped from it, relishing the cold antiseptic taste of the gin. Pelleira held his wife's hand and stared at me through his one good eye. His hair was turning silver and he had a fine nose and dark, well-scrubbed skin. He gave the impression that even his guts were clean. Old money.

"Are you having a pleasant stay?" asked his wife, in her textbook English. Señora Pelleira had a magnificent bone structure, and blond-ish-gray hair that was pulled back and hidden beneath a large black bow.

"Educational," I said. "My driver knows a lot about politics."

Señor Pelleira leaned over and said something to his wife in Portuguese. She smiled, and said, "Señor Pelleira believes there are no politics in Argentina, only economics."

Señor Pelleira spoke to his wife again and slid a padded case from beneath the table. He placed it across his lap, the clasp toward me. "We have something Mr. Greenstein thought you would be interested in," said Señora Pelleira while I followed her husband's movements. "It is a rare and expensive item."

Some polo players came in from their practice and clattered over the stones without a word and went into the bar. They smelled of horses and the perspiration had soaked through their jerseys. Señor Pelleira waited until they had passed.

He flipped open the case. Inside was an armorial crest, perhaps five inches in diameter, of the sixteenth or early seventeenth century, featuring a horse and rider etched on a silver disk and surrounded by raised heraldic designs. It was an exquisitely detailed piece. I leaned forward, but not too far, and looked it over.

"It is interesting, no?" asked Señora Pelleira. "It has been in my husband's family for a long time."

I said nothing. The horse was armored, rearing on its hind legs, and the rider brandished a sword. The plate would sell to a collector for forty or fifty thousand dollars, maybe more. My commission was sixty-five percent on the net.

"I'll give you seven thousand American for it."

"No," said Señor Pelleira, looking at me from his single blue eye.

"You will make a profit in your later dealings, but still, we must have a fair price," Señora Pelleira said.

The Pelleiras knew what their little treasure was worth, even under miserable conditions. I had twelve thousand dollars in the money belt—the maximum that Sol would allow on this kind of thing. There was no sense fooling around.

"Pick it up and examine it, if you like," Señora Pelleira said.

I reached into the case. The plate was half an inch thick and heavier than I expected. Its surface shone like a mirror and my face, worn and puffy around the eyes, glanced bleakly at me when I held it up.

"Nine thousand," I said.

Señora Pelleira shook her head no and a mass of tiny wrinkles formed on her throat. "Twelve," she said.

Her husband lit a cigarette, pushing it to one side to keep the smoke out of his eye. I unclasped the money belt and counted out the money, some of it in small bills. All I had left was a handful of australes and my return ticket for the morning.

"Here it is," I said, pushing the money across the table. Señor Pelleira barely even looked at it.

Señora Pelleira recounted the bank notes and I tucked the silver plate inside the waistband of my pants and drank some gin.

"Why did you sell it?" I asked. Señor Pelleira said something in Portuguese and his wife translated: "You cannot invest with the skeletons and bones of history. For that you need cash."

On the way back, less than a mile from the Plaza, we encountered dozens of people in the street. They poured in our direction, and the cab driver stalled against the tide they offered, tooting his horn. One man leaned in the window. "Go back. There was a bomb on the Plaza," he said. "Four were killed and now the soldiers are everywhere." I paid the driver with some australes and got out of the cab.

My hotel was blackened with soot and there was a large jagged hole where the door had been. The concierge was lying in the rubble covered by a sheet. I could see his shiny boots sticking out. Everyone was wearing boots. I approached the hotel and a soldier motioned me away at gunpoint.

My luggage was gone but I had the silver plate and my airline ticket. Also, my cash was running out. Soldiers were arriving by the truckload. I decided to walk over to the San Francisco Hotel and look up the baseball players.

Butch was sitting in the lobby with a beer. A few other players were half-dressed in their uniforms, talking and drinking beer. "Hi, Mr. Williams," said Butch. "Game's cancelled. Coach K.'s on the phone making sure we can get out of here in the morning."

"My hotel was blown up. If you don't mind I'll just tag along with you fellows."

"Sure," said Butch, hoisting his beer. "We're getting bombed ourselves."

Crab joined us, in his uniform pants and a long-sleeved undershirt. He sat down, crossed his legs and opened a can of beer. "I'm gonna get drunk and wake up in Texas," he said.

Coach K. turned out to be Kelly Rudd, a wiry, youthful man of perhaps thirty-five, the Tiger's coach and a first baseman that still swung the bat pretty well, Butch said. Rudd came into the room and gained everyone's attention by placing his hands on his hips and glancing around. The lobby fell silent.

"Our flight to Houston is scheduled for seven-thirty tomorrow morning. We leave here at five sharp. You're on your own until then. Just remember, people are getting killed out there."

Rudd came over and Crab introduced me and explained my situation.

"Congratulations," said Rudd, gesturing at the surroundings. "You've just been named General Manager of the Beaumont Tigers."

"I'm honored."

"You shouldn't be," said Rudd. "I'm the coach and I have to clean the toilets."

Crab and Butch sprang up. "Coach K., we're gonna go have a look around," said Crab.

"I'll go with you," Rudd said. "I didn't come all this way not to see."

*

The streets outside the hotel were quiet and empty, except for some sirens in the distance. It wasn't yet dark. Rudd walked along with his hands in his pockets, watchful. Crab still had on his uniform pants and he and Butch both wore their caps.

We entered the Plaza de Mayo. Several streets were blocked off and across the center strip, soldiers were erecting barricades and stringing razor wire between the buildings. In a patch of gloom just ahead sat the peasant women, keeping their vigil. One of the women rose to her feet, small and frail in a black habit like a nun's, and coming over to us, took hold of Crab's large rawboned hands.

"Gaston," she said, smiling at the tall straight American. When the woman was through gazing into his eyes, remembering her own son, he bent down so she could kiss him on the cheek.

Beyond the Plaza were more pedestrians, and some of the cafes were lit up and doing business. We found a kiosk called the Bar Europa and ordered four beers at the tall zinc counter and drank them under the awning. A nice-looking girl in stretch pants walked by, and Crab leaned out and said, "Pssst." The girl ignored him, clicking away in her heels. Butch laughed, and Crab put him in a headlock and they swayed over the cobblestones.

Rudd turned from them with a faint smile and leaned his elbows on the bar.

"No girls for you, Coach?" I asked.

"My range isn't what it used to be," said Rudd. He drank some beer and looked sideways at another pretty girl. "But even a blind squirrel finds an acorn once in awhile."

I leveled my gaze at him. "What are *you* doing here?"

Rudd laughed. "Dropping pop-ups and missing fastballs, mostly," said the compact Texan. "I'm here because I love baseball. You put your uniform on and go out there and take your chances." He peered into his glass. "It beats the hell out of teaching school or tending bar, let me tell you."

"Okay," I said. "But you can't play forever."

Rudd grinned at some private reflection and then raised his sharp brown eyes to mine. "When I was younger, a prospect myself, I was always picturing myself higher up. Now when I'm out there, I love every single pitch like it's my own flesh and blood." He waved his hand. "My old man was a roustabout who always did just enough to get by. He'd just as soon watch me play football or baseball as go to work. When my stepmother was on him about it, he used to say, 'Iris, I never seen no Brinks truck following no hearse.'"

A few more Tigers in their caps and maroon and gold warm-up jackets congregated with Butch and Crab under a streetlight. Some beggar kids ran out of an alley and began pestering them with kung fu kicks. A moment later soldiers appeared, flushing the square in the direction of the hotel, and the Texans drifted down the cobblestones, calling to each other in light amused voices.

"I guess it's time to mosey along," said Rudd.

One of the little beggars approached the bar and asked for a glass of water. He was only about 7 or 8, dressed in rags, and his arms and legs were thin as rails. The bar man cursed and took a swipe at him.

Rudd called an order to the bar man and he poured four glasses of milk. Rudd signaled to the kid that the milk was for him but the kid said no. Rudd motioned again and the emaciated youngster took one small sip and put it down, never taking his eyes off Rudd. The other glasses were for his friends who were now several blocks away. The urchin hesitated a moment, then ran after them. Rudd and I waited and when they returned, they fell upon the milk like they were starving, their hands barely reaching around the pint glasses.

A policeman came along and gestured at us. Rudd paid for the milk and we entered the foot traffic heading back toward the Plaza. "Poor little buggers," said Rudd, his hands dug into the pockets of his jeans. "They'll never get out of this place."

The soldiers and police were sealing off the downtown and we managed to reach the San Francisco just ahead of the paddy wagons they were using to pick up stragglers. I went in behind Rudd and

53

we were met by the sound of cymbals, maracas, gourds and other little-known instruments as the team crashed through a version of "Deep in the Heart of Texas." Players were draped over the furniture, in manic trios and quartets, tootling and strumming and banging, a truly berserk philharmonic. Rudd smiled and put up his hands.

"Stow that junk," he said, the hands back on his hips. "We have to keep a low profile tonight, Tigers. We're staying right here, in the lobby." He glanced at his watch. "Come five o'clock, we're history."

There was a mock cheer. Several players went upstairs to fetch their luggage, and backgammon boards and cards were produced. It was like a rain delay. Rudd was busy organizing the canvas equipment bags and I went over and spoke to him.

"Listen, Coach, I'm in a tough situation and—"

Rudd cut me off. "Don't worry about it."

I went to the bar and bought Rudd a beer and myself a glass of gin. "That's the last of it," I said, handing him the cold brown bottle. "The well is dry."

"Now you're a free man," joked the Texan.

The hotel brought out some little round meat pies called *empañadas* and the Tigers devoured them. After dinner I joined a game of poker with Rudd and Butch and two other players. Using a small loan from Rudd I won several hands and soon sat behind huge stacks of australes. This worst of all possible nights in Argentina was swinging around to me.

"Luck ain't visitin' this end of the table," said Rudd, throwing his cards down. He laughed.

Something about him reminded me of my colleague Peter Reilly, though he was much younger and without Reilly's boiled Irish face. One afternoon I was having lunch alone at Durgin Park and realized I'd left my billfold in the office. Peter Reilly was at the bar and hearing me explain things to the waiter, he lurched over to my table, glass in hand. At the staff meeting that morning he had drawn the long straw for Cambodia and was out celebrating.

"Caught short?" he asked.

Reilly reached into his pocket and drew out a wallet fastened to a tarnished silver chain. He spread it open, revealing an array of currencies from around the globe, British sterling, rupees, bahts, cordobas, the Polish zloty and Brazilian cruzeiro. They fanned out, guilders and francs and pesos as thick as my fist, in a myriad of colors and sizes, decorated with the faces of dead kings and queens and ugly, pockmarked generals in badly tailored uniforms.

"Here," said the Irishman, letting a fifty dollar bill drift down to the table. "That should do the trick." Above the dazzling bouquet of money his face was pale and his eyes fixed and staring at the wall. "Pretty paper, but if you look close, its got blood all over it."

Remembering this, I felt the metal disk pressing against my abdomen, the accumulated weight of icons and artifacts hunted down in every treacherous backwater I had ever visited. Coach Rudd jerked his chair back to the table and stretched. "At least I have my health," he said, waving his hand at the australes. "Too bad I can't afford the ride to the airport."

"There's your bus money, Coach," I said, pointing to my winnings. "Just let me have a team cap. I'd like a souvenir from this particular trip."

"Hell, I'd give you one of those anyhow," said Rudd.

The Texan unzipped his carryall and rummaged through, pulling out a stiff new maroon cap. He flexed the brim once or twice, popped the crown outward and handed it to me. "There," he said, when I put it on. "You're a Tiger."

The bus arrived after a while and I was roused from my chair and went outside in the darkness. The players filed on and then it was quiet. Gears grinding, the bus rattled over the cobblestones, alongside the barbed wire and sandbags and the soldiers staring out from behind them. Soon the Tigers were asleep, snoring amid the odor of damp cotton uniforms, their legs thrust into the aisles. As we glided through the checkpoints, the shadowy interior of the bus diffused them into particles and it was like they had become invisible somehow, finally going home.

God's Work

Welch's pond lies on the border of Carter, Massachusetts and Delham, New Hampshire, a small blue vessel of water amidst two hundred acres of pine forest. As children, my younger sister Louise and I often visited there to escape the dense, sticky heat that invades New England in July and August. I remember sitting in the backseat of my father's car, gliding through the pines, the diving float strangely black and unmoving on the fiery white surface of the pond.

Just beyond the town forest, at the base of Cronin's Hill, was a rambling, gray-shingled farmhouse that belonged to the only black family in Delham. There were six Harrison children, five girls and one boy, and when they jumped off the long painted dock and came up bobbing from the depths, their skin shone a rich, purplish color I had never seen before. My father called them "wards of the state."

Richard Harrison was two years younger than I was and half a foot taller. Huddled in my terrycloth jacket, I would watch the tall, long-faced boy laughing and playing with his skinny little sisters, tugging on their waxen braids and racing through the shallows. He ran so fast he left footprints, empty spaces that remained for half a second before the water filled them back in again. By the eighth grade, Richard Harrison was over six feet tall and I don't recall ever seeing him without a basketball under his arm. Nailed to a dead tree by the pond was an old rusty hoop and he would practice for hours, jumpers and lay-ups and hooks, often alone and sometimes with white boys from Carter High. They treated him roughly but by the time Richard was a freshman, no one could stop him and the games at Welch's pond came to an end.

I went away to college. Louise got a job as a lifeguard at the town beach and she sent me newspaper clippings of Richard Harrison in his blue Delham singlet and glossy shorts, with a huge Afro and shining white teeth. During his senior year he scored fifty points against Carter and there in the background of the photograph were the boys who had fouled him at Welch's pond. They were walking away with their heads down while Richard Harrison held up his index finger and grinned at the camera.

One day my sister came home and said that she was going to the prom at Delham Regional with Richard Harrison. Louise went to an all girls' Catholic school and was very excited about wearing a gown and corsage and riding in a limousine. My father was busy reading the *Eagle-Tribune* and when Louise finished telling us, he adjusted his cigar and raised the newspaper. "You tell Richard he better behave himself," he said.

The night arrived. Pacing up and down, my father held a little Kodak camera and the trio of flashcubes he had purchased for the occasion. "Take it easy, Dad," my sister kept saying.

"Louise: I am taking it easy," he said.

There was a lilac bush in front of our house, and a couple of years earlier, when I had escorted Elaine Bellorado to Carter's prom, we had our pictures taken there. My mother picked out a corsage for Elaine that matched the lilacs, and the neighbors all came out to see the lovely, dark-haired girl and her spray of white roses.

Richard Harrison arrived in an old jalopy with half its tailpipe missing. Drawn by the roar, several people gawked as a six-and-a-half foot black man in a powder blue tuxedo unfolded himself from the driver's seat. His Afro formed a halo above his head and he carried a large bouquet of purple and red carnations. My mother placed her hand on my father's back and we all moved onto the front lawn to greet Louise's escort.

Rising only as high as her date's breastbone, Louise was resplendent in her pink taffeta and silk dress, framed against the lilac bush. As my father snapped pictures, old man Roosevelt tottered outside to water his lawn, although it had rained plenty that week and I had seen him watering it an hour earlier.

Without taking his eyes off Roosevelt, my father spoke to my mother. "Honey, would you go into the kitchen and get that other roll of film, please?"

"You've already taken a whole roll, dear," my mother said.

His gaze still fixed on our decrepit neighbor, my father said, "I want to have my picture taken with Richard and Louise."

My mother went inside and we waited in the hot silence of the yard. It would have been a lot easier for my father to hustle Richard and Louise inside and take the photographs there, away from the neighbors. But that wasn't my father's way.

*

I didn't see Richard Harrison much after that. Later I heard that he enrolled in the community college but dropped out after basketball season. I finished law school and took a job with the Massachusetts district attorney and then one afternoon, when I was standing in line to mail my Christmas cards, I ran into my sister's old prom date.

He emerged from a door marked *Authorized Personnel Only*, dressed in gray-blue trousers with blue piping, a white shirt, and a zipped gray cardigan with the stylized head of an eagle on the left breast. On his head was a blue knit cap with the eagle logo on the brim. The cap fit his head tightly, indicating that Richard's Afro was long gone. Our eyes met, and he came over and shook my hand.

"So you're a mailman," I said.

"Postal worker," said Harrison, towering over the two nuns who were behind me.

"That's super. You look great." We struggled for something more to say, as the line of customers inched toward the single barred window of the post office.

"How's Louise?" asked Richard.

"She got married about a year ago. They're expecting a baby."

"Who'd she marry?"

"A guy from North Andover. He's a stock broker."

Richard Harrison also understood that my sister's husband was white. Facing another long silence, I blurted out, "What are you doing New Year's Eve?"

"Nothing."

"A friend of mine bartends in Portsmouth and I'm going up there. Why don't you come with me?"

"All right," said Richard, with the enthusiasm of someone making a dental appointment.

I offered to pick him up and then another postal worker came through the door. He was a short, unhappy-looking fellow with an oversize stomach and tangled eyebrows. In each hand was a loaded canvas bag and with a short pendulum motion, he deposited the two bags at Richard's feet. "Get going," he said.

Richard Harrison raised the bags to his shoulder and crossed the tiled floor and went outside, into the cold gray afternoon. A white panel truck with the eagle on the side pulled up and Richard slid open the door and climbed in with his bags of mail. Then the truck drove off.

The two nuns watched through the window and the older one, in a starched black habit and white cowl, said, "God's work is varied and difficult."

*

It was bitter cold and there were no lights showing when I arrived at the Harrison's early on New Year's Eve. Looming above their house, Cronin's Hill was a large, dark shadow, bristling with pine trees. For a moment I thought Richard had forgotten our appointment, but then a long pair of legs scissored across the beam of my headlights and the car door opened and he was seated beside me, his head cropped almost bald and a gold hoop shining in his left ear. The musk of his cologne was fruity and wild.

"Happy New Year," said Richard, shaking my hand. He reached into his leather jacket and took out a pint of Wild Turkey. "Have a drink."

"No thanks."

Richard was wearing pointy-toed boots, black trousers, a white silk shirt opened to the waist and a gold Zodiac medallion. He gestured with the bottle, and said, "You goin' to a funeral or something?"

I was dressed in a white oxford shirt, crew-necked sweater and a tweed jacket, with khakis and penny loafers. My bartending pal, Mike McGrath, called it my lawyering costume.

"You better have a snort," Richard said. Taking the whiskey from his enormous, white-palmed hand, I said, "Just a small one." I sipped from the pint, gasping for a moment as the Wild Turkey burned a trail to my stomach.

"Here. Give it to me," said Richard. He tipped the bottle to his mouth.

Richard Harrison drank and I drove, and the former basketball star told me about his life since he had graduated from Delham Regional. He'd torn up his knee at nineteen and soon learned there would be no big-time scholarship for a six-foot five-inch center that couldn't run. After dropping out of college, he enlisted in the Navy and was discharged for getting in a fight with a sailor from Kentucky. His mother was dead, from pancreatic cancer. Two of his sisters, Clarice and Donna, were addicted to drugs. Occasionally they came to the house looking for money. Another sister, Belinda, who I remembered as a beautiful, wide-eyed child, lived at the house with her two sons.

The job at the post office was paying him $9.87 an hour, and with four mouths to feed and a mortgage, Richard Harrison was having trouble keeping it together. On Saturday nights, he worked the door at a strip joint called the Chez-Wen in Lawrence. He had been seeing a dancer named Tiffany, but they broke up when the father of one of her children—a biker—objected to the sort of person his daughter was being exposed to. This objection left Tiffany with a broken nose and missing front tooth.

"I guess he don't like postal workers," said Richard, drinking from the pint.

The parking lot at the Swordfish Authority was full, so I squeezed my car into the alley. I was eager to see Mike McGrath, a friend from college who worked as a lobsterman and tended bar on the side. A disheveled, charming fellow, my old roommate calls himself "the lord of lobstering and bard of Hampton Beach."

A gigantic swordfish hung above the bar and dozens of swords taken from fish of various sizes covered the walls. Mike McGrath was at the beer taps, entertaining a couple of blondes. "We build up our health with proper nutrition and exercise," said the sandy-haired lobsterman, his voice breaking amidst the general clatter of the bar, "then destroy it with alcohol, tobacco, and—" he leaned over the bar, wagging a finger at the blondes—"with unbridled and gratuitous sex."

The girls laughed like maniacs, exposing their perfect teeth. "Build and destroy," said McGrath, placing glasses of beer onto the dented copper surface of the bar.

Revelers were three and four deep, some in their holiday finery and others wearing canvas-backed jackets and rubber boots. The Swordfish Authority was that kind of joint, a posh dining room overlooking Great Bay and a rowdy saloon where intemperate songs were sung and occasional fights broke out. The trophy above the bar was adorned with red and green garland, and when a large tip landed at Mike McGrath's elbow, he threw a switch that lit up the words EAT ME along the swordfish's flank.

McGrath spotted us. "Another asshole in a tweed coat," he said. I introduced my companion and McGrath extended his broad, freckled hand and Richard shook it. "What's your poison?" asked McGrath, smiling at his new acquaintance.

"Wild Turkey, rocks," Richard said.

"Oh, a philosopher," said Mike McGrath, snagging the appropriate bottle.

McGrath tapped a pint of stout for me, and Richard and I stood there against the heavy dark wood of the bar, palming our drinks, and breathing in the odor of cigar smoke and old seawater. The two blondes were pinned beside us and the nicer-looking one, who wore her hair in a ponytail, gazed up at Richard and said, "You're a big man."

Her friend giggled. Richard leaned against the bar, smiled at her and said, "I am big."

"How big are you?" asked the blonde, and her friend laughed a second time.

Richard pitched his voice beneath the din, so only the two blondes and I could hear. "Big enough to sit at the table and eat," he said.

The blondes laughed some more and then two men left off their game of darts and pushed through the crowd. "Our table's ready," said one of them. He wore a green flannel shirt and battered overalls and his jaw was coarse with stubble. Taking his girlfriend by the elbow—a little roughly—he steered for the dining room, his gaze locked upward on Richard, who regarded him calmly. When the four of them were gone, Richard said, "I guess he don't like philosophers."

Over the next two hours, Mike McGrath served us fish chowder, T-bone steaks with fried clams and several drinks apiece. When another bartender came on and my buddy was free to leave, McGrath presented us with a bill for just nine dollars. "Gotta cover the taxes," he said, "but there'll be no taxation without inebriation."

I wanted to stay, competing in the Eye Olympics with this pretty brunette across the room, but Mike McGrath had been pouring drinks all night and was ready to go somewhere else. The three of us went outside and lurched across the parking lot, beating our arms against our chests to ward off the cold. A few stars had appeared in the night sky and over by the harbor, someone was launching a battery of fireworks.

"Let's go to Toomey's house," McGrath said.

Thomas "Chick" Toomey was an old high school pal of McGrath's and the hottest developer on the seacoast. Beginning with a small real estate company inherited from his father, Toomey bought up dozens of old beach cottages, tore them down, and built luxury hotels in their place. His annual New Year's Eve shindig had become a hot ticket among all the young go-getters.

"How'd you ever get invited?" I asked McGrath.

"I entertain the local gentry with various seafaring yarns," said Mike, who wore a moth-eaten peacoat over his golf shirt with the swordfish insignia. "Then at midnight I turn into a pumpkin."

*

The Toomeys lived in an 18th century farmhouse surrounded by rustic stone walls. Situated on a little rise, the house and adjoining barn were painted Colonial blue with dark gray trim, and a crescent driveway bisected the stone wall and led up and past the house and then back down to the street. Through the windows we could see women in long dresses and men in neckties drinking cocktails and laughing.

Someone had departed early—a rare occurrence, Mike McGrath said—leaving a parking space right in front of the entrance. We emerged from my car and stamped over the flagstones into the house. "No prisoners," said McGrath.

Inside, the warm scent of roasted turkey and sage enveloped us, and although several guests smiled in our direction, no one offered to take our coats or introduce us around. The place was filled with antiques—Shaker rocking chairs and spinning wheels and a coffee table made of beveled glass. In the foyer was a twelve-foot evergreen, decorated with strings of popcorn and illuminated by candles in little brass sconces. The smoke from the candles made swirling gray patches on the ceiling.

A large fireplace dominated the main room, lined with soapstone and framed with mahogany planking. The host of tonight's gala leaned against the mantle, which was decorated with the horned head of a stag and an old flintlock rifle. Chick Toomey was plump, florid, haughty and rich, with a neck that spilled over his collar and hair in little spikes atop his head. Almost every remark he made drew laughter from the circle of young men and women that surrounded him, and he talked in a wheezing voice that came from his sinuses. Chick was dressed in a smoking jacket and green silk ascot.

"Is he kidding with that outfit?" I whispered to McGrath.

"He's a kidder," Mike said aloud. "Right, Chick?"

Toomey pointed to several trays of hors d' oeuvres, which were arranged on a table beside pitchers of eggnog and a crystal bowl filled with punch. "Try the smoked salmon," said Chick, in his high-pitched voice.

Mike McGrath glanced at the food, shaking his head. "I wouldn't eat that shit if you paid me," he said. "The French come into our waters and catch it, then they smoke it aboard ship and hold it out to drive up the price."

"Fuck the French then," said Toomey, and his entourage

laughed.

Mike McGrath waved Richard and me over to the bar, and while cold air seeped out of our jackets, we mixed ourselves some drinks. Richard was a curiosity, his earring and medallion glinting in the candlelight. A woman in a black cocktail dress approached him and asked if he played basketball. "I used to," said Richard, gazing down at her spectacular décolletage.

The woman smiled up at him. "And what do you do now?"

"Get asked about playing basketball."

Laughing, the woman said, "Touché."

"Yeah," Richard said. "Two points for me."

The pretty brunette from the Swordfish had arrived at the party, and emboldened by liquor, I went over and spoke to her. Lauren Lupo wore a beige poorboy sweater and beige corduroys, a string of pearls, and little suede boots. I extended my left hand and saw that she wore no engagement or wedding ring. "I'm still shopping," Lauren said.

"Excuse me?" She repeated herself, and I asked, "Shopping for what?"

Lauren smirked and said, "Why would a single girl come here if she wasn't looking for a husband?"

"That's pretty cynical."

Her gaze penetrated to various corners of the room and she laughed. "Open your eyes, Huckleberry," said Lauren. "The world is a pretty cynical place."

In jurisprudence there's a doctrine known as *res ipsa loquitur*, which means "the thing speaks for itself." One arm encircling his wife's narrow waist, Chick Toomey stood beside the portrait of his twin daughters and a fellow in a checked sports jacket said, "Tax-deferred annuities," and everybody laughed. Suddenly I realized we were a generation that had fought for nothing but money, believed in nothing but ourselves, and wished for nothing but dominion over others.

Lauren was still smirking. "Let me ask you something," she said. Crooking her finger, she led me toward the dining room. Lauren peered into the shadows to make sure no one was concealed there, and asked, "What are you trying to prove?"

"I don't know what you're talking about."

Lauren stared into my eyes. "Don't put me on," she said.

"I'm not. What do you mean?"

She jerked her thumb toward the bar. Richard Harrison now entertained three admirers: the one with the cleavage, a bucktoothed redhead in a pair of harem pants, and another woman who was six feet tall and wore a dress that looked like snakeskin. "I'm talking about the basketball player."

"He's a postal worker."

Lauren Lupo shook her head. "I don't care if he's the head of the NAACP. I mean, this is New Hampshire, you know."

"And in fifteen minutes," I said, looking at my watch, "it's going to be 1983."

Lauren glanced around the room. "Not on this plantation, it ain't."

At midnight, our host commanded everyone's attention and we counted down from ten and then groped all the women. Lauren and I lingered beside the Christmas tree, while Chick Toomey hugged his bankers and presented them with Cuban cigars. Then he dry-humped his wife to general applause and several champagne corks bounced off the ceiling.

"Silly little Huckleberry," Lauren said, embracing me.

*

On a butcher block in the kitchen was the huge, ravaged skeleton of a turkey, its flesh hanging from the bones and encircled by wilted garnish and jellied cranberries. Four large drumsticks were lying beside it, and a platter of stuffing that looked like road hash. I was on my way to the bathroom when Chick Toomey intercepted me, banging through his cabinets in search of something.

"What do you do for a living?" asked Toomey. Under his arm was a dusty bottle of Beaujolais.

"I'm an attorney."

"Do you do criminal work?" Toomey found the corkscrew and punctured the foil atop the Beaujolais and twisted it in. "Because I know a tax attorney who needs a good criminal lawyer."

"I work for the Mass. District Attorney's office."

Chick and I were standing on either side of the turkey, picking at its carcass. "Why would anyone want to work for the government?" he asked.

"To put the bad guys in jail," I said.

"The really bad guys don't go to jail. I should know," said Toomey, filling a wineglass, " 'cause I borrow money from them."

Chick's wife appeared to tell him so-and-so was leaving and I excused myself and went into the bathroom. When I came out Lauren Lupo was beside the turkey skeleton, talking to Richard Harrison and the bucktoothed girl in the harem pants. Chick Toomey was gone.

"You haven't lived until you've been in a café on the Boulevard Montparnasse," the bucktoothed girl was saying, Looking a little glassy-eyed, Richard pinched together a ball of stuffing and tossed it into the cavity of the dead bird. The girl in the harem pants asked if he'd ever been to Paris and when Richard shook his head, she squealed, "You have to go."

Richard Harrison had his arm inside the turkey skeleton just as Chick Toomey re-entered the kitchen. "WHAT IS THAT NIGGER DOING WITH HIS HAND IN MY TURKEY?"

At first I thought he was kidding, as if you kid about something like that. But then a snarl erupted in his throat and Toomey lunged for his guest with both hands. The two men grappled for a moment and their combined weight knocked the turkey to the floor. Only a large grease spot remained on the butcher block, surrounded by cubes of red jelly and tattered garnish.

"Get the fuck off me," said Richard, pushing Toomey away. But the shorter man had a low center of gravity and he came back, his arms flailing. The bucktoothed girl screamed. While I dragged Richard toward the living room, the man wearing the checked jacket rushed in, followed by several other guests, and they shoved their host in the opposite direction.

"Get that nigger out of my house," said Chick.

I could feel the disapproving stares, heavy like syrup, as Richard and I made for the exit. Conversations were frozen in mid-sentence; the young woman in the décolletage shrank into a chair and her new escort, a man in a cashmere sweater, gazed hotly at us.

Just as we reached the door, Chick Toomey ran through the foyer and leaped on Richard's back, clawing at his neck and attempting to gouge out his eyes. "I'll fuck you up," said Toomey, his voice high and strained. They swayed close to the decorated fir tree, tulips of candlelight glittering across the fabric of their clothes. As the mob surged past, I thought of my father standing against the lilac bush with his arm draped over Richard's shoulder. *God's work is varied and difficult.*

I sprinted over the carpet. "Leave him alone," I said, smashing into Chick. Together in a tight, wriggling mass, the three of us plummeted onto the antique coffee table, shattering it to bits. With a shriek, Toomey's wife threw herself down and began scooping up the pellets of glass like they were diamonds. Chick lay dazed on the floor.

Richard and I bolted through the front door. Part of the company had moved outside to smoke a joint and as we ran by, someone said, "Look. Chase-the-coon." I flung myself against the car just as Mike McGrath popped up in the backseat, followed by the six-foot woman, their hair and clothes in disarray.

"What the...?" asked McGrath.

"Trouble," I said.

Chick Toomey ran outside, pursued by his wife, the man in the checked sports jacket and several others. "That table cost me eight thousand dollars," said Toomey.

Mike McGrath scrambled to his feet and charged up the walk, tackling Chick in mid-stride. "Build and destroy," said Mike, as they disappeared over a snowbank.

I started up the car and shoved it into gear. Richard Harrison was crammed into the seat beside me and as we sped off, he craned his neck out the window. People were fighting all over the great white blanket of snow that covered the property. "Fucking crazy," he said.

At the end of the drive the car skidded and as we flew into a snowbank, my tires hit the stone wall underneath. We spun sideways, jumping the wall, and ended up facing the other direction. I glanced over at Richard, his face underlit by the dashboard, and wondered if any of the players in this little drama had in fact been doing God's work. Above where we sat Mike McGrath was trying to hold them off, but several figures ran through the drifts toward us, clad in silk and cashmere, shouting about the nigger.

The Landscapes of Dr. Aboud

Forty-seven Mexicans died when the volcano at Chihuahua erupted: farmers in straw hats, brown-skinned children, and women with gold teeth and plaited hair. Standing before an easel, Dr. Aboud gazed at the volcano from his hotel room window. His impression of the mountain, scorched at the base with streaks of fiery ooze from the summit, didn't include its victims—only the rising earth, blue smoke and a vivid yellow sky.

While Dr. Aboud painted, three men went to the morgue at Cristos las Paces hospital on the outskirts of Chihuahua, where they bribed the attendant with twenty-dollar bills and a fifth of Jack Daniels and then plunged syringes into the forty-seven pituitary glands of the dead villagers. In total, Aboud's henchmen extracted nine ounces of Human Growth Hormone, enough to turn a high school football team into a ferocious band of 300-pound animals.

There was a rap at the door and Dr. Aboud moved the canvas away from the window and put on his shoes and jacket. Then Luis came in and handed Dr. Aboud a glass container. "Here it is, *jefe*," the man said. "A very strange thing."

"Biological engineering is the future," said Dr. Aboud, placing the vial on ice. He gave Luis a stack of bills.

Luis had one thick eyebrow that ran across his forehead. Outside Dr. Aboud's room, in the heat of the Chihuahua sun, Luis's two cousins sat drinking beer beside a dented old truck. "The bodies stunk like hell," said Luis, counting the money. "Three hundred dollars is not enough."

"That was our agreement," said Dr. Aboud.

"There was a girl who had no face, it was melted right into her skull. I paid the attendant ten dollars and he finished the work for me. I need more money."

Dr. Aboud sat on the bed in a pinstriped jacket and linen trousers. He was a small, mahogany-colored man, with fine bones and brilliant yellow hair. "I'm not responsible for your sub-contracting arrangements," he said to Luis. "You insisted on bringing your cousins."

"They only get twenty-five dollars," Luis said, glancing at the two men in the parking lot. "But still there is not enough."

The Mexican loomed above the bed, reeking of hard liquor. His foot lay beside the plastic cooler where the hormone was stored and he nudged it, keeping his eyes on Dr. Aboud. "Give me the money," he said.

Dr. Aboud reached into the pocket of his sports coat. He withdrew a syringe and opened the cooler and took out the vial filled with thick yellow fluid. Then he pulled the stopper and loaded a small amount of the Human Growth Hormone into the syringe. Dr. Aboud beckoned to Luis and the foul-smelling man came forward. Probing with his fingers, Dr. Aboud selected a vein on Luis's arm, sprayed a circle of disinfectant and injected the hormone.

"Soon you'll be the most fearsome man in your village," he said.

Luis looked down at the tiny hole made by the syringe. "Good for business," he said.

His eyebrow wavered for an instant, and then he turned on his heel and went outside. There was some pushing back and forth, and Luis struck one of his cousins a punch that sent the man reeling. The other man helped his brother into the truck and Luis got behind the wheel and they drove off, the tailpipe rattling across the parking lot.

"You'll certainly grow," said Dr. Aboud, lying on the bed. "Your muscles. Bones. Everything." He watched a spider walk across the ceiling. "You'll be Chihuahua's biggest, strongest man for a while. After that, who knows?"

*

In the morning, Dr. Aboud proceeded to the Acapulco Hilton. From his suite, he ordered a magnum of champagne and set up his easel on the balcony. Beyond the hotel were cliffs and then the shimmering blue expanse of the Pacific, but Dr. Aboud was staring straight down. There was a gorgeous woman sunning by the pool. He studied her awhile and then dressed in his bathing trunks and descended to the ground floor.

Stopping for a bundle of roses, Dr. Aboud marched out to the pool deck. The woman was six feet tall, with brown arms and legs and perfect, lustrous skin. Her body arranged itself in tilted planes, and there was a ruthless sexual slant to her shoulders and taut brown stomach. From behind a pair of sunglasses, her eyes fixed themselves on Dr. Aboud. A cascade of shiny dark hair fell over her breasts and her teeth showed themselves for a moment, square and white.

"Yes?" she asked.

"I was in my room," said Dr. Aboud, "and couldn't help noticing you."

It was plain the woman was accustomed to being admired. "My name is Raza," she said.

"Dr. Aboud," said the yellow-haired man, bowing low. "Of Los Angeles, California. Cosmetic and corrective surgery."

Even from the aerie of his suite, Dr. Aboud had detected the single flaw in Raza's carriage. The flowing sheen of her hair could not disguise it from him. "I can give you breasts that Rudolph Valentino couldn't distinguish from those of his own mother," he said.

Raza stood up. Her bust was not small, just out of proportion to her height. Where the breasts should have continued, round and swelling and tipped with hard red nipples, they stopped. Raza's jaw quivered and her mouth opened to reveal a pink tongue and her wonderful teeth. The sun glinted off her dark glasses, exploding in two white fireballs.

"I would never let you touch me," she said.

She stalked away and Dr. Aboud raised his hand in the air, summoning a waiter. "Some papaya for my ladyfriend," he said.

In five minutes Raza was back, her breasts covered by a red kimono. Dr. Aboud gestured toward a chair, but the Brazilian refused.

"Who do you think you are?" she asked.

"I wasn't talking about me," said Dr. Aboud.

The waiter brought papaya juice in bamboo cups, then clipped the stems from the roses, placed them in a crystal vase and centered the vase in the shade of a huge green umbrella. Raza kept silent until he departed. "I refuse to sit with a man who has insulted me," she said, folding her arms over the kimono.

"Not many can be made perfect," Dr. Aboud said. He stood, extending his hand. Raza took it and together they sank into the chairs. "I only bother with the top one-half percent," said Dr. Aboud. "You, my dear, are in that number."

Everywhere Dr. Aboud went, men approached him who wished to be larger—professional football players, bodybuilders, even Secret Service agents and matadors. If they had good bone structure, he would start a course of treatment. But many of them shied away after the initial side effects: swollen breasts, a droopy, shriveled penis, and uncontrollable episodes of anxiety and paranoia.

"To become ultra-masculine one must first be feminine," said Dr. Aboud.

Women were Dr. Aboud's specialty. They wanted the faces of angels, the flanks of thoroughbred horses, breasts like Venus. "You must be rich," said Raza.

"Artists seldom think about money," Dr. Aboud said.

It was late in the day and the pool was deserted. Shedding her kimono, Raza bared her breasts for Dr. Aboud. They were the shape and weight of large peaches, beautifully orange in color with areola the size of Spanish doubloons. "What do you think?" Raza asked, her breasts suspended there in defiance of gravity.

Dr. Aboud took hold, pinching the nipples with his index fingers and thumbs. Slowly Raza's eyes closed and a moan escaped her lips. Squeezing and probing her flesh, Dr. Aboud maintained a clinical demeanor. Finally, he cleared his throat. "I suggest we go to my suite," he said.

Raza followed Dr. Aboud to the elevator. As the glass cube ascended the building, Raza fell to her knees and fumbled with the drawstring of his bathing trunks.

"Doctor-patient relationships are changing," Dr. Aboud said, "and there's nothing the AMA can do about it."

*

From their seats in first class, Dr. Aboud and Raza were treated to a panorama of sea and sky. Below them toy buildings appeared, the freeways made of ribbon and string. Raza gripped Dr. Aboud's hand when the pilot announced they would be delayed above Los Angeles. "I don't like flying," she said. "All the control goes to the pilot."

"You cannot fly a plane by committee, my dear," Dr. Aboud said. "But if you command your niche, you have sway over all."

"That's nonsense," said Raza.

Dr. Aboud shook his head. "Be impetuous if you like, but don't be stupid."

"I am not stupid," Raza said. She folded her arms across her chest.

"When you're attacked, you cover up your weaknesses," said Dr. Aboud. "Soon you won't be doing that."

Raza glanced about the cabin. The skin stretched downward along her cheekbones, and her full red lips tightened into a pout.

"I'm in control here," said Dr. Aboud, gesturing with his hand.

Raza laughed. "You're no more in control of this flight than I am."

"If the pilot chokes on a chicken bone, I would take charge," said Dr. Aboud.

A telephone buzzed on the wall and a flight attendant picked it up. The woman looked stricken for a moment, then she went past Dr. Aboud and Raza into coach.

"That's so unlikely, it's not worth thinking about," said Raza.

Dr. Aboud shrugged. "Regardless, the pilot is dependent on me, because I can save him," he said.

The first-class stewardess returned to the cabin and knelt beside Dr. Aboud. Her face registered worry at the eyes, but she maintained an artificial smile. "Doctor, I'm sorry to bother you," she said in a voice that only Dr. Aboud and Raza could hear. "But a passenger in coach is suffering from chest pains. The captain was wondering if you

73

would take a look at him."

Dr. Aboud did not hesitate. "I'm retired," he said.

Raza and the stewardess gaped at Dr. Aboud. "Excuse me," the stewardess said. "But you're the only physician on board. The man is in terrific pain, or I wouldn't bother you."

"I'm sorry, but there's nothing I can do."

The stewardess clamped her lips together and marched back into coach. There was a brief silence, then the plane began its descent.

"You just said you could save the captain," said Raza. "This man is probably having a heart attack, and yet you do nothing."

Dr. Aboud smiled. "He's not the captain."

*

The receptionist buzzed to inform Dr. Aboud that there was a man called Bonecrusher Jameson in the lobby. "I'll see him in room A," the doctor said.

He was busy with Mrs. Cohen, a 45-year old woman who wanted collagen injected in her lips and her thighs sculpted with liposuction. Dr. Aboud had just suggested grafting kidskin into the hidden curve beneath Mrs. Cohen's buttocks. The goat hide was soft and pliable and could be used to replace sections of her damaged skin.

"But Dr. Aboud, I don't want the legs of a goat," said the woman.

"Leave it this way and you'll have the legs of an elephant."

Dr. Aboud let Bonecrusher Jameson wait another ten minutes. When he entered Room A, four men greeted him. Jameson's stocky little manager was white. His chin and the top of his head were covered in stubble and he chewed a wad of tobacco. Behind him two gigantic black men wearing jackets inscribed with "Bonecrusher Jameson, 49-0" sat reading *Highlights* magazine.

Bonecrusher was seated on the examination table. He had broad shoulders with inverted tulips of muscle at either end. His hands looked three sizes too big for him.

"Sorry to bust in on you," said the white man. He introduced himself as the Sultan. "But the champ needs to put on forty pounds. In eight months we take on Razor Williams at Caesar's Palace."

"Stand up, please," Dr. Aboud said to the fighter, who was dressed in a pair of gray athletic shorts. The champ raised himself off the paper that covered the examination table. He towered over Dr. Aboud, his skin a glistening purplish-black, striated with muscle.

"Six-foot-two-inches tall," said the Sultan, working over his tobacco. "One hunnert-ninety-three pounds. Power in both hands and the reflexes of a cat. Light heavyweight champeen of the world."

The physician probed the fighter's muscles and lifted each hand and looked at it. Then he took the man's blood pressure and checked for hernias. As Dr. Aboud continued the exam, Jameson followed him with his eyes.

"Very good ratios," said Dr. Aboud, measuring the expanse from the champ's neck to the point of each shoulder. He took a tiny flashlight from his pocket and shined it into Bonecrusher's eyes. "The comprehension necessary for the task at hand."

"When Bonecrusher was an amateur, he killed a guy in the ring and then went out for chow mein," the Sultan said. "I knew right there I had a champeen."

The bodyguards remained engrossed in their magazines. Lowering himself back onto the examination table, Jameson stared at the wall.

"I heard you got something that puts on good weight, fast," said the Sultan.

Dr. Aboud took a pad out and wrote something on it. "First, I would shave his knuckles to present a greater punching surface," he said. "Then I would detach some of the nerves in his wrists so he won't feel pain in his hands. And I have something that will allow Mr. Jameson to gain forty pounds and perhaps grow two inches. My only suggestion would be to postpone the fight long enough for the surgeries to heal."

"Can they test for this-here serum?" asked the Sultan.

"HGH is produced by the body," said Dr. Aboud. "Mr. Jameson will just have more of it than most people."

The Sultan's chaw of tobacco stopped moving. "Give 'im the first shot," he said.

"It'll take nine visits, at ten thousand dollars per visit," Dr. Aboud said.

The Sultan began to pace. "His purses ain't so big right now."

"We can make other arrangements," said Dr. Aboud. "Sign over twenty-five percent of future gross revenues and I'll complete the procedure."

"You want a quarter of the champ?"

"Of the future undisputed heavyweight champion of the world," Dr. Aboud said. "In five months, Mr. Jameson will be bigger, stronger, with an increased ability to inflict and control pain. In other words, he'll be a new man."

The Sultan stepped on the pedal attached to a trash can and spit his tobacco into it. "I only got thirty-five percent myself. The rest is investors," he said. "And with sparring partners and training expenses and all, I ain't made diddly squat so far."

"Ten percent of millions is more than thirty-five percent of 'diddly squat'," said Dr. Aboud.

The Sultan mulled this over and then stuck out his lower lip and agreed.

Bonecrusher Jameson made a gesture and one of the bodyguards crossed the tiles and leaned toward him. "The champ don't want this fool touching him," the bodyguard said.

All eyes swerved to the Bonecrusher. He remained silent with his hands resting in his lap and his gaze fixed somewhere on the wall.

"This is like the space race, champ," said the Sultan. "The man in the white coat gets you to the moon and you do the walkin'." Bonecrusher sat motionless on the crinkled paper of the examination table, his gaze falling straight ahead.

"Your trainer is right," said Dr. Aboud. "I supply the propulsion and the know-how and you take it into the ring. What you do there is your business."

The champ motioned to the bodyguard closest to him. Again he spoke into the man's ear and the bodyguard took the gray T-shirt from a hook on the wall and helped him on with it. Bonecrusher Jameson headed for the door.

"Stick your propulsion up your ass," the bodyguard said.

Just before noon, Dr. Aboud retired to the basement. He removed his lab jacket and trousers and hung them in a closet. Naked, possessing very little body fat, the doctor set up an easel with a blank canvas on it. In front of the canvas he arranged various pots of egg tempera he had mixed himself.

He dipped the big toe of his right foot into one of the paint tins and raised his leg to place a dab of color on the canvas. As the work progressed, he increased his speed, using every toe on both feet. Dr. Aboud twisted and contorted himself backwards and sideways, while beads of perspiration dappled his forehead. Gradually the picture took shape: a pointillist café situated beside the strong green curve of a river.

Exhausted, Dr. Aboud lay down on a straw mat and fell asleep. An uncanny internal clock woke him after thirty minutes. His receptionist was at lunch and Dr. Aboud spied the television squirreled away beneath the counter. On screen was an image of Raza sauntering across a beach, her sandals in one hand and a bottle of iced tea in the other. The music swelled, her monumental breasts jounced together, and the announcer drew a connection between Raza's sexual desire and this particular brand of tea.

Dr. Aboud watched as Raza's throat tensed and relaxed, and the bottle of iced tea emptied itself. "Your talents are boundless, my dear," he said.

Several messages were impaled on a spike. Scrawled across the top one was a note that a man named Luis had called. There were a million Luis's in Los Angeles. A few were successful, and the rest rode on the back of garbage trucks. Amused by this, Dr. Aboud performed a half-Windsor on his necktie as he crossed the vestibule. He punched some numbers into a keypad, locking his office, and then strolled down the block to a restaurant called Pancho's Villa.

Parked in front was an ancient truck splattered with mud and smelling of chickens. Behind the truck was a car with Nevada plates that read "49-0." Dr. Aboud walked up the cactus-lined path and into the restaurant.

Waiters in shiny boots scurried in and out of the kitchen hoisting silver trays. Dr. Aboud paused in their wake and the Sultan beckoned to him from one of the tables. Bonecrusher Jameson was dressed in a black nylon running suit, staring into space. On the plate in front of him was a pile of kidney beans encircled by slices of kiwi fruit. A short distance away, the bodyguards were drinking margaritas and throwing dice into the jointed corner of the bartop.

Beyond them, Dr. Aboud could see a patio that contained some tables and a small copper fountain. Several people were dining on the flagstones and bits of conversation floated here and there on a breeze scented with flowering Judas. Dr. Aboud approached Jameson and his manager.

"We been talkin' sense," said the Sultan. "Dollars and sense."

Bonecrusher's forearms rested on either side of the untouched food. His short, unseeing gaze indicated that rational arguments would have little effect. Slipping his right foot from its loafer, Dr. Aboud saw his toes stained vermilion and azure and canary against the carpet. He swept his leg toward the ceiling and then deposited a smear of yellow on Bonecrusher's nose before returning his foot to the ground.

"Excuse me," Dr. Aboud said. Then he raised his left foot and dotted over the boxer's nose with magenta. "But I'm suggesting that quickness cannot be augmented. Only brute strength, which is a language I think you understand."

In response, Bonecrusher Jameson stood and unleashed a torrent of punches that came within a hair's breadth of Dr. Aboud's face—like an infinite number of flying crows. Diners at the other tables began using their cell phones to call the police.

But Dr. Aboud was undaunted. "I can add seventy-nine-hundred foot-pounds of pressure to each one of those punches," he said.

At that moment, an enormous Mexican vaulted the fence onto the patio. A woman fainted at the sight of him. Luis grabbed a burrito from the woman's plate and wolfed it down, shreds of lettuce hanging from his fist like currency, while those around him upset dishes of guacamole scrambling to the perimeter.

"Now *that's* a heavyweight," the Sultan said.

Luis entered the dining room, tipping himself sideways to fit through the doorway. The Mexican had calves like two bowling balls and a gigantic eyebrow that seemed to go all the way around his head. In the four months since the volcano had erupted at Chihuahua, he had grown several inches and his girth had increased.

"I need another shot," Luis said. He lumbered toward Jameson and the bodyguards scrambled from their stools, intercepting him.

"Put on the brakes, Jake," one of them said.

Luis delivered a single clubbing blow to the bodyguard and he went down. He sat shaking his head, like a man resisting an idea, and then struggled to his feet. "Ho now," the bodyguard said, signaling his partner.

The two men sprang at Luis. For a moment the Mexican's towering figure was obliterated as they swarmed him, their gold chains jumping in various geometric shapes as punches flew. Then Luis straightened up and flung the bodyguards aside. They sprawled on the floor, rubbing their knees and elbows.

Ahead was Bonecrusher Jameson, his chin held low and fists clenched at his sides, the sweat popping on his neck.

"Easy, champ," the Sultan said. He glanced at the bodyguards. "You're gettin' paid mighty good to handle this kind of thing."

"Takin' it on the chin ain't the way to win," said the bodyguard.

He shimmied between the tables and the other bodyguard rose and followed him out. "So long, champ."

"If Mr. Jameson is still conscious a minute from now, I'll become his personal physician at no charge," Dr. Aboud said to the Sultan.

"What's the catch?" asked the Sultan, worrying his tobacco.

"If he gets knocked out, you'll train my Mexican friend here—for five percent of the gross."

The Sultan said, "It's a deal."

The champ shuffled forward, his head darting back and forth. Twice he stuck his jab into Luis's beard, following with a right hook to the vicinity of the Mexican's liver.

It was like hitting a sandbag. "Ow," said Bonecrusher.

Luis reached out and grasped Jameson by the shoulders, yanking him downward while raising his knee with tremendous force. Upon receiving the blow on his right temple, Jameson rolled his eyes and collapsed, his wrists bent at funny angles.

A man wearing an oversize sombrero ran up and began pointing at him: "...*ocho, nueve, diez!*" he said, struggling to raise Luis's arm. "*El premiado.*"

Sirens ululated toward Pancho's Villa like the cries of deranged women. Bonecrusher remained on the floor, and several patrons began pushing and shoving each other as they crowded forward. "Y'all just cancelled my meal ticket," the Sultan said.

But Dr. Aboud gestured at Luis. "Meet your new protégé," he said.

"You wanna fight professionally, son?" asked the Sultan.

Luis raised his fists, which were like two hams, and glanced at Dr. Aboud. "Can I make money doing this?" he asked.

"In this country, you can be king," the sultan said.

Four police officers rushed into the dining room with their nightsticks raised, followed by a team of paramedics dragging a stretcher. An LAPD sergeant with a face like a matinee idol pointed his truncheon at Luis. "On your knees, wetback. And quit eyeballing me," he said. Hitching up his belt, the sergeant addressed Dr. Aboud: "We got reports of an ethnic disturbance."

Bonecrusher Jameson groaned from his position on the floor, and then sat up and began rubbing his eyes. "The nigger's moving," one of the police officers said. Guns were drawn.

"Everybody down on the floor," said the sergeant.

The Sultan stood waving his arms. "Don't shoot! He's not insured."

"Get back," the sergeant said, clutching his weapon. "I'll pop a cap into both these monkeys if anybody so much as breathes on me."

The Mexican and the prizefighter were forced to spread-eagle on the carpet. Bonecrusher Jameson was bleeding and his right eye was swollen shut. The paramedics rolled their gurney past him and began ministering to the woman who had fainted.

"All these underclass types look guilty to me," said the sergeant. "Everybody goes in the wagon."

Luis resisted attempts to handcuff him—first by pushing the officers away and then, as they rushed from all sides, flailing at them with his hands. The sergeant was hit in the nose and it exploded across his uniform like a rotten tomato. While the largest of the police officers applied a chokehold on Luis, another officer chopped at his knees with a nightstick and they wrestled him to the ground.

"My face," said the sergeant, touching his broken nose. "He hurt my face."

"If you need surgery, give me a call," Dr. Aboud said, handing over his business card. Then he hurried across the dining room, past the uncomprehending face of the Sultan. His feet left dimples of color on the floor, tracks that diminished until the carpet was blank again

The Tex Cameron Show

Years later, after my father had died, I saw Tex Cameron on late night television selling excursions to Florida. Standing beside a bail of hay, he looked old and shrunken beneath the huge white Stetson he was wearing. I remembered him as a young cowboy leaping on the back of Gold Dust, the horse rearing majestically, and with a circular wave of his hat galloping off toward the horizon. Every Sunday morning after the first set of commercials, Tex Cameron would ride under a hanging wooden sign that said "Tombstone" and the live segment of his show would begin. In the corral Tex would dismount from the horse and, looking straight into the camera, in a low sure voice he'd say, "Howdy, kids."

And the studio audience would thunder back, "Howdy, Tex!"

From the wings his sidekick, Sagebrush Billy, would amble out and he and Tex would talk about riding cattle or fighting Indians or their days together in the Texas Rangers. I never questioned why they moved to Massachusetts to go on television or how they managed cattle drives from downtown Boston.

In 1967 when I was 10 years old, my father had a new station wagon with an extra seat that popped up in the back. By the time summer ended, the Red Sox were in first place and my father took me to buy my Cub Scout uniform. Riding home dressed in the stiff blue shirt and yellow neckerchief was like being a war hero in a parade. The rear window was cranked down and Jim Lonborg was pitching for the Sox on the radio, working so deliberately we could hear the whistles and catcalls and *Hey, peanuts here!* between tosses. My father drove up Tauvernier Street to our house on that warm clear afternoon, the new car smelling of vinyl and moving at a crawl so we wouldn't miss a pitch.

"This is the life," he said.

At our first Scout meeting they told us Pack 45 was going to be on the Tex Cameron show. The next few days were like waiting for Christmas. All we talked about was what we would say to Tex Cameron. "I'm gonna ask him where Tombstone is," said Donald Ketchum. "It's probably fake."

Up early on Sunday, I buttoned myself into my uniform with the moon still hovering above the D'Amatos' house next door. My mother and baby sister were sleeping and I tiptoed downstairs. The rest of the house was gloomy with shadows, but the kitchen was lit up. At the table my father sat looking over the newspaper.

"Want some breakfast?" he asked. Admiring the uniform, my father glanced at me from head to foot. We were two men alone in the wee hours.

"I'm not hungry."

My father gestured at the clock. "Trust your old man," he said. "It's a lot more comfortable sitting here than in the school parking lot."

I took the sports page. My father sipped his coffee and I could feel him looking at me over his black-rimmed glasses. He was smiling but there were sad little wrinkles in the corners of his eyes.

When we arrived at the school there was the bus, silver and gleaming, with little red lights across the top. "Look at that," my father said. "Perfect timing."

I ran for the bus without answering him. Pack 45 streamed aboard the glowing hulk and I glanced back over my shoulder as I was carried up the grooved silver steps. The outline of my father's crew cut was visible in the front seat of the car, his glasses like two shining discs as a pair of headlights passed in front of him. I could feel his gaze steady on me and it didn't seem right to be going to meet Tex Cameron without him.

Earlier that summer, at a baseball card show, I waited for Carl Yastrzemski to sign my autograph book. For half an hour, I was shoved back and forth by bigger kids and pushy, sweat-smelling parents until

I heard my father's voice, loud and steady from where he stood behind the line: "Hey, Yaz! Sign the kid's book, for crissakes." And the Red Sox left fielder glanced over all our heads to where his eyes met my father's, and he beckoned me forward.

*

Donald Ketchum speared me in the ribs and I went down to the back of the bus. My best friend Sonny D'Amato was waiting there. He turned his neckerchief around and slipped it over his nose and mouth. "This is a stick-up," he said. Then he pulled the neckerchief down and wore it bunched up like an Apache tie.

The sun rose above the highway and everyone was talking at once about Tex Cameron and Sagebrush Billy and the jumping ability of Gold Dust. We drove into an industrial park, and the scoutmaster said we were getting close. In the slanted morning light, we gawked out the windows at the huge buildings. Every inch was paved and there wasn't so much as a squirrel skittering across the parking lot. Then the bus pulled up to a corrugated metal building that looked like a giant tool shed.

"There ain't a pack of cows within ten miles of this joint," said Donald Ketchum.

Still, we were excited as we paraded into the lobby of Channel 19. There must have been 200 kids in there, overflowing among the potted plants and a circular reception desk emblazoned with the station number. Rope tricks were being practiced; hats scaled in the air. It was like a convention of midget cowboys.

A man wearing a golf shirt with *The Tex Cameron Show* on it addressed us through a bullhorn. "Gold Dust isn't feeling well this morning and Tex would appreciate it if you'd be on your best behavior," the director said.

"That dumb horse was sick last time I was on," said a boy behind us. Sonny turned and gave him a drop-dead look. If Tex Cameron wanted us to be quiet, we were made of stone.

Ushers led us into the studio. Tombstone seemed like a shrunken replica of itself, crowded by television cameras and miles of thick rubber cable snaking over the floor. Instead of seats there was a tilted concrete slab fenced in with metal railings. Pack 45 was herded down front.

"We'll be able to count Tex Cameron's nose hairs from this spot," Ketchum said.

We leaned over the rail trying to get a clear view of the flimsy-looking storefronts and tiny corral. Technicians were scrambling back and forth with big, spongy headphones clamped over their ears, running last-minute checks and throwing switches. Everything looked much smaller than it did on television—it couldn't have been more than twenty feet across Main Street. I saw an old man in a blue workshirt and buckskin trousers carrying an armful of hay and some apples. He put them down inside the corral.

"Who's that—Tex Cameron's grandfather?" asked Sonny.

The director sat up front in a canvas chair. Another man dressed in a silk prizefighter's robe was talking to him. The guy in the robe gestured toward the audience with a lit cigarette, upset about something.

The director turned on his bullhorn. "Kids, say good morning to Tex Cameron," he said.

Our eyes roamed up and down the set. There was no sign of Gold Dust or the tall lean figure of Tex Cameron. But the director continued smiling, his hand extended toward the man dressed in the silk fighter's robe.

"*That's* Tex Cameron?" Sonny asked.

The man in the robe wasn't smiling. He had a smug look on his face and continued smoking with his gaze fixed on the floor. He was a small guy without his hat and boots but it was Tex, all right. The man with the bullhorn said something about choosing contestants and he and Tex came along the red metal railing, a cloud of smoke hovering between them. The director questioned some of the kids and others he simply pointed to and Tex shook his head yes or no.

"I need a sheriff and deputy," said the director.

Every hand went up in a Hitler salute. Voices all around were saying "Me! Me! Me!"

"Give us your best 'Howdy, Tex!'" the director said to one boy. The kid fumbled it and Tex shook his head in disgust.

Someone else was given a chance and answered with a bellow. They had their sheriff. Tex pointed straight at Donald Ketchum and the biggest mouth in Pack 45 couldn't even manage a whisper. The finger shifted to me and I went deep for it: "*Howdy, Tex!*"

Tex nodded, and the director jerked his thumb over his shoulder. "Okay, kid," he said. "See the man over there."

"Holy shit," said Sonny, boosting me over the railing. "You're gonna be on the show."

I landed without feeling the floor. Passing by Tex Cameron, I glanced up and recognized the profile, lean in the jaw with dark squinty eyes. He grinned at me for a second, flicking away his cigarette. "Don't screw it up," he said.

The man in the headphones took me and the sheriff aside to explain our duties but I had seen it done a hundred times. "Don't look into the camera. Look at Tex," he said. "He's the star."

The director called for quiet. All the technicians froze in place and there was a brief countdown. The theme music started playing. Sagebrush Billy came out from somewhere in his faded cavalry uniform and stood right beside me. He had curly hair and a drooping mustache and smelled of liquor. At the rear of the set, a curtain parted and Tex rode in on Gold Dust. As soon as the horse's rear end cleared the curtain, Tex dismounted and led Gold Dust to the corral. There was barely enough room to prevent the giant yellow horse from bumping into things.

Tex looked more like himself. In his snakeskin boots, chewing on a piece of hay, he came to an x marked on the floor and said howdy. He was shining under the bright lights, a sponge-covered microphone poised just above the crown of his hat. When he spoke, a great crackling wave of sound came from behind me—*Howdy, Tex!*—but I didn't pay any attention to it. Gold Dust was only about fifteen feet away, her long yellow head thrust between the top and bottom rails of the corral. She was a beautiful tawny gold color, heavy with muscle at the chest, but her eyes were almost dead. The hay and apples were right there, and she didn't even flare her nostrils at them.

The old man in the workshirt was closest to the horse. He had a plastic bucket filled with water and he was staring at Gold Dust with a worried look. After Sagebrush Billy came out, the cameras swung in his direction and Gold Dust was out of the spotlight for a while. The man in the workshirt moved over to the corral and stroked the horse's nose. Raising the bucket, he whispered in Gold Dust's ear and got her to take a little drink.

The man was broad in the shoulders and had a face like an old catcher's mitt. None of the technicians or cameramen acknowledged him but they got out of his way. With his water bucket and hay and that old leathery face, he looked like a farmer who had wandered into Channel 19 by mistake.

Sagebrush Billy started the first contest. In the middle of Tombstone, five kids stood with coils of rope in their hands. Sagebrush Billy took an adult-sized lasso and with a quick toss, threw it over a fence post.

"There you go, boys," he said. "Easy."

Tex Cameron unlooped his own rope and started circling it with his right hand held downward in front of him. The whirring rope formed an inverted cone that hovered above his boot tops. The cameras dropped in their mounts, following him. "Jes' makin' a tee pee," Tex said.

The star moved aside when the camera turned back to the contestants, and the hatless old man came out and stood on the x twirling Tex's rope. All his tricks were down low, or out to one side—never anywhere near his face. The rope spun and made changing liquid shapes, like a ghost that shifted around with a tiny buzz.

Tex was a few feet away, watching the rope and describing it in that slow drawling way I had heard so many times. "Figure eight...over to a backward loop...this one ain't nothin' but showin' off...made it up myself." The cameras moved over to the stuffed longhorn, and the roping contest began and ended quickly. Sagebrush Billy presented a chuck wagon overflowing with toys to the winner and then the show broke for a commercial.

Tex took his rope back from the old man. "Nice work, Tom," he said.

"I been practicin' a little," said the man.

During the commercial, Gold Dust splashed the ground with

manure and Tom cleaned it up. Smoking another cigarette, Tex Cameron waved his hat in front of his face. "Spray that with something, will you Tom?" he asked. "It stinks."

The old man shoveled the lumps into a plastic bag and mopped over the pavement. "It ain't licorice," he said.

The next segment was filmed inside the jailhouse. Tex and Sagebrush Billy sat at the table examining the wanted poster and talking about when the sheriff and his deputy would be riding into town. My heart began hammering in my chest and I glanced over to the space beside the corral. Tom was standing there with the plastic bag and mop, and he winked at me.

At the next break, Sagebrush Billy and the director and two assistants lined up the studio audience. My job was to lead all the kids down Main Street. Then I had to double back and help the sheriff compare the faces of the kids going by to the disguised face on the poster. If we picked the right kid, we would each win a wagon full of prizes.

A technician called out, "Ninety seconds," and half the kids were still crowding around the gap in the railing where they were supposed to line up. A man wearing headphones took me and the sheriff by the elbows and guided us over the tangled cables and behind the flimsy wall of the jailhouse. The lights were very bright and we shaded our eyes.

"Get your hands down," the technician said. "It's meant to look real."

He left us alone for a moment in the heat of the spotlights. There was a camera pointed at us and a microphone above our heads but they weren't turned on yet. The sheriff was a chubby kid wearing a brown cowboy hat and glasses. He looked scared to death.

"What the hell am I doing?" he asked.

A good part of the audience remained inside the railings. We could hear them through the cardboard wall, pawing the ground like cattle. Tex was in front of the jailhouse with Sagebrush Billy, getting ready for the next shot, and he clomped over the wooden sidewalk in his boots and passed by the barred window of the jail.

"Shut up and get in line," he said in a shrill voice. "I'm on in ten seconds."

Silence fell over the set. Through the window I could see Tex Cameron and his sidekick lounging against the hitching rail out front. The little red light on top of their camera came on.

"The sheriff's in town," said Tex, back in his drawl again.

"I hear-ed," Sagebrush Billy said.

Tex was busy chewing on a piece of hay. "Reckon we should go in and see about that wanted man," he said.

Sagebrush Billy nodded. "I reckon."

The director cued us and Tex and his sidekick ambled through the door. I was sitting at the table smiling my guts out. The sheriff turned bright red and I thought he was going to faint from holding his breath.

"Sheriff," said Tex, nodding across the table as he sat down. The kid blinked in terror.

"Hi, Tex," I said. "Thanks for coming in."

A flicker of surprise registered on Tex Cameron's face. But he shifted his gaze to me, bringing the camera to his profile as he did. "Deputy, we got a problem here in Tombstone and we need you and the sheriff to help us out," he said.

I nodded my head, looking him in the eye. "That's what we're here for," I said.

Sagebrush Billy almost burst out laughing. Already I had spoken more lines than three years' worth of deputy sheriffs. "I like a lawman with some brass," he said.

"This outlaw we're after is an ornery cuss," said Tex, with a hint of irritation in his voice. "There's never been one like him in these-here parts."

He handed me the wanted poster. On it was a person wearing a heavy false beard and thick eyebrows and a coonskin cap. Because of the disguise, only the pink tip of a nose and two small blue eyes were visible. Tex Cameron smirked at me—discovering the identity of the wanted man in less than a minute on live television was practically impossible.

"You're right, Tex. He's a dangerous man," I said, handing the poster to the chubby kid. "Have a look at this, Sheriff."

"I feel a lot better about it with you two fellas in town," ad-libbed Sagebrush Billy. "We gotta make our streets safe for decent, law-abidin' folk."

"We aim to," I said.

I thought Tex was going to fall off the chair, but he set his jaw, stood up and adjusted his hat. "Let's take a gander at them suspects," he said.

He and Sagebrush Billy and the sheriff went out through the front door of the jail. Led by a technician with a flashlight, I passed behind the cardboard facade and took the first kid by his cold, sweaty hand. With the rest of the studio audience coming behind me, I marched down Main Street toward the bright lights. Tex and Sagebrush Billy and the sheriff were reviewing the faces as they passed. A technician held me by the arm, watching for the precise moment between shots when I could join the others at the hitching rail.

The sheriff reached for Donald Ketchum and declared him to be the wanted man just as I stepped onto the wooden sidewalk. The chubby kid turned to me with a fierce triumphant look, his eyes shining behind his spectacles.

"I got him," he said.

Sagebrush Billy tied the prisoner's hands behind his back with one of the miniature lariats and the director signaled a commercial. "We're back in two minutes," he said. Then he turned to Ketchum. "Are you the one on the poster?"

"No, sir."

The only time one of the audience could have been taken aside, dressed in the disguise and photographed was in the lobby before the show. Ketchum was with me and Sonny the whole time.

"You're not him?" asked the sheriff, looking like he was going to cry.

"Not even close," said Ketchum, who had brown eyes and a big nose. "But thanks a lot. Now I'm gonna be on tee vee"

The director called for the real wanted man. He was a head taller than Donald Ketchum with the close-set blue eyes and snub nose from the photograph.

"Back in fifteen seconds," a technician said.

The true identity of the wanted man was revealed while the sheriff and I smiled dumbly at the camera. Clutching our plastic Tootsie Rolls, we walked out of the shot. The two chuck wagons with all the prizes were given to Donald Ketchum and the boy from the poster. Sagebrush Billy leaned down and mussed their hair. "Cagey as two foxes," he said.

"I'm Tex Cameron," said the star, smiling into the nearest camera. "For me and my sidekick, Sagebrush Billy, that's all from Tombstone. Keep ridin' and ropin' and we'll see y'all back here next week."

Suddenly I realized that my turn as deputy sheriff was over, gone for good, and the secret dream I had of being a regular on the show—greeting Tex and Sagebrush Billy each week from the blacksmith shop or the hotel—was gone with it. As soon as the bright lights were turned off, Tex and Sagebrush Billy walked off the set and disappeared. They wouldn't remember any of us.

The studio audience began to file out, laughing and talking as they climbed the arcade to the exit doors. Technicians rolled up cables and wheeled away the cameras and light stands and dismantled Main Street. "I'm not gonna be able to carry all this stuff," Ketchum said, sitting in the middle of Tombstone with his prizes.

Each week when the show ended, Tex Cameron rode Gold Dust through a field of tall yellow grass. Hoofbeats echoed across the screen and the camera tracked man and horse until they were just a speck on the horizon. But now Tex was gone and Gold Dust stood quietly against the rails of the corral.

"Go ahead and pet her if you want," said Tom, who had appeared with two currycombs and an old horse blanket. "Just move slow. She gets a little funny under them lights."

I reached over and stroked Gold Dust's nose. "Is Tex going to come and ride her somewhere?"

The old man shook his head. "After the show I bring Gold Dust back to the farm where she lives."

"Are you a cowboy?" I asked, watching Tom brush the horse.

"Used to be."

He had the combs moving real good now, and the broad flank of the horse swayed toward him with each long pull. Gold Dust's coat was piled deep like velour, glistening under the lights. "Tex Cameron isn't a real cowboy, is he?" I asked.

"No, but he's a pretty good actor," said Tom.

The horse pivoted and then lifted her tail, firing a stream of manure to the ground. "Tex is a horse's ass," I said, repeating a phrase I'd heard my father use.

The old man threw the tattered blanket over Gold Dust and she let out a whinny. "Adios," Tom said, disappearing behind the curtain with the horse.

I ran to the exit and through the lobby to the bus. Ketchum was sitting up front, gloating over his new skateboard and basketball and swim fins. Sonny had a seat saved for me in the last row.

"There was no hotel, no town, nothing," he said.

"I'll never watch that show again," I said.

*

My father was waiting at the school with a box of doughnuts. "You guys were fantastic," he said.

I climbed into the station wagon and my father started the engine and drove to the end of the school driveway. "So what was Tex Cameron like?" he asked, handing me a cruller.

"A guy there told me he's just an actor," I said.

With one foot poised on the brake, my father was holding the station wagon at the corner of Tauvernier Street. His crew cut was turned the other way, studying the cars rolling toward us.

"Anyway, you were the star," he said, timing our swing into the traffic. The station wagon accelerated with a smooth powerful sound and my father turned and smiled at me, shooting us toward home.

Sages

His vision blurred by last night's *Ron Rico*, Tom Ryan saw a young man lurching toward him beneath the elms. There was a medieval scattering of crows, black and screaming, and the man seemed to rise up, struggling toward him on the smoky yellow air.

"Mister Doctor," the man said. "Thank God it is you."

Ryan searched the campus for somewhere to hide but he was alone on a huge sea of grass. He could hear a lawnmower in the distance and it seemed that his life was being held in mechanical jaws and shredded by rapidly turning blades.

"I don't have much time," said Ryan, checking his watch. It had stopped at two o'clock.

Ossama Siddiqi was the color of a pecan. His eyes watered behind his spectacles and he had the small rosy mouth of an infant. "I need you to tell me, Mister Doctor," he said in his thin musical voice, "what I must do."

Ryan nodded. He was charitable with useless information—the accumulated detritus of a middle age spent in outer offices, reading magazines and serialized books.

"Mister Doctor," said Siddiqi. "Now I am a pharmacist with good position. And I have a girlfriend, Audrey Robillard." Leaning backwards, he wet his lips and looked into his old professor's eyes. "But my family has arranged a marriage for me in India. Please, what should I do?"

"Fifty percent of American marriages end in divorce," Ryan told his former student. "On the other hand, ninety-eight percent of arranged marriages are successful. Marry the Indian."

Siddiqi looked disappointed for a moment. Then he clasped Ryan's huge hand in his, smiling with perfect white teeth. "You are always right, Mister Doctor," he said. "I want my marriage to be successful. You must come with me to India."

*

Ryan was an English professor in the night school at Shawsheen Technical College. Over the years, his love of language had dwindled. Mostly he stared out the window at the great blankness that filled the sky, while people whose names he never bothered to remember scratched away at their composition books.

Near the end of class one night, a student approached him. He came up timidly, clutching his theme. "Mister Doctor," the man said. "How sorry I am to bother you."

Ryan glared at him over the evening newspaper. "What is it?"

The man was in his twenties, slightly built and round-shouldered, his eyes magnified by the thick lenses of his spectacles. With a trembling hand, he thrust the paper under Ryan's chin. "Please, to get your instruction," he said.

Ryan folded up the sports page and spread the man's theme on the desk. The topic for the evening was "The Most Important Person I Know." In tiny green script, Ossama Siddiqi had written: *Mister Doctor Ryan is the most important person I know because for a great man a doctor to fix sickly people and to help at night my writing Composition is important to my accepting Medical School. Mister Doctor Ossama Siddiqi to be like M. D. Ryan to help people always. Not to speak to see out window and think of people many ways to help.*

Siddiqi looked eagerly at Ryan. "My most important person I know," he said, revealing a mouthful of crooked teeth. "My Mister Doctor."

"I have a doctorate in English," said Ryan. Under the glaring lights, the rest of the class scribbled at their themes. "The world's most useless degree."

Siddiqi's puzzled face hovered over him. Ryan coughed into his fist, squinting again at the miniature green handwriting. It wiggled on the page like the legs of tiny insects. "You have a real problem here with run-on sentences," Ryan said.

On Monday evenings, Siddiqi lurked in the parking lot when Ryan arrived at six o'clock. He maintained a belief that Ryan performed heart transplants and other daring surgery by day and revealed the mysteries of the semicolon at night. But near the end of the term, Ryan found Siddiqi under a tree, his face buried in his hands. He was weeping.

"I am unable to get into your medical school," he said. "That was my one dream of America. Mister Doctor—what should I do?"

Ryan asked if he was strong in chemistry. "It is my best subject," Siddiqi said.

"Go into pharmacy then," said Ryan. "It's easy, indoor work."

Siddiqi considered this for a moment. He stood up, brushing the grass from his clothes. "This is my new dream for America," he said.

"And get your teeth fixed. Nobody wants to see a bucktoothed pharmacist."

*

At the college, Ryan shared an office the size of a broom closet with Matthias Hornblower. "Thomas—I'll be out of your way shortly," said Hornblower, as Ryan filled the doorway. Papers were scattered across his desk. "I'm speaking on the principles of Victorian rhetoric at the Chancellor's Symposium. I hope you'll be there."

"When is it?" said Ryan.

"Four o'clock sharp. In the Faculty Lounge."

Ryan laughed. "I'll be at a lounge, all right." He entered sideways, his own desk bare except for yesterday's *Boston Globe*. "I wish I was there right now."

"But you have a class," Hornblower reminded him. "And teachers love to teach."

Unscrewing a bottle of aspirin, Ryan made a wry face. "I have *tenure*," he said. "And I love my paycheck."

Arrayed in houndstooth, flecked with pipe tobacco, Hornblower had that lean, half-starved Cambridge look—bald on top, white hair pushed behind his ears and worldly, inquisitive eyes framed by reading glasses. "An Indian gentleman was here to see you," he said. "An ex-student of yours."

"Siddiqi."

"Pleasant chap," Hornblower said.

Ryan pulled the wad of cotton from the aspirin bottle and tore it in half. In class, the cotton would make a nifty pair of earplugs. "The man's naivete could set buildings on fire," he said.

"Mr. Siddiqi mentioned something about an arranged marriage," said Hornblower. He gathered his papers and stood up. "Apparently this fellow sees you as some kind of *bodhisattva*. I hope you're giving him good advice."

The old newspaper went into the trash and Ryan unfurled the new one. The solid, ink-smelling weight of it crackled in his hands. "I'm sorry," he said, lost in the pleasant haze of the *Globe*. "What did you say?"

Hornblower frowned. "I was just saying that a mistake in marriage could ruin Mr. Siddiqi's life."

"I told him to go to India," said Ryan.

Hornblower laughed in a single braying note. "You did what?" He had his hands full of papers; his upper body twisted around like a question mark with white hair.

"Mail order brides last longer. I've seen the statistics."

Hornblower sat down and smoothed an errant tuft of hair with the palm of his hand. He looked like someone about to play the piano. For a long moment, neither man spoke.

"Obstructing love is a dangerous business," said Hornblower. "The entire canon of Western literature is fixed on the notion of love: romantic, familial, fraternal, unrequited, doomed, erotic, homosexual, heterosexual, misplaced and ambivalent. A *sine qua non*, love is interwoven deeply into our cultural ideals, our values."

Ryan glanced up from his newspaper. "So what?"

"By coming here to the west, Mr. Siddiqi is trying to free himself from the Old World," Hornblower said, waving some papers like a manifesto.

"You want to take over, go ahead," said Ryan.

There followed a long silence while Hornblower selected a dusty volume from one of the shelves and leafed through it. Satisfied, he clasped his hands over the book in prayer-like fashion, then cleared his throat. "Please recall, Thomas, that the sage, the enlightened one, is a trusted guide, but he's denied the journey himself," Hornblower said.

"That's me," said Ryan, opening the *Globe* to the travel section. "Always a bridesmaid, never the bride."

He began reading about a trip someone had made to the Far East. Hornblower's presence hovered for a few minutes beyond his line of vision, eclipsing the light. There was a soft rustling noise, then the shape carried itself off, the heavy air in the doorway rippling for a moment afterwards. Ryan descended into the newspaper story. His body seemed to narrow itself and enter the white space between the words. After some time a noise outside the office brought Ryan back to his desk. His left leg, bent against the chair, was asleep and he stamped it up and down.

Ryan got on the elevator thinking about Siddiqi. His former student was headed toward marriage and the comfort of an all-night drugstore. He might even get rich, a possibility for a smart pharmacist. The elevator stopped, and then the doors opened with a revelatory hiss of air. It struck Ryan that the humble Mr. Siddiqi might have a better life than his own.

*

Tom Ryan, monumentally hung over, was waiting to get his hair cut when he noticed a young woman on the sidewalk outside the barbershop. She was carrying an infant and staring in his direction, her face a white moon above her black cape and boots. The wind came up, throwing grit against the facade of the building, and the woman turned away for a moment to shield the baby, her cape whipping against her legs.

The huge window distorted the woman as she reached the doorway. In the thick wavy glass, the shape stretched itself until it separated into twin images: one woman coming nearer, armed with a baby; an identical woman continuing down the sidewalk. Chimes rang above the door and the woman entered.

She came straight to Ryan's chair. "Are you the famous Mister Doctor?" she said. It was strange to hear it in the flat sarcastic tones of the Merrimack Valley. *Mistah Doctah.*

"Who wants to know?" asked Ryan.

A blue blanket with horses on it covered the baby, who gazed at the wall.

"Me," said the woman. She smelled like cigarettes and coffee. "Audrey Robillard: Siddiqi's girlfriend."

The baby was only about two months old, milky white, his head perfect and round like a baseball. "Siddiqi was gonna work at the drugstore and we were gonna get married," said Audrey. "Now he's going back to India, thanks to you."

"Is that Siddiqi's kid?" asked Ryan.

"No. He's my kid," Audrey said. "Siddiqi said he didn't care, he loved Eugene."

The professor noted that babies often resembled famous politicians. This one looked like Eisenhower. He was bald, his brow was crooked, and one blue eye was faintly cocked. Wearing a checkered vest over his undershirt, tiny Ike maintained a wise and steady silence.

Audrey pointed at the child. "What the hell am I gonna do?"

"I don't know," said Ryan.

"Whaddaya mean—you don't know?" asked Audrey in a rising voice.

One of the watery-eyed barbers glanced over, still snipping at the fringe of a bald man asleep in his chair. Then another customer came in, shaking his fur-trimmed overcoat and stamping his feet. Sensing a tightness in the air, the well-dressed man detoured to the magazine rack and remained there, pretending to read *National Geographic.*

Ryan stood up, buttoning his old stadium coat. He could wait another week to get his hair cut.

"Don't walk away from me," said Audrey.

"I'll see ya, Willie," announced Ryan to the barber—musically, for the chimes above the door rang at the same time, depositing him on the sidewalk.

It was cold and a thin gray light filled the street. Audrey caught up to Ryan and wheeled him around by the elbow. His eyes bloodshot, the professor shivered in his battered coat. "What gives you the right to keep me and Baby Eugene from having a decent house?" asked Audrey. "A decent life."

Ryan said nothing, his hands deep in the pockets of his coat. His stomach was sour, burning at the edges. In his left-hand pocket, he knocked against a little plastic vial and remembered his other errand.

"Are you going to answer me, or not?" Audrey asked.

The baby stared blankly ahead, his arms dangling at his sides. "The entire canon of Western literature is fixed on the notion of love: romantic, doomed, etc.," said Ryan. "Not once did you even mention it."

Audrey was speechless for a moment. Then her eyes, heavy with mascara, flickered over Ryan in a quick appraisal. "You're drunk," she said.

"Very observant," Ryan said, wagging his finger at her. "You must be a detective."

Audrey cursed and stomped off. Facing backward, Baby Eugene gripped the edge of the blanket. "Adios," said Ryan, waving at him, and the baby laughed.

Ryan walked down the length of Tauvernier Street in the brisk penetrating air, then crossed over Broadway to Rex-All Drugs. It reeked of disinfectant and crowning each aisle was a shiny collection of crutches, canes and aluminum walkers. Dressed in a lab coat, Ossama Siddiqi hailed his old professor from a platform in the rear of the store.

"Mister Doctor. I have something for you," he said. Siddiqi's hair was neatly combed and he looked like a ship's captain, with a commanding view of the drugstore.

Ryan took the vial from his pocket and held it up. "Paxil," he said.

Siddiqi descended to him, clutching an envelope. At ground level, the top of his head reached only to Ryan's shoulder. "I will fill your medicine to the rim," said the pharmacist, beaming. "But I want you to be a guest at my wedding."

Inside the envelope was a round-trip ticket to India. Siddiqi and his bride had scheduled the wedding to coincide with Ryan's vacation at the end of the term. *"Chandra,"* said Siddiqi, his eyes huge and moist behind his spectacles.

Ryan shook his large head from side to side. "I can't go."

Siddiqi was crestfallen. He pushed the ticket toward Ryan's chest. "Mister Doctor Ryan, you have given us our life together and you must be there to start us happy. This is Usha's one and only dream."

It was a first-class ticket Ryan held in his hand, worth over a thousand dollars. He was fifty-seven years old and except for army training in Ohio and a blurry week in Atlantic City, he had never been anywhere. "What the hell," Ryan said. "But I want to pay for the ticket."

A smile burst across Siddiqi's face. "No, Mister Doctor," he said. "I paid for it with all your advice, which is every time as true as a dollar."

Another customer entered the drugstore. It was the man in the fur-trimmed overcoat, sporting a fresh haircut. He stood for a moment looking around and then his gaze fell on Ryan, and he gave a start. "You again," the man said.

"Don't worry," Ryan said, holding the ticket up. "I'm going to India."

*

Chaipur, the so-called pink city of Ragistahn, was the site of the wedding. From New Delhi it took Ryan several hours to reach it by train. On the journey he met Mrs. Penelope Baird, a divorced woman who had been living in India for seven years.

"A sense of humor is essential in an Indian survival kit," Mrs. Baird said to Ryan near the train station, as they detoured around an elephant that was squatting in the road.

Penelope Baird was a Scottish tea broker, dressed in sandals and khaki shorts, her graying hair drawn back in a loose ponytail. They were going up a steep lane between two palace walls, crowded on either side by hovels made from torn blankets and newspapers. There was the stench of urine, elephant manure, disease and decay, interrupted only by the occasional smell of incense burning on prayer altars in front of the shacks.

Beggars sat under lean-tos with their hands extended, or else blocked the lane, staring out from beneath their filthy bandages. "You can't help looking at them," Mrs. Baird said. Ryan had never seen such a circus, and one man hesitated in front of him and thrust out his arms. They were infected with some kind of larvae, a voracious parasite that lived beneath the skin. "Sweet Mother of Jesus," said Ryan, digging in his pocket for some coins. He gave the man a few rupees without touching him and for a moment, they were in danger of being overrun by beggars.

"This way," said Mrs. Baird. She grabbed Ryan by the wrist and they escaped into the lobby of a hotel.

"If I do that again, give me a good swift kick," Ryan said.

Mrs. Baird led them out another door into the brightness of the market square. "If you insist," she said, hailing a *tonga*, or donkey cart.

Wandering about the market were Ragistahni men with sweeping mustaches, their faces wizened by the sun. They were taller than Ryan had expected, striding about in their white tunics and embroidered slippers, their heads covered by massive turbans of royal purple and gold and scarlet. They stood in little groups drinking tea, or inspected the various bazaars, looking serious and purposeful.

The women were much more industrious. In rainbow skirts and shawls, dripping with gold—ankles, toes, ears, wrists and fingers—they were everywhere at once, buying and selling. Ryan had seen women laboring on construction sites, and down on the Ghats by the lake, pounding and pummeling great heaps of linen and damask. They went about these tasks with great fervor, in contrast to the men, and while they worked they were laughing and shouting and gossiping.

"What a place," said Ryan, as the tonga moved through the crowd.

"India can be foul and it can be wonderful," said Mrs. Baird. She touched Ryan on the arm. "It's all a test and you're living in the question. The Hindi word is *chandra*."

"What's that?" asked Ryan.

"Joy of life," Mrs. Baird said. "*Chandra* is the line between living and dying."

They disembarked at a tea stall on the perimeter of the market. Ryan paid the fare while his companion secured one of the outdoor tables and ordered sweet tea and *dosas*, large crepes with potato and coconut chutney as filling. The waiter, in a sky blue turban, bowed and went into the stall where he stood gazing out at the market and smoking.

"Keep in mind that ten Indian minutes are like two European hours," said Mrs. Baird. She took some cheese balls that had been dipped in sugar from her bag. "I always bring along *rasgulla* when I go out for tea."

Ryan had not seen Siddiqi for over a month and was anxious about their meeting. India amazed him, and he did not want to say or do anything that might be taken as an insult. Having Mrs. Baird along made him more at ease. She spoke English, of course, as many locals did, but she could also drop into Hindi. Like notes on a flute, it carried them throughout the city and into whatever Ryan needed: currency exchanges, hand-made gifts, clean water.

When Siddiqi approached, in a long dazzling white shirt and stiff fez, Ryan didn't recognize him. Trailing a short distance behind Siddiqi was an old man. In his shaggy gray hair and beard and gray diaper he looked like Matthias Hornblower gone native. The old man stopped in the middle of the square, gazing after Siddiqi.

There was plenty of livestock in the market: baby elephants, camels, cows in every size and shape, and exotic birds. As Siddiqi came upon a muster of peacocks, they spread their enormous tails, dragging them on the ground until they rose, forming a bower of vivid turquoise for the pharmacist to walk through, his arms held in the air. "Mister Doctor," he said, doubling his pace. He grasped Ryan by the elbows. "Welcome to Chaipur, my teacher and friend."

They embraced and Ryan felt a strange rush of kinship. Then the professor introduced his Scottish companion and Siddiqi issued Mrs. Baird an invitation to the wedding. "This is a celebration of two hearts, and all hearts beating should share in it," he said.

They sat down and the waiter brought out the tea in a samovar. While he poured, Mrs. Baird asked Siddiqi about the woman he was to marry.

"Usha Bangeshkar," the pharmacist said. "She is from a very old family."

The three days of music and feasting would take place at the Bangeshkar home on the west side of the city. And by tradition, when the bride met the groom in front of the house, they would be seeing each other for the first time.

"Ever?" asked Ryan.

Siddiqi bobbed his head up and down. "Usha means dawn," he said. "This will be my life's beginning."

Mrs. Baird wished him well in Hindi, and they began a long tuneful exchange. His eyes popping, Siddiqi gestured at Ryan. Halfway through, Mrs. Baird reached across the table to the pharmacist. Then she turned to Ryan, still holding Siddiqi's hand.

"You're the guest of honor," Mrs. Baird said. She mused a while, and added: "They all want to meet you and ask your advice."

After the tea, Siddiqi excused himself and went to see the Hindu priest. The old man in the diaper followed him at a distance. Ryan stood gazing as they crossed the square, trumpeted by miniature elephants. "Incredible," said Ryan.

"It's simply marvelous," said Mrs. Baird. She indicated Siddiqi just before he disappeared into the temple. "That boy worships the ground you walk on."

*

At the crest of a dusty hill, the Bangeshkars lived in a large stone house with a flowering jasmine plant in the yard. Its petals decorated the ground and perfumed the air. Buttoned into a poplin suit with a striped club tie, Ryan felt like an ambassador. He smiled at Mrs. Baird as another of the bride's relatives pumped his hand.

"You have done a great thing, Doctor Doctor," said Uncle Ragu. Tiny-chested, his arms and shoulders bare, Ragu clung to the American. "Where do you think Ossama and Usha should live?"

Ryan shrugged. "Near the Rex-all, I guess."

Uncle Ragu marveled at the idea, his teeth bunched together when he smiled. "Should I work in a drugstore?" he asked.

"What do you do for a living now?" asked Ryan.

Uncle Ragu let go of Ryan and raised his arm. "Elephants," he said.

They were interrupted by music coming up the hill. The wedding guests surged over the dirt yard and gathered along the low stone wall or else spilled into the street. The groom was seated on a white horse, his family walking alongside and a small group of musicians out front. Siddiqi was dressed in white trousers and a powder blue jacket. On his head was a white turban with a multi-colored garland obscuring his face.

"When the bride comes out, it will symbolize leaving her home for the boy's house," Mrs. Baird said.

The band halted at the gate, ankle deep in flower petals, and the groom dismounted. Relieved of Siddiqi's weight, the old sway-backed horse splashed the ground with manure, but only Ryan seemed to notice. Then the music stopped and the tall double doors of the house opened. Out came the bride, in a red sari and gold bracelets and bangles. A Hindu priest assisted Usha down the stairs.

At the end of the walk, the priest, dressed in leggings and wearing a turban with a long white tail hanging in the back, took Usha and Siddiqi by the wrists. Praying softly, he joined their hands. The bride and groom turned toward each other and the priest uncovered their eyes. Round-faced, with reddened lips and cheerful dark eyes, Usha smiled and her tongue darted out in a nervous gesture. Siddiqi blinked a few times and then he and Usha held their hands aloft. Everyone cheered.

"Now Mister Doctor Ryan will tell about this marriage," said Siddiqi.

Ryan felt his knees wobble. Towering above the other guests, he smelled jasmine and the thick spicy aroma of the wedding feast that was being prepared in the backyard. Siddiqi and his bride and all the guests were waiting for Ryan to speak. The old man in the diaper came to the gate. He was barefoot and had no possessions.

"Thank you for inviting me," Ryan began, drawing on his many years behind the lectern. "I..." A lump rose in Ryan's throat and he choked it down. "In marriage, you need faith as much as you need anything, and Ossama and Usha have plenty of that. God bless them."

The priest led the wedding party inside. The sway-backed horse wandered off down the hill, and the guests and musicians and then the old man went into the house. Heaped on three low tables in the main room were mounds of silk and carved teak and ivory, ruby-encrusted gold statuettes and baskets filled with bananas and figs. "Usha's dowry," said Mrs. Baird as they crossed the stone floor.

Ryan's shoes made noise against the flagging. "It looks like Fort Knox," he said. The old man sailed by without a glance, and Ryan and Mrs. Baird followed him into the backyard.

Tied to each other with holy thread, the two young people were sitting beneath a flowered canopy. A small fire was burning on the ground in front of them, and the priest threw rice and holy oil into the flames while he chanted. Guests were sitting on the ground. Some of them watched the ceremony, and the rest were clustered in small groups eating and talking.

Ryan and Mrs. Baird sat with Uncle Ragu. Against the stone wall, some of the men smoked *bhang* in little clay pipes. The sweet crude smell of the hemp mingled with the strange music and Hindu chants. Ryan felt the cool earth through the seat of his trousers, and his knees began to ache. Uncle Ragu asked him if he enjoyed the outdoors.

Ryan laughed. "I haven't been outside in twenty years," he said.

During a pause in the ceremony, Usha came over to kiss Uncle Ragu and was introduced to Ryan and Mrs. Baird. Many of the guests had finished eating and as the band continued to play, they danced over the petal-strewn yard.

"In my happiness I thank you," Usha said to Ryan. Elaborate designs made from a crushed leaf called *mehndi* decorated her hands and feet. The bride removed a flower from her headdress and placed it in Ryan's lapel. "Welcome," she said.

Siddiqi beckoned Usha to the dancing. Leaning against Ryan, Mrs. Baird smiled and tapped out the rhythm on his arm. She got up when Uncle Ragu asked her to dance. Across the yard, the old man in the diaper was sitting on the wall. Ryan struggled to his feet and brought him a bowl of rice.

"*Chandra,*" the old man said. He took one bite of the rice and then set it down.

Behind him was an empty slope that turned bluish in the distance. "What should I do?" Ryan asked. The old man looked at him for a moment. Then he swung his legs over the wall and dropped into the rough grass on the other side.

Ryan watched the old man descend until he was lost in the dry sedge of the hillside. The music traveled over the dusty ground, flying outward until it scattered across the landscape. Ryan stripped off his jacket, careful not to damage the flower in his lapel, and then his tie and shoes. Calling out to Usha and Siddiqi and Mrs. Baird, he danced toward them on the foamy blue air.

Two Mississippi's

The school bus let me off in front of my father's store and I went inside, the sacks of flour stacked along the wall like sandbags, and a pyramid of grape and apple juice decanters glowing purple and gold under the fluorescent lights. Beneath the slanted glass of the meat case were slabs of beef and sausages bundled together and wrinkled joints of ham. I stacked my books in the corner and took my football from its cubbyhole, like pulling a roast out of the oven.

My father was waiting on an old woman. His broad white apron was stiff with blood, extending to his knees, and he regarded the customer from his usual position behind the meat case.

"A dollar twenty-nine a pound for stewing beef is quite expensive," said Mrs. Doyle, a wire basket hanging by the crook of her arm. "At the First National it's only a dollar nineteen, and the T-bone is much cheaper, too."

I could hear the narrow planks of the floor creaking as my father shifted his weight, grasping the door to the meat case. "I buy two sides of beef when they buy fifty," he said, with a distant look in his eyes. "If you want meat at those prices, Mrs. Doyle, I'm afraid you'll have to buy it over there."

The woman glanced down through the holes in her basket, and then swung her gaze back to my father. "I'm only stating a fact, Mr. Carling," she said, her voice echoing throughout the store. "Now, I'll take three pounds as I always do. Only please see that you trim the fat. My husband likes it very lean."

My father slid the door open and pulled out the tray filled with

107

meat. Heaping some onto the cutting board, he hewed away at the whitened rind clinging to the pieces he had selected, cubing them with a special thin-bladed knife.

"I'd like that in three one-pound packages," said Mrs. Doyle. She lifted her chin for emphasis, and the flesh underneath quivered like pudding. "If you don't mind."

"Not at all," my father said. He divided the stewing beef into three equal piles and wrapped them in green paper, sealing the bundles with long strips of masking tape. Mrs. Doyle raised her basket and my father nestled the packages inside like three swaddled up babies. "Will there be anything else, Mrs. Doyle?" he asked.

"Just some cornstarch."

"That's on the left-hand side, right next to the golden syrup."

"Thank you, Mr. Carling." Mrs. Doyle handed my father a bill and he subtracted the final item along with the stewing beef, returning her change. "I'd like to keep the basket," she said.

"Go ahead. Bring it back next week."

Mrs. Doyle marched down the aisle, stopping for a moment to locate the cornstarch. When she exited, three little chimes above the door played a fragment of "God Save the Queen." My father said it gave the place an old-fashioned British air, even though hardly anyone on Tauvernier Street spoke English anymore. The mills were out of business, most of the old shops and markets were being boarded up, and the people who were moving into the neighborhood ate mostly rice and beans.

"Hello, son," my father said, looking at me for the first time. "How was school?"

I said "Ehh" and my father laughed, sliding open the door to the meat case. He pushed aside some chicken quarters and removed one of the four-inch pork pies, chopping it in half with a cleaver. On his share he poured a dab of Worcestershire sauce, then sat down on a three-legged stool and we ate in silence, the pork pie cold and heavy in my palm. Over my father's shoulder was a picture of him and Grampa Wray in front of the store. The window behind them had been freshly painted, and the tall white wedge of my father obliterated one of the letters that spelled out ARLING & SON, BUTCHERS AND BAK-

ERS.

"Game today?" my father asked, nodding at the football.

I rolled the instep of my sneaker over the curve of the ball. "Kevin's father is gonna be visiting."

"Whoa, that'll be something," my father said, finishing the pie with two quick snaps of his jaw. Crumbs had fallen onto his bulging stomach and he pinched them into his mouth with large red fingers.

"Maybe you can come and watch," I said.

My father shook his head, smiling at me. "There's a loin to be butchered, and then I have to juggle the books for a while."

I pictured the old man tossing my schoolbooks into the air, then adding a rib roast, some pork pies, and his cleaver until it all revolved about his head in a giant wheel. For a long time now, business had been bad. My mother said it made no sense for two people to sit around waiting for customers, so she applied at First National and got work as a cashier. In the evenings, she watched television while my father cooked meatloaf or chops for supper, and I would take out my box of football cards and arrange them on the floor. I wasn't supposed to make any noise.

When I finished the pork pie, I pulled the earholes of my helmet apart and slipped it on, looking at the meat rack from between the bars. I stood up and my father snapped the chinstrap into place. "Score me a touchdown," he said.

Picking up the football, I circled the meat counter and went down the single aisle of the store. "Supper's at six," my father called out.

With one hand I raised the ball over my head and stepped through the doorway between the warm, meat-smelling shop and the brittle air outside. The chimes rang out and then were muffled behind the heavy glass, sealed inside with the vague white shape of my father. A couple of guys in leather jackets hustled across Broadway, and then the strip was quiet except for some papers blowing along the gutter. Above me, the sky was gray and smelled of winter.

Climbing Tauvernier Street, I could hear Kevin Reese's voice rising between the shadowy gray bulk of the houses. Then a figure darted out from behind a parked car and knocked Kevin down; it was his brother Ted.

"Cut the crap," Kevin said. He was wearing his New York Giants helmet and Ted's old corduroy jacket zipped over a pair of shoulder pads.

"Don't be a puss," said Ted, slapping him on the helmet. "What would Spider think?"

Kevin loved the Giants, especially Spider Lockhart. My favorite player was Gino Cappelletti of the Boston Patriots. Kevin and I argued all the time about who was better, Lockhart or Cappelletti, but Ted said that was just kid stuff. His helmet was a high school model, plain white with a blue stripe down the middle, and he went around with the chinstrap undone. Kevin was my best friend in the neighborhood but he semi-ignored me when Ted was there, and it got worse if his father was visiting. Then I was like the invisible man, with a dotted line around me so there would be someone for the Reeses to play against.

I could see Mrs. Reese through the kitchen window, a tall, lumpy woman with red hair, putting a pan on the stove. A cigarette smoldered at her elbow and she still had on her secretary's outfit and high heels. She and Kevin's father were the only divorced people I knew. Mr. Reese was an insurance salesman and, once in a while, when his collections took him into the neighborhood, he would stop and play football with us. He had a cannon for an arm and could throw spirals the length of Tauvernier Street.

Ted practiced his punts, tall arcing beauties, and Kevin fielded them, sometimes catching the ball over his shoulder and then swerving down the sideline. Ted was fifteen, three years older than Kevin and me. He had veins in his arms and frizzy hair that stuck out like a waffle from the side of his head. When Ted and Kevin teamed up they were unbeatable in just about everything. It made me wish I had a brother.

I tried catching some of the punts, but when I looked straight up I got dizzy and it felt like my legs were rooted in the pavement. The first one bounced off my shoulder and the second one I misjudged completely, lurching forward just as it sailed over my head.

"Get a bushel basket," Ted said, laughing at me.

A car turned the corner. "Here's Dad," said Kevin.

Mr. Reese drove up in a glossy cream-colored sedan with a convertible top. The chrome was so perfect I could see myself in it: stretched wider than I was tall, with a plastic bubble on my head. Mr. Reese emerged from the car with a brand new Duke football, which he lofted toward Kevin just by flicking his wrist. The ball streaked across the sky, and as it reached a point almost directly above us, it dropped nose-first into Kevin's catching range and he grasped it out of the air. He sure had gluey hands.

"Look. A real pro football," said Kevin. He turned the ball over to examine it, and I could see Gino Cappelletti's autograph in gold above the laces.

"Afternoon, men," said Mr. Reese, looking from Kevin to his brother. He was tall and husky, with a nose that had been broken several times and thinning blond hair. "Ready for some pigskin?"

"Yessir," said his sons.

"Save the new ball," he said, picking mine off the ground. "This one's already scuffed up."

To make the teams fair, it was me and Mr. Reese against Ted and Kevin. Mr. Reese was wearing his business suit and loafers, so he couldn't run very well. Ted punted to us and Mr. Reese faded back a few yards and caught the ball, then lateraled it to me. I tried to make a move, but I wasn't quick enough and Kevin tagged me.

"Who did I get—the human snail?" asked Mr. Reese.

We huddled and Mr. Reese gazed over my head at his sons, who crouched with their facemasks together, whispering back and forth. "Do a curl," he said.

The storm drains were running and I could hear the water rushing beneath the street. I hiked the ball through my legs to Mr. Reese, wondering how far out I was supposed to go. Ted called out "One Mississippi, two Mississippi's" in his metallic voice and I streaked along the gutter with Kevin on my right shoulder, then stopped sharply and turned back toward the ball. It was already there, on a breath of wind, tearing through my hands. My fingers burned and the ball flopped onto the pavement. I retrieved it, trotting back for second down.

Mr. Reese looked at me with his cold blue eyes. "Whatsamatter—can't you catch?"

"It was kind of a fast one," I said.

On the next play I went deep and Mr. Reese faked a throw, causing Ted to vault in the air, and Mr. Reese limped past him for a pretty good gain. When Ted caught up from behind, Mr. Reese shoved the ball in his son's belly. "Just keeping you honest," he said, rubbing his sore knees.

Gloom over the housetops meant it was close to six o'clock. When we turned the ball over, Mr. Reese just stood on the line of scrimmage and let Ted practice his passing. Kevin was tricky: darting and curving, stutter-stepping all over the street. He scored on the second play, getting behind me for a long bomb.

The door opened, and Mrs. Reese came to the top of the stairs. "Ted, Kevin," she said. "Supper's in five minutes."

Tossing the football in the air, Mr. Reese stared at his ex-wife from the gutter. With a tiny sound, he spit between his front teeth and a drop of white fell on the pavement and then disappeared. Nobody said a word, and Mrs. Reese puffed on her cigarette. "Do you hear me?" she asked. "Five minutes."

"*Okay*, Mom," Ted said.

"Just make sure," said Mrs. Reese, her voice quavering in the stillness.

Mr. Reese continued to flip the ball in the air. It went up in a banana-shaped pattern that bowed outward and rose to a spot about ten feet above his head, hovered for a moment, and then dropped back into his hand.

Mrs. Reese glared at him and then went back inside. Her high heels echoed like gunshots and when she slammed the front door it shook in its frame.

"Next touchdown wins," said Mr. Reese. He elected not to receive the kickoff and we started our possession from the telephone pole. Just before the first play, he said to Ted, "Let me have Kevin, and you take this guy."

Ted nodded from inside his helmet. "All right, Dad," he said.

Kevin gave me a quick glance as he crossed over; we both knew what was up. It was almost like he was apologizing for his speed.

"I'll cover my brother," Ted said to me. "You stay on the line.

Don't let the old man run it."

Kevin snapped the ball to his father, and I called out the Mississippis and then just stood there feeling useless. The play lasted forever. Kevin danced and dashed and skipped all over Tauvernier Street, but he couldn't shake Ted for very long and Mr. Reese held the ball by his ear and smiled. "Get loose, Kev," he said. "The pressure on me is incredible."

I took a chance and ran in. Flailing at Mr. Reese, I nearly had him when he released the ball, sending it thirty yards with a motion that I couldn't even see. The pass cut the air like a rocket and Ted leaped high to knock it down.

"Lucky," said Kevin.

Ted shook his head. "Nope," he said. "Skill."

On the next play, I rushed immediately and Mr. Reese completed a short one to Kevin and Ted tagged him so hard he fell down on the pavement. Scrambling to his feet, Kevin threw a punch that got beneath Ted's facemask, clipping him on the chin.

"Watch it, little man, or I'll knock your block off," said Ted.

With his father there, Kevin was pretty brave. "This is tag, not tackle," he said, giving Ted a shove. "Let's get out on a real football field, and you won't even touch me."

"Screw you," said Ted. "I'll play a freakin' tune on you."

The front door opened again, and Mrs. Reese leaned outside. "Supper is ready," she said.

Mr. Reese held up one arm like a pro quarterback trying to silence the crowd. "Last play, Madelaine," he said.

In the gathering dusk, Mrs. Reese looked pale and furious. "I wasn't speaking to you," she said. For a moment they glared at each other and then Mrs. Reese ducked back into the house. This time she closed the front door so gently I couldn't hear it click.

Mr. Reese arranged things so I was covering Kevin, who snapped the ball and sprinted out on a fly pattern. My elbows jerking upward behind me, I back pedaled as fast as I could. At the sewer cap, Kevin threw a fake to the outside that stymied me for an instant and then he shot past, one hand waving in the air. Speeding after him, I knew the pass was coming by watching Kevin's eyes. They grew wider and his mouth opened in a perfect O and he swerved off his right foot toward the sideline. Turning at the same instant, I heard a hissing sound and threw my hands up, wrenching the ball out of the sky.

Kevin made a last desperate grab for it, crashing onto the sidewalk. Up ahead I could see Ted attempting to block his father, elbows thrust out like chicken wings and his fists together. Mr. Reese's eyes were serious and he knocked Ted away with one hand, holding his ground in the middle of the street. I veered to the right and Mr. Reese freed himself and drifted that way. As Ted scrambled to cover his father's move, I cut into the space he had left, the ball tucked under my arm, light as gas with nothing but empty pavement in front of me. Just then Mrs. Reese came onto the porch again, her face all wet from crying.

At the end of Tauvernier Street, I could see my father mounting the hill dressed in his old pea coat and a trilby hat. I looked back at Mr. Reese frozen there, his shoe tops gleaming in the streetlight. He thrust a hand in my direction like he meant to reel me in somehow. But I hugged the ball to my chest and kept going, my father rising toward me, arms upraised, signaling a touchdown.

Latin Kings

Tauvernier Street starts from the gutter on Broadway, rising between the abandoned houses and tenements, the cars parked in the dirty slush on both sides: battered Toyotas and Datsuns and rusty old Fords with plastic bags for windows and Christmas lights strung over the racks. When I was a kid there was a ragman with a blind horse who drove his wagon over the hill. The horse dropped turds the size of baseballs and we'd throw them at passing cars.

Today I'm banging around town, driving with my left foot out the window and drinking cherry brandy. It tastes like Kool-Aid with glass in it. Playing chicken with the mailboxes, I get so close to one I scrape my door and now I'm trying to Zen my way to a dent on the other side. I've been up and down Broadway and Jackson and Prospect and Berkeley looking for Olivia, although I pretend I'm just out kissing mailboxes.

Near the top of the hill is a mansion with huge pillars in front. A long time ago, a dude named Axelrod used to live there. He owned the Axelrod Patent Medicine Company and was 98 when he died. Olivia says it's now divided into eight apartments—Rodriquez, Carerra, Melendez, Soong, Boles, Preciado, Bundzinski and Gutierrez. Not a fucking Axelrod in sight. Sometimes she hangs out with Gutierrez, this Latin King dude who has a cat named *Muerte*.

Olivia read my palm once and said I'd have a lot of trouble in life. But I'm smart. I read books and shit. At the end of Essex Street is a museum that used to be Axelrod headquarters. One day I was reading *Axelrod's Almanac* from 1889, "Second in Circulation Only to the Bible," and found a letter from Yang-seu-Tsing, Minister-in-Chief to the rebel Emperor of China.

"To Dr. Axelrod in America, the great curing barbarian of the outside country:

"Your present of sweet curing seeds and fragrant curing drops ... of the Cherry smell, has been brought to Hug-seu-Tsene – the Mighty Emperor ...of the terrible, stout Ming dynasty ... Be profoundly happy, O wise barbarian! for I, Yang-seu-Tsing, say it. Your curing seeds and sweet curing pills were given to the sick in his army of the Winged-Sword, and have made them well. Be profoundly happy while you live, for this is known to the Mighty Emperor of China, who approves your skill and permits you to send more of your curing Medicines for his fierce armies of myriads of men.

"They may be given to Chiang-Lin, chief Mandarin of the Red Button in Shanghai, who will repay you with Tea, or Silk, or Gold.

"The high Mandarins of China have heard of your great knowledge, surpassing all other foreigners, even aspiring to equal the divine wisdom of our own healing teachers, who make remedies that cure instantly. We are pleased to know you bow in terror before our Mighty Emperor."

*

Even while they're thanking him, these Chinese dudes are saying 'don't fuck with us.' Give us your sweet curing drops and bow in terror, or the army of the Winged Sword will smite your ass but good. That's why those chinks have been kicking it for so long. They're all street.

There's a flat stretch in front of Axelrod's house where the white dudes play football, huffing in their workboots and tackling each other on the pavement. Every beat town along the river is the same: all the mill owners are dead and the mills died with them. Now it's just the Latin Kings and Latin Gangsta Disciples and these football-crazy white boys and one big, long hassle over Tea and Silk and Gold. I go around like the chief Mandarin of the Red Button, nothing gets to me.

Some dipshit on the radio is saying that lesbians really turn him on. Olivia went with chicks for a while. I saw her at the Cedar Crest one day, eating scrambled eggs and kissing some bitch from North Andover, which slit my heart like a bag and squeezed out all the juice. A week later Olivia came back, with food from DeMoulas and a pack of Trojans, like it never happened. She said the old sweet potato wasn't for her.

The white boys stop playing while I drive through. I hear the football thump against my window and someone says *rican* and I throw the bottle out and it smashes into a thousand pieces. My mother is three-quarters Dominican. My dad's name is O'Hara or something. He works at Cristobal Auto Body on South Union. One time they brought in a stock car and we followed it on our bicycles. It was a Chevy, painted black with a white "8" on the hood, riding down South Union on a flatbed. They got to the garage and Mr. Cristobal was there and a bunch of guys in nylon racing jackets and my old man wore a helmet with the visor down and everybody stood back when he lit his torch. There he was, my *father*, as hard as any brick dick out of South Lawrence, barbed wire tattooed around his biceps and veins popping out. When he took off his mask, he had red hair and a broken nose. So I'm not Puerto Rican; I'm nothing.

I drive slow down Tauvernier Street, eyeballing each of the football dudes like I'm inspecting his soul and they all look straight back at me, but I don't have any soul. There's a dozen churches on the block: St. Patrick's and Sacred Heart and Saint George's Orthodox and Salon Del Reino De Los Testigos De Jehova and Redeemer Lutheran and Iglesia Bautista Biblica and Third Baptist and the Spanish Free Methodist and Iglesia Evangelica Hispana and United Pentecostal and El Lirio de Sion and Hispanic Seventh Day Adventist. They got nothing I want.

Down the back slope, the sidewalks are filled with dead Christmas trees and large cardboard boxes filled with little boxes and hunks of wrapping paper. The manger outside St. Patrick's has been taken away and the baby that was lying there is gone. Everybody is back to playing Keno and stealing checks and fucking each other's wives. It's so cold the hairs freeze in my nose and the sky is filled with a hundred jagged fires and so is the city.

On Berkeley Street, I'm just another dude with a high-and-tight

117

haircut. The regulars in front of Primo Likker think I'm crazy, that I see ghosts in the street and skeletons walking. But I'm just following the history, man. A long time ago General Lafayette visited here and old soldiers from the Revolution came out in wheelchairs and crutches, just to shake his hand. Lafayette was a French dude. A survivor.

I see a spot near Primo's and pull in, leave it running. A dude named Jesus is leaning against the wall. He has dreadlocks and wears sandals and shorts, even in January. I know he's going to ask me for a smoke and I have my pack out as I walk up.

Hey-zeus. You seen Olivia anywhere?

Jesus removes a baggie from his pocket, takes out a chunk of hash and packs it into the cigarette. He lights it, presses the smoke for a while, and then exhales. No, he says. Wait. Yeah. I seen her near the Common.

She say anything?

Not to me.

Jesus calls when I walk away. What about that Lafayette dude?

He was a warrior. Straight up.

Word, says Jesus. It's so cold, tears are running down his face.

Back in the car, I skate past some delivery trucks, run down an alley and turn onto Common Street. Inside the park the trees are bare, snow hangs from the bushes, and three crows are eating something on the ground. I don't want to look at it.

I run back on Jackson, cross the singing bridge. It's all body shops and chink restaurants in South Lawrence; mostly I stay on my side of the river. One night I got in a jam with some Latin Kings in front of Mr. Tux and got hit with a chain, but I kept on fighting. Jesus says he knows who hit me. He's in the Kings, but doesn't represent. The windows of Mr. Tux were filled with mannequins. They were staring at me, in their top hats and tails, the fierce army of myriads of men.

Near the Axelrod Mill I see a chick in a fake fur, standing under the archway. The mill is huge and dark behind her, broken windows and shattered bricks, *No Trespassing* stuck up everywhere. Six thousand workers used to pass through these gates, talking in twenty-five languages, going to make cherry pectoral, sarsaparilla, ague cure, hair-restorer and other patent medicines. Now there's nothing but old mattresses and crack pipes and rubbers.

The chick is Olivia. Small and beautiful like a rodent. She sees me and ducks between the two halves of the mill. I leave the car there, start running. It's not mine anyway.

Under a sign that says *Livery*, there's a dude and some black chick lying on pieces of cardboard. The dude has a shaved head with a small blue crown tattooed on his forehead: Gutierrez. Never fuck with a dude who's getting busy. But I gotta find Olivia. I live in the olives of her eyes, man.

Chick go by here? I ask.

Inside the stable there's hay on the ground but the horses are all dead. Gutierrez reaches under the cardboard and pulls out a knife that looks like a sword. I keep on walking.

The two sections of the mill stretch ahead for half a mile. A cherry smell lingers, overpowering the garbage and pigeon shit. As I go along, a car pulls into the alley. It's a Ford Galaxy with no windows and a crown—the Latin Kings insignia—painted on the side. Olivia runs and gets in and the car drives away.

Me and Olivia never had any happy times. One night I took her to the Lobster Pound in Methuen. Methuen has trees and farms and shit. Follow the river and it's right over the city line. A little gray shack with fishnets and buoys. The lobsters were crawling all over each other like bugs. When they dropped 'em in the pot, Olivia stuck her arm in and got burned pretty bad. Later I ate both the lobsters. They tasted like nothing.

A city bus rolls by, with something printed on the side: *Feel desperate? Call the Samaritans*, but the number is scratched out.

*

Now I'm on foot, cars racing over the bridge and dudes are swearing at me. The river is filled with eels. Back in the day they used to call them "Merrimac beef." Nobody eats them now, except the Dominicans. Once I was standing outside Lawton's Frankfurt Stand, crumbling my roll into the canal. An eel came swimming up like a broom handle. Within minutes, there were thirty gangbangers with fishing poles, laughing and singing in Spanish. One dude brought his

119

grill and fired it up on the sidewalk. I got the hell out of there.

I walk by the old jail and Mohammed's Bakery where they make soft bread rounds like a kangaroo's pouch. The city is shaped like a bowl, with the river cutting across and the smell of gas from the sewers. In the old days people worked their way up in the mills, and climbed out to Methuen or North Andover. First the Irish, Italians, Germans, then the Jews, Polish, Lithuanians and the French Canadians. Now it's all Spanish and there's nowhere to go. No jobs, nothing.

Tenements in faded pastels grimed with salt and dirt from passing cars crowd the street. Between a check-cashing place and a three-decker is Al's Time, Inc. Al Nussbaum is an old dude with hair growing out of his ears. His shop is filled with clocks: cuckoos and grandfathers and ship's captains, all of them set to different times and ticking like a million crazy insects. Al is perched on a stool beside the cash register. He grunts at me and looks back at the tiny gears spread over his bench.

It's later than you think, he says.

Al Nussbaum was eight when he took a tour of the Axelrod mansion. As the kids trooped along a hallway, looking at the portraits and shit, Al saw this dude sitting in an office. Old man Axelrod beckoned to him and Al went in, ready to piss himself.

Like it here? the old man asked.

Al was terrified. He said yes.

Then come back when you're goddamn good and ready.

Al has one of Axelrod's clocks. He bought it from the estate when the old man died. It's the only clock he owns that doesn't keep time and isn't for sale.

I'm looking for Olivia, I say.

Al stops tinkering with his screwdriver and put his eyes on me. They're gray and runny. Don't bother, he says. When his back is turned, I reach into the drawer and grab a ten-dollar bill.

See ya, Al.

I'll see the inside of a grave before I see you, he says.

Outside, a greasy wind is blowing. Up ahead is the Galaxy with the Latin Kings in it. After his company failed, old man Axelrod would drive through town and people would throw stones and rotten vegetables at him. Someone had proven that Axelrod's cure was mostly alcohol. Stories appeared in the Boston newspapers and the old man was ruined. But he climbed in his Stanley Steamer every week to visit his boarded up factory. By the time he died, there wasn't a single piece of glass left in the old mill, and his car was a wreck.

In the back of the Galaxy, Olivia kisses the dude with the shaved head I saw with the black chick by the stable. The light changes just as I throw the rock and it arches above the traffic, homing in. For a second I'm not sure whether I want to hit anything or not. Then the rock skips through the back window and rattles around inside. Gutierrez looks over his shoulder and sees me. He smiles and says something to the driver and they keep on going. I keep walking.

Along Broadway, past the taxi stands and *Breakfast All Day* joints and a funeral home with bars on the windows. Dude with peanut skins in his teeth sells me a pack of smokes and two nips at Jacquinto Liquors. He says there's crank on the street and do I want to buy some? Ten bucks. I drink a nip, buy another one and go out.

By the old fire station a dude is selling the same shit for eight bucks. Says it's an after Christmas sale. On the wall there's a rusty hook that the firemen used to hang their buckets on. Dude that ripped off the Kings had his head hung there last week. Nobody dies of cancer around here.

Jesus is missing from Primo's and the streets are getting dark. Climbing Tauvernier Street, I see a kid delivering papers with nunchuks in his hand. One of the football dudes is standing under a street light. He looks at me from inside his hood like he's in a cave.

You seen a car with no windows? I ask him.

Saw a dude with no legs. Ain't seen no car.

I lay one of my nips on him and we drink. I light two darts, give him one. I'm looking for a chick in a fur coat, I say.

He nods toward the old brick mansion. In there.

I give the dude my smokes. Keep 'em, the dude says.

I throw the little nip bottle away. I'm gonna quit, I say.

Me, I'm adding things, says the football dude.

*

121

Outside the Axelrod mansion I find the name Gutierrez and press the button.

What? asks a voice.

I'm looking for Olivia.

There's laughter but no one says anything. Then the buzzer sounds, unlocking the door. The hall is poorly lit and smells of garbage and burnt spoons. Little alcoves that housed Dr. Axelrod's paintings and antiques are soiled with urine and rolled up diapers. LATIN KINGS RUEL is spray-painted across the ceiling.

At the top of the stairs I find #8 and tip the door open. There's no furniture except a legless couch and a hotplate on a stand against the wall. Two dudes are wrestling in the middle of the room and Gutierrez is cooking a spoon on the hotplate. A window is broken and the place is freezing.

For an instant I catch sight of Olivia. Then she's gone behind another door, like a single frame clipped from a movie. Gutierrez is holding the rock I threw at his car.

I want to see Olivia.

The two dudes stop wrestling and stand up. One of them is huge, with cobwebs tattooed on both hands. Lots of prison time. The other King is short, his chest like a stove. Beneath his colors is a T-shirt that says *Genes by Birth, Strong by Sweat.*

Gutierrez puts down the spoon and the other door opens and the black chick comes out. She starts cooking the works, tilting her head and cursing in Spanish. Gutierrez unzips his pants and takes his dick out. It looks like an old yellow worm.

Olivia ain't here, he says.

I am as tall as the short dude, as heavy as the black chick. I am chief Mandarin of the Red Button. My great knowledge surpasses all others, and I am profoundly happy while I live.

Gutierrez's cat slides out from whatever hole it hides in. *Muerte* is just a bunch of wrinkled skin. It looks at me through black eyes rimmed with green and walks away, tail in the air.

C'mon Olivia, I say to the closed door.

Gutierrez reaches into his jacket and takes out the knife. The blade is almost a foot long.

The big dude steps forward. A chain falls from his sleeve. He swings it back and forth like a pendulum. Half a second I'm looking at the chain and the knife comes like a snake in Gutierrez's hand and rips into my shoulder. Blood drips over my fingers.

I was seventeen and Olivia was fourteen. We were on the Common, beneath a hemlock tree that had a plaque cut into its trunk. The bark had grown around it like skin. I sank into her; the scent of lilacs, the softness of petals. Then she took a string and tied it around my *cojones*, releasing it a little at a time. There was a sharp, sweet pain in the middle of my pleasure.

Gutierrez slashes downward, hitting my rib. The blade snaps off. I hear the chain singing through the air. I am in need of sweet curing seeds and fragrant curing drops. I'm on my knees, the Kings all around.

Jesus appears, carrying a baseball bat with nails sticking out of it. He swings the bat at the stove-shaped dude, puncturing his side. Blood squirts out and he falls to the floor, his legs twitching. *Hombre*, what are you doing? asks Gutierrez. But Jesus pulls the bat free and sinks it into Gutierrez's leg. He goes down, the top of his head turning purple. *Ave Maria*, he says.

The big dude swings his chain, pulls the bat from Jesus's hands. Bat and chain fly across the room. Leaping from God knows where, *Muerte* hurls itself at my face. I take the blade of Gutierrez's knife and kill the pink hairless thing called Death.

Jesus grabs the broken haft of the knife and jams it into the big dude's neck. He runs into the hallway screaming.

Now Gutierrez has the bat. He swings it at Jesus, hits him under the arm. Jesus yanks the bat from Gutierrez's hand, unwraps the chain from the handle and begins whipping him with it. Gutierrez is on his knees, saying no, no. There's a wound in Jesus's side and cuts across his forehead. I'm bleeding from the ear.

The black chick comes out naked. You're fucked, she says.

Olivia bolts through the door and down the stairs. The black chick races over to the hotplate, grabs the spoon and a plastic bag and runs out. Jesus has the bat in one hand, the chain in the other. He goes to the window. The Galaxy skids into the parking lot and six

Kings get out.

See you later, Jesus says.

I jump down the back stairs while the Kings pile through the front. There's a rotten cherry smell in the air. I start running down Tauvernier Street. The sky is black and the moon is like a spotlight, shining on me. I race for Salon Del Reino De Los Testigos De Jehova, where I'm supposed to meet Jesus.

Fear of Earnshaw

W rapped in blankets, Max Talbot sat deep in a folding chair, his hair reduced to fuzz and eyebrows hanging in clumps from his forehead. The loose, papery skin of his neck was as yellow as the dandelions covering the lawn. And for a long time very little happened on Tauvernier Street, no cars went by, no deliveries were made, and Max just stared into the abyss.

His mind was depthless and black, but on its inner walls flashed an image of something familiar. Here he was middle-aged again, emerging into the spotlight while a beautiful woman with blonde hair beckoned to him. Max smiled and continued toward her, a great hum of anticipation throbbing in his midsection. Descending from the sky was a huge baritone voice singing, "My Heart Cries for You." But then the spotlight melted away and Max realized it was just his wife, Eleanor, playing his old Vic Damone records.

Upstairs in their apartment, Eleanor cleaned the toilet with a wire brush and swept all the floors, humming along to "Tzena, Tzena, Tzena." For a while she watched her husband through the window but it was impossible for her to sit still for any length of time. Finally, Eleanor crossed the dusty living room and dialed Rita Bachop across the street.

"Dear, how are you?" asked Rita. Beyond her, the sibilant voices of talk radio murmured in the distance.

"Confidentially," said Eleanor, "Max is driving me out of my mind."

"Confidentially" was often the first word out of Eleanor Talbot's mouth, and then everything she said afterward was far from it. Nothing was sacred to her, but she was such an indefatigable source of new gossip that the older women of Tauvernier Street had made her dingy second-and-third floor apartment their headquarters. In those high-ceilinged rooms, judgments were passed on everything from the quality of Lawrence tap water to the digestive rate of its pigeons.

Rita hung up and scraped the rest of her eggs into the wastebasket. She stretched her rubbery cheeks in the mirror, applying rouge, and donned a green nylon cape and daisied hat that Mrs. Talbot had often remarked upon. Then she went outside. The old salt boxes lining Tauvernier Street were empty at this hour—all the children were in school and their parents at work—creating a vast concrete playground for Rita Bachop and Eleanor and their other friend, Mrs. Gurney. Heading up the sidewalk, Rita glimpsed Mrs. Gurney's face for a moment behind the sash and then the octogenarian slammed through her front door and appeared on the street. Together they approached the apartment house where the Talbots lived.

Rita cried out, "Yoo hoo, hello there, Max."

Max Talbot's gaze passed straight through them, and the two women hurried into the house. In the foyer, they could hear Vic Damone singing "On the Street Where You Live" to a brass accompaniment. The haft of Eleanor's broom clunked against the woodwork above them.

"Cleans and cleans to no visible effect," said Rita.

"Dirt sweeping the dirt," Mrs. Gurney said, as they went up.

The door opened before either woman could knock. "Enter, dear neighbors," said Eleanor, flourishing a tray of store-bought cookies. "But wipe your feet," she reminded them.

The apartment smelled of death. Rita Bachop and Mrs. Gurney scraped their Buster Browns against the hairy doormat, peering up another staircase toward Max's bedroom. Along the hallway were several photographs of Eleanor, a plump, dark-haired woman in ski pants and candy-striped sweaters. Old newspaper articles depicted her behind the bar at the Knights of Columbus, one inscribed with the quotation: "In a hundred years, what difference will it make?" Eleanor called this her philosophy of life.

Seated in the parlor now, Rita Bachop motioned for Eleanor to turn down the record player. But their hostess was already riding the exercise bicycle that occupied the middle of the room, churning the pedals with her fat little legs. Facing her, Rita and Mrs. Gurney were sunk into moth-eaten armchairs.

"Go ahead, dear," Eleanor shouted over the music. "Turn it down to your own comfort level."

Rita scraped the arm of the phonograph across *Linger Awhile with Vic Damone*, producing a noise like the singer was being stabbed in the throat. "That's my comfort level right there," she said.

"Why, Vic Damone was a sensation," said Eleanor. "Remember 'Rich, Young & Pretty'? Jane Powell goes to Paris with her father and meets the Frenchman of her dreams, played by Vic Damone. They go splashing through the fountains and the father tries to break them up but they're in love." Eleanor pointed her finger into the air. "Now *that* was a movie."

"And so believable," Rita said. "With a wop playing a frog who sings in English."

"Max always *loved* Vic Damone," said Eleanor, gazing toward the window like her husband was in the ether instead of on the front lawn.

"I never could stand that old dago," said Rita.

Mrs. Gurney grunted her agreement. "Joey Bishop and Sinatra and all the rest of them. How can you entertain anyone if you can't keep your pants on?"

"Hubba-hubba," said Eleanor, the wheel of the exercise bike whizzing around.

"Frank Sinatra never did anything for me," Rita Bachop said. "Ol' Blue Ass."

Mrs. Gurney smacked her false teeth. "I was a dyed-in-the-wool Jolson girl myself," she said.

"That terrible old fart," Rita said, rolling her eyes. "Prancing around in black face like a dimestore nigger. I never had any need of *him*."

"Ladies, have a cookie," Eleanor said from atop the bicycle. "I made them myself."

Mrs. Gurney snorted at the idea. "Made them in a blue and yellow wrapper," she said.

Beside her, the television was like a great sightless eye. Eleanor reached into the smock she was wearing and produced the remote control. "Time for *The Jack LaLanne Show*," she said.

"Time for lunch," said Mrs. Gurney.

On screen appeared a man in his seventies dressed in a tight jumpsuit with massive arms and a smile full of dentures. He did toe touches and jumping jacks while Eleanor rattled the exercise bike, her eyes glittering.

Rita Bachop had to shout over the television. "What is the doctor saying about poor old Max?"

"It's just them hospice people now, wanting to know if he'll donate any of his organs," said Eleanor, spinning the wheel of her exercise bike. "Max had his fun. It's time for me to fill *my* cup."

This shocked even as diligent a busybody as Rita Bachop. Why, Eleanor and Max Talbot seemed wonderful together. Of course, like any couple who had been married for so long, they were a little eccentric. Eleanor dressed her aged husband in shorts and fluorescent T-shirts printed with legends like "Stud Muffin" and "No Fear." Arm in arm, they walked among the handsome young joggers who filled Tauvernier Street after supper. Some evenings, if Max was off socializing at the Knights of Columbus, Eleanor and Rita would sit on the porch tracking the hard curved behinds and jouncing penises of their neighbors. "Look at the striped bass on that one," Eleanor would say. But nothing in her behavior indicated anything but love and respect for Max.

Tapping a finger against the small glass face of her wristwatch, Mrs. Gurney said, "Are you saying Max is *kaput?*"

There was a commercial on the television and Eleanor slowed her pumping legs until the wheel of the exercise bicycle was barely moving. "Any time now," she said.

"That's awful," said Rita. She paused diplomatically. "Do you have insurance?"

"Max paid into something that'll cover the funeral, thank God. Because, confidentially, we don't have a pot to pee in."

The foyer door creaked below them and they heard Max on the stairs. "We better be going," said Rita, glancing at Mrs. Gurney.

Eleanor heaved herself off the exercise bike while Rita and Mrs. Gurney bumped along the hallway. They slowed, came to a halt, and began retreating when they realized there was no way to avoid coming face to face with the dead man. The door opened and he was standing there, yellow and aggrieved and stooped, with a look of mortal terror in his eyes.

"What's your hurry?" Eleanor asked her friends. She had followed them down the hallway with the serving tray in her hands. "Have a cookie."

Clutching their handbags, Rita Bachop and Mrs. Gurney wore terrified smiles and made a quick detour around Max without addressing him. "Toodle-oo," said Rita, as the women plunged down the stairs. Outside they hid behind the scabbed trunk of an oak tree, measuring the distance they had come.

"That knocks the eyes out of the potato," said Rita.

Mrs. Gurney was leaning against the tree in her car coat. "He's carrying all that cancer 'round in him like it was coal," she said.

"Ugh. Would you go to sleep with that in the house?"

"I most certainly would not," said Mrs. Gurney.

Rita muttered something about laundry and then veered toward her apartment. In a second she had disappeared inside, locking the door behind her. Still clutching the oak tree, Mrs. Gurney remained hidden, gazing upward at the contaminated house.

*

Max stood in the hallway while Eleanor washed the breakfast dishes. When his wife had screwed the taps shut and slammed through all the cabinets, he called out in a quavering voice, "Whatcha doing, Mama?"

Emerging from the kitchen with a large slice of cake and diet soda, Eleanor said, "Go upstairs, Max."

"What about my medicine?"

"You don't need it," Eleanor said, indicating the way to his room. "Now get up there, and let me have some peace."

129

Max Talbot started his body in motion by leaning, and then swung a leg out to catch his weight. Propelling himself that way, he stalked to the foot of the stairs and began trudging upward. He glanced over his shoulder, but his wife was still there.

"Go on," she said.

When Max reached the halfway point, Eleanor picked up her soda and cake and bustled into the other room. On the landing Max gripped the banister with both hands. His head swam with stars, and he felt like he was trapped in an immense void. Then he pitched forward again until his leg rose involuntarily, and he began mastering the upper flight.

The pungent odor of fried ham filled the top floor, although the thought of food made Max sick to his stomach. He felt all right in the morning, good enough to watch Eleanor cook her early meal. Then his strength began to waver and the nauseating smell of breakfast would chase him upstairs. He spent most of his time there now—time that he sensed was growing short.

Nudie magazines spilled out from beneath his bed. They formed a slippery layer underfoot and he nearly fell, catching the edge of the mattress with his slim behind. Large velvet portraits of women covered the walls, squatting on their haunches, their great varnished breasts protruding like artillery shells. On the nightstand his television depicted a quivering field of snow and Max lowered himself onto the mattress, keeping his gaze there.

He fidgeted with the rabbit ears and the television came into focus. Three young women were exercising as strange, syncopated music pounded away in the background. Their flesh jiggled and Max turned away, groaning. "Stop," he said.

Max had fancied himself a ladies' man until age sixty-seven, when it grew impossible to drink and carry on at his old rate. Then, after ignoring pain in his abdomen for some time, he was diagnosed with liver cancer. Neither surgery nor chemotherapy offered any hope, although the doctor said certain drugs could "mitigate" his distress. Max began taking the pills on a very strict schedule, as if he expected to recover. But their effectiveness soon faded, and he was left with a growing ache in his midsection.

Max turned off the television. Groping over the side of the bed, he picked up a *Hustler* magazine and flipped through the pages. Vic Damone was singing again, his voice creeping upstairs. After a few moments, the invalid tossed the magazine aside and faded into reverie.

Once long ago, a carnival performer named Wicked Wanda had selected Max from among the audience and led him over broken peanut shells into the spotlight. Forcing him to his knees, Wanda grasped Max's head and one shoulder. Then she told him to stand and he struggled upward, legs trembling. As Max rose into the brilliant cone of light, he felt Wanda jackknife into a handstand. Gripping the bony knob of his skull, she flicked herself into the air, somersaulting twice against the inky backdrop of the canvas. The acrobat rocketed past in a torrent of yellow hair, elongated breasts and flashing legs. An instant later, she landed in the sawdust, her arms thrown up. There was prolonged applause and Wanda crooked her hands, welcoming it.

Later that night, Wanda fastened Max to the bed with bright silk handkerchiefs. Then she did a handspring onto the mattress and squatted over him while Vic Damone sang "An Affair to Remember" from a transistor radio. Loosening her hips until she grasped Max's pecker with her silky inner muscles, the acrobat went thrusting up and down. "How's that for a trick?" she asked, but Max was speechless.

For months afterward Max brought one blonde after another into the Knights of Columbus, even when Eleanor was working behind the bar, yet he never approached the bliss of that night. As time advanced, the thought of what had occurred inside that circus trailer left him feeling angry. No woman ever seemed as exciting again, certainly not Eleanor, who satisfied herself by eating cake and pedaling across her living room.

The velvet nudes stared down at Max with expressions of disgust and recrimination. He took Eleanor's rosary from the bedpost and felt the polished nuggets between his fingertips. But his Hail Marys wouldn't go anywhere—they stopped at the thick dull membrane of the ceiling. Abandoning his prayers, Max's growl started low in his chest and then spilled over into wrenching sobs. From the lower floor Vic Damone's baritone again rose toward him, crying in a great tremolo over lost youth and lost love.

*

The next day Eleanor was sitting on her front porch when the ambulance arrived. Seeing this, Rita Bachop threw on a housecoat patterned with tiny raspberries and hurried over. The attendants were already inside the apartment, and their voices could be heard coming from the upper floor.

"Confidentially"— Eleanor began, cocking an ear. She held up her hand to prevent Rita from speaking. "Wait. Here they come."

The paramedics carried Max outside. Clutching a set of rosary beads, he turned toward the women with a helpless look on his face. Then the attendants slid the stretcher into the ambulance and zoomed off with a howl of sirens.

"—I never let that old buzzard touch me," said Eleanor.

Rita couldn't think of a reply. She pulled at the joints of her fingers and then glanced downward, where the raspberries on her housecoat looked like tiny brains.

"When I cut the thread, that's it," Eleanor said. "You just wait and see."

In the fragrant June morning there were hints of an earlier time, and Eleanor recalled her life as a young woman. She was twenty-six years old when she had married her first husband, a Navy reserve pilot named Alfred Earnshaw. Other than the usual wedding night activity, the gallant young pilot barely touched her or said a word. She chalked it up to nervousness, the strain of the coming war in Korea, and perhaps an element of self-denial that kept her husband poring over flight manuals and lifting weights in the basement.

The day he left for Portsmouth, Eleanor awoke at dawn and prepared an elaborate breakfast of sirloin steak and eggs, with a pot of coffee and fresh orange juice. Earnshaw came downstairs in his dress whites, carrying his sea bag. He passed through the kitchen, ignoring the carefully arranged table and Eleanor's best silver, which she had received as a wedding present. *Ain't you gonna eat before you go?* she asked. Earnshaw didn't look at her; he had hitched the sea bag over his shoulder, and stamped through the tiny hallway and out the back door.

Mrs. Gurney emerged from her apartment on a pair of crutches and was laboring up the sidewalk. She had a large bandage around her knee. "Oh dear, what happened?" asked Rita.

"I gashed myself with a peach pitter," said Mrs. Gurney.

Her friends rushed down the stairs. "When I get my beads back, I'll say a rosary for you," said Eleanor.

"I didn't know Max was such a good Catholic," Rita said.

"There's no atheists in foxholes," said Eleanor. "I've looked more than one in the eye and said 'Go to hell, you bastard.'"

*

In the chapel of Higginbottom Funeral Home, Vic Damone was singing "You Were Only Fooling (While I was Falling in Love)" from a tape Eleanor had provided. She sat flanked by Rita Bachop and Mrs. Gurney among a sea of empty folding chairs.

The lone Knights of Columbus representative, Mr. Cote, was a small man with cheap hearing aids in each ear. He wore a crimson sash across his chest and stood at parade rest next to the coffin. Inside it, Max Talbot aimed his waxy nose at the ceiling. A search through Max's closet had produced only some Hawaiian shirts and a pink Nehru jacket, none of which were acceptable burial outfits. So Eleanor had purchased a blue serge suit from Higginbottom for a hundred and twenty-five dollars—a good deal, she remarked to her friends, if Max was going to wear it more than once.

Faint dots of blush colored the dead man's cheeks, and the hair inside his ears had been trimmed. "Anyway, he looks his best," said Rita.

Mrs. Gurney signaled her agreement. She had donned a shiny, blue-gray wig for the occasion but it was a bit too large and she felt it slipping whenever she nodded her head. "Everything is hunky-dory, as far as Max is concerned," she said.

Mr. Cote crossed to where Eleanor was sitting. He spoke with a French Canadian accent, mingled with the static from his hearing aids. "Pardon me, Mrs. Tal-bot," he said, tapping the plastic seashell in his right ear. "I have to go make water."

The tape ran out and silence reigned. Then the roar of a miniature lion could be heard and at once the ladies realized it was coming from Mrs. Gurney's stomach. Covering the sound, Rita gazed toward Max's body and said, "It must be hard to say goodbye after all those years."

"*Sayonara*," said Eleanor. "He had tons of women but he never had me, the poor sap."

This was like gold to Rita Bachop and Mrs. Gurney, currency for all those nights on the stoop. They sat and waited for more.

When her first husband had shipped overseas, Eleanor thought she was pregnant and began drinking milk shakes to soothe an upset stomach. Alfred Earnshaw would serve for a year, and in the delicious early quiet of their separation she wrote to him about the baby that was on its way. A daughter, she imagined, something soft for them to cuddle and fuss over. Writing it down like that made the child seem definite. But after a month of increasing discomfort Eleanor went to see a doctor, who probed with his metal instrument and said there was no baby inside her. And because of a cyst, which was removed, there never would be. Then came a visit from the Navy chaplain and the news that Earnshaw had been shot down and captured by the North Koreans.

A year passed, and then one day Eleanor received a telephone call from the chaplain. Hours later, a car arrived and Earnshaw limped up the front walk. He was so thin his ribs showed all around and he had scars on his neck where the North Koreans had attached electrical wires. Eleanor threw open the door, with lipstick carefully applied and her hair colored a rich shade of brown, but Earnshaw stumped past her into the house. *Where's my daughter?* he asked. *Where's my little girl?* In a fumbling minute Eleanor described her mistake. Standing on the carpet in his baggy dress uniform, Earnshaw's face was blank with the hate showing only in his eyes. An odor of scorched linens filled the room. Then he threw down his sea bag and descended into the basement.

For six months Earnshaw avoided going out. But the Navy requested that the ex-POW attend a Knights of Columbus dinner for local veterans. Fortified by bourbon, he lasted through one speech—something about his "heroic incarceration"—then got up and left the hall. When Eleanor arrived at their apartment a short time afterward, Earnshaw came up from the cellar and struck her across the face. The beatings, administered in silence, became routine after that but Eleanor never told anyone.

Except for Max Talbot, who came into the bar every afternoon and drank Gin & Squirt. Only once did Max offer a comment, after learning that Earnshaw liked to masturbate into her cold cream jars: "That's what divorce court is for," he said. This piece of advice intrigued Eleanor. Overall, she knew very little about Max until one day he announced that his wife had died of pneumonia. Since his nine-year-old son, Maxie, had no mother, getting one was his first priority. A few days later, with Vic Damone singing "Say Something Sweet to Your Sweetheart" from the Wurlitzer, Max and Eleanor agreed to get married.

"When I worked at the Knights, Max would take his bosomy blondes in there," Eleanor said. Her gaze moved away from the coffin, settling on one of the cheap ceramic vases littering the room. "We never loved each other."

The chapel door swung open to reveal a tall, middle-aged man wearing a seersucker jacket and orange silk tie. His hair was combed back with some sort of goo that shone under the recessed lights of the entranceway. Eleanor hadn't seen Maxie for almost twenty years. While she remembered him as pale and slender, the red-faced man approaching her was stuffed into his coat like a sausage.

Max Talbot Jr. stopped several feet away. "Hello, Eleanor," he said, without extending his hand. "You look good."

"As good as anyone with two dead husbands can look," she said.

An obese man in a friar's outfit entered the room. The rope around his waist cinched his bulk into upper and lower flab that rolled beneath his tunic as he moved. Whispering for a moment with the undertaker, the friar came before the tiny congregation. He cast a meaningful glance at the corpse behind him and then his eyes rolled back in his head. "Oh, Gawwd, let us pray," he said.

Mr. Cote tapped at his hearing aids, and the friar continued: "To-day we will lay to rest the mortal remains of" —here the friar referred to a scrap of paper— "Mack Talcum. What is a sad time for his wife Helen—Ellen—is a joyful time in the Kingdom of Gawwd. For life on earth is like a diseased tooth. It aches us and it pains us. But Gawwd has filled the cavity of Max's life with the silver of heaven."

"I didn't know Max had such lousy choppers," said Mrs. Gur-ney.

The friar plunged ahead. "So join me, brethren, in praying that Gawwd will soon uproot us all from the pain of this life and fill our many cavities with his heavenly grace. Ahh-men."

The friar blessed the coffin, and then swung around to grasp Rita Bachop's wrist. "I'm sorry for your loss, Evelyn," he said. "May Gawwd comfort you in these trying times." Then the friar moved off, his flesh sloshing back and forth beneath his tunic like motor oil. He accepted an envelope from Higginbottom and departed through the front door.

The undertaker cleared his throat. "That concludes services here at the funeral home," he said. "Now I'd like to ask the pallbearers to step forward."

Eleanor nudged Mr. Cote and the little man sprang up, per-formed several deep knee bends, and took his place at the head of the coffin. Supported by her friends, Eleanor bent close enough to see the glue holding Max's lips together. "So long, pal," she said, making a noise between her teeth.

As Higginbotton began closing the coffin, Eleanor scolded her stepson. "Maxie! Say something to your father."

Maxie looked like a man peering over a cliff. "Good luck," he said.

The undertaker motioned for Mr. Cote to pick up the front end, and he and Maxie hoisted the rear. As they rotated toward the front door, Mr. Cote allowed the nose of the coffin to dip and the body thudded against the flimsy inner wall.

"Steady now," said Higginbottom. "Let's not tarnish Mr. Talbot's memory."

The ride to the cemetery was short and bumpy. Several cars intruded on the procession and Mrs. Gurney, sitting beside Eleanor in the limousine, made a harumphing sound. "They won't be in such a hurry when it's their turn," she said.

Seeing the cemetery jarred Eleanor into thinking about her first husband. The newspaper had reported that Alfred Earnshaw's death was accidental, but at the time Eleanor remarked to Rita and Mrs. Gurney that no one, leastwise a decorated war veteran, cleaned his gun by looking down the barrel. On the day of Earnshaw's funeral, she took a taxi up to Bellevue. It was a rainy November morning, and there still must have been close to fifty cars in the procession. The ceremonial *pop* of rifles and an echoing version of taps reached Eleanor where she waited outside the gate. When the last car had driven away she approached the grave, which was covered by a tarp with the name of the funeral home printed on it.

The headstone lay among thousands of identical white markers decorated with American flags. Footprints dimpled the muddy ground, and bits of metal that turned out to be shell casings. The coffin, suspended across the grave on canvas straps, was fixed with a plaque that contained a replica of Earnshaw's war decorations. Red geraniums were scattered all around.

From a concrete building some distance away, Eleanor could make out several workmen with shovels coming toward her. Quickly she drew a wedding ring from her pocket. It clattered over the coffin, slipping into the space on the other side. "In a hundred years, what difference will it make?" she asked.

For Max Talbot, the Knights of Columbus had purchased a cemetery plot that was very close to the road. Balancing the front end of the coffin, Mr. Cote crossed a springy plank running lengthwise across the grave. There was a breathless moment when the little man almost lost his balance, but he danced sideways, righting himself. Then Higginbottom removed the plank and the three men lowered the coffin onto canvas straps.

Passing cars and the whir of heavy trucks obliterated every other sound. Across the street, an old man was clearing brush with a chainsaw. As the traffic cleared, Higginbottom opened his mouth to say a prayer but the roaring chainsaw blotted him out. Twice the undertaker paused and began again, only to be interrupted by the saw. *"Jesus Christ!"* he said in the abrupt silence, recovering with, "Redeem us, O Lord."

The canvas straps groaned, then one broke and the coffin pivoted downward. The body fell against the clasp and tumbled out. Fingers still laced together, the corpse was suspended over the remaining strap wearing only the shirt, tie, and suitcoat, which was split up the back to make it one-size-fits-all. "Where the hell are his *pants?*" asked Eleanor.

"My suits don't come with trousers," said Higginbottom.

Mrs. Gurney and Rita Bachop gasped. Down in the hole beneath their feet Max Talbot looked like the victim of a crime. His jaw had come unhinged and a great piece of cotton batting hung out of his mouth. Confronted by a withered, half-naked version of himself, Maxie ran away, tramping over dead flowers and wreaths. Meanwhile, Higginbottom was straddling the corpse, arms encircling its waist, his soft white face puckered from the effort. The coffin was half in and half out of the grave.

"It's like a goddamn circus," Mrs. Gurney said.

Tears streaking his face, Mr. Cote said, "He was my friend." Leaping into the grave, he hoisted Max's translucent ankles. With Higginbottom lugging the corpse's shoulders, they forced it upward into the gaping coffin.

Breaking into sobs, Eleanor wobbled off in her high heels. Some distance away was a marker with the inscription: *Alfred P. Earnshaw, United States Navy.* "You son-of-a-bitch," Eleanor said, stamping on the sod. Her heel caught in the turf and she fell onto the grave.

"Please, dear," said Rita, hurrying over. "A hundred years from now, what's it gonna matter?"

Eleanor remained face down, pounding the grave with her fists. Hands curved into talons, Rita and Mrs. Gurney grasped at her.

The Philosophy Shop

Business was slow. People I had known all my life went by on their way to mail a letter or out for a quart of milk, and a few waved or mouthed hello. But most of them ignored me.

It was only in jest that my father had said, "What are you going to do with a degree in philosophy, open a little philosophy shop?" But after I graduated *summa cum laude* from Johns Hopkins, and a dissatisfied client had shot my father to death, his law office was empty, *ergo*, I took my modest inheritance and negotiated a lease with the landlord. It occurred to me that the good people of Carter, Massachusetts, had more than enough information on the divorce rate, the unemployment rate, the incidence of hair loss among men in a certain economic bracket— "of sailing ships and sealing wax," as it were—and what they really needed was knowledge, or *gnosis*, a pure intuitive way of seeing. And the idea was for them to pay for it, a valid notion, because as Benedict de Spinoza had written in 1671, all ideas are always true.

The October sky was bright and shining and I was about to close up when the door opened, letting in a gust of cold air and a young woman. She was no more than five feet tall, with the huge dark eyes of a bunny. "Is this a pottery shop?" she asked.

"This is the Philosophy Shop."

"Oh, sorry," said the woman, her eyes drifting over the shelves and glass display cases and finally back to me. She was standing at the counter, smiling faintly, hands on her neat little hips, and I couldn't help noticing the curious antiseptic odor that followed her when she

139

moved. "I washed my bra in dish soap last night and it smells funny," she said.

"I don't find it at all troublesome."

She introduced herself as Hilda Holloway, and we shook hands. "Max Berman, Jr.," I said. "Call me Mickey."

"So Mickey, what sort of philosophy are you selling?" asked Hilda.

"It's not a commodity, per se. I deal in philosophical inquiry."

Hilda seemed confused for a moment. "People...give you money for that?"

"A little. I haven't exactly worked out my fee structure yet."

Hilda thrust out her lower lip and nodded. Her hair looked soft, gleaming in the afternoon light that fell through the windows. Once or twice I caught a whiff of her bra and had to stop myself from speculating what color it was, whether it was made of silk and hitched in the front or the back.

I reached into a paper bag under the counter and took out an apple left over from my lunch. "An apple is 'good.' But 'good' is not round or sweet or nice-smelling. You can't take 'good' out of an apple like you can take out the seeds. Can 'good' exist by itself in time, not as a property? No. As G.E. Moore wrote, 'Everything is what it is, and not another thing'."

Hilda fished in her pocket and took out a crumpled five dollar bill. "I'll buy that," she said.

The door opened again and one of my few regular customers bustled in: Walter Wnek. Besides my shop, there was a bakery, liquor store, florist, dance studio, tavern and gas station in the town square. Walter owned the garage at the bottom of Tauvernier Street. With little formal education, he had discovered philosophy only recently and was learning that his common sense approach to life had deeper roots. Walter was a big, hairy man, about sixty years old, wearing filthy overalls with his name stitched on the breast pocket.

Walter Wnek took off his greasy workboot and banged it on the counter. "Here is a material object, therefore, material objects exist."

"Have you never been fooled by what appeared to be a material object?" I asked him. "Have you never dreamed of being chased by a horrible monster, only to wake up and find yourself safe in bed? So if your senses have been deceived before, isn't it possible that you are forever being deceived? That this room and everything in it—even the three of us and our accumulated history—do not really exist?"

Walter Wnek, his lips set in a grim line, exerted pressure through his sinuses that caused his face to turn crimson and his eyes to pop out in horror. The boot fell to the floor.

"Mickey Berman, you're a real pain in the ass," he said. Hilda handed him the workboot and he put it on the counter. "What about this morning, when I was banging on Billy Nagle's transmission and whacked myself in the thumb?" asked Wnek. "That wrench and my thumb felt pretty real then, goddamnit."

"Real objects are based on a sequence of repeated impressions," I said. "The pain in your thumb was real because you had performed that action before, and each time, the sensation was the same."

"I never stuck a knittin' needle in my eye before, but if I did it just once I'd probably say it was real," said Wnek. His hands, grimy and unadorned except for a gold wedding ring, clutched the front of his overalls. The thumb on that hand was twice its normal size and the nail was missing. "I don't need a philosophy to know when my eye's been put out."

"The wrench you hit yourself with—it's back at the station," I said. "You're not experiencing it at this moment. Is it an object, or an idea?"

Wnek pulled at his grimy hair. "It's a damned wrench," he said. "It's an object."

I picked up the boot. "Like this? Even though we aren't experiencing the wrench with our senses, like we are the boot, it's an object like this?"

Wnek twisted his hair into whimsical shapes, pulling his lower lip down until it nearly touched his chin. "It's different, I guess," he said.

"It's an object when we're experiencing it, an idea when we're not," said Hilda.

Wnek seemed grateful for the help. "I'm picturing the wrench in my mind," he said. "It's an idea."

"The wrench is inside the gas station. So it's an idea inside an idea?" I asked.

I thought Wnek was going to lunge over the counter at me. "Look, for crissakes, Mickey, I know the goddamned wrench is there on the floor of the garage where I left it," he said. "I don't know how I know, I just do."

"When you're not thinking about the wrench, it's no longer an idea. Does it cease to exist?" I asked.

Wnek seized the apple on the counter and took a gigantic bite out of it. Three more snaps of his jaw and it disappeared, seeds and all. "Where is it?" he asked. "I can't see it, but I know it exists. You're not aware of it, but you know it's real. It's not an object, and it's not an idea. It's an apple."

"Walter, you have cut the Gordian knot," I said.

He shook his head. "No, I ate the goddamn apple, is what I did."

"That's it. Now you're doing philosophy."

Wnek flashed a grin. "I'm the only empiricist around," he said. "Shit, I have to get back to work." He crossed to the door and was outside and turning up the sidewalk before he realized he only had one boot on. He glanced through the window at us with a look of surprise on his face and rushed back in for the boot. Hopping in a circle as he pulled it on, he said, "Do a little philosophy and you don't know whether to stand on your head or whistle Dixie."

Over by the window, Hilda watched him rush off down the street. "So that's how it works," she said. "People come in with questions and you ask questions about their questions. Next thing you know, the customer is walking out with one shoe on and there's enough unanswered questions lying around, if they were bricks, you could build a house."

"Like I said, I haven't worked all the bugs out yet."

"To put it mildly," Hilda said. Eyes dancing, she added, "I don't think the world is ready for Philosophy Shop franchises."

I came out from behind the counter in my frock coat and leggings. "Why, what do you do for a living?"

"I teach dance."

"Oh, that's real lucrative, no doubt," I said. "There must be a dancer lurking behind every bush."

Hilda wagged her finger at me. "I believe that's an *argumentum ad hominum*—arguing to the man and not the issue."

"Well, it's good to see your mind is not a *tabla rasa*—blank slate."

Hilda squeaked with delight. "You are relentless," she said.

Cleaved by the afternoon light, she stood half in darkness and half illuminated. All her curves and small protuberances glowing with St. Elmo's fire, Hilda was transformed into what Aristotle called *entelechy*, a thing fully realized. Thus transformed, she entered through my eyes and lodged herself in my heart. From that moment on, I would have to reconcile my frequent intellectual dissatisfactions with the various twinges and agonies Hilda Holloway put me through. The early Greeks called it *agape*; the Latin poets, love.

"I've never danced," I said, drawing near her, careful to step around the spot on the floor where my father's body had lain. Our faces were almost touching. On the windowsill a plaster bust of Plato stared at me with eyeless sockets, and my courage wilted.

"What's the matter?" asked Hilda.

"This seems...premature. The actions of men are not the same as stones falling. Physical love was of little interest to a figure such as Plato."

Hilda looked at me with those deep, dark, bunny eyes. "But you're not Plato, are you?" she asked. "Don't be a donkey and pin the tail on yourself."

I grasped her in my arms. "Oh, Hilda," I said. Then I kissed her: *pneuma*, life's hot breath, a mingling of souls. The inside of Hilda's mouth was warm and sweet; it beckoned to other pleasures. I wanted to run into the square and kiss her on the traffic island. After a long moment, we broke and I said, "Have dinner with me tonight."

"I can't," said Hilda.

A sudden gloom descended, and my arms dropped to my sides. "Fate," I said. "Only humans are free to believe they are predetermined—this is the ultimate irony."

"I'm not married or anything like that," said Hilda. "I'm just busy tonight. We'll have dinner some other time." She raised herself on tiptoes and kissed me on the cheek. "You think too much."

The door opened and closed, and she was gone. I started to dance around the shop but caught myself. The world's greatest philosophers were gazing at me, in their pince-nez and mustaches and glossy white hair, or else skullcaps and vestments or pleated togas; mature men, not given to such outbursts.

Decorating the walls of the shop were pictures of Bertrand Russell and Augustine and Jean-Paul Sartre, Friedrich Nietzsche and Thomas Hobbes, the crusty Scotsman David Hume, all my idols. Left behind like didactic grandfathers by most students of philosophy, I intended to deliver them from the forgotten corners of the library into the mainstream. Like so many business partners, they lined my pockets, if not with money, then with solid good sense.

I stopped in front of a lithograph of Augustine, the angry saint, and a conflicted, mystical and sensuous man. "Hilda is really cute," I said.

"God, give me chastity, but not yet," said Augustine.

Further along the wall, Aristotle spoke up. "One swallow does not make a summer."

"I know that. But upon seeing her, I just felt there was a connection, what Plotinus called, 'the flight of the alone to the alone,' " I said.

"Don't say 'felt,' say 'concluded'," advised Thomas Hobbes.

"I was looking for a kind of passionless, cool life," I said. "And now, if I think of myself, I can't help being 'self-ish.' "

Hume said, "It is not contrary to reason to prefer the destruction of the whole world to the scratching of my finger," and Aristotle finished the discussion with, "The bird of youth is soon on the wing."

Before locking up, I filled a pail with warm water. Then I got on my knees and scrubbed the fading bloodstains on the floor. My father had left a real mess and I was forever cleaning it up. I was a regular Lady Macbeth about that.

It was dusk. At the top of the square was Barr's Tavern, standing black against the sky. The glow of its lower windows curved into the soft yellow light of the doorway, welcoming me. Bent nearly double, I pushed against a strong wind on my way up the street, the ends of my coat snapping like a flag, my Jean-Jacques Rousseau haircut streaming out behind. Leaves flew past me in frenzy of red and gold, scratching along the pavement and spun into miniature tornadoes that rattled against the beveled glass entranceways of the shops and then disappeared. A town truck passed through the square with three workmen on the back and they jeered me, their voices ringing in the empty street.

"Hey, it's the philosopher."

"Get a job, you fucking sissy."

The third man was silent, gripping a stanchion fastened to the truck bed, his face wreathed in shadow. "*Gnote se auton,*" I called to him. "Know thyself."

Heavy, vaporous light mingled with the smell of roasting meats inside the tavern, blurring the figures ranged along the bar and in front of the fireplace. Beneath the low ceiling, the rumble of conversation was punctuated by clattering silverware and the steady clink of glasses.

Walter Wnek was having dinner with one of his employees, Gus, the tow truck driver. In front of them were T-bones that had been picked clean. They were drinking highballs. "Walter," I said, coming to the table. "As gold is exchanged for wares, wares are exchanged for gold."

He mumbled something and stuck his nose in his highball glass.

"*In vino veritas,*" I said. "C'mon, fellas. The next round is on me."

Gus cut at the air with his hand. "No, thanks. My doctor said if my dick was as hard as my liver, I'd be in the movies."

I went to the bar and ordered highballs for Walter and me. "Fivefifty," said the bartender.

"The metallic existence of money is only the official sensuous expression of the very soul of money existing in all branches of production," I said, quoting the young Karl Marx.

"Five-fifty," said the bartender.

I rewarded him for his alienated labor and turned back with a drink in each hand. Walter Wnek gestured toward the door, staring in that direction. At the entrance, waiting to be seated, was a middle-aged man with slicked back hair. He was wearing an iridescent green suit and talking into a portable telephone. It was Rocco Savinelli, making a spectacle of himself, watched over by a baby-faced hulk whose muscles bulged through the raincoat he was wearing in spite of cloudless weather.

Savinelli was a well-known extortionist and wheeler dealer. He was also the man indicted by a grand jury for shooting my father.

"What the hell is he doing out of jail?" asked Wnek.

"An excellent question," I said.

Accessorized by a thousand dollar suit, the telephone and his goon, Savinelli commanded a great deal of attention until Hilda Holloway came in. She wore her hair loose to her shoulders and a snug skirt, drawing wolf whistles from Gus.

"She's got an ass like a little paint can," he said.

As the object of my love eclipsed the object of my loathing, then separated into two distinct entities, like a cell dividing, I felt my heart tumble in my chest. I wished for an instant that I was a man of action: a swift karate movement on the bodyguard precipitating Savinelli's total surrender, followed by an appreciative Hilda arrayed like Venus on a rumpled bed. But I was more of a dualist than a duelist; a "thinking thing," standing there like a statue of Descartes, the highballs numbing my hands.

Savinelli turned and began flirting with Hilda, who smiled and tugged on the edge of her skirt. Black waves of jealousy swept over me, and I had to remind myself that the object of my idea is never a body-out-there, as I apprehend it; rather, it is merely a statement-of-my-body-caused-by-a-body-out-there.

"That son-of-a-bitch killed your father," said Walter Wnek. "You're not just going to let him stand there, are you?"

"Reason itself does not move men to action. Passion animates us," I said.

Wnek thrust his chair aside. "If you're not going to do anything, I will. Your old man was a friend of mine. I beat Uncle Sam out of a few bucks every year thanks to Max Berman."

Before Walter Wnek was even halfway to the door, bulldozing through the tables, Savinelli's goon had spotted him. Closing in,

Wnek reached for Savinelli, apparently to tap him on the shoulder. The guy in the raincoat turned and broke Walter's hand with a single sharp pop.

A little shove from the goon and Wnek stumbled out the door, clutching his damaged hand. "When the other guy is that big, keep your seat," said Gus. "You ain't fixin' no transmissions with a busted hand."

"In my sympathy, I am not feeling Walter's pain," I said. "I am only re-feeling a similar emotion I once experienced myself."

Ignoring the disturbance, Savinelli offered an arm to Hilda and pointed to a vacant table. Her eyes searched the room. Finally noticing me, Hilda broke his grip and came over—floating, it seemed, and attended by a glowing blue outline of aromatic mist.

"I made it," she said.

"Your arrival, coinciding with the appearance of Rocco Savinelli, underlines the Greek notion of deity," I said. "Although most are followers of Christ, not Plato, it is evident there is a 'logos' steering through this universe, not a 'nous' outside of it. A crazy quilt of interconnectedness." The din of the tavern enveloped us and I ran my hand across Hilda's aura. "Don't you see—the soap in the men's room looks like pink lemonade. This demonstrates the waywardness of man."

"Sit down," said Hilda, pulling up two chairs. "I was with you right up till the pink lemonade."

Over by the windows, Savinelli and his bodyguard, down to their shirtsleeves and suspenders, were talking in loud voices. I told Hilda about Savinelli's bogus real estate company and the strong arming that had left my father in a bloody heap on the floor of his office.

"He shot your father?" asked Hilda. She reached for my hand and held it. "How terrible."

"Walter was right," I said. "Evil should not be ignored. The criticism of weapons can never replace the weapon of criticism." Springing to my feet, I took a plastic bottle from the condiments on our table and rushed toward Savinelli. "Philistine," I said, squeezing a yellow stream of mustard in a double zigzag across his shirt and tie. "An unexamined life is not worth living."

The mustard container made a deep gasping sound. When I felt the container re-inflate itself, I squeezed again. The projectile of mustard landed in Savinelli's eye.

"I can't see," he said.

The bodyguard knocked the mustard container to the floor and grabbed me by the collar. Dangling above the table like a marionette, I said. "O, men of Athens, while I live I shall never stop exhorting you and pointing out the truth."

"Mr. Savinelli?" the bodyguard asked, holding me in the air with one hand. Hilda flailed at him with her tiny fists. I felt my heels swinging and customers at the other tables stared with their mouths open, stunned into silence.

"Put him down, Bruce," said Savinelli, dabbing his eye with a napkin. "No harm done."

The bodyguard released me and Hilda fluttered into my arms. "Did he hurt you?" she asked.

"Only insofar as rendering someone totally helpless is painful," I said. "I sustained a fractured ego and nothing more."

A waiter arrived and made an attempt to remove the brilliant yellow M that decorated Savinelli's chest. He sent the waiter away and his bodyguard out for some cigars, insisting that Hilda and I join him for a drink. I refused.

"Then don't drink," said Savinelli. "You're one helluva talker. Let's talk."

Recalling something from Thomas Hobbes, I said, "Words are the counters of wise men and the money of fools."

"Then what I'm going to tell you is like money in the bank. Sit down," said Savinelli, raising his pulpy face to mine, the mustard staining one eye. Reluctantly I took a seat and Hilda perched on the arm of my chair. "Max Berman and I were in business," said Savinelli. "A very complicated investment business. He wanted a bigger return. I said no. He produced a gun, we struggled over it, and I was the lucky one."

"That's not the truth," I said.

"The prosecutor thinks so. I have papers with your father's signature on them. His prints are all over the gun. That's how it happened."

It was true that my father's fingerprints were on the murder weapon and that there were no eyewitnesses. It didn't follow that Savinelli had acted in self defense. His guilt had disappeared behind an eclipse of circumstantial evidence and legal maneuvering. But the law was not the truth. According to Montaigne, the law was whatever was plausibly asserted and vigorously maintained.

"My lens and compass do not focus on eternity," I said. "However, your version of what happened in my father's office is a lie."

Savinelli rested his large hands on the table. "Then you tell *me* what happened, wiseguy," he said.

I reached in my pocket and found a quarter. First holding it up for inspection, I threw it across the table and Savinelli caught it. "There—that's the truth," I said.

"Twenty-five cents?" asked Savinelli.

"Not the object—the action. There is an undeniable reality to the kinetic transaction that just took place, a validity that can neither be enhanced nor diminished with words. It simply is, or more exactly, *was*. My father *was*. He existed in space and time. The motion of your body, activated by your mind, modified by the velocity inherent in the muzzle of the gun, produced an irresistible kinetic force—a truth—that transformed Max Berman from 'is' to 'was.' Or from our perspective this evening, from *was* to *is not*. That conclusion is irrefutable."

Hilda pinched me on the earlobe in concurrence. Savinelli was dumbstruck. He looked at the two of us, and at the quarter nestled between his thick red fingers. "I don't have the slightest fucking idea what you're talking about," he said.

Hilda and I stood up. "You're right. Philosophy is a science fiction adventure of the mind," I said, opening the flaps of my coat. "And the philosopher is like a flasher. Take that."

"Don't push your luck," Savinelli said. "I'm not someone you want to fuck with."

"As my father certainly discovered," I said.

Savinelli rose from his chair. "You squirted me with mustard. And said some kind of bullshit"—he threw the quarter down—"to make fun of me. Now you've pissed me off. That ain't too smart."

His bodyguard came back in with a fistful of cigars. "I got two kinds, Mr. Savinelli."

"Just pay the goddamn check, Bruce," said Savinelli, wrestling with his coat. He pointed at me. "I'm about to make an investment in your little business."

"The Philosophy Shop is a sole proprietorship," I said.

"Now you've got yourself a partner," said Savinelli. With that, he spun around and left the tavern.

Hilda clutched my arm. "Do you know what you're doing?" she asked.

"Calculating the consequences of every action is for politicians, not philosophers," I said. "I have no idea what I'm doing."

Going outside, we heard the sound of breaking glass. In front of the Philosophy Shop, its window marred by a gaping black hole, Rocco Savinelli stood on the sidewalk unearthing another brick with the toe of his shoe. A persistent wind blew leaves through the square, and I ran toward him, shouting Zeno's paradox: "Before any distance can be traversed, half the distance must be traversed. These half-distances are infinite in number. It is impossible to traverse distances that are infinite in number."

Behind me came a sweep of headlights, the grinding of gears, and Walter Wnek's tow truck rumbled into view. Savinelli took no notice of it. "This is your lucky day, smart ass," he said.

A few feet from him, I tripped on some loose bricks and stumbled forward. Hilda grabbed at my coattails to steady me and I went headlong into Savinelli, who stepped backward off the curb and was knocked out of his shoes by the tow truck. He landed in the street with a vicious thump, his tongue hanging out and his chest peaked in the middle like a tent.

Brakes squealing, Wnek flung open the door and leaped to the pavement. "I was on my way to the hospital. I didn't even see him."

Hilda and I got up from the sidewalk. It was obvious that Savinelli wasn't breathing.

"He needs an ambulance," said Wnek, and dashed off toward the tavern. We approached Savinelli's inert, mustard-stained body lying in the gutter, and Hilda said, "We should do something."

I looked down at the dead man and a pair of kidskin loafers, size 13. For the second time today, Walter Wnek had cut the Gordian knot. It occurred to me that the ancient Greeks were right: what appeared as randomness in the world is merely our inability to comprehend. The steering of all things through all things.

Taking Hilda by the hand, we stood in silence for a moment and then I recited the skeptic's prayer. "O, God, if there is a God; save his soul, if he had a soul."

The Messenger

A short while after the end of our marriage left me weeping in a courthouse stairwell, I realized that my ex-wife Delores was sending coded messages via our eight-year-old son, Riley. Because of what had occurred on a rainy Saturday afternoon not long before our hearing, the judge ordered Delores and I not to have any contact with each other, but one day when I picked Riley up from school, he was wearing a wrinkled green T-shirt that hung on his scrawny frame like a rag. LAS VEGAS was emblazoned across the front of the jersey; the city Delores had escaped to during the first weekend of our legal separation, whisked there by a mysterious suitor and in whose draped and overdecorated rooms my wife of nine years had performed acts of salacious and gymnastic wriggling that I could only begin to imagine.

I work in a paint store. Ten hours a day, six days a week, thinning, mixing and stacking gallons of oil and latex and satin, explaining the nap of rollers and the nozzle velocity of sprayers and the coverage capability of over forty different brushes, imported and domestic. Tauvernier Street Paints is family owned and I'm not a member of the family that owns it, and can only hope after all these years that I might work my way up to assistant manager some day.

Right before our son was born I had saved enough money to buy a nice little cape on a half acre of land and used my discount to paint every square inch of that house: Navajo white ceilings; canary in the kitchen, burgundy in our bedroom, and sienna and magenta in the foyer and halls. Afterwards, Delores went through with her stencils and printed a frieze of giraffes and hippopotamuses around the upper edge of the baby's room and then painted our ceiling black and edged it with a hundred gold stars. We finished at sunset on the third day and stood on the lawn gazing at the house, which glowed resplendently in its new coat of vermilion. And although we were both freckled with paint, chips of eggshell white turning up in our pubic hair days later, we went to bed that night beneath an apron of golden stars and slept the deep, contented sleep of children. We had made a home for ourselves.

Delores is a six-foot redhead with a flat chest and slightly bucked teeth. But she has marvelous green eyes and an ass as round and hard as an overinflated volleyball. We met one sultry June evening, at a church carnival. She was walking through the midway when a giant spinning teacup broke loose from its moorings and crashed through a retaining fence, scattering nuts and bolts and causing old women to scream in fear.

Delores went down like she'd been shot and I was right there, holding a plume of cotton candy the size of a hibiscus and feeling a little like Saint Sebastian as shards of metal flew past on all sides without touching me. In the welter of shouts and sirens and calliope music, I knelt beside Delores and she looked at me, her eyes a bright surreal green with a trickle of blood running down from where she gripped her upper arm.

When I reached over, my cotton candy brushed against her and the blood melted a hole through to the plume's core and at once I felt Delores' gaze eating straight through me.

"I'm hurt," she said, as I grasped her wrists and pulled her up.

Immediately the air was charged with a million curved and vibrating particles that migrated across the space between us and into the halo of lights strung across the churchyard and over and through our body tissues and bones. It wasn't love at first sight; it was chemistry, and chemistry is guided by laws that human beings are powerless to resist.

We fought a lot. But there were days when we never got out of bed, thrusting at each other like demons in a half-blissful and half-tortuous and ultimately failed attempt to either merge into one person, or be rid of each other for all time. Instead we rubbed ourselves raw

153

and lied there panting in the sheets, determined that the next bout would be our last.

Riley came from that sort of effort. A short while after he was conceived, we were married on a dock extending into Cobbett's Pond, the water flat and black all around and the minister in his frock coat and long white hands declaiming the verse in a baritone that rang to the other shore. It was cold there in October, the leaves down from the trees and rotting in the shallows, and a small knot of friends and relatives huddled together on the stony beach. Delores wore a garland in her hair and when the reverend fixed me with his pale blue eyes and announced that I could kiss the bride, I held Delores by the hand and we plunged into the frigid water, our breath escaping in large, wobbly dirigibles as we sank to the bottom, cleansing ourselves.

Riley was our treasure, our reward. He's small and smart and funny and weak, with his mother's green eyes and my hair, blond and spiked up in the back like a crown of thorns. The day that Delores and I split up he crouched behind an old wooden rocker on our front porch for an entire day, refusing to answer his mother, who insisted that if he ate something he'd feel better. A couple days later, when we met in a city park for our first visit after "the incident," Riley said that his mom tried to fill the hole in his life with chicken soup. But the soup ran through the fissures of his heart like blood and he fell on the kitchen floor and convulsed like someone possessed by the spirit.

The Las Vegas shirt was an insult, an affront to my manhood and as damning as any pornographic photo. Because even to the last minute I couldn't believe I'd be divorced; before I knew it, I was living on this guy Jerry's sofa, all my belongings jammed into a trio of cardboard boxes and stowed in the hall closet. Digging through them I found a T-shirt that would fit Riley and surprised the boy by ripping the Las Vegas shirt from his back and tossing the remnants into the wastebasket.

"Mom bought me that," said Riley.

I was standing in front of him, my chest heaving. "I know she did, and I can't stand looking at it."

*

Leaving Jerry's place after dinner the tailpipe fell off my old station wagon and I had to rummage around in the crawlspace for a roll of duct tape and some rope. It took fifteen minutes but I was able to cinch the ragged ends of the pipe with the tape and then wrap a length of rope around it. Then I cut off the excess rope with a hacksaw and threw the saw, the rope and the duct tape into the backseat and headed across town.

I was late bringing Riley home, and stopping the court-ordered 150 yards from my house, I could see Delores standing outside. Riley kissed me and walked away, his backpack slung over his shoulder, crossing the demilitarized zone between his mother and me like a little refugee. In the faded evening light Delores was there at the edge of the sidewalk, her hair dyed blonde and a tilt to her carriage from the high heels she was wearing. It had been many weeks since I had seen her. From this distance all I could make out was the staring skull holes of her eyes and the flash of her mouth as Riley approached and she smiled.

He was wearing the same T-shirt I always sent him home in; different shirts, to be precise, but always hanging to his knees and always with the same logo on the front; they contained the only thing I had to say, imparting the one sentiment I could be firm about—the place where I spent all my time and expended the effort that put food on their table and a roof over their heads: *Tauvernier Street Paints.*

Delores put an arm around Riley and led him into the house. Neither of them looked back, and I climbed into my car, slammed the door and drove away, the tailpipe rattling. An old Procol Harem song that Delores loved came on the radio, and I felt the blood rush to my face and my skin grow hot. For years I had marinated my soul in the half-truths and lies of our union and now it was roasting in the fires of jealousy.

The messages continued, and so did my agony at the dissolution of my marriage. No one can tell when a relationship begins to go south, but I can pinpoint the exact moment when my connection to Delores was severed for good. She was on her way out for the evening, dressed in a pair of black leather pants that flattered her rump and a maroon jersey that dropped over the pale white flesh of her shoulders.

Her mouth was reddened with lipstick and she wore dangling silver earrings that caught the light from the ceiling fixture in our kitchen. I was on a stepladder, painting the inside of the cabinets. The floor was covered in newspaper and the space around me was redolent of paint thinner and brewing coffee while rain beat against the windows.

"Where you going?" I asked, glaring down from my perch.

"Out."

Descending from the ladder I blocked my wife's path to the door. "This is the third night in a row," I said.

"It's a free country," said Delores.

We had fought so much over the previous month that we were hardly speaking to each other. Things were so tense, Riley was staying at Delores' mother's house and I busied myself every night after work repainting what I had painted only six months before. On Sundays, I'd put on my old white pants and a store T-shirt and paint the kitchen or the hallway or the bathroom from before sunrise to well after dark. It's what I am.

Delores stood there on the paint-spattered newspaper with a cold green look in her eyes. The ions that for so long had migrated between us had disappeared and staring across the gulf of our tiny, acrid-smelling kitchen was like encountering a space too large to comprehend, like the distance between stars.

"You're not going anywhere," I said.

Delores continued past me. "Like hell I'm not."

Without thinking I dipped my paintbrush in the open gallon and applied a long broad stripe from the side of Delores' face to the hollow behind her left knee.

"How's that?" I asked.

She glanced back at me with abject hatred and pushed through the side door and into the gloom of the yard without looking back. A moment later, I heard the car starting up and the beam of the headlights swept across the windows and into my eyes and Delores was gone. I didn't see her again until we went to court.

*

I studied Riley's shirt every day like a scholar poring over a tablet of cuneiform. Sometimes I could divine next to nothing from an empty sweatshirt or turtleneck. But even when his torso was blank there was her scent when I embraced him: rich, yeasty, warm, like the smell of coffee grounds and fresh baked bread. Things went day to day, my spirit rising and falling on the tides of domestic geography. Often my heart would enter a black and desolate country as places I'd never been scrolled across my son's chest—*New Orleans; New York City; Virginia Beach is for Lovers*—the content of Delores' life in those places remained an enigma and I mourned the lost hours and what she had done there. Then my hopes soared when I'd spot a conciliatory *Hampton Beach, New Hampshire,* where we had honeymooned, or Riley's navy blue pullover from the *Cape Cod National Sea Shore,* where the two of us had walked hand in hand, eating fried clams from a striped cardboard container while Riley ran ahead, flying a kite.

That afternoon we spread Riley's homework over a TV table in Jerry's living room and I sat on the couch beside him while he tackled the long division.

Gathering my nerve, I asked, "How's your mother?"

Riley glanced at me. I never said much about Delores in his presence, although I hectored Jerry through entire Sunday afternoons on the subject of my ex-wife. He'd be watching a football game with a tumbler of whiskey in his hand and I'd stand there orating like a demented Socrates.

"She's the same," said Riley.

"The same as what?"

Riley stuck the blunt end of a pencil in his ear and began turning it. "Same as always."

I was not the same, nor would I ever be. "Get that pencil out of your ear," I said.

"Mom lets me do it."

I grabbed the pencil and threw it across the room. "I don't care if she lets you stab yourself in the eye with needles. You're not gonna do that here."

Riley shrugged. "You are who you live with," he said.

"Yeah, and you live with me," I said.

We both knew that wasn't true and Riley just looked at me with his mother's eyes, embarrassed somehow, like I had just stubbed my toe on a church pew and uttered a vulgarity.

*

At Delores' mother's house last Thanksgiving, our little family had sat around a table groaning with potatoes and peas and gravy and asparagus, drumsticks the size of a man's arm, and little crystal bowls containing wax beans and herring in cream sauce. The smell was a medley of roasted meat, warm pumpkin pie, sweat diluted aftershave, and Delores, always Delores, and her invigorating personal scent of lavender and yeast.

When the coffee was brought out, Delores stirred in a tiny spoonful of sugar and knocked the edge of the cup against her bucked teeth. We had quarreled about money before dinner. Money was always shorter than a pygmy at our house.

Riley was buttering a roll. Delores' mother was there, in her turkey print dress and woolen shawl, deaf as a haddock and looking like a mannequin with dentures.

"If you had any balls, you'd open your own store," said Delores. She had been drinking wine all day.

We kept our voices low and Delores' mother looked at us with a smile on her face, uncomprehending. But Riley had stiffened. "I could go broke in my own store," I said.

"At least you'd go broke in *your* store, not somebody else's," said Delores.

Later that night, we were driving along the highway in the rain when we came upon an accident. Smudge pots had been laid in the roadway and here and there the spent cylinders of road flares were lying amongst two or three that still fizzed and sputtered white-hot against the pavement. A large number of emergency vehicles were lined up along the guardrail, throwing blades of red light. At the end of the long row of fire trucks, police cruisers and resuscitation vehicles of every sort was the victim's car: a squashed block of a sedan, all four tires missing, lying on its roof beside the highway like a discarded toy.

Just as we rolled onto the scene, a vignette unfolded on the shoulder of the road: a dozen firefighters in their long-brimmed helmets and canvas coats stood in tableau around an unfolded tarp, with something lying inert at its center. In the strobe of revolving light the firefighters heads were bent, their faces dirty and grim. They looked exhausted, out on a holiday night answering calls. At that instant, a hearse entered the cordon and glided up to the firefighter's heels, shiny and black in the rain, arriving like some harbinger out of the gloom.

Over the next few seconds, Delores, who was sitting beside me in the passenger seat, was illuminated in three different attitudes by the light that flashed into our car. It looked like the strip of photos you get from a booth at the beach; the smooth planes of her features registering only mild interest in the first pose. Darkness inhabited the car for an instant and when the light arrived once again a subtle change on Delores' face produced an expression of fear mingled with prurience, like she had witnessed something carnal by the side of the road. The space around us went black like in an old vaudeville skit and in the final image, my wife had turned toward me, her lips parted, the small dark secret of mortality—hers, mine, Riley's, and the dead man's on the highway—revealed in her eyes.

In that unexpected and tender moment I realized that the end is always coming closer, and that I had hurried it along through my own foolishness, as people often do. At a costume party that Halloween I'd sneaked out to the car with a girl wearing harem pants and a glittering bikini top. Delores and I had quarreled and I was drunk. She never had an inkling that I had cheated, but there at her most vulnerable I looked into her eyes in the dim reflected light from the roadway and she knew that she had been betrayed. If I could have exchanged places with the dead man on the tarp, I would have. I had thrown away the most valuable thing in my life, all for some Spanglish fuck puppet from Dorchester.

On the other side of the highway, police and fire were arriving at a second accident: rubbernecks gazing across the median at the fatality had collided, and now there were more travelers down on the pavement. Some people. They just don't know when to fucking quit.

*

By Christmas I was out of the house and living at Jerry's full time. Jerry is a crazy, wild-haired kid who has few interests besides drinking whiskey and watching porn. He's late to work at the paint store three or four time a week and would've been fired a long time ago if he wasn't the owner's nephew. His apartment is on the top floor of a three decker on the corner of Broadway and Tauvernier Street; four rooms filled with stinking throw rugs, mismatched furniture and at least a dozen empty Jameson's bottles.

Hoping that Riley would be visiting me on Christmas Day I went down to the YMCA and bought a stunted pine tree and nailed it to a cross made of two boards and while Jerry lay on the couch nursing his hangover I decorated this humble little tree with a string of colored lights and a dollar's worth of tinsel from the Five & Ten. In her absence the figure of Delores had grown to Brobdingnagian proportions, looming on the horizon, a giantess whose laugh was like thunder and whose approach on those days I was allowed, a glimpse of her rattled the horizon.

Jerry doesn't have a phone and I spent all of Christmas day in the parking lot of the Li'l Peach calling my old number. Either they weren't home or Delores wasn't answering and I looked up her mother's number and started calling that. The old lady is hard of hearing and no one answered there either, and I switched back to the other number. I did it all on the same fifty cents.

Stamping my feet, I stood on the frozen pavement blowing on my hands and watching the cars go by. During the morning hours I bought a large coffee and a guy from the bowling alley came by and spiked it with rum. It seemed like every other car contained a smiling husband and wife and their handsome children, the extra space piled high with brightly wrapped packages. As the afternoon waned there were more solo riders, empty taxicabs and cop cars, Broadway gradually taking on the desperate character that inhabited it the rest of the year. One by one the lights went out along the strip and as my telephone calls became less frequent I lost all hope of visiting with my son. Finally the heavy metal screens were lowered on the Li'l Peach and the clerk, a twenty-year-old kid with a lot of piercings and tattoos locked the front door and strolled away. When he crossed the filthy parking lot the kid was whistling little bits of "White Christmas" in a pure sweet tone. By seven o'clock even the punks and junkies on lower Broadway had somewhere else to go.

In complete darkness I went up the six flights of stairs leading to Jerry's apartment, my boots heavy on the treads. Pushing open the door I smelled the old whiskey and a thousand microwave burritos along with the paint smell that was woven into all of our clothes. Jerry was lying on the couch watching a video starring a skinny black girl, a man large enough to be a Sumo wrestler and a collie. Without a word I crossed the room, threw open the largest of the windows and grabbed the Christmas tree by its base. With one swift movement I stuffed the tree through the window and it fell with a bristling thump into the alley.

Jerry sat up. "What'd you do that for?"

"Christmas is over," I said.

*

In May, huge flocks of ravens and starlings roosted on the wires above Broadway. I was promoted to assistant manager, found an apartment half a block from the store, and was buoyed by the soft east wind. Tufts of grass were flourishing among the vacant lots, and Riley's T-shirts began to acquire a milder tone: *Give Peace a Chance*, *Jesus Christ Superstar*, and *Ask Me if I Care*. Then, one day, I picked Riley up from school and he was wearing a clean, pressed *Tauvernier Street Paints* T-shirt. I had sent those home on him for weeks and he'd never worn them and now they appeared five days in a row, like an apparition of the Virgin Mary materializing on a slice of toast or a dirty windowpane.

On that fifth day, Riley was supposed to go to a Cub Scout meeting at Iglesia Evangelica Hispana. I never could stand those things and made arrangements for another dad to keep an eye on him while I went out to kill some time. Over on Broadway, I ran into Jerry and the two of us went to the Ace of Clubs around six PM and drank beers. After two or three, we began chasing them with shots of Jameson's. I played a skein of old country songs on the jukebox and draped myself over the bar, with the heavy, beveled mug in my hand.

"She still loves me," I said, finally.

Jerry dropped a shot of whiskey into his beer. "Who?" he asked.

"Delores."

Jerry shook his head. "That ship sailed a while ago," he said.

I swallowed the whiskey buried in my own pint. "It's coming around for me," I said.

Jerry stared into the bottom of his glass. "I saw Delores the other day. At the post office," he said. "I didn't mention it to you because, well, I didn't." On the jukebox, Lefty Frizzell was singing about a woman from Tennessee. "She was at the counter, mailing a letter or something."

Jerry gazed at the shining row of liquor bottles above the bar like he was scanning the horizon for something. "When I saw her—" He turned to me, his eyes dark and earnest and sad, booze lines carved into the sides of his face. "She was...you know. She looked happy."

The clock over the bar showed 8:15; I was supposed to pick up Riley at eight. I left Jerry in the company of the bartender and raced along Broadway to my car and fired up the engine. Delivery trucks and vans and low riders with mag wheels and tinted windows crowded the roadway, blasting Latin music. I inched along, sweating and cursing and pounding on the dash.

After dark, the neighborhood around Iglesia Evangelica Hispana was no place for an eight-year-old boy, when the gangbangers and crank dealers and streetwalkers came out. It occurred to me that Riley was only half mine but when he was staying with me, I was responsible for both halves. What sort of Old Testament king would have split our son down the middle; a lung, a kidney, a testicle apiece; ribs popped off one by one; his blood pulled away from itself like the parting of a sea, and each of his cells divided into their proprietary halves until his genetic code unraveled and his mother and I were each left with a jellied mass of protoplasm.

When I arrived at Iglesia Evangelica Hispana just after 8:30, the church was dark and the parking lot was empty. A wild rush of panic surged through me and I stopped the car in the middle of the road, sodden with whiskey, enervated by fear and burdened by a host of my own mistakes. Without thinking I stomped on the gas and headed for my old neighborhood, where Delores and I had once been happy; where Riley had been safe.

Driving along I noticed the fluorescent orange "Violation" notice stuck under my windshield wiper. One of my headlights was broken, I knew, and the side mirrors had been snapped off the car while it was parked. As I entered my old street, the revolving light of a police car swept across the house fronts, illuminating the underside of shrubs and the ghostly limbs of the trees. I felt drawn toward the spot where Delores stood, crying and hugging Riley, the sturdy figure of a policeman nearby, his hat in his hand.

Every single good I had ever done was blotted out and, gliding forward, the car expanded around me like an airship, skimming the clouds. I closed to within fifty yards, ten, five, ruined by drink, the backseat of the station wagon crowded with rolls of duct tape, lengths of rope and hacksaw blades. In his Cub Scout uniform beside the policeman Riley looked militaristic and stern. Delores glanced at me, her blond hair cut into a pageboy and falling over her eyes, and I knew I was doomed.

Radio Call

It was after midnight, the sky obscured by clouds and threatening snow with piles of it already lining the road. With the chill seeping in the windows of his cruiser, police officer Rick O'Keefe was talking to his wife Tammy on his cellphone when he got a radio call about a fight inside a bar across town. Static filled the cruiser and O'Keefe reached over to turn his radio down.

"Is that for you?" Tammy asked.

"Yeah, it's just a fist fight or something."

"Where?"

O'Keefe switched on his revolving lights and pressed on the accelerator. "The Rabbit Hutch," he said.

His wife snorted. "You love their waitresses."

"I'm a regular," said O'Keefe. The hood of the patrol car rose as he zoomed down the center of the road. Claireborne, New Hampshire was a little retail town on the Massachusetts border, population 23,000, and very few cars moved along the town's main thoroughfare at this hour.

"Well, be careful," said Tammy. "Call me."

"I'll see you in the morning."

"Love you. Bye."

It was true; Rick O'Keefe had visited the Rabbit Hutch six times in the past two and a half weeks: unruly patron, bar fight, counterfeit fifty dollar bill, driving under the influence, another fight, and serving alcohol to a minor. The waitresses at the club were tired-looking former cheerleaders and strippers dressed in skimpy black outfits—

most of the trouble at the bar spread outward from there. With its collection of bikers, local hard guys and drunks, the Rabbit Hutch was a little bit of hell on earth.

O'Keefe confirmed for the dispatcher that he was, in fact, on his way to the Rabbit Hutch. Estimated time of arrival: three minutes. A lot could happen in those three minutes. Most often, fists fights were over, wives had been beaten, husbands were two counties away, and banks had been thoroughly robbed by the time the cops arrived. Therefore, good people skills were more important than marksmanship or physical strength when it came to police work.

O'Keefe pulled up to the Rabbit Hutch at the same moment as another patrol car, driven by his friend, Kevin Imbriacco. O'Keefe and Imbriacco were both pushing forty, with young children and stay-at-home wives, working seventy or eighty hours a week to cover their mortgages. The biggest difference was, O'Keefe had only been on the cop job for three years, after a stint in the Coast Guard, six years as a boat salesmen, and seven years as an insurance investigator. Imbriacco was a sixteen-year police veteran, having taken the examination and gone straight into the academy right after the Marine Corps.

"Hey, rookie," said Imbriacco, as he emerged from his cruiser. He slammed the door shut, shoved his nightstick into the loop on his utility belt and stood there on the pavement. "Heart rate up?"

"I pissed myself on the way over," O'Keefe said. "Feeling much better now that you're here." He was half a foot taller than the other cop, dark-haired, jug-eared, with large hands and a bump in his nose where it had been fractured playing hockey as a kid.

Imbriacco grinned. "Pay attention," he said. "You might learn something."

The Rabbit Hutch was little more than an old storefront, pressed right up to the street, with a broad, steel-reinforced door flanked by two plate-glass windows. The name of the bar was printed on each of the windows in large block letters with a pair of stylized bunny ears underneath. In the moment before the cops headed for the door a patron emerged; he was about sixty years old, wearing Gas Company overalls and a dark blue woolen cap with earflaps.

"Was there a fight?" asked Imbriacco.

The man was drunk; his eyes spun in the revolving light from the two cruisers and he planted and replanted his feet, struggling to remain upright. "No fight in there, officer," he said.

Imbriacco moved closer to the man. "You're not driving, are you?" he asked.

The man glanced at the parking lot across the street, where nine or ten cars occupied the spaces closest to the bar. "No, sir," he said. "I'm walking."

"Wise choice," said Imbriacco. Following the man's gaze he noticed that one of the vehicles in the lot, a rusty green Town Car, was lit from within and a man in the driver's seat was lolling over the wheel.

Hitching up his belt, Imbriacco spat into the roadway and started toward the parking lot. "I'm gonna check that out," he said to O'Keefe. "Go look inside."

"Roger," said O'Keefe, slotting his nightstick into the metal loop on his belt.

Imbriacco approached the Lincoln with his hand on the butt of his service revolver. When he got close, the sturdy Italian cop signaled to O'Keefe that it was all right, and O'Keefe approached the door of the Rabbit Hutch.

"What should I do?" asked the man from the Gas Company.

"Go home," said O'Keefe.

The tall, dark-haired cop pulled open the door and went inside. Last call had already come and gone, and a half dozen inebriated customers were blinking in the glare of light from the bar, their drinking and their alcohol saturated fantasies interrupted by the incursion of state law. There was an odor of beer and toilets, and a mixture of cheap shaving lotions also hung in the air. All of the patrons but one were male, and all of these men, except for a husky young fellow in a motorcycle jacket, were over the age of forty. The kid in the black leather jacket was perched on a stool, talking in a low voice to a woman nearly twice his age, a peroxide blonde wearing thigh-high boots and a purple mini-skirt. *Warlords* was stenciled across the back of the man's jacket.

"Who saw the fight?" O'Keefe asked. It was obvious to him that the combatants, whoever they were, had departed some time ago.

Behind the bar, a redhead wearing a tight leotard was building a wall of clean beer glasses brought up from the dishwasher. When she bent over, this young woman, who was no more than twenty years old, displayed a significant amount of cleavage that Rick O'Keefe tried not to look at.

"Who was fighting?" O'Keefe asked the barmaid.

"Not me," she said.

Halfway down the bar, a middle-aged man in a soiled dress shirt was restocking the coolers from a hand truck piled high with cases of beer. It was Mike Hutchinson, the bar's owner, an oily character who had moved to New Hampshire from Rhode Island and had done a stretch in federal prison for extortion. Married for the third time, Hutchinson was known for sleeping with his waitresses, which was another source of turmoil at the club. Most only stayed a couple of months, when they figured out they weren't about to become the fourth Mrs. Hutchinson.

"No fight in here, officer," said Hutchinson.

O'Keefe moved down the bar. "I took the call," he said.

The kid in the motorcycle jacket spoke up. "It wasn't much of a fight," he said. "One guy did the punching, and the other guy did all the bleedin'."

Over the radio attached to his collar, O'Keefe heard his partner tell the dispatcher that he was in the parking lot across from the Rabbit Hutch with the victim, a 29-year-old Caucasian male named Tommy Broscoe. He had multiple lacerations of the head and face, one eye had been damaged, and his tongue was partially severed. Imbriacco requested that an ambulance be sent.

"Oh, those guys," said Hutchinson. "They didn't fight in here." He gestured toward the darkened windows. "Whatever happened, happened outside."

O'Keefe turned and stalked out of the bar, the kid in the biker jacket right behind him, pulling the middle aged blonde by the wrist. When they reached the sidewalk, the kid stepped in front of O'Keefe and said, "I ran out here with some dude from the Gas Company and broke it up. Tommy was hurt pretty bad."

"He was bleeding," offered the blonde.

Their breath formed little white plumes in the air. "The other guy was really drunk," said the biker. "All night long he was saying how he had a gun, and how he was gonna come back and use it on Tommy."

"He specifically said he was going to shoot him?" asked O'Keefe.

The biker nodded. "He said he'd been cleaning his gun all day and that he would blow Tommy's head off with it."

"What's the guy's name?" O'Keefe asked.

"I don't know."

"What does he look like? How big is he? Big as me?"

Sizing O'Keefe up, the biker said, "A couple inches shorter. About two hundred and something pounds. Military haircut."

"Where did he go?"

The biker pointed down Main Street. "That way. He was on foot."

Two weeks earlier O'Keefe had arrested a husky ex-Marine with a criminal record, who lived in a small apartment a few blocks from the Rabbit Hutch, on Pleasant Street. His name was Chip Murtaugh and a look at his file indicated that he'd been arrested six times for assault and battery and convicted twice since his discharge from the service eleven months ago. All but one of the arrests had occurred in the proximity of the Rabbit Hutch.

Although the mention of Chip Murtaugh's name had zero effect on the biker and his frazzled blonde conquest, O'Keefe jogged the kid's memory by describing the tattoo on Murtaugh's right forearm. "Yeah," the biker said. "USMC in red and black."

Writing down the biker's name, address and telephone number in a small, wire-bound notebook, O'Keefe handed the kid a pasteboard card with his own name printed on it and the non-emergency number at the PD.

"Will I have to go to court?" the biker asked.

"I'm sure you know the way," O'Keefe said.

Across Main Street, an ambulance had entered the parking lot, its beacon striping Kevin Imbriacco's face as he stood up and waved the EMTs over. O'Keefe met Imbriacco over near his cruiser, which was still running, and the two cops stood there in the well of light from a streetlamp.

"How is he?" asked O'Keefe.

"I think he's gonna lose his eye," Imbriacco said.

The two EMTS had propped the beating victim against the side of the ambulance and were inspecting his wounds. Even from sixty feet away, O'Keefe could make out a large Rorschach of blood on Tommy Broscoe's shirtfront. More blood covered the interior of the car.

"He won't say who did it," Imbriacco said.

"It was Chip Murtaugh," said O'Keefe. "One of the guys who broke up the fight said Murtaugh has a gun. He's been talking about it all night."

Imbriacco reached inside his cruiser and reported these facts to dispatch. The sergeant on duty ordered both cruisers to proceed to Murtaugh's residence. "See you there, rookie," said Imbriacco, jumping into his patrol car.

His siren keening, Imbriacco made a quick turn out of the parking lot and roared down Main Street. Just as O'Keefe reached his car, there was a general radio call, "Code Three," ordering all nine cruisers in service to Murtaugh's address.

"Shit," said O'Keefe. He grabbed the radio. "One seventy-six. On my way. Out."

It was just a few blocks to Pleasant Street and O'Keefe raced along at eighty miles an hour. Glued to his dashboard was a strip of photographs depicting his nine-year-old twins, Dylan and Fiona, and his wife. They had been taken at the beach the previous summer, the kids tanned and rimed with salt, dressed in swimsuits and little terry cloth jackets. In the first two pictures, they appeared together, arms around each other's necks, smiling at the camera. In the final image, Tammy had popped up between them, her mouth describing an exclamatory "O", all three of them laughing. O'Keefe wasn't there; he'd been working an overtime shift that day.

As he skidded onto Pleasant Street, a second general call erupted from the radio. This time, the dispatcher, a calm, rotund fellow who had been moving police cars around the grid for ten years, was shouting in a thin, high-pitched voice. "Code Three. Officer reports shots fired. Repeat: shots fired. Everybody *get there now*."

Ahead, Pleasant Street was empty but for the two police cars already in front of the rickety gray Colonial where Chip Murtaugh lived. Jumping on his brake, O'Keefe stopped behind Imbriacco's patrol car and leaped out. It had begun to snow. Falling in large flakes across the yard, the dots of snow brought a weird tranquility to the scene; they were as fat as goosefeathers and just as light.

The snow was deep here and O'Keefe labored up the slope toward the house, which was fringed with bushes. It was like running in a dream, the house moving away from him as fast as he could approach, plunging through the crust to his knees, unholstering his weapon as he came. The acrid smell of gunpowder hung over the yard. Keith Imbriacco was off to one side, crouching with his service revolver in both hands, aimed at a figure lying prone among the bushes. The other cop, Larry Wasilowski—31, unmarried, a former prison guard—was edging closer to the man on the ground, also pointing his weapon.

"Get up," said Wasilowski. "Let go of the gun. Show us your hands."

A series of groans came from the man in the bushes. O'Keefe leveled his weapon at the suspect and glanced over at Imbriacco. His friend looked back at him; although he was less than fifteen feet away, it was like Imbriacco was staring across a chasm. Before tonight, neither man had ever fired his weapon, except at the training range. Now, Keith Imbriacco had shot a man.

Wasilowski was talking into the radio transmitter attached to his collar. "The suspect is down. He has a gun. Shots have been fired. Repeat: shots have been fired."

Sirens were approaching from every direction. "He has a shotgun. It's underneath him," Imbriacco said to O'Keefe. "We're not sure if that's all he has."

Everything was happening fast for O'Keefe, but each image became frozen for an instant in a snapshot. The falling snow added to the sensation: the façade of the house was seared forever into his memory, the darkened windows, the shrubs capped with new flurries; Imbriacco in silhouette, arms and weapon extended, like an action figure, a policeman made of wax. Each little movement that O'Keefe made was deliberate and clear. His hearing was especially keen; behind him, half a football field away and thirty feet off the ground, a squirrel clambered up the trunk of an oak tree.

O'Keefe's training took over and he did and said things without thinking of them first. Little things he had picked up, as far back as the academy, directed his actions like the hand of some unseen assistant. *Keep moving. Don't put your finger on the trigger unless you have a target. You're not being paid to get beat up or shot. If there's a threat of serious harm, shoot him before he shoots you.*

The area between O'Keefe, the other cops and the suspect, who was still obscured by the bushes and falling snow and the darkness (*Why is it so fucking dark?* thought O'Keefe), was called the "funnel of death," a triangular shaped zone that was mapped out by their intersecting fields of fire. An hour ago, it had been just another patch of snow-covered front yard and now it was as dangerous a place as anywhere in the world.

"I'm gonna move him," said O'Keefe, gesturing at the suspect.

Just as O'Keefe stepped forward, a woman wearing green pajamas and an old peacoat ran across the yard, barefoot. "Chip. What did they do?" she said.

Without a word, Rick O'Keefe holstered his weapon and grabbed the woman as she ran toward the suspect. Encircling her waist with both arms, O'Keefe dragged her through the snow.

The woman struggled against him. "They shot Chip."

"If you get anywhere near there, you're gonna get shot," said O'Keefe.

He managed to drag the woman around the corner of the house, where he tripped over a rake or shovel buried in the snow, but somehow maintained his grip on her. Rising to his feet, he saw a man rushing at him through the spinning blades of snow, a large fellow in a red and black hunting shirt and khaki pants. "Get your hands off her," the man said.

Holding onto the woman O'Keefe reached out and grabbed the man by the throat as he arrived, lifting him in the air. The man pulled at O'Keefe's forearm and wrist with both hands, sputtering and choking.

"I'm trying to help her, you stupid shit," said O'Keefe. "Back off."

His eyes bulging, the man looked toward the street where a horde of police cars were arriving and back at O'Keefe; he nodded, indicating that he understood. When O'Keefe released him, the man took the woman by the arm and they retreated toward the rear of the house.

"They shot Chip," said the woman, staggering through the drifts.

The man pulled her along. "Shut up," he said.

All this took only a few seconds. O'Keefe ran back to the scene as a New Hampshire State Trooper in his broad-brimmed hat and wielding a large, black revolver, charged up the snow covered walk. Imbriacco and Wasilowski remained a short distance from the suspect, yelling at him to show his hands. The man groaned, thrashing in the undergrowth.

On instinct, O'Keefe slipped behind the shrubs and alongside the house, grabbed the suspect by the collar and dragged him out of the bushes. The man was over two hundred pounds of dead weight; O'Keefe pulled him through the knee-deep snow, digging in his heels and straining backward. The suspect's coat rode up, exposing three bullet wounds in his torso. The holes were small and red; very little blood came from them.

It was Chip Murtaugh, all right. He was groaning from deep inside his chest and writhing in the tamped down snow. O'Keefe recognized his tattoos and thick, heavy shoulders. He had talked to Murtaugh a week earlier. The ex-Marine was drunk and belligerent. He had beaten another man into a bloody stupor but the victim insisted that the cuts on his head were the result of falling off his barstool.

On that occasion, Murtaugh was short in his answers, a recalcitrant bully with little to recommend him. Now he was beyond talking to. His eyes were rolled back in his head and he was making a guttural noise that sounded like an animal caught in a trap. As Murtaugh rolled back and forth in the snow, O'Keefe could make out five more bullet holes in his lower back. He had been shot at least eight times.

"There's the gun," said the State Trooper, putting his revolver in its holster. He stepped over Murtaugh and shined his flashlight into the space between the bushes and where Murtaugh had been hiding. "Don't touch it. Make sure he doesn't have a second piece. I'm gonna tape this whole area off."

Lying in the groove where Murtaugh had been dragged out of the shrubs was a Mossberg .12 gauge shotgun. O'Keefe used his flashlight and counted ten unexpended shells on the ground near Murtaugh's feet. Searching the ex-Marine's pockets for another weapon he found six more shotgun shells and lined them up in the snow. Nearby, Larry Wasilowski was pacing the front walk as he called for an ambulance. Already the State Trooper was marking off the crime scene and directing the other cops, who were arriving in bunches, away from the place where Murtaugh had been shot.

Kevin Imbriacco still had his gun drawn, his face pale in the glare of spotlights from the dozen cruisers now filling Pleasant Street. "I fucking shot a guy," said Imbriacco, in a voice that only Rick O'Keefe could hear.

"He had a loaded shotgun," said O'Keefe.

Imbriacco dropped to one knee in the snow. "When we came up, we didn't see him there. Larry noticed the footprints going into the bushes." Imbriacco turned and gazed at the street, noting the path he and Wasilowski had taken. "He could've shot us to shit."

Later that morning, O'Keefe would learn that he had missed the shooting by less than ten seconds. Just as he turned onto Pleasant Street and heard the second general radio call, announcing that shots had been fired, the actual events were unfolding a scant one hundred yards from his location. Wasilowski spotted Murtaugh first, lying in the shrubbery at the conclusion of his footprints. The two police officers drew their weapons and approached, telling Murtaugh to stand up and show them his hands. In a drunken voice the ex-Marine said that he'd shoot anyone who came near.

There was some yelling back and forth. Seizing the initiative, Wasilowski holstered his own weapon and leaped on the suspect, wrestling with him briefly. Unable to keep his footing in the snow, Wasilowski collapsed on top of Murtaugh, who had something long, heavy and metallic gripped in his hands. For an instant, Wasilowski had the barrel of the shotgun in his right hand and his left arm in a chokehold across Murtaugh's throat. But the ex-Marine was powerful; struggling to his feet, he threw the 200-pound cop off his shoulders, bringing the shotgun up in the same motion.

Wasilowski scuttled out of the bushes, regained his feet and drew his weapon. Chaos ensued, as Wasilowski and Imbriacco shouted at Murtaugh to drop the gun and the wild-eyed man, dressed in snowmobile pants and a heavy jacket, yelled that he'd kill them both. As Kevin Imbriacco inched forward, Murtaugh leveled the shotgun.

Shoot him, Wasilowski said.

Simply by depressing the trigger on a police-issue Glock .40 caliber handgun, the officer can discharge continuous hollow point bullets until his entire 9-shot clip has been exhausted. In the space of a few seconds, Larry Wasilowski fired three rounds and Imbriacco five; all were hits, three in Murtaugh's abdomen and a group of five across his lower back.

*

An ambulance pulled up to the house and two EMTs ran through the snow carrying a backboard. One took Murtaugh's pulse while the other man used a pair of shears to cut away Murtaugh's jacket and shirt. "Jesus Christ," said the EMT with the shears. He exchanged glances with his partner.

Steam rose from the bullet wounds. "Just get this shitbird out of here," said the big state trooper.

The senior EMT began to say something and the trooper waved him off. The state trooper had a fringe of gray hair beneath his wide-brimmed hat and projected a sense of authority even among the other police officers. "Until the Attorney General gets here, this is my crime scene, and the perp—" he indicated Chip Murtaugh, who was strapped to the backboard— "is no longer useful to me."

O'Keefe's supervisor appeared, plodding through the drifts, a hefty, liquor-faced sergeant named Tomba, with 38 years on the job. He took one look at Murtaugh, trussed up on the backboard, and asked, "We all right?" Assured that no police officer had been hurt, Sgt. Tomba instructed Wasilowski and Imbriacco to have someone take them back to the station for a debriefing.

"Get a cup of coffee, and sit your ass in my office," said Tomba. "The A. G.'s gonna be there all week."

The Attorney General's investigator, a man named Kilgarriff, had just arrived in his plain black Crown Vic with state plates. He was talking to the gray-haired trooper and using a digital camera to photograph the crime scene. Kilgarriff grimaced for a moment when he took Chip Murtaugh's photo and then turned away, spat into the bushes and resumed his conversation with the trooper.

When Sgt. Tomba heard that O'Keefe had not fired his weapon, and seeing O'Keefe at the edge of the property, blowing on his hands and shifting his weight back and forth to keep warm, Tomba gestured to him and the tall, jug-eared cop stuck his hands in his pockets and trudged over.

"Follow the ambulance," Tomba said. "If he says anything at the hospital, write it down." The two cops glanced at the EMTs, who were laboring over the snow-packed yard with the stretcher.

"I don't think he's gonna say much," Sgt. Tomba said.

Only when Rick O'Keefe had slammed himself inside the warmth of his patrol car, the engine still running, did he realize that it had been snowing the entire time. The house's façade, tilted up against the dense, gray sky, the huge pine trees that framed it, and the steep slope of the lawn were obscured by the storm. All along it had seemed to O'Keefe that it wasn't snowing; that every action that had occurred in the past hour had taken place beneath a clear, starry sky. But the two inches of fresh snow that had accumulated on his cruiser meant he'd been wrong about that—that his senses had been fooled and his memory regarding something that had just happened and that he'd witnessed was less than accurate.

Ahead, the ambulance pulled out from the curb and O'Keefe was right behind it, easing past the fire trucks and police cars and S. W. A. T. vans clustered along Pleasant Street. When they cornered onto Main Street, bright under the klieg lights and newly plowed and salted, the big square ambulance and the following car headed toward the closest major hospital, St. Magdalene's, just over the Massachusetts border, their sirens ululating in tandem.

It was two AM. For a moment O'Keefe considered phoning his

wife to tell her what had happened, but Tammy had been asleep for hours and Rick didn't want to disturb her. They would talk about what a crazy night it had been when he got home, just after eight o'clock in the morning, and he was certain that he and his wife would discuss the events in detail over the next several mornings, drinking coffee and eating buttered toast. Just of the thought of it was a comfort to him.

Surrounded by a stone wall, a forest of snow-laden pines and a number of small, darkened outbuildings, St. Magdalene Hospital stood on the crest of Tauvernier Street topped by a 75-foot neon crucifix. The ambulance and then O'Keefe's patrol car entered through the front gate of the property and climbed the long, winding drive, their lights illuminating the woods, as the cross atop the hospital loomed above them, like a wonder of the world.

The emergency room was around back. Near the entrance was the giant oval of a helipad, the orange windsocks hanging limp in the blizzard and the X at the center of the pad covered by all the new snow. Although there were better, more fully equipped hospitals in Boston, less than ten minutes away by air, no helicopters were flying tonight.

Describing a curved T in the snow, the ambulance made a three-point turn at the end of the drive and backed up to the sliding glass doors of the emergency room. While the EMTs hustled Murtaugh out of the ambulance, O'Keefe parked his cruiser a short distance away and jogged toward the hospital, sheathing his nightstick as he came. The doors opened for him with a pneumatic hiss and he was thrust into the dim, antiseptic-smelling lobby. The front desk was vacant, two rows of hard plastic chairs stood empty, and on the wall opposite the door hung a large, framed portrait of Arcadia; three nymphs holding hands and gliding through a forest in their diaphanous gowns.

Just then the news of a "Code Ninety Nine" burst over the PA and O'Keefe rounded the corner and walked rapidly toward the examination rooms. Murtaugh's gurney was in the first cubicle, attended by the two EMTs, a stout, middle-aged woman in an old-fashioned nursing cap, and a doctor. The doctor was a short, trim fellow with salt and pepper hair, dressed in white trousers and a lab coat with a pack of cigarettes in his breast pocket.

Everyone in the room stared for a moment at the lone police officer. Their looks were hard-eyed and penetrating. In the nurse's eyes, particularly, O'Keefe could read a sentiment he had experienced once before, in his first week on the job, when a kid was killed after robbing a jewelry store and crashing into a tree. Back then a nurse had said, "You cops, you break people and we have to fix them."

O'Keefe stared back at the nurse. There was a little placard hanging in the locker room back at the station that read: *People sleep peaceably in their beds at night only because rough men stand ready to do violence on their behalf.* Rick O'Keefe did not doubt for a moment that Chip Murtaugh would've killed one of his colleagues or even a passing motorist, if Imbriacco and Wasilowski hadn't shot him first. So the nurse and glum-faced paramedics and the short little ER doctor could go fuck themselves, for all he cared.

The doctor slipped the ends of his stethoscope into his ears and bent over the stretcher and listened to the gurgling sounds coming from Murtaugh's chest. There was blood everywhere, soaking the hard white linens covering the stretcher and the examination table beneath it.

"Wrap him up and ship him out of here," said the doctor, after a very brief exam. "He's bleeding out as fast as we can put it in." He frowned at the row of bullet wounds, took up a clipboard from a stainless steel table that was nearby, and motioned for O'Keefe to reenter the hallway.

"What happened?" asked the doctor.

He wasn't a native New Englander—his vowels were too raised and rounded for that—but he'd grown up in a rough little city somewhere, maybe even done some boxing; there was a ridge of scar tissue above each eye and his nose was off-kilter.

O'Keefe was staring down at the old flyweight's salt and pepper hair. "Let's go somewhere private," he said.

The doctor gestured at the nurses and paramedics amidst the clatter of the PA. "There's nowhere to go," he said, clicking the nub of a ballpoint pen. "What happened?"

"Hey, doc," said O'Keefe, furrowing his brow. "I'm not talking to you in here."

The doctor looked at him for a moment and threw the clipboard onto the night nurse's desk and headed for the lobby. "Come with me," he said.

He led O'Keefe through the electric doors onto the concrete bulwark outside, the empty ambulance with its doors still open, and a mess of bloody dressings covering the floor. The doctor reached into his breast pocket, retrieved the package of cigarettes, shuffled one into his hand, and produced a match from his trousers and lit up. When he exhaled, clouds of smoke mingled with Rick O'Keefe's breath and drifted away on the frosty air.

"Asshole—" O'Keefe jerked his thumb back toward the ER—" was hiding in the bushes with a loaded shotgun and pointed it at two other cops, friends of mine. He said he was gonna kill them. So they shot him."

Cocking his head and shutting one eye, the ER doctor pulled hard on the cigarette, expelled a long plume of smoke and then looked at the glowing ember in his hand and flicked it over the railing into the snow. "Fuck him, then," he said. "He got what he deserved."

O'Keefe and the pugnacious little doctor went back inside. Excusing himself, the doctor stepped into a tiny office just off the lobby to fill out his paperwork. The thin but penetrating sound of endless, aimless music had crept into the ward. Coming along the hallway, O'Keefe was surprised to find the first examination room deserted except for Chip Murtaugh; the nurse and EMTS were busy elsewhere.

Murtaugh had been unstrapped from the backboard and was lying there in just his snowmobile pants, his hair matted with sweat and blood, and his gaze fixed somewhere on the wall. He had rolled up on his left side, panting and choking, his booted feet occasionally kicking at the air. O'Keefe took a couple of steps into the room. Suddenly, the patient sat up and threw his legs over the side of the table. He groaned in a loud voice and began rocking back and forth with his arms crossed over his midsection. Lines of fresh blood ran down from the wounds in his back and were absorbed into the waistband of his trousers.

O'Keefe was only a few feet away and for a moment, their eyes met. Murtaugh was aware of his surroundings, and for that instant something like familiarity registered in his gaze; he knew where he was, and what was happening to him. But the light that had come into his eyes just as quickly subsided.

Then Murtaugh fell back onto the stiff bloody linens of the examination table, his eyes closed now, his lips pale and quivering. In a strange way O'Keefe felt that a mantle had been taken from him, and he recognized the song that played in the distance as "The Girl from Ipanema." Murtaugh emitted a long, gurgling sigh and began rubbing his ankles together and gathering the edges of the linen with his hands. In his twisting and turning, he reminded O'Keefe of an animal trying to get comfortable enough to die.

The EMTs came back into the room and fastened the straps that kept Murtaugh on the gurney. Unlocking the wheels, they rolled him into the hall.

"You taking him to Boston?" asked O'Keefe.

The older man shook his head. "He's going by private ambulance."

O'Keefe followed the stretcher back through the pneumatic doors onto the concrete loading dock. It had stopped snowing and the sky was clear and black. The younger EMT climbed into the ambulance and moved it out of the way just as a red and yellow *Superior* ambulance crested the drive and backed in to take its place. They were a third-rate outfit and the EMTs that emerged from the garish-looking van were pale, fat, young and nervous. The driver's hand shook as he signed for the patient.

His partner rolled a clean, white stretcher alongside the gurney. He and the driver unbuckled Murtaugh, and with the help of the Claireborne EMTs transferred him to the new stretcher and rolled it into their ambulance. The driver shut his partner up in the bay and hurried around front, his keys jangling as he moved. The ambulance backed out from the loading dock like a ship leaving its moorings, and as its beacon swung across the wintry landscape, the *Superior* ambulance began descending the slope.

On the loading dock, the senior EMT spat over the railing. "That poor sonofabitch doesn't have a prayer," he said.

The two EMTs climbed back into their ambulance, revved it up and dropped over the brow of the hill and out of sight. On the way back to his patrol car, O'Keefe halted in the snow and glanced up at the roof of the hospital. At three o'clock in the morning the glowing cross atop St. Magdelene's was the most prominent object in the sky.

O'Keefe shut himself inside the cruiser and eased it into gear. Turning in a wide arc, he followed the twin tracks of the ambulances downward, toward the street. The vestigial forest bordering the drive, part of an old growth of timber that had once stretched all the way to Canada, rose in a jagged wall on either side. The gigantic fir trees, in particular, were burdened with snow and their long blue shadows extended across the road. Above the trees the sliver of a new moon had appeared.

At the terminus of the driveway, the old fashioned traffic light went quickly from yellow to red. One set of tire tracks veered south, toward the highway and Boston, and the other went in the direction of the New Hampshire border. While he waited for the light to change, O'Keefe considered those few moments he had spent alone with Chip Murtaugh in the examining room. There was something about the look in Murtaugh's eyes when he sat up. It was a look of fear, certainly, of horror; fear of the unknown; a fear of pain and the distinct mark of pain itself; the anticipation of death; and the primitive and agonizing emotions connected with the body's failure, its ultimate exhaustion. But in the shifting gradations and the changing quality of light in Murtaugh's eyes there was something more. O'Keefe had noticed it—it had struck him—just before Murtaugh dropped back down on the gurney and turned his face away.

Now, as the traffic light changed, and O'Keefe swung north in the dim light from the moon, he felt an unexpected pang for his wife and children. He couldn't wait for his shift to be over—the kids in their pajamas, the coffee smell, and Tammy wearing an old police sweatshirt with her toenails painted red. He was a lucky man. For back in the emergency room, he'd seen pity in Murtaugh's eyes; not pity for himself, or the cops, or what they had done to him and how they would suffer for it—because there was always guilt and sleepless nights. What O'Keefe had seen was broader and more encompassing than that; it was pity for the world, and everything in it.

Pinholes

Shinbones and wrists slanting from his pajamas, Rommy lay in bed covered by Martin's old leather jacket. The ten-year-old was exhausted from shuttling between his grandmother's house here in Connecticut and Amanda's deejaying gig in Boston, especially the extra trip for the hospital visit and Martin's funeral. Amanda closed the bedroom door and followed the faint blue glow of the television back to the sofa. Then the screen went blank and Amanda heard her own voice talking about the late news coming up.

Two years and Channel 23 still had her on tape. Martin's voice, which ranged only a couple of notes in any direction, had kept him in a band like the Pinholes doing local clubs. He could write songs, though. When he and Amanda were going together, he'd sit on the edge of the bathtub in his old apartment and put the seat down on the toilet and play the new ones for her. The can was the place for his songs, Martin would say. Acoustics like Symphony Hall. By the second chorus Amanda would know the words and they would make it a duet, her rich merry voice and his slightly nasal one, swirled together, ringing off the tiles. They'd laugh and call it a hit, a definite gold record. Then his smile would fade and Martin would pick at his guitar, old riffs from old songs, pieces of someone else's gold record. Amanda always felt guilty that her one accidental talent was pushing her into bigger things and Martin was stuck in Windsor, Connecticut, auditioning songs in his bathroom.

Amanda's boyfriend, Nouri, had been torturing himself all week with retroactive jealousy. "Why do you cry for this man who never called you?" he asked, looking absurd in his boxer shorts and black socks. Outside of his silk suits he was not so impressive. "Do not cry in my bed for another man, a dead man."

Nouri was enraged by her feelings for Martin. It was a nice break from his usual Middle Eastern indifference. In the eight months they had been living together in Nouri's townhouse, Amanda spent most nights after her shift curled up with Rommy in his room, as happy to see her son as she was to avoid Nouri's brief, careless lovemaking.

At first Nouri had taken Amanda to trendy restaurants like Davio's, where he spread twenty dollar bills across the room, landing them at the best table in the place. Glancing around, Amanda was self-conscious in her velvet mini and bomber jacket, the other women with their hair up, wearing long dresses and furs. But while the champagne was being poured, Nouri reached over and took her hand, his shirt and his teeth white against his skin and the dark fabric of his suit.

"You are a jewel," he said, "shining in the night."

"That's just my fillings," said Amanda, freeing her hand.

She was rock 'n' roll—sleeping until noon, eating a lot of fast food and hanging out with an assortment of musicians, bartenders and record salesmen who only handed over a twenty when they wanted two fives and a ten. Such elegant surroundings were new to Amanda, and as the waiter uncovered the gaudy red shell of her lobster, she decided she could get used to them.

Rommy was a different story: he missed the scene. And of all the local bands and their singers, Rommy liked Martin the best. On his birthday he and Amanda caught the Pinholes' Saturday afternoon set at Chicken Jimmy's, and Martin invited Rommy on stage to sing du-wop. After that Martin was like God to Rommy. In his room the boy had huge posters of the Squirrel Nut Zippers and Rancid, and a small black and white photograph of the Pinholes. Down in one corner Martin had written *Don't stop rockin' until you stop walkin'*.

Martin had done just that. He finished a set at midnight and wasn't two blocks from Chicken Jimmy's, on dry pavement and without leaving any skid marks, when he smashed his car into a utility pole, crumpling it like a tin can. At two in the morning Amanda took a call at the radio station from Tony, the Pinholes drummer, who said Martin had been in an accident. An hour later, Tony called back to say Martin wasn't going to make it. He was in a coma at Hartford General and if Amanda wanted to see him before it was over, she should come straight from work.

Twice she got as far as the hospital lobby. The first time Amanda went through the electric door and out again before it closed. From behind the wheel of her car she watched Tony and the other Pinholes cross the parking lot in single file. A short time later, she followed them inside. But something wouldn't allow her beyond the plastic palms and blue Naugahyde couches, into that acrid hospital smell that closed on visitors like a fog. Occasionally the triangle above the elevator doors lit up when the car arrived and Amanda expected to see Martin standing there, bandaged perhaps, saying something smart-ass about life in the fast lane. But it would just be a nurse in her rubber-soled shoes or a man pushing a gurney.

Amanda felt helpless. Upstairs, machines were keeping Martin alive. Keeping that hand warm that hadn't picked up a phone to call her in months. Two break-ups and they still planned to get back together someday, when they were both in town and available. Martin was a great one for never burning his bridges.

Amanda imagined the Pinholes around his bedside, singing *a cappella*. But one look at the band getting off the elevator and she knew there hadn't been any singing. They drifted into the lobby like shell-shocked gypsies, nobody saying a word, aiming for the electric door in their motorcycle boots and fringe. Amanda reached out and grabbed Tony by the sleeve. The unshaven percussionist looked awful, his eyes huge and watery behind rimless spectacles.

"How is he?" asked Amanda.

It took Tony a moment to focus on her small, pretty face. "You better go up," the drummer said. "You won't be able to stay very long."

Amanda bit her lip, glancing toward the elevator. "I don't want to remember him like that."

"Neither do I. But I went," said Jennifer, standing apart from them, her blonde hair tangled into points. She clutched her elbows and smirked. "Of course, I'm not a big radio star."

Tony frowned at her and then looked into Amanda's light gray eyes. "Martin was proud of you getting that gig. We all were."

All but Jennifer, it seemed. She gave Amanda a bitchy look. Jennifer could sing all right, but nothing special, and it had more to do with her cup size than her vocal range when Martin added her to the band. That was the trouble with Martin. He made a lot of important decisions between his legs. Amanda used to say that it was an enormous responsibility for such a small area.

A horn erupted in the street. Fitch, the bass player, had wandered into the path of an oncoming car. The driver leaned on his horn and gestured the skinny guitarist to the curb. In his scruffy buckskin coat and hair to his shoulders, Fitch looked like a demented pioneer. The car roared off, and they all stared in that direction.

Jennifer ran outside. "Jesus—now what?" asked Tony. He gave Amanda a kiss on the cheek. "I guess I'll be seeing you," he said.

"I guess so," said Amanda.

After the Pinholes were gone, she stood in the middle of the lobby, her heart pounding. Amanda heard a buzz of voices behind her and names being paged on the intercom. Then she walked out of the building, as if it was on fire and she had been instructed not to panic.

*

Amanda was beside Martin's casket in her black miniskirt, in a room half filled with black miniskirts, when Jennifer took something small and flat from her purse and slipped it under Martin's elbow.

"What was that?" Amanda asked.

Jennifer giggled. "Martin's cell phone," she said. "I'm gonna call him."

Amanda retreated to the rear of the chapel. Propped up in the casket, Martin was dressed in a baggy blue suit and polyester tie, his long hair pulled back in a ponytail. He appeared to be sleeping and holding his breath at the same time. He even looked a little bloated, when Amanda remembered his hard narrow body was like holding a bundle of ropes. The stillness in his chest frightened her.

Rommy had surprised Amanda by asking if he could go to the funeral. She always took such requests seriously and sat him down for a talk. As gently as possible, she described the embalming, display and burial of Martin's body. Soon the boy's face indicated he no longer wanted to go. Looking into it was like gazing at her own reflection: the short spiked hair, passive gray eyes and full mouth. Always wanting to know, and then finding the weight of that knowledge unbearable.

Tony came into the chapel with lanky, gray-haired Jimmy Watson, the owner of Chicken Jimmy's. The two men stopped at the casket and then made their way to the back of the room. Tony had acquired a limp and his face was sunken and dark.

Embracing him, Amanda smelled his boozy breath. "Oh, Tony," she said.

The drummer sniffled in her ear. "There goes Martin," he said, "and there goes the fuckin' band."

Amanda began to cry. "Just get another singer," she said.

"None of us can read music. Martin played, and we followed him," said Tony, pushing Amanda to arm's length. His eyes were bloodshot and weary. "Nope, the Pinholes are just as dead as he is."

They separated. "I need a smoke," Tony said, heading outside.

Jimmy Watson bent his pockmarked face toward Amanda and kissed her on the cheek. "I'm so sorry," he said.

His condolences seemed strange to Amanda. "Jimmy, for crissakes. I'm not the widow."

"I know, but I thought of you as soon as I heard," he said.

In a rumpled corduroy jacket, his gray hair loose to the shoulders, Jimmy Watson nodded and spoke to several people as they passed by him. Voices occasionally broke the level of decorum, and the smell of marijuana wafted in from the parking lot. Amanda recognized a lot of faces: rival band members, club owners and managers, even a couple of minor record company people who would never listen to any of Martin's songs. A real gathering of the clan. For most of them the event was an obligation, the prelude to a lot of drinking and carrying on later in the day.

Jimmy Watson surveyed the room. "I wonder what Martin would

make of this," he said.

"He wouldn't be caught dead in that suit," said Amanda.

"Where did they get that thing?" Watson shook his head. "It's awful."

"They should have dressed him up like a pirate or a cowboy," said Amanda. A woman in the crowd laughed. "So long as everybody's entertained."

"Martin loved sticking it to the establishment," said Watson, sniffing the marijuana in the air. With a quick gesture he referred to the undertaker, pacing back and forth across the carpet in silent outrage. "And there's no greater absurdity than the American funeral. What a fucking joke."

Jimmy looked through the crowd, to the waxen figure in the cheap blue suit lying among the flowers. "Whatever shenanigans are going on today, you know Martin would've been right in the middle of 'em," he added.

"Martin would be right in the middle of all those girls," Amanda said, gazing at the casket for a moment.

"The women sure went after Martin with a vengeance," said Watson. "All that delicate young flesh gunning for you makes the job seem important."

"And it makes the people who love you miserable," said Amanda.

"Martin came up short in the talent department," Watson said. "Don't hold that against him. If he had no talent at all, you never would've met him." He rustled his coat. "Hey, you should come by the club? Dream Wagon is playing." Watson started to go and then turned, clasping one of Amanda's hands. "Jesus, I almost forgot. Congratulations on making the big time. How does it feel?"

Amanda watched the miniskirted young girls hovering around Martin's body. "Like I missed something," she said.

*

Chicken Jimmy's was dark, smelling of cigarette smoke and stale beer in the carpets, woven into the curtains, and in the woolly black acoustic tiles lining the walls and ceiling. Amanda found the nightclub as indistinct as a cave and it took a moment for her eyes to adjust.

"Martin and I were going to get married," a blonde woman was saying to the bartender. "No one really knew."

Amanda laughed. "No one knew because it's bullshit," she said. "Don't go making up lies just because he's dead."

Amanda and Martin had once attended a wedding together. In her brilliant white dress, trailing silk along the floor, the bride passed by, her polished, haughty face turned toward the altar and the object of her long successful campaign: the drummer from Martin's old band.

"Poor bastard never knew what hit him," Martin said. Afterward, getting drunk at the bar, he said, "I'd like to have a wedding and not actually get married. That's the trick."

"Some trick," said Amanda, pressed against him, her tequila held under her chin.

"It would be great," Martin said, waving his glass at all the commotion, "to be the center of attention and not be stuck with a wife when it was over."

"That's called a funeral," said Amanda.

"Wedding, funeral—same thing," Martin said, tossing down his drink.

Amanda wasn't too keen on marriage either. Her first husband, Rommy's father, was a mistake of youth not to be repeated. Until Martin came along. Then the memory of all that heartache vanished, just as the actual pain of childbirth faded and left her with the notion—which she knew was false—that it hadn't been that bad. Amazing that she could forget either sensation. As soon as Martin began cheating on her, she felt that familiar stabbing thrust in the pit of her stomach.

"Amanda. Over here," called a voice. Chicken Jimmy's was about a third full, most of them left over from the funeral. Tony stood up and waved his arms. "Join the party," he said.

The party consisted of the remaining Pinholes and a few members of Dream Wagon sitting together at a back table. Jennifer and Roxie, the singer from Dream Wagon, were side by side with their hair teased into fantastic shapes. They were both dressed in leather and drinking Sombreros. All the guys drank vodka.

The keyboard player from Dream Wagon, Rex Monaghan, a barrel-chested man with a mane of dirty blond hair, grabbed Amanda and planted a kiss on her spiky head. "I love ya, so look out," he said, in a voice made hoarse by cigarettes and lack of sleep. Amanda scrunched down under Rex's weight and when her eyes came level with the table, she saw the cellphone beside Jennifer's purse. The thought of what was at the other end almost made her sick. Then the first blast of recorded music shot out of the speakers, and Tuesday night at Chicken Jimmy's had begun.

Rex bought Amanda several tequilas and kept an eye on her until Dream Wagon was ready to go on stage. "Show time," said the keyboard player, yanking her into an improved posture. Then he whispered in her ear. "I know how it is, baby doll, but you just gotta swing with it."

Amanda went to the bar and ordered another tequila. Martin used to say that her Mexican-Irish heritage gave her a taste for the hot stuff and the stubbornness to keep it down. They had met one night on the spot where Amanda was standing. After the Pinholes' first set that evening Martin walked straight to the bar, perspiring in rivers, and smiled at her. "Hi, sugar," he said, an attractive long-haired man in a leather jacket and matching pants. "Can I buy you a drink?"

"No, but I'll take the money," Amanda said.

Martin had reached into his pocket and took out three dollars. Extending it toward her in jest, he laughed when Amanda snapped it out of his grasp. "Hey, thanks," she said.

A voluptuous redhead approached Martin from behind and covered his crotch with her hands. "Don't leave me alone tonight, babe," she said. Martin sent her back to the table with a placating remark.

"Your girlfriend has nice breasts," Amanda said. "You must be very proud of her."

"She's not my girlfriend."

Amanda snorted. "Whatever she is, she grabbed onto your dick like it belonged in her back pocket."

Finishing his beer, Martin said, "Well, I gotta split. Maybe I can give you some more money later."

"We'll see," said Amanda, smiling into her glass.

Martin led the Pinholes without the usual stage antics; a pretty fair guitar player, Amanda decided, and not a great singer but distinctive. When the show was over, Martin had hung around until Amanda surrendered her telephone number. A week later the redhead was history, and he and Amanda were an item.

Rex let out a shout and Dream Wagon struck up their first tune, a burst of snare drum ripping through the dark smoky air. They were accomplished musicians and, between Rex and Roxie, capable of mimicking more than a dozen vocal styles. In recent months, Dream Wagon had been invited to open some arena shows and was playing top clubs in Boston and Hartford. Martin used to party with Rex and loved to complain that a cover band was no better than recorded music. *Why bother,* he'd say, *when monkeys could be trained to play other people's songs.* At the suggestion Rex would drop into the guise of an ape, which he resembled, and begin shrieking and chattering and swinging his arms.

As long as the two bands were equal in bookings and status, it was all in fun. But Dream Wagon began outdistancing the Pinholes, opening for big name acts at the Orpheum and the Tweeter Center, and the effect on Martin was definite. His attacks grew sharper, his tongue more acid.

"'Wagon is playing the same shit every night," he said to Amanda during one of his piques. "They might as well have Roxie come out and blow the crowd."

Martin was used to performing for noisy drunks at Chicken Jimmy's and other small clubs; he liked the life. But he was almost thirty, crawling across a long plateau in his "career," and Amanda knew it irritated him to see a garage band like Dream Wagon reaping the applause and bigger money. And when Rex started getting a lot of female attention, Martin's womanizing became ridiculous and Amanda left him.

Going to Boston made it easier; Amanda and Martin didn't speak for months. Through the grapevine, she learned he was still with the Pinholes but moonlighting with a band called the Stolen Roans. They dressed and performed as the Rolling Stones of the 1970s and Amanda heard they had a prancing, strutting, sneering lead singer who was an actor by trade.

"It was sad," a friend told her after seeing the show. "Martin was trying, but you could tell he was miserable up there."

Amanda watched Rex playing to the crowd at Chicken Jimmy's and thought of Martin, of all people, giving up his music for someone else's. It was sadder than looking at him in his coffin. Suddenly Amanda felt regretful, once again abandoned by Martin in a smoky nightclub. She started to cry. A friend of Rex's who had been at the funeral walked up and folded her in his arms. "Hey," he said. "It's not the end of the world."

Amanda got loose and ran straight into Nouri. There he was, marvelous skin and glittering white teeth, dressed like a millionaire. "What are you doing here?" Amanda wanted to know.

"Your mother called me," said Nouri.

Amanda flung herself against Nouri's chest, and began sobbing while he stroked the back of her head. "Come home," he said.

Nouri fished in his suit pocket and removed a small velvet box, turning Amanda so she could see it. Her crying stopped. Then Nouri flipped open the box and the contents gleamed with its own phosphorescence. It was a diamond ring; the facets of the huge gemstone captured the light over the bar and scattered it into soft floating points.

"For you," Nouri said.

Amanda gazed into the deep brown reservoir of his eyes. Her options seemed limited. She closed a hand on the velvet box and hugged it against her neck. "All right," she said. "Let's pick up Rommy and we'll go."

Nouri stiffened inside his suit. "About that," he said. "Rommy cannot stay with his grandmother?"

"No," said Amanda. "I'm his mother."

"But I am not his father," Nouri said. He opened the velvet box again right under Amanda's nose. "This is a 3-carat diamond. I bought it for you. No one else."

Amanda thrust herself away, reeling in a small drunken arc. The people around them were beginning to stare. "Nouri, you're such a prick. It would be a miracle if you ever thought of anyone besides yourself."

"I am a prick?" he asked, his precise diction making her laugh. "I will be a prick, then. When will you pay back the money I loaned you?"

"What money?"

"The money for your car. One thousand dollars."

Amanda couldn't stop shaking. "You gave me that money for Christmas," she said. "It was a gift."

"Now it is a loan."

"Get the fuck out of here, Nouri," said Amanda. She sat down and covered her face with her hands. "If it wasn't for Martin's accident I wouldn't even be talking to you."

"Accident?" asked Nouri. "There was no accident."

Amanda looked up and saw something terrible in the faces gathered around her. *There was no accident.* It was a fact that she already understood, like seeing a guitarist play a chord, then a moment later, having it crash through the amplifier.

"You keep the ring," said Nouri, pressing the velvet box into her hand. He was on his knees beside the chair. "Pay me for the car later."

"Tell you what," said Amanda, looking him in the eye. "Exchange it for a 2-carat diamond, and we'll call it even."

Nouri left and Amanda groped her way over to Jennifer, who was playing with her cell phone. Coming from behind, Amanda took it from her and listened to the constant ringing sound. Then she smashed the phone against a chair and threw it down, pounding it with the heel of her boot.

"What are you doing?" asked Jennifer.

"Wrong number," Amanda said.

Jimmy Watson drove Amanda back to her mother's house. When she looked at him, he was divided into sections that revolved in a dizzying kaleidoscopic effect.

"In you go," Watson said to Amanda when they pulled up in the driveway.

Amanda slumped against the upholstery and shut one eye to pull the jigsaw of his face together. "I'm sorry," she said. "It's just that I couldn't stand those people and the things they were saying."

Jimmy Watson kept silent.

"Why didn't anyone tell me Martin killed himself?" asked Amanda, meeting his eyes.

"That's only a rumor," Watson said.

"Oh, Jimmy, for crissakes, *everybody* knew," Amanda said. "Even Nouri figured it out. I feel like such an idiot."

There was a long silence. "Remember when Martin changed the name of the band to the Pinholes?" asked Watson.

"They were the False Cures and The Cure made it big, so he changed it."

Watson grunted. "Martin told me he chose the Pinholes because life poked a lot of tiny holes in you, and if you looked close, you were always bleeding," said the club owner. "Listen, I don't know what happened the other night. But Martin never changes again in any way, and you keep going." He made a gesture with his hand. "Kind of a rotten deal, actually."

*

Amanda dimmed the volume on the television and went into the kitchen. Outside the moon rode across a patch of silver sky, that old Windsor moon, gilding the lawn furniture and casting a shadow behind Rommy's bicycle. Amanda felt like she had reached an appointed hour, but no one approached.

"Mom, what time is it?" Rommy was in the doorway, Martin's leather jacket hanging over his pajamas.

"It's late," said Amanda. She brushed the hair from Rommy's forehead. "Want something to drink?"

"Yes, please." Rommy climbed onto a stool and waited for Amanda to pour him a glass of milk. "Moo," he said.

Amanda chuckled. "Mmooo."

Rommy whitened his upper lip with the milk and gazed at his mother. The leather jacket hung down to his knees, and he looked like he had been abruptly reduced in size, by a magic spell or a wizard in a fable.

"What happens when you die, Mom?" he asked, blinking at her.

"You go to heaven," said Amanda.

"How long do you stay there?"

"You get to stay there forever," Amanda said.

In a small voice, Rommy asked, "Then what's all this for?"

"I don't know, baby," she said, leaning close to him.

Rommy slipped his arms around her neck and pressed himself—she could feel his heart beating—against the warmth of her upper body. "You can sleep with me, Mom," the boy said. "Just for tonight, okay?"

"Cool beans," she said.

Amanda shooed Rommy off to bed. She rinsed their glasses in the sink and went to turn off the television. It spiraled down to a white dot, leaving her in darkness, and she moved through it toward her son.

Jailbird

Eddie Trembley was over six feet tall and wore his black hair with a curl in front and slicked into a duck's ass at his collar. Standing in the doorway with an old seabag over his shoulder and his eyes darting back and forth, he looked like he was going to prison, not getting out.

My father said Eddie was my cousin and would be staying with us for a while. I didn't know whether to clean my room or what—I had never met an ex-con before.

"Hey, chief," Eddie said to me. He didn't offer to shake my hand. "How's it hangin'?"

Eddie was 35, with deep lines in his face, narrow brown eyes and a panther tattooed on his left forearm. In the mornings, he shaved over the tiny sink in our bathroom, stripped to the waist, hunching over to see himself in the cloudy mirror. I was 15 then and a great collector of muscle magazines, thick glossy ones with advertisements for the Charles Atlas Dynamic Tension Program and different kinds of protein powder and "How To Build Unbelievable Calves Fast!" Each month there would be some new giant splashed across the cover, with bulbous forearms and a deep chest and abdominal muscles that looked like glazed kitchen tile. But I had never seen anything like Eddie Trembley. He was a monster.

The muscles that started halfway up Eddie's back flared outward to his shoulders. Each fiber in his torso and down the arm that held the razor worked like a little mechanical wire as he scraped the shaving cream from his chin. And although Eddie put away huge greasy meals at our kitchen table and never worked out, there wasn't a speck of fat on him.

I pounded the heavy bag in my bedroom and curled over 75 pounds, but next to my cousin I was a little white smudge, floating in and out of our tiny apartment while Eddie occupied one spot for hours, his long legs thrust out beneath the television set.

My mother died when I was two and I lived at my aunt's house most of the time. Because of his night job at the Fruit Salad company, my father couldn't take care of me until the weekends. Then I went home to my dark little room and my weights and Manson, my Burmese python.

My father got up one Saturday afternoon to work an extra shift and found Eddie snoring in my bed. "That's my son's room," he said. "You sleep on the couch." Eddie rose up, wearing jeans and nothing else, his eyes hollow from sleep. He loomed in the doorway, towering over my father who was dressed in his rumpled gray work uniform.

"Sure thing, Uncle Lou," said Eddie on the way to the icebox.

My father followed Eddie into the other room and sat opposite him at the kitchen table, slumped over his potbelly. He took out a pack of Camels and offered one to Eddie, and he and my father sat there for a few minutes smoking in silence.

"You been home two weeks and you haven't even looked for a job," my father said. "You're a big strong guy, when you gonna make something of yourself?"

Eddie stiffened at the mention of the word *home*. He cupped his cigarette and smoked it in a quick tender fashion like he expected to have it snatched away from him. "When I have a job, I work," Eddie said. "When I don't, I don't."

"Come with me Monday night and talk to the foreman. Maybe we can get you in," my father said.

"I don't like working nights."

My father kept his weak eyes fixed on Eddie. "Nobody says it has to be nights. I'll introduce you and you take it from there."

My father had two rules for Eddie staying with us: no drinking and no drugs. That weekend, Eddie pushed things a little bit. My father couldn't get to sleep on his nights off and sat up watching movies and eating cookies from a bag. I heard Eddie come in around 3 a.m. He lurched up the stairs and then banged the door open, stumbling in the hall. My father clicked off the television.

"One more time like this and you're out," my father said. "I won't allow this kind of behavior in my house."

Eddie sneered. "This house don't belong to you," he said. "It belongs to the man. Just like the fruit company and everything else."

"I pay my bills and this here is mine," said my father.

Behind the closed door in my room I could imagine him pointing at the floor but meaning the apartment, his car, his job—all the things he worked so hard for. "That's your problem, Eddie," my father said. "You don't respect other people and what belongs to them."

Eddie's voice dropped low, like he was tired or just sad. "I got nothing belongs to me, so what's the difference?"

On a wicker stand beside the sink in our bathroom was a huge dusty bottle of red mouthwash that had been full for over a year. In the space of only a few days the level of the bottle dropped to practically nothing. Eddie had lousy teeth but he sure used a lot of that mouthwash, his breath coming out in sweet fiery clouds.

United Fruit Salad offered Eddie a janitor's job on second shift. He started working, and things went well for a few weeks. Eddie didn't like wearing the gray custodian's uniform, but he had a few bucks in his pocket, giving my father a little toward expenses and buying himself two beautiful rayon shirts. One was beige with yellow palm trees and the other had a brightly colored pattern of musical notes and piano keys.

*

One day after work Eddie came into my room and watched me pound the heavy bag. I had the shades open and Manson's tank moved out from the wall so he could sun himself near the window. "You got a good punch there, chief," said Eddie, when I had exhausted myself. The bag hung by a heavy chain in the center of the room. "Twist your wrist as you throw it," he said.

Eddie came closer to the bag. In a heartbeat, he threw two bare-knuckle lefts and a straight right hand that exploded like gunshots against the canvas. Before I could be certain he had thrown the punches, his hands were back dangling at his sides. Eddie spit a tiny white fleck between his teeth that landed on Manson's head. Then he turned around and went into the kitchen. The heavy bag swung back and forth, creaking on its chain like someone had hit it with a sledgehammer.

My aunt was not crazy about Eddie staying with us. When my father picked me up for the weekend, she said Eddie was a drug addict and thief and shouldn't be around a teen-ager like me.

"If I put him out, he's got nowhere to go," my father said.

"His own family won't have him, and why do you think that is?" my aunt asked, her thin arms folded across her chest. "Once a junkie, always a junkie."

My father was sitting halfway on a kitchen stool, winded just from walking in from the driveway. He sagged to one side, the tiny red veins visible in the pouches beneath his eyes. "I can't argue with a single thing you're saying," he said, rubbing the tattoo on his forearm. It was the severed head of a snake with a dagger through it. "But for however long it lasts, I'd like the kid to have a roof over his head and clothes on his back."

My aunt was an O'Connell like my mother and she used to tell me there was a mean streak in the Trembleys. They drank and fought and got thrown in jail. Even my father had been a hell raiser, living at home with my grandmother until he was 40. Every morning he pretended he was getting ready for work. He packed a lunch and put on dungarees and a work shirt and went downtown. At the Wonder Bar, he would trade my grandmother's homemade *tourtiere* and strawberry rhubarb pie for drinks. When those were gone, he'd hustle pool until closing time.

"There wasn't one Trembley who turned out right," my aunt told me. "The last thing your mother said to me was how much she worried about you and your father."

Before he met my mother at the discount bakery where she worked, my father had never held a job longer than six months. Then he got married and moved into veterans' housing and got hired at the Fruit Salad company. There was a photograph of my father pushing me around in a stroller between the barracks-style VA buildings, his sleeves rolled up over his tattoos. He was smiling with his bridge out and a tooth missing in front. Buried inside the carriage, I looked like a little stroke victim wearing a hat.

Everything was okay until my mother caught pneumonia. The doctor said it was under control but she was dead in two days. By the time I was 13, I had a skull and crossbones tattooed on my hip, where nobody could see it. I drank whiskey with Goat Arsenault in the woods behind the junior high. I kept my mouth shut and did pretty much whatever I wanted, especially on weekends.

Goat Arsenault was almost as tall as Eddie, but skinny with red hair. One Friday afternoon, we were in my room listening to records and Goat had Manson out of his cage when Eddie came home. Manson had been eating more white rats than I could afford and was seven feet long. I heard the icebox click shut and then Eddie passed by without looking at us and went out the front door.

"Is that the jailbird?" Goat asked.

"That's Eddie."

Manson undulated along Goat's shoulder and dropped a coil across his neck. Goat's eyes got really wide for a second and he flipped Manson onto the floor.

"He don't look all that tough," said Goat.

We both sat there feeling the muscles in our arms. "Then you didn't get a good look at him," I said.

*

From the backseat of Goat's car on Saturday night, I saw Eddie outside one of the Puerto Rican liquor stores at the bottom of Tauvernier Street. It was pretty dark and I would never have noticed him except he was wearing the shirt with the yellow palm trees. Eddie stepped out from the sidewalk and reached in the window of a car parked next to us. When he straightened up, his hand went into his pocket and he turned and looked at me. A girl came out of the apartment house and met Eddie and they walked down the sidewalk. Eddie looked smaller on the street, his hands jammed in his pockets and the lazy curl falling across his forehead.

I didn't move. They went past us and then before I could breathe Eddie ducked back and was leaning in my window, smelling of sweat and aftershave and booze, all in one nauseating wave. "What is this, amateur night?" he asked. "Get the fuck out of here."

I was drunk when I went home and didn't mention anything to my father. He was in his chair smoking a cigarette and watching an old Claude Rains movie. "Did ya have a good night?" he asked without looking up.

"Nothing to write home about," I said.

My father's hobby was collecting coins and he had the blue cardboard books filled with Indian-head nickels and Kennedy halves and two-headed pennies spread on the coffee table. Beyond him, Claude Rains descended some stairs in a smoking jacket and said something debonair to Ingrid Bergman.

"This is a 1911 dime," my father said, holding up a coin. "It's worth three hundred bucks."

"Don't give it to the paperboy," I said.

My father folded up the books and put them in the polished wooden box he kept hidden in his bureau. The box looked like something you'd keep dueling pistols in.

"That's the funny thing about coins—a dime might look like ten cents unless you got the eye for it. But these nickels and dimes are gonna put you through college someday." My father looked at the wooden box like it contained the Hope diamond. "I'm not the smartest guy in the world, but I got a sharp eye," he said. "And I'm a saver. Your mother used to say that's why she married me."

Above the television was a picture of my mother with dyed blond hair piled on top of her head like cotton candy. There was a sad gleam in her eyes like she knew she would get sick, even though she was smiling and looked healthy.

*

Eddie came home two days later and my father threw him out. No one said a word as he packed the little seabag with his rayon shirts and underwear and the gray work clothes he'd been required to buy. He stopped long enough to take a pee and finish off the mouthwash.

Coming out of the bathroom he walked a little stiff-legged and his eyes were glazed over.

"The man," was all he said.

It was school vacation and my father took a few days off so we could go fishing and have long smoky breakfasts at Perrault's Diner. At night we went to Canobie Lake Park and rode the flying swings and the roller coaster, and my father knocked over three cement milk cans with a baseball. He won a rubber snake and threaded it up his shirtfront so the head popped out at the collar.

"Something's sneaking up on me," he said.

We went home with our hands smelling fishy and the rubber snake dangling around my father's neck. "I guess you're not too old to go out and have fun with the old man," he said, trudging up the stairs.

"It was all right," I said.

My father unlocked the door and reached for the light switch. The television and video player were gone. Running to my room, I discovered my stereo was missing and the toaster and microwave oven. It was like Santa Claus in reverse.

My father went into his room and stood looking down at the empty drawer of his bureau. The wooden box was gone. "He's such a stupid son-of-a-bitch he'll probably get nothing for them coins," my father said.

Manson was dead. He was lying in the cage with his head just about squeezed off. There were two handprints on his neck and the skin was all loose and ropy and his eyes were bugging out.

*

Hard work and all those Camels finally killed my father. My aunt and I put him up at Racicot's Funeral Home. In the back of the chapel, accompanied by a sheriff, was a muscular guy in an orange jumpsuit and shackles. Eddie stared straight ahead at the coffin, not speaking until my aunt had a word with him.

She came back up front. "Go say something," my aunt said.

When the chapel cleared out I went back there. Eddie looked the same except for a new tattoo on his right arm. It was an angel carrying a syringe with the word "Heaven" underneath in fancy script.

I was 19 then, big and solid. "You're the man," said Eddie.

"Stealing from your own family is as low as it gets," I said.

Eddie flashed a quick look at me, like a man glancing up from the bottom of a tunnel. "It was easy," he said with a shrug.

"Those coins meant everything to my father," I said.

"They didn't mean nothing to me, chief. That's how it works."

The funeral director came out of the back room in his striped gray suit and was with my aunt by the coffin, motioning to me. It was time to screw on the lid. My mother and father were dead and Eddie Trembley had shot himself full of junk and was still alive. Alive and stacked with muscles.

"Why'd you come here?" I asked.

Eddie looked at me. "Don't be a sucker like your old man," he said.

The Thorndikes
of Tauvernier Street

My mother, eight months pregnant, was scratching up the ragged leaves into piles and Dad was burning them in the gutter. Flanked by a gigantic oak tree on one side and a pine on the other, our house was an old yellow Colonial, streaked with pigeon droppings at the eaves. It needed painting but my father could never find the time because he was working so hard at the bakery. We had waited until spring to get rid of all the leaves and now there were millions of them.

I scooped the leaves onto a plastic tarp and dragged it out to the street and dumped them with the rest. The pile ran the length of our property and my father had lit it at both ends and in the middle. The fire ate toward itself in all directions and smaller piles, thrust into the street by the wind, had also caught fire and were sending thin columns of smoke up from the roadway. My father told me to get the other rake and I was standing in the middle of Tauvernier Street with the smell of burning leaves filling my sinuses when I first saw the Thorndikes coming up the hill.

Of course I didn't know they were the Thorndikes, then. They had an old woody station wagon loaded down with baby furniture and mattresses and heaps of clothing, and following behind the wagon was a metal trailer like what they used to haul sailboats. Except instead of a boat there was a fifteen-foot cone of riveted aluminum with "United States" printed on the side and two holes where the window and hatch were supposed to be. The trailer sported a Florida license plate and a bumper sticker that read "Visualize Whirled Peas."

"Would you look at that," said my mother. She had a rag tied in her hair and stood leaning on her rake.

"Lousy Democrats," my father said.

I lingered in the street and Dad put up his rake and whistled at me. "Get out of the way, Joe," he said, his eyeglasses reflecting little wicks of flame.

From inside the station wagon we heard them singing "My Wild Irish Rose"; a spare, curly-haired man behind the wheel, a woman in a kerchief beside him, and three blond children in the backseat. I stepped aside as they reached the flat and the car passed through the columns of smoke and rolled by; the three of us frozen there, mouths agape, holding our rakes like spears. Smoke enveloped the road, and car, trailer, space capsule and Thorndikes disappeared into the blankness like images from a dream.

Standing empty at the end of the block was the old Axelrod mansion, the grandest house in our neighborhood. I dropped my rake in the middle of Tauvernier Street and hopped on my bike and rode after the station wagon. As I cleared the smoke, my father said, "Hey. We've got a lot of work ahead of us."

"Let him go, Jim," said my mother.

I raced past the Nazarian's and the Panebianco's just as the station wagon turned in, crunching over the gravel toward the tall wooden doors of the mansion. The place was three stories of red brick, with wooden shutters and gingerbread trim hanging from the roof. Standing catty corner was a barn that had once contained the Axelrod horses.

"Hallo," said Mr. Thorndike as I leaped off my bicycle and it crashed onto the gravel. He was standing beside the wagon as the kids piled out, a tall, green-eyed man in an old polo shirt and chinos with a length of rope for a belt. "What's your name?" he asked.

The three children and Mrs. Thorndike, holding the baby in one arm, were scrambling around the car untying ropes and disassembling the boxes and parcels that were stacked all over it. With a great heave, they loosened the space capsule and it rolled off the back of the trailer and made a loud noise against the gravel.

"My name's Joe."

Mr. Thorndike threw a plaid suitcase into the air and I caught it. "I hereby christen you an honorary Thorndike," he said. "And all Thorndikes are expected to help unpack."

"Yes, sir!" I grabbed the suitcase and stuck a pillow under each arm and followed the procession into the house. Mrs. Thorndike was just ahead with the baby, carrying a stack of linens, and her husband grabbed her around the waist and kissed her, spilling the linens onto the floor. Squealing, Mrs. Thorndike said, "Quit it, George. Look at my sheets," and the baby laughed and gurgled.

"My sweet Martha," said Mr. Thorndike, his arm still cinched about his wife's narrow waist. "How about mixing us a couple high-balls?" Mr. Thorndike swiveled his head around and winked at us. "Kids," he said. "Go upstairs."

Peter was my age. His white blond hair stood up in a cowlick and he wore a blue and yellow striped T-shirt and hiking shorts. "Dad, which room can I have?" he asked.

"Go pick one," said Mr. Thorndike.

We all went running upstairs, carrying suitcases and pillows and screeching like banshees. On the landing the girls, Marybeth and Lulu, were attracted by the light through a stained glass window and Peter and I raced up to the third floor.

At the end of the dormer was a snug little room paneled in lac-quered oak with a built-in dresser and two bunks notched into the wall. Each of these featured a mattress with a blue velvet slipcover and matching headrest with gold tassels. Peter leaped sideways like the high jumper Dick Fosbury and smashed against the wall, landing on the far bunk. I jumped onto the other bed and lay there, panting.

"We'll have a secret society and this'll be our clubhouse," said Peter.

"Right-o," I said, an expression of my Dad's.

Peter extended his hand and we shook on it. "The Ancient and Honorable Secret Society of...," he began.

"The Captain's Cabin," I said. "Members identified by the code words..."

"Boola, boola," Peter said.

Mr. Thorndike was an honest-to-goodness rocket scientist who had worked on top secret missions, Peter said. But one day his father burned some papers in the garage and they packed up and left. Mr. Thorndike was going to start teaching at Merrimack College in the fall.

On the eve of their departure, Mr. Thorndike drove through a gate at Cape Kennedy marked "Authorized Personnel Only" and the children watched as their father and a man in a lab coat rolled the space capsule, which was an old practice drone, onto the trailer and fastened it with elastic cords. Mr. Thorndike handed the other man a bottle in a paper bag and they shook hands and then the Thorndikes drove back through the gate and over a long sandy road with their headlights turned off.

"Another guy took his job," said Peter. "A stinking German."

I got off the bed and stood looking out the window. Across Lawrence Street was Ye Old Burying Ground, the town's first cemetery with its thin gray headstones dating back to the early 1700s. It contained farmers who had been scalped by Indians and Revolutionary War heroes and men slaughtered at Gettysburg and Bull Run. An iron fence surrounded it and grass grew in thick patches between the crypts.

A voice called up the stairs: "Joe! Your father's here."

Peter and I thundered down stairs and then rode the banister over the last stretch, crashing to the floor. Mr. Thorndike yanked us to our feet; he was wearing a moth-eaten sweater that said "Yale" across the front and a battered yachting cap. Outside it was growing dark and my father stood in the well of light from the entranceway, his T-shirt marked with soot and gray, wispy pieces of ash resting in his crew cut.

"Time to go," Dad said, his eyes crinkling up behind black frame glasses.

"Aw, Dad," I said.

Although the car was only half unpacked, Mr. Thorndike was busy tearing all the shutters from the house. Halfway between the barn and the space capsule he had built a campfire using the rotten old wood and the flames made leaping shadows against the barn.

" 'Aw Dad' nothing," my father said. "Your mom's going to worry."

"Jim, I'll have the wife go and invite your missus up to the house," said Mr. Thorndike. "The kids are having a ball."

My father and Mr. Thorndike were calling each other "Jim" and "George" and it was plain that they had become friends in whatever span of time had passed before Peter and I were called downstairs. My father was drinking a can of Ballantine and there were three other empties pyramided on the windowsill. Except for Christmas and Fourth of July, when the bakery was closed, Dad never drank or stayed up past eight o'clock at night. He worked six days a week, and his Sundays were taken up with odd jobs around the house—the first one he had ever owned. He and my mother had known each other since they were kids, when their families lived in three-deckers near the Axelrod mill. Now that he had a house and a little plot of land, Dad said, he'd work until his fingers were bloody to make the payments.

Just then Lulu, who had something wrong with her eye, and Marybeth came skidding around the corner, followed by their mother who was still carrying the baby, and a yellow cat named Tango that belonged to the Nazarians. Mrs. Thorndike wrinkled up her nose at the sight of the campfire. "George, what on earth are you doing?" she asked.

"Improvising," he said. "Right, Jim?"

A profile came into view along the fence and then my mother turned in at the gate, both hands holding her swollen belly like she was presenting a gift. "Here comes the missus now," my father said, his voice cracking a little. "Mae, come and say hello to the Thorndikes."

Her lips in a brief, tight line, my mother stopped on the gravel and listened to the introductions. She was a small, nervous woman with auburn hair, dressed in stretch pants and my father's short canvas jacket worn over a maternity blouse. "It's a pleasure to meet you," my mother said, dazed by the profusion of Thorndikes. "But Jim, you have to work tomorrow."

Mr. Thorndike opened two more cans of Ballantine and handed one to my father. "Please, Mae," he said. "Sit awhile by the fire."

The girls ran to the station wagon and retrieved two folding chairs and half a dozen campstools, setting them around the heap of burning shutters. Rummaging in a pile of sundries, Mr. Thorndike hauled out a bag of potatoes and a copper kettle. "I wish we had more to offer," he said, straightening one of the lawn chairs for my mother. "But we'll heat you a cup of tea."

Mr. Thorndike tossed the kettle to Peter, who ran over to a spigot and filled it halfway with water. Then Mr. Thorndike placed several of the potatoes near the coals and balanced the teakettle on a shutter that hadn't caught fire. Mrs. Thorndike took the seat next to my mother and let her hold the baby. His hair was fine and white and he snorted as my mother brought her nose to his and then pulled back.

"What a wonderful child," Mom said. "He's so quiet."

Martha Thorndike sat back with her legs crossed, an empty teacup in her hand. She had removed the kerchief and her hair was blonde and curly and I could tell in the firelight that she was at least a dozen years younger than Mr. Thorndike. "He doesn't get a word in edgewise around here," Mrs. Thorndike said.

Somewhere in the goods strewn across the yard, Mr. Thorndike had located his ukulele and sat on a campstool strumming it. "Who knows 'John Jacob Jingleheimer Schmidt'?" he asked.

We all screamed that we knew it and Mr. Thorndike launched into the first verse, holding the ukulele right beneath his chin and singing in a rich, quavering voice. My Dad beat time against the arm of the chair with his beer can and my mother was smiling at him. Across the way, Marybeth Thorndike sat in the gravel hugging her knees, long white legs slanting down from the hollows of her shorts and her eyes glistening in the firelight. In the middle of the final verse, she looked straight at me and smiled and it felt like something beautiful was laughing inside my heart.

After a while, Mr. Thorndike rolled several dark objects from the fire and skewered them with the end of a stick. "Who wants a black Murphy?" he asked, and we each took one of the burnt, shriveled potatoes, hard on the outside like a volcanic rock. Bouncing it on my lap until it cooled somewhat, I broke open the potato and ate the smoking hot white innards while Mr. Thorndike strummed his ukulele and sang "The Tennessee Spud."

It was getting late. Cockeyed Lulu was asleep in her father's lap and Tango the cat had gone leaping over the gravel and disappeared between pickets in the fence. Half a dozen beer cans littered the yard, and my mother had drunk three cups of blueberry tea and was staring a hole in the side of my father's head.

"We should be going," Dad said. "Thanks for such a great night."

Petting Lulu's fine, white hair, Mr. Thorndike grinned at us. "I hope you're looking forward to a thousand great nights," he said.

Walking my bike home, I followed behind my father and mother, who held hands and gazed at the darkened windows along Tauvernier Street. "What nice people," Dad said.

My mother cupped her protruding stomach. "You're going to have a wicked head in the morning," she said.

Something ran across in front of us and an owl hooted from the trees. After dark, you couldn't tell we lived so close to the city. With one arm around my mother's waist Dad waltzed her down the sidewalk. "Remember the day we got married?" he asked.

My mother laughed and shook him off. "Don't push your luck."

*

Before he could paint our house, my father had to get rid of all the pigeons. One day after work, he unlocked the bulkhead and hauled a roll of chicken wire up from the cellar. Still dressed in his cooking whites, Dad strapped on a tool belt and leaned the ladder up against the house. Then we went inside and climbed up to the attic with an old phonograph player and a stack of Trini Lopez records, and with three extension cords strung together Dad plugged in the phonograph and turned the volume all the way up. We heard wings rustling under the eaves and my father shouted over the music. "First we have to drive the buggers out," he said.

We ran downstairs past Mom, who was two weeks shy of her due date and reclining on the sofa, and she asked us what we were doing.

"Making life miserable for the pigeons," my father said.

"Not just the pigeons," said Mom.

We bolted through the kitchen, into the hazy green softness of the yard. Sure enough, one pigeon after another stuck its dull gray head from beneath the eave, hopped along the ridgepole and flapped away. Delighted with this, my father hurried over to the ladder and climbed toward the roof with the bale of chicken wire slung over his back. I clambered up after him with the tack hammer.

When he reached the top of the ladder, my father took a pair of pliers from his belt and began clipping a large sheet of wire from the bale. The pigeons were still emerging from the dark jagged hole above us and my father choked on the stench that was emanating from beneath the roof. "Dirty, stinkin' things," he said.

At the far end of Tauvernier Street, I saw the door of the old Axelrod place open up and Mr. Thorndike marched outside, followed by Peter, Marybeth and Lulu. Mr. Thorndike was carrying a rifle and Peter had an old steel helmet on his head and Marybeth was lugging their picnic basket and Lulu wore the helmet liner. My father had such a helmet and liner in the attic; every G. I. who went to Korea owned one.

The Thorndikes made a neat military turn onto our walkway. Dad was fussing with the wire, tangling it over the points of the ladder and scratching himself with the cut edges.

"Sergeant," said Mr. Thorndike.

Dad looked down through the apertures in the ladder. Removing the rifle from his left shoulder, Mr. Thorndike executed a "port arms," and deposited it on his right shoulder.

"Go 'head down, Joe," said my father, as two more pigeons emerged from the hole.

My father tossed the bale of wire onto the lawn and threw the pliers down after it. He chased me to the ground and laughed at the sight of the white-haired Thorndike children, standing at attention and lined up for review. Mr. Thorndike handed the rifle to Peter and groped inside the basket Lulu was carrying and removed two sweating cans of beer and gave one of them to my father.

"Hair of the dog," said Mr. Thorndike, his eyes encircled by dark rings and sunken into the hollows of his face.

"Don't let the wife see," Dad said, turning his back to the house.

My father touched his beer can against Mr. Thorndike's and while they drank, Peter showed me the rifle. It was a Daisy .22 with a long black barrel and a sight mounted on top. "I shot an alligator with it once," said Peter. "But it didn't die."

In the weeks since the Thorndikes had moved in, Peter and I played catch in the street and rode our bicycles to the Axelrod mill to throw rocks at those few windows that still had glass in them. One rainy afternoon we all gathered in the Thorndike living room for the Saturday matinee starring James Cagney, about a family of entertainers. When it was over Mr. Thorndike and Lulu tap-danced on the marble floor, singing "Yankee Doodle Dandy" while the rest of us howled like a bunch of lunatics. My father stayed at the Thorndikes' pretty late that night, and the next morning he overslept and didn't arrive at the bakery until six AM. It was the first time in twelve years that the bakery hadn't opened on time.

Up in our attic, Trini Lopez played his guitar and sang and a raft of pigeons ululated and cooed in protest. They beat their wings against the eave and one became trapped in the wire that has half-stapled to the roof. "Peter," said Mr. Thorndike. "Give me the gun."

"You can't be serious," said my father.

"Serious as a heart attack," said Mr. Thorndike.

Dad had been a cook in the Army and never got farther than a base in Munich. Mr. Thorndike was a Navy carrier pilot who was shot down twice and decorated for bravery.

Mr. Thorndike set his empty beer can in the Nazarian's driveway and raised the rifle to his shoulder and sighted along the barrel. Just then a pigeon crawled out of the hole and Mr. Thorndike whispered to himself, "Steady," and squeezed the trigger. Going *ffffffftttt* through the air, the bullet sped toward the eave and the pigeon fell to the ground, dead.

"Bingo," said Mr. Thorndike.

He shot three more in succession and then my father had a go at them. His first attempt missed, and then he killed a large gray pigeon with a crimson ring around its neck. It fell in the gutter and was so big we called a cease-fire and I poked it with a stick just as the ring began to fade and its eyes glazed over.

They killed nine birds and drank three Ballantines apiece before the last record dropped onto the turntable in the attic. Dad was instructing me on how to use the rifle when my mother stomped onto the porch, holding her swollen belly.

"Mae, honey, I'm sorry," my father began. "It's just such a damned nuisance to—"

My mother leaned against the railing. "My water broke," she said in a quavering voice.

Taking advantage of the respite in firing, a pigeon sneaked from the hole and flew across the yard. Dad spotted the bird and in a single, unhurried movement raised the rifle to his shoulder and killed it with one shot. The pigeon landed on Tauvernier Street and the Nazarian's cat ran out to look at it.

"That was a fine piece of shooting, Jim," Mr. Thorndike said

.

*

Mr. Thorndike drove my mother and father to the hospital. It began to grow dark and Peter and I walked back to his house and found a couple of old sleeping bags and went outside to the space capsule. That day we had ridden our bikes to Lawlor's for a horde of atomic fireballs, tiny wax bottles of flavored syrup, tar babies and sticks of red and green licorice. Gorging ourselves now on the candy we watched Tango the cat go inside the barn to hunt for mice. The air was mild and sweet with the lilacs blooming along the fence and after half an hour Marybeth and Lulu crept out of the house in their nightgowns and went giggling into the loft above us.

Their heads poked out of the open bay and Marybeth said "Hi, Joe" and they collapsed with laughter.

Peter snorted with disgust. "A couple of comedians."

A while later we went around the barn and climbed the trellis to the back window. Slowly we raised our eyes above the sill and saw the two girls lying flat on their stomachs peering down at the yard through the bay door. I motioned to Peter that we should climb in and scare them. He nodded and we muscled up and over the sill and began crawling toward the girls.

I headed straight for Marybeth. As we drew closer Peter grinned at me and I could hear the back door to the house swing open at the instant we pounced on the girls. They screamed.

I straddled Marybeth's slim behind and tickled her while she squirmed beneath my weight. Down in the driveway Mrs. Thorndike, holding little George, looked up at us and said, "Get out of there, you kids," and in those hysterical seconds Marybeth grabbed my hand and squeezed it and the two of us laughed in unison.

Mrs. Thorndike ordered the girls into the house. She wore a denim shirt tied at the midriff and smelled of talc and her hair was pinned up in the back, revealing her long slender neck. "You boys can stay in the yard until your father comes home," she said to Peter when we had climbed down from the loft.

After his mother went inside, Peter and I took large pieces of gravel from the driveway and threw them over the barn. Some pieces must have weighed half a pound and we watched them rise until they hovered for an instant against the sky, and then began their descent. All things that flew intrigued us in those days. I speculated that gravity was a humongous magnet beneath the earth's crust but Peter said that couldn't be, as most things weren't made of metal but everything fell back.

The wind was blowing through the treetops and we crawled into the space capsule and a while later fell asleep, rocked on a sea of gravel. Sometime afterward, a rush of light streamed into the yard, illuminating the rivets inside the capsule and rolling a huge weight over the driveway. The old woody stopped a short distance away, the headlights were extinguished, and Mr. Thorndike got out clutching several white bags from Kelly's Hamburgers.

"Hungry, boys?" he asked.

Mr. Thorndike produced six hamburgers wrapped in waxed paper and two large envelopes containing French fries. The wind died down and we leaned against the car and squirted ketchup and sprinkled salt from little packages and had a feast. There were two tall paper cups filled with Coca-Cola and Mr. Thorndike drank something else from a ceramic mug. He said that my parents were still at the hospital, waiting.

"Let me propose a toast," said Mr. Thorndike. "To all the babies born in the world tonight, and all their big brothers and sisters, and all their crazy neighbors. To the health of said babies, the wealth of their brothers and sisters, and the fortitude of their neighbors' livers."

"Dad, can we stay out here tonight?" asked Peter.

"Sure," said Mr. Thorndike, his hair unkempt in the darkness. "Why not?"

When he had lurched against the car and gone inside, I crawled back into my sleeping bag. "Your old man is the greatest," I said.

Peter crumpled the leftover hamburger papers and tossed the spiky ball onto the gravel. "Boola, boola," he said.

In the morning I walked down Tauvernier Street with the sun halfway up and motes of pollen descending from the trees. My father was on a ladder against the house, scraping the clapboards with a wire brush. He waved at me when I came up, saying, "Your baby sister's name is Jocelyn."

It had been a rough delivery and my mother was going to be in the hospital for a while. My Dad's plan was to scrape the house in one day, prime and paint the trim the next, and finish the entire job before Mom came home. I was instructed to change my clothes, have something to eat and report back in five minutes. The enormity of the task weighed upon me as I plodded up the stairs; my father had been busy since dawn and only a few square feet of clapboard had been scraped of old paint. Here in the first days of summer I would be chained to this peeling wreck of a house with an old putty knife and my father's stubbornness, while other kids played in the street and rode past on their bicycles.

My only hope was that Dad would leave for work but after I got started, chipping at the first row of clapboards, he said that Mr. Titone had opened up the bakery and would handle things for the day.

"Why don't you just hire somebody?" I asked, jabbing the putty knife at a bubble of old yellow paint. Immediately I regretted saying it.

On the ladder above me Dad kept working in silence for a minute or so, the paint chips falling to the ground. "In life, you'll have to do a lot of things that you don't want to do," he said.

We worked all through the morning, and didn't stop for lunch until one o'clock. I had a ham sandwich and an apple and glass of milk, all smelling of paint chips, and then went back out. After seven hours my father and I had only managed to scrape one irregular section on the north side of the house. A van pulled into the yard sometime after five o'clock and delivered several gallons of primer and red paint, along with some wooden mixing sticks and one fine, new horsehair brush. Dad said that the red paint would cover the yellow and make the job easier.

A while later Mr. Titone drove up in the truck and delivered the keys to the bakery. He was a thin, denture-wearing fellow with a brush cut, dressed in stained whites and trailing the pleasant odor of bread. My father gave him a cigar wrapped in cellophane that said "It's a girl!" and he and Mr. Titone stood in the driveway smoking.

"How's the missus?" asked Mr. Titone.

"Tired," Dad said. "It wasn't easy."

Mr. Titone gazed up at the scaly bulk of our house. "Be a shame if it was," he said.

My father and I scraped until dark and left the ladder against the porch and went into the darkened house. We set up trays in the living room and ate TV dinners and watched in silence as Roger Mudd announced the bombing in Cambodia. A while later I climbed into bed, thinking of the unfinished work that surrounded me, not even a quarter done. Before drifting off I heard an insistent noise and realized that Dad was out there, rubbing the house with his wire brush until well after the neighbors had gone to sleep.

The next day my father left at four AM for the bakery and there was a note on the kitchen table saying that I should keep scraping the front of the house. I took my time making rye toast and boiling an egg, sweeping the crumbs into the sink and washing my glass and plate with gallons of hot water. Finally I went outside. A peewee called from the treetops and I could hear the Nazarian's radio playing "That's Amore."

Dad must have worked most of the night because two sides of the house were done and he had primed all the window sashes. I went around to the front and began scraping the bottom row of clapboards. After a while Peter Thorndike came up on his bicycle and watched me from the street.

"Boola, boola," he said.

I looked over at him, waved the brush and returned to my work. Peter straddled the thin blue frame of the bicycle, gripping the handlebars. "Dad's taking us to the beach," he said. "You wanna go?"

"Can't."

Peter watched for another couple of minutes before he climbed into the saddle and rolled away. After a few minutes Mr. Nazarian came out of the house with the *Herald-Traveler* under his arm. The retired pharmacist unlocked the door of his Buick and started the engine and sat behind the wheel reading his paper. He had brown skin and wore a narrow-lapeled suit and a little alpine hat that rode the crown of his head. Just then Tango the cat shot through our yard, leaped onto the Buick and ran across the hood. Mr. Nazarian didn't even look up.

The Nazarians had a nineteen-year-old son named Aram who had joined the Marines right after high school. He was killed a few months later at a place called Hué when a stray bomb from an American B-52 landed in the wrong spot. Mr. and Mrs. Nazarian were quiet people to begin with, and now they were like ghosts. A man came twice a month to cut their grass and the market delivered a box of groceries to their house every Friday. Once in a while my dad took over a loaf of bread and if Mr. Nazarian was at home, he would come out to the screen door and they'd make small talk for a while. Their son had been dead for a year.

The voice of Dean Martin was cut off mid-warble and Mrs. Nazarian emerged from the house in a clatter of high heels, wearing a round straw hat with plastic roses attached to the brim and clutching an oversize pocketbook. She climbed in beside her husband and Mr. Nazarian folded up his newspaper, deposited it in the backseat and puttered away without saying a word.

A while later the Thorndikes drove past, their car filled with inner tubes, plastic pails and shovels, and an inflated rubber chair bent double by the roof. Mr. Thorndike wore a green eyeshade pulled low on his forehead and Mrs. Thorndike, her shoulders bare and freck-led, waved baby George's hand as they went by. The woody glided to the corner like a hearse and I saw Marybeth in the rear-facing seat, fiddling with a diving mask and looking at me.

For a long time after they'd gone I stood with my cheek pressed against the hot clapboard, scouring the same little place over and over and breathing in the scent of the exposed cedar. Leaning there, I pictured various items in the attitudes that I'd left them: a wadded up towel on the bathroom floor; my baseball glove lying ajar on the sofa, the ball having rolled onto the carpet; the glass and dish from break-fast standing in the rack by the sink, and all of it ticked over by the clock. At school I had learned that the men who painted the Golden Gate Bridge began at one end and by the time they were finished two years later, had to go back to the beginning and start all over again. Every so often, one of the men would go insane and jump off.

I cursed the great scabby edifice that rose before me, and my father and mother and the squalling, red-faced infant they would be bring-ing home. Just for a moment I hated the unvarnished, oven-smelling bakery that I soon would be expected to work in, and imagined what it would be like if my own father owned a yachting cap and golf clubs and wanted to spend his afternoons at the beach.

The day stretched ahead with monumental indifference, the heat and silence of our yard an endless purgatory. As luck would have it, I was taking a rest in the cool sticky shade of our pine tree when Dad's truck rolled up to the house. He climbed out, squat and beetle-browed in the flaring light of the yard, hands on his hips, surveying what I had done: three clapboards in five hours. I expected him to yell at me but my father just picked up the wire brush and started scrubbing the next clapboard, the chips falling fast, and told me to go inside and make us a couple of sandwiches.

It was cool inside the kitchen, the hum from the refrigerator cast-ing an Egyptian lull over the premises. I stood before its open door, the slab of olive loaf wrapped up in butcher paper and heavy in my palm. Bread, mustard, cheese and butter piled up on the sideboard and I arranged the sandwiches with careful precision and took them outside. Already my father had scoured two additional clapboards and started on a third. He had the ladder up against the house and a fresh gallon of primer was opened on the lawn.

I handed my Dad one of the sandwiches and he folded it in half and began eating without a hitch in his work. "Take the putty knife and go around back," he said.

Retreating into the shade, I climbed onto the bulkhead and ate my sandwich, chewing like a metronome. The sun had baked the neighborhood into reverie and not so much as an insect droned over the yard. When I was through eating, I unraveled the garden hose and turned on the spigot. Hot water gushed out for several seconds and I held the nozzle away, spattering the pavement. Then I took a long cold drink and poured the water over my neck, trickles running down inside my shirt and into my Chuck Taylors. Dad yelled something and I cranked the valve shut and got busy with the scraping.

My father worked at a pace that seemed manageable enough and for a while I could keep up with him. He just never slacked off or took a rest and while I always found some diversion—a trip to the bathroom or the garden hose for a drink—he just went on and on, scraping and chipping and scouring until his arm should have fallen off.

Around five o'clock Dad announced that he was going up to the hospital for a visit. Not bothering to enter the house, he disconnected the hose and washed his face and hairy arms right there in the back-yard, instructed me to finish the section above the bulkhead that I had been working on, and then walked across the lawn, stepped into the bakery truck and rumbled away. Immediately I went inside, took a quart of peach ice cream from the freezer, and sat on the linoleum and ate some of it. Feeling guilty and bloated, I returned to the yard and just as I took up the putty knife the Thorndikes drove over the crest of the hill, their sunburned faces turned toward me, clamoring and waving and honking the horn.

Mr. Thorndike beached the woody on the shoulder of the road and the whole family piled out: Lulu in a pair of water wings; Peter wearing a brand new sailor's cap; little George toddling forward while Mrs. Thorndike held his arms, beaming at his new trick. Her breasts, like two reddened puffs of dough, hung from her top and swung along with George's rhythm.

"Huzzah," Mr. Thorndike said, taking in the house. "The lad who can accomplish all this in a day will end up being president."

Mrs. Thorndike crinkled up the lovely planes of her face and smiled. "You're doing a nice job," she said.

"My father did most of it," I said, nudging a pebble with my shoe.

"Where is the old man?" asked Mr. Thorndike, gazing about the yard. "Doesn't he know there are child labor laws in this state?" He was laughing, his nose pink with sunburn and flecks of mica glistening on his arms. The entire Thorndike clan was tousled and salty, wrapped up in their beach jackets and running around the yard barefooted. Lulu stepped on the nubby edge of a pinecone and came yelping into her father's arms.

"Dad should be back any minute," I said. "We're gonna try to paint the whole house before Mum and the baby come home."

"If you'll give me time to fetch my painter's cap, I'll be happy to join you," Mr. Thorndike said.

Peter came running up. "Can I help, too?" he asked.

"Sure," said Mr. Thorndike.

Mrs. Thorndike had the baby at her shoulder. "He's getting hungry again," she said.

"Homeward," said Mr. Thorndike, shooing his family toward the car. "Would you like to come along, Joe? We're having pepper steaks."

"I better stay here, thanks."

"Tell your father the cavalry is coming," said Mr. Thorndike.

They filled the woody and drove off and I began scouring again with renewed energy. Dad came home and said we could use the help, since my mother and sister were being released around noon the following day.

Positioning myself with a view of the street, I kept an eye open for the Thorndikes. Any minute I expected to see father and son trooping along the sidewalk in their old clothes and imagined the doubling of our present speed as well as the company of my best friend and the effervescent Mr. Thorndike. Even my father brightened under the possibilities, whistling to himself as he finished the west end of the house and primed the bulkhead.

Dusk crept over the neighborhood. My father joined me on the last section and we worked there in the twilight without speaking to one another. His whistling died away and I stopped looking toward the old Axelrod place and got on with my work. The Thorndikes weren't coming.

Sometime after dark we finished scraping the house and my father drove the bakery truck over the lawn, training the headlights onto that last wall so he could primer the window sashes and bulkhead. When that was accomplished, he switched off the lights, plunging the yard into darkness, and we went inside the house to clean up. Dinner was a can of spaghetti heated on the stove, and I was so exhausted I couldn't even watch television. On the way to bed, my father emitted a loud belch and neither of us laughed. He turned on the light in the baby's room and brought in a droplight and spread newspapers over the floor and began working. I shut the door to my room and stuffed a towel into the crack and went to sleep.

In the morning the smell of new paint filled my room and I got up, blinking and rubbing my eyes, and staggered down the hall. In the baby's room my father was applying a second coat of white paint and the sun reflected brilliantly from the walls. By the time I had washed up and flushed the toilet, Dad was in the back yard, mixing his first gallon of red paint.

Chips of the old paint speckled the gutters and the smooth, raw clapboards shined in the early sunlight. While I ate a chocolate doughnut, my father ascended the ladder and great sections of the house began disappearing under the red paint. I was allowed to open another gallon and, wiping the chocolate dust on my trousers, I pried open the can and stirred the oily red soup until the two parts were blended together. Dad instructed me to apply the paint in even strokes with the grain of the wood and to use the very tip of the bristles to first seal the edge of the clapboard. My hand shook in excitement and I had to resist the urge to slap on the paint to make it go faster. House painting, my father said, was an art.

We covered the north wall in just over an hour. Eight windows broke up the expanse of the west side, requiring a great deal of brush-work around the sashes. My father cut in the most difficult trim while I started on the open spaces but still our work slowed down. Dots of red paint covered my father's overalls and the crushed yellow dust of our scraping powdered his old shoes. He moved from window to window gripping the paint can by its handle, his jaw pressed together and the sun reflecting from the disks of his eyeglasses. Over the next thirty minutes the only thing he said was to skim the excess paint from my brush on the edge of the can, otherwise I'd get blotches.

As noon approached, two sides of the house were completed and we had started on the third when the telephone began to ring. Its steady purring could be heard through the wall and Dad finished his brush stroke without hurrying and wiped his hands on a rag and went inside to answer it. A few minutes later he returned wearing an old lumberjack's shirt over his painting clothes and he smiled at me and said, "They're ready to come home."

I rested my brush on the upturned lid of the can. "What about the surprise?" I asked.

"Once your mother and sister are home, we'll come out and finish," Dad said.

"That's not the same thing, is it?"

My father smiled and shook his head. "No," he said. "But it's pretty good."

Soon after my father had driven away Mr. Thorndike appeared in the yard carrying a mop handle and three cans of Ballantine dangling from their plastic web. "How's it going?" he asked.

From my perch on the ladder I could make out the bald spot in the center of Mr. Thorndike's head. "My dad went to pick up Mom and the baby. They should be back in an hour."

"And when they arrive, you'll be the hero," said Mr. Thorndike. His yachting cap stuck out of his back pocket and there was a carpenter's pencil behind his ear and a tape measure clipped to his belt.

Even the two of us could not finish the job in an hour. But Mr. Thorndike was a very smart fellow and I was curious to see what could be done, given the circumstances.

Carrying the ladder, we moved around to the last unpainted façade of the house. The east wall, which faced Sunrise Ave., contained only the small frosted window of the bathroom and was otherwise empty, scraped clean. Mr. Thorndike took a long drink from his beer and raised the ladder to the top right-hand corner of the wall, ordered me to stand at the foot, and climbed to the uppermost rung and produced the tape measure. Fixing the tab just beneath the eave, he let the metal cylinder drop down to me, unreeling the tape as it came.

"Bring it right to the ground," said Mr. Thorndike.

I called up that it was thirty feet and, making an x with his pencil, Mr. Thorndike descended a few rungs, left another tally halfway down, and a final mark near the base of the wall. Sending me inside for a roll of tape, he continued with his notations and by the time I had searched the cellar and attic and everywhere in between, I returned to the yard and found the ladder on the opposite end of the house and Mr. Thorndike making the last of several dozen marks.

I sat down on the stubble of our lawn, engrossed. Using an old shoelace retrieved from the gutter and strips of tape from the roll my Dad had used to mask off the windowsills, Mr. Thorndike fastened the horsehair brush to the mop handle and dipped the bristles into a gallon of red paint. He climbed the ladder halfway and, extending the mop, painted a stripe from his uppermost mark to one a few feet below it. Then he came down, drained a good portion of his beer, and went back up with the gallon of paint and a hook that fixed it to the ladder.

"What are you doing?" I asked.

Mr. Thorndike used his contraption to describe a large red "W" on the side of our house. "Being creative," he said.

On the fourth letter, which was a "C," Mr. Thorndike misjudged the curve and had to wipe it off with his handkerchief, leaving a faint smear. "Christ on a bicycle," he said. Then he drank from the can of Ballantine he had wedged in his pocket and threw the crumpled tin into the yard.

Twenty minutes later, spattered by paint and with three beer cans lying in the yard, Mr. Thorndike climbed down from the ladder and stooped to wipe his hands on a rag. "*Voila,*" he said. "*C'est le fait accompli.*"

Just then my father drove up in the truck. Emerging from the open bay, he gaped at the house with a mixture of pride and chagrin on his face. There in gigantic red letters Mr. Thorndike had written:

Welcome Home
Mama & Baby

Hugging a tiny bundle to her chest, my mother walked around the truck and joined my father in staring at the house. "My, my," she said. "You boys have been busy."

She stood on the crushed cinders of our driveway, looking at the house like it was the Eighth Wonder of the World. Mr. Thorndike gathered up his beer cans and we all converged on the lawn. My mother peeled back the upper folds of the blanket covering my sister, a tiny, black-haired thing, her little fists squirming at her throat.

"See your new house?" asked Mom, rubbing Jocelyn's cheek with her finger. "Your big, new, red house."

Suddenly Mr. Nazarian appeared with his Kodak and said he was going to take a picture. "What a baby," he said. "What a paint job."

He marched us to the center of the yard: my Mom and sister in front, Dad beside them, me kneeling in the grass, and Mr. Thorndike to one side, his cap at a jaunty angle. Just as we stiffened to be shot, Mr. Nazarian waved his arm, moving the entire tableau several feet to a new location near the edge of our property.

He looked through the viewfinder, satisfied that the painted message was visible behind us. We smiled until our cheeks hurt and finally Mr. Nazarian clicked the shutter. "There," he said. "For posterity."

*

Over the next three days Mom stayed in bed most of the time, feeding the baby and watching her sleep. I heard vague rumblings very early as Dad went off to work and a while later it was my job to go down to the kitchen and prepare my mother's breakfast and carry it up to her. Jocelyn slept in a shallow, open-faced crib that had once been mine and that my father had painted when he painted the baby's room. But one day, as I crept upstairs, she was propped up in my mother's bed, her hair a single tuft of shiny black fuzz, eyes opened and staring at a point somewhere beyond me. Mother smoothed the little silk ribbon on the baby's jumper and motioned for me to sit in the chair beside the bed.

"Put your arms like this," said Mom, forming a cradle.

My mother rolled over; the skin on her back impressed with the rumpled sheets, and lifted the baby with a hand beneath her head and her padded bottom. Crouching on one hip, mother placed Jocelyn into the web of my forearms.

"Don't worry," Mom said. "She's not going to jump out."

The baby weighed next to nothing. But trills of air ran from her nostrils and when I put my thumb in the baby's hand, she gripped it with her thin red fingers. It was still very early and the sun angled in, shining on the headboard of the bed. Suddenly I was struck by the responsibility of having a sister, and began to hand her back. "Here," I said.

"You're doing fine," mother said. "Talk to her."

"What should I say?"

My mother laughed. "Whatever you like."

Gazing down at Jocelyn I cleared my throat. "I helped paint the house when you were in the hospital."

"Is that all?" Mom asked.

I deposited the baby in my mother's arms. "I like to play baseball and to listen to music," I said, as lines of perspiration ran down my back.

After his twelve-hour shifts at the bakery Dad finished painting the house, hung new yellow awnings over the windows, and erected a flagpole on the corner of our lot. After work on Saturday afternoon he dragged three old snow tires up through the bulkhead and using a utility knife, split them into tulip shapes, double-coated them with leftover white paint, and installed them beside the house as flower planters. On Sunday, Mom and Jocelyn came outside for the first time in a week and toured these improvements while my father doted alongside.

"I hardly recognize the place," mother said, looking pale in the sunlight.

"We're just getting started," Dad said, naming the other chores that he had planned. He bent to clear the garden hose from our path, the folds slithering through the newly mown grass. He pointed ahead at the discarded pieces of snow tire. "Pick those up," he said to me.

I ran ahead and collected the warm, heavy strips of rubber and threw them in the ash can behind our garage. Tauvernier Street was bowered over with trees, and a chorus of birdsongs filled the air. I hadn't been anyplace since school had let out and was itching to jump on my bike and go fishing in the Spicket or off to play ball somewhere. My mother noticed me staring in the direction of the old Axelrod place and nudged my dad's arm.

"Why don't you let him go?" Mom said.

Dad glanced around the yard. "There's still a lot of work to do," he said.

But Mom stood there looking into my father's eyes and finally he laughed and shook his head. "All right," he said. "Go."

I sprinted for my bike and rode away without looking back. Seconds later I was crunching over the gravel in the Thorndike's driveway and calling for Peter to come out. He exploded through the back door carrying his baseball glove and Mr. Thorndike followed him with the bat over his shoulder, tossing a new white baseball into the air.

"Howsabout I hit a few fungoes?" asked Mr. Thorndike.

I yanked my glove from the handlebars, stuck it on my left hand and pounded my fist into the greasy leather pocket. "You bet."

Amid the drone of lawn mowers, we spread ourselves down the middle of Tauvernier Street. Peter used the sewer cap for a pitcher's mound, I crouched on the asphalt forty feet away, and Mr. Thorndike took several swings with the bat. His wrists were loose and easy, and the bat windmilled through the air in a smooth, easy blur. Mr. Thorndike flipped the bat around and struck the asphalt three times with the handle, then tossed it up, grabbed the thin end and cocked the bat over his shoulder like he meant to smash the ball into next week.

"Let's see what you got," Mr. Thorndike said.

I threw the ball to Peter and he went into his Jim Kaat windup. They were both lefties and had a big leg kick. Peter coiled up, his right foot in the air, and thrusting his right arm and leg forward at the same time, unfolded himself and snapped off a beautiful fastball that streaked toward me and went into my glove with a pop.

Still looking at Peter, Mr. Thorndike raised his left hand and called "Time." He winked at me and said, "Be right back" and then strode over the driveway and into the house. I threw the ball back to Peter and he raised his glove and caught it and we stood there for a minute looking at each other.

The door swung open and Mr. Thorndike returned wearing an old maroon baseball cap with a faded "Y" on the front and carrying a drink in his hand. "Needed my hat," he said. He took a pull on the highball, the ice making a little music in the glass, and when it was empty he set the glass on the curbstone and took up the bat again.

"Show me," he said.

I pounded my fist into the glove and Peter went into his motion. Again the ball cut through the heavy, sweet-smelling air and Mr. Thorndike, motionless until the last instant, flashed at the pitch with his hands, bringing the head of the bat around with tremendous speed. The noise it made was like splitting a log and the ball jumped on the line toward the Nazarian's house and passed straight through their front window, tinkling the glass. All at once we saw the curtain go *poof*, and Mr. Nazarian leaped off the couch while the ball chased him around his living room.

"Holy shit," I said.

Peter and I dashed from the street into the Panebianco's yard. The two of us went up and over the chainlink fence, collapsing it in a great metallic spasm, as the fence sprang back and threw us into the weeds on the other side.

For an instant Mr. Thorndike remained in the middle of Tauvernier Street admiring his hit and then he tossed the bat aside and ran after us. As it pinwheeled around, the skinny end of the bat struck the highball glass, throwing the ice cubes onto the pavement where they shone like diamonds.

*

As the days grew longer and my father began opening the bakery an hour later and closing it earlier, he was around the house more often and my chores grew in number. We scraped and painted the garage to match the house, built flower boxes for all the windows and replaced or repaired most of the screens. While the baby watched from a tiny swinging chair, my mother filled the window boxes with soil and planted geraniums and Dad and I carried them outside and fixed them to the house. Every day I was expected to rake out the cinders in the driveway and mow the lawn once a week. Still, I got away to the Thorndikes as much as possible and by mid-July I was going in the back door without knocking and helping myself to whatever goodies Mrs. Thorndike had made.

In the three months since the Thorndikes had moved in, they had stripped and burned most of the shutters from the lower part of the house, and all of their winter clothes and a good number of household items were still boxed and baled and stacked against the wall in the foyer. The grand staircase was littered with terrycloth beach jackets and sneakers and hula hoops, and stray roller skates and the occasional empty beer can had found their way into various nooks and crannies and onto the mantelpiece. In general, the old Axelrod place looked like it had been invaded by a troupe of circus acrobats, with their wooden-sided station wagon and bright clothes and dented space capsule occupying a good part of the driveway.

Lulu could do this trick with her left eye. She had been born without a certain muscle and had learned to control the eye through the supreme effort of other tiny muscles holding it in place. But if she wanted to, Lulu could relax the eyeball and the pupil would fall against her nose with the weight of a marble dropping into a slot. The first time she did it in my presence I said "fucking A" and the other children, incited by this, ran about the driveway screaming.

With baby George against her chest, Mrs. Thorndike descended into this bedlam and grabbed Peter and Marybeth by the wrists. "Lulu showed Joe her eye," said Marybeth.

"Stop that," Mrs. Thorndike said.

"I can't," said Lulu, whose eye would not uncross. Her arms and legs were tanned very dark and her good eye shone like a pilot light. She sat in the dirt, crying.

Mrs. Thorndike peeled back Lulu's eyelid and made a quick study of the tendrils adhering to her eyeball. "We're going to the hospital," she said. "Peter, go tell your father."

Peter ran into the house and Mrs. Thorndike helped Lulu into the front seat and started up the car. "I can't take you, Joe," she said.

"That's all right. I have to go, anyway."

Peter came back outside and jerked open the door and got into the backseat. "Dad's staying," he said. Mr. Thorndike had been scarce lately and my father had mentioned at dinner the night before that the two hadn't spoken in over a week.

With Lulu pressing both hands to her eye, they backed out of the driveway, swung in an arc, and roared off down Tauvernier Street. My baseball glove was in the house and kicking a stone so hard it skimmed along the gravel, I hauled open the screen door and entered the suddenly quiet, suddenly gloomy old mansion. On the sideboard was a loaf of bread, half out of its sleeve and toppled over, one slice set aside and covered with peanut butter. The jar was open and the knife lay smeared on the counter and beside it was a container of grape jelly with the lid still on.

My baseball glove was lying on the stairs but for some reason I went right past it and kept going. In the silence of the house I could hear a noise coming from somewhere and headed for the second floor. When I reached the landing, the tiny noise distinguished itself, although I couldn't quite tell what it was or where it was coming from.

Creeping along the hallway I passed the girls' room, with their unmade beds and stuffed pandas and monkeys askew on the window-sills. The bathroom door was ajar and there were large puddles spread over the tiles. Farther along was another room that Mr. Thorndike used for a study and that door was halfway open and the ticking sound, whatever it was, came from there. The blinds were drawn inside the room and small amounts of light seeped between the bands. Against the wall a television was playing with the volume off. Images of the war appeared on screen: men in helmets and fatigues with their sleeves rolled up, helicopters rising from stands of elephant grass, and fighter jets zooming nose down across the delta.

Mr. Thorndike was in a rocking chair against the wall. The air was clammy and an odor like stale bread and mothballs filled the dank, enclosed space. The sound echoing throughout the house was the squeaky chair, as Mr. Thorndike held his guts and rocked back and forth. He was wrapped in a sheet he had pulled from the day bed when he heard me coming upstairs. On the table beside him was a bottle of Epsom salts and a ceramic pitcher. Mr. Thorndike drew a glass up from the floor, poured water into it, and spooned in a large dose of the salts.

He drank half of it and replaced the glass on the floor "*Salud, mon frère*," he said. The slatted blinds cast shadows over the room, masking the expression on Mr. Thorndike's face.

My heart pounded like a machine gun. "Are you all right, Mr. Thorndike?" I asked.

"Sometimes the cure is worse than the disease," he said. "But still, the cure must be taken."

Whatever was racing through his bowels suddenly gripped him and he threw off the sheet and hurried to retrieve a bucket that was hidden behind his chair. Mr. Thorndike was wearing only his under-pants. "You better go," he said.

Backing up, I collided with the edgewise door and then dodged into the hallway and ran down the stairs.

*

August was a slow month at the bakery and with those extra hours Dad completed all the major improvements to our house and yard: painting, glazing, trimming, mowing and watering his little estate into such eye-pleasing form that passing motorists slowed down to look. Maintenance was ongoing and while I kept up the lawn and driveway my father ripped out the walk to install new flagstones and marked a place in the backyard for a patio. After removing the sod and squaring everything with a carpenter's level, he staked it out and let things settle overnight. The next day he mixed his own concrete, poured out the slab, and impressed the remaining pink and green flagstones into the dense, sticky mass and troweled it off. When he was through, sweating in the oppressive heat, my father smoothed a little triangle in one corner and I was allowed to scratch in the date with a roofing nail.

In the midst of the dog days my father built a picnic table in our garage and then announced his plans to host a barbecue for the neighbors. Mom phoned the Nazarians and Thorndikes and Mr. Titone and early on Sunday morning, when the cement had whitened into a solid tablet, Dad threw open the bulkhead and hauled up our grill, a sack of charcoal, and the rusted, book-shaped tin of lighter fluid. Struggling over the lawn, the two of us carried the picnic table out and placed it in the center of the slab and I dumped the briquettes into the grill pan. They sent up a cloud of black dust and I stood waving my free arm and holding the empty sleeve, which seemed as light as air.

"That's why I let you do it," my father said, chuckling at me.

He donned a pair of gloves, arranged the briquettes into a pyramid and soaked them with the lighter fluid. My Dad handed me a wooden match and I scraped it on the flagstones and then tossed it at the briquettes. There was a small explosion.

"Holy shit," I said, jumping out of the way.

Dad laughed. "Don't let your mother hear you say that."

With his hands on his hips, my father surveyed his new patio, the smooth, planed surface of the picnic table, the mums and asters that had sprung up along the foundation, and then the edifice of the house itself, shiny in the light and patterned with leafy shadows. We had been living on Tauvernier Street for a year and a half, and his labors on that small rectangle of land had been many and unceasing, and now, on a beautiful Sunday morning where the earth seemed to pause for a moment and even the trilling of birds was suspended, my Dad seemed a little embarrassed by it all.

"Well..." he said, working his jaw and then glancing down at his boot tops. "Lots to do."

By the time the air was wavering above the grill and the charcoal had gone white, Mom and I brought out television trays filled with hotdogs and hamburger patties and thick, heavy joints of Italian sausage. In a large bowl chicken parts floated in soy sauce, where they had been marinating all night, and on a separate tray Dad pounded a quartet of T-bone steaks with his wooden mallet and coated them in salt and pepper.

Mr. Titone arrived in the bakery truck, carrying two sacks brimming with dinner rolls, and he and my father inspected the T-bones while sipping on cans of beer. "Those are real heavyweights," Dad said.

"Keep them out of the hands of women and children," said Mr. Titone, who wore a plaid sports shirt, his crewcut stiffened with wax.

When all was made ready, Jocelyn's bassinet was arranged in the lee of our garage and Mom sat beside it, reading *Life* magazine and sunning her legs. "If nobody else shows up, we're going to be eating all day," she said.

Just then Mrs. Thorndike appeared pushing little George in a carriage with a large vat of macaroni salad tucked inside, and behind them came Lulu and Marybeth pulling a toy wagon that contained an enormous watermelon. Peter rode his bicycle alongside, balancing a plate of deviled eggs on the handlebars.

"Martha, I told you not to bring anything," said my mother, rising to greet them.

"It only took five minutes," said Mrs. Thorndike. She wore a sleeveless white blouse and a pair of Navy clamdiggers and her toenails were fire engine red. "Anyway, I needed to use up the eggs," she said, handing over the plastic tub.

Trussed into his apron and holding a two-pronged fork, Dad looked over from the grill. "Where's George?" he asked.

"He's got a terrible headache," said Mrs. Thorndike.

"That's too bad," my father said. Turning to Mr. Titone he said, "Wait 'til you get a load of this guy."

Mrs. Thorndike unfolded a small plastic enclosure for baby George while Peter and I set up a game of lawn darts on the other side of our house. "Don't you girls get near those darts," said Mrs. Thorndike. "I don't want anyone losing an eye."

Dad flattened the pyramid of briquettes and fit the shaft extending from the grill into the center hole and laid on six hotdogs. Their aroma filled the air and Peter and I abandoned our dart game and crowded around. "You boys hungry?" my father asked.

"I could eat a horse," said Peter.

My father winked. "One horse coming right up," he said.

Right after Dad and Mr. Titone went inside for a minute, there was a noise from across the yard and Mr. and Mrs. Nazarian came through their side door. Despite the heat, Mr. Nazarian had on a brown suit made of some nubbly material, along with a white shirt and a tie with a little cedar tree emblazoned on it. His wife was clad in a long floral dress, gathered at the waist and topped by a white crocheted sweater and matching wide-brimmed hat.

Mrs. Nazarian carried a tray filled with squares of baked kibbee and her husband brought over a platter of something called lamajoun. They were floppy discs of bread covered in lamb paste and when the Nazarians had placed these strange dishes on the picnic table and taken seats on the hard narrow bench there, my mother smiled at them. "Thank you for coming," she said, in a louder voice than usual.

Mr. Nazarian removed his tiny alpine hat. "Thank you for inviting us," he said.

The Nazarians sat hip to hip, yoked by the sadness that had not dissipated over a year's time and attended by the unmistakable sour odor that permeated their house, clothing and automobile.

Peter and I were chucking a football and it tipped off my fingers, took a crazy bounce and then waddled over the patio and settled next to Mr. Nazarian's foot. He looked down at the ball like a skunk had curled up beside him and then picked it up, and with an awkward motion of his arm made a little toss. The ball flopped to the ground and rolled between my feet.

"Thanks," I said, and ran off.

My father thrust open the bulkhead and climbed into the yard, followed by Mr. Titone, the back of his pants smeared with dust. Rushing over to the Nazarians, Dad stuck out his hand and asked, "Can I get you something to drink? Would you like a beer, Nabib?"

It was the first time I had ever heard Mr. Nazarian addressed by his first name. "Do you have any tea?" he asked.

"Tea? Hot tea? Sure, I think so," said Dad, laughing like it was funniest thing he'd ever heard. "We have some, don't we, Mae? We must have some tea somewhere."

Mom rose from her chair and peeked into the bassinet at Jocelyn and the Nazarians stood as one. "I'll be right back," my mother said.

"A wonderful drink, tea," said my father, shaking his head at the idea. "Just great."

Drinking his beer, Mr. Titone watched as Peter, Marybeth, Lulu and I loaded our plates with deviled eggs and macaroni salad, while Dad bestowed a crinkly, smoking frankfurter on each of us.

"I wonder what the poor people are doing," I said, walking away.

Peter followed with his overflowing plate and we sat against the bulkhead, holding the food in our laps. "Painting their houses," he said.

Carrying the last of the television trays, Mother emerged from the house with a ceramic teapot and cups, a pitcher of milk and a china bowl filled with sugar cubes wrapped up in light blue paper. She used her elbow to ward off the screen door, descending into the yard with a beatific look on her face.

"Tea," she said.

Mr. and Mrs. Nazarian took only a cube of sugar in theirs, stirring it for a long while, and Mrs. Thorndike joined them. She added a generous amount of milk in order to cool her tea, and nibbled on a wedge of lamajoun. "Mae, try some," said Mrs. Thorndike. "It's fabulous."

The two women sat in the arc of shade cast by the garage and drank tea with the Nazarians, while Dad and Mr. Titone stood in the sunlight, tossing down beers. Four empty cans littered the patio and Lulu stamped the heels of her shoes into two of them and tap-danced over the new walkway.

"I'm one of the seven little Foys," said cock-eyed Lulu, banging her heels against the paving stones.

"That's great, honey," said Mrs. Thorndike, over the racket. "Now stop."

Mr. Thorndike arrived a short while later, clad in old golf clothes and looking tired and unwell. He refused a can of Holihan's and erected a lawn chair beside his wife and sat down opposite the Nazarians with a grim look on his face. His eyes sagged beneath a wrinkled forehead and his gaze was dark and baleful.

Mr. Nazarian, with his brown skin and thick wavy hair, remained in the sunlight, his flesh-toned socks covering up his legs where they extended from the cuffs of his pants. The retired pharmacist hadn't eaten a morsel of our food; he held a strip of lamajoun between his fingers and a teacup in the other hand. Beside him, Mrs. Nazarian sat with her knees pressed together and anklebones touching. She was being eclipsed by the shade creeping out from the garage, and her expression was like that of a person who could not hear or speak.

I got up and leaned over the bassinet to check on my sister, wrapped up in a thin yellow blanket, her hands moving back and forth like she was shaping a ball out of the dense, humid air. Over the past few weeks I had felt myself drawn to Jocelyn, especially as she had grown more active and her personality had begun to emerge. On those bright, sunlit mornings with my father gone to work and mother preparing breakfast, Jocelyn scrutinized the kitchen with a wry look on her face, content that we would do her bidding. These had become my happiest moments, sitting at the kitchen table getting to know my little sister.

"Isn't the weather lovely?" my mother asked. "I can't remember a nicer August."

Mrs. Thorndike held out her arms. "I'm brown as a berry," she said. "And that's just going from the car to the supermarket and the driveway to the house."

We heard the drone of a propeller and then a small plane appeared in the sky, towing a banner that read "Eat at the Clambox." The airplane was headed for Salisbury Beach and the thousands of bathers and picnickers lounging on the coast.

Mr. Titone manned the barbecue, turning the bloody hanks of meat. "That's the life," he said, pointing at the sky with his fork. "Up in the clouds, not a worry in the world."

"Sometimes," said Mr. Thorndike.

"Are you a pilot?" Mr. Titone asked.

"Used to be."

"Whereabouts?"

"George was in the Navy," my dad said. "Flew nineteen missions over Korea."

Mr. Titone was impressed. "That so? I was in the Big One myself. Third Marines: a ground pounder."

Holding the brim of her hat, Mrs. Nazarian watched the single engine plane chug toward the horizon. She studied Mr. Thorndike for a moment and in a quiet voice asked, "Did you drop bombs on people?"

Mr. Thorndike did not seem insulted or even surprised by the question and kept his pale green eyes fixed on Mrs. Nazarian. "That I did, ma'am."

Mrs. Nazarian's back was stiff, like iron rods were holding her erect. As the plane and its banner faded into the distance, the only sound was the meat sputtering on the grill, and then the *chink* of cup on saucer as Mrs. Nazarian lowered her tea. "How can you live with that?" she asked.

His gaze unwavering, Mr. Thorndike said, "Some days are better than others."

"Who wants dessert?" my father asked us.

"Me! Me! Me!" we all shouted.

My father halved and quartered the watermelon and then dissected one of the sections into bright muscular wedges that gleamed in the light and emitted a fruity aroma when we came near. "Come and get it," Dad said, motioning with his butcher knife.

Gnawing the melon to the rinds, we stood on the edge of the patio and made a contest of spitting the seeds onto the lawn. Afterwards, our stomachs full to bursting, the other kids and I went through a dormant period, lolling on the grass while we contemplated the huge blue vault of summer sky. Gradually our energy returned and Peter and his sisters raced alongside the house in a game of tag and I went round the other side and began toying with the lawn darts.

Each dart was made of a heavy steel ingot outfitted with plastic feathers. Pinching the blunt end with your thumb and forefinger, you were meant to toss the dart in an underhanded motion toward a hula-hoop lying on the ground about thirty feet away. Darts touching any part of the hoop scored one point and those landing inside were worth two.

I soon grew bored tossing all six darts by myself and tried to find a new use for them. Our pine tree, stunted by the wind blowing over the house, was about forty feet tall, with thickset branches and a squat, Christmas tree shape. Weighing a dart in my hand, I wondered if I could send it clear over the top of the tree into the lawn on the other side. The laughter and screams of the other children traveled over the house; their game brought them no closer than the front yard.

Something was ticking in my bowels as I threw the first dart high in the air, its feathers whirring. Just as it cleared the treetop Marybeth rounded the corner, followed quickly by Peter, who was stretching out his fingers to tag her. Running hard, Marybeth veered onto the lawn, squealing as she came. Peter lunged forward to keep up, skirting the pine tree, and made a last, desperate grab for his sister.

Just missing Peter's head, the dart passed clear through his foot, sneaker and all, and penetrated deep into the earth. For a moment he was pinned there, wriggling to free himself, and then he fell over and I saw the heavy tapered steel of the dart protruding through the sole of his Chuck Taylors. His face was blanched white and he sat there gaping at his foot like it belonged to someone else. There was very little blood, only a tiny smear on the shaft of the dart.

Marybeth doubled back, stared at Peter's foot, and twisting up her lovely smooth face, screamed blue murder. Lulu tore around the side of the house like a cheetah and joined in, and half a second later all four of us were like a barbershop quartet, bass, alto, soprano, and tenor, our cries as beautiful and organized as music.

"Get it off," Peter said.

"Oh *shit.* I'm sorry. It was an accident. I'm so sorry."

Peter looked at me with absolute terror in his eyes. "Just get it out," he said.

I knelt and tugged on the dart but it wouldn't budge and as Marybeth fell keening to the ground beside me, I leaped up and ran around the edge of the house toward the patio. It was all just a dream, slowed down and hollowed out like we were moving in syrup; all the various noises distorted into something unintelligible except for the scrape of my shoes on the cinder driveway.

My father was already running toward us, his apron flapping. My mother's chair was upset on the lawn and she and Mrs. Thorndike rounded the picnic table like two thoroughbreds, their hair flying behind them, and Mr. Titone came up on the outside, waving his fork at the air like a jockey flailing his whip.

Mr. Nazarian was right beside them, his hat still on his head, knees rising to his belt buckle as he struggled to keep up. Her eyes crazy with fear, Lulu ran across his path and Mr. Nazarian had to make a shifty move to avoid a collision. "Look out," he said, crashing to the turf, and Mr. Titone hurdled him and continued on.

Still seated, Mrs. Nazarian had her teacup poised in mid-air and Mr. Thorndike wore an expression of profound sadness on his face. "Live by the sword, die by the sword," he said.

*

Just before school began I learned that Tauvernier Street was named for a French viscount, Marcel du Lac Moray Tauvernier, who, after reading dispatches from the War Between the States that appeared in a Paris newspaper, traveled to Boston in 1863 and enlisted as a common soldier in the Union Army. His unit was comprised of Massachusetts farmers and mill workers, including several men from our town, and when the viscount was killed at the Second Battle of Bull Run, a letter found among his belongings indicated his wish to be buried alongside his friends.

Late one afternoon I found the grave, a simple plaque hidden by pine trees in Ye Olde Burying Ground, just a short distance from our house. It said TAUVERNIER across the upper margin and included the following epitaph:

> I lie in this ground
> Amidst my comrades
> Proud of their victory
> Despite death;
> For we are all men
> And all mortal.

Acknowledgements

Near the end of his classic account of World War I, *Good-bye to All That*, the British writer and rugby player Robert Graves describes a meeting he had with the venerable poet Thomas Hardy. Over cups of tea in his garden, Hardy remarked that he could "sit down and write novels to a time-table, but that poetry always came by accident."

The way that Hardy felt about his poems is the same way I feel about the stories in this collection. Pretty much without exception they arrived unheralded, and through a variety of means. Some were fashioned out of events that I participated in, or that occurred to me; some were related to me by a friend or a stranger on the next barstool; still others grew out of fleeting moments in my childhood, or after a comment overheard in the street led me to scribble in my notebook. Once or twice, on a lucky occasion, an entire story appeared full blown in my head like it was being transmitted from someplace else. Those days were rare.

I'd like to thank some of the folks who helped me write these stories, and certainly the editors who published them. Joe Taylor of Livingston Press is a fine editor and gentleman and has probably done more for my fiction writing career than anyone else. Certainly, R. T. Smith of *Shenandoah* and Tim Holland of the late, lamented *Crescent Review* are near the top of that list, as well; professional literary men (and women) like these are fast disappearing from the contemporary landscape. We probably won't see editors the like of them again. Special thanks to *Boston* magazine, *Pacific Review*, *West Branch*, *Aethlon*, *Pinehurst Journal*, *Coe Review*, *Kiosk* and *Hawaii Review* for publishing my fiction. Space is dear in those magazines, and I was happy to be included in all of them. Yumi Araki and Kelly Chow of Boston University wrote, produced and directed a short film for this book and I am grateful to these whiz kids for bringing an old man into the multimedia age.

Dr. Richard Davies of Acadia University's English Department and Dr. Alistair Duckworth at the University of Florida provided early advice and encouragement regarding my short fiction. My friend, the late Dr. William Coughlin, U. S. Army veteran and long time writing teacher at the University of Massachusetts Lowell contributed to a pair of stories in this book. Salem New Hampshire police detective Mark Donahue, his wife Maureen, and the hardworking men and women of the Salem PD; Revere Massachusetts police lieutenant John Goodwin, United States Marine Corps Lt. Colonel Ron Martin (retired), USMC Second Lieutenant John Hearin (USMC Reserves, also retired), rugby teammates Conrad Merry, J. David Civil, Carlos Ballbe, and Chris "Stinky" Hynes; childhood friends Bob and Bill Corey, Dash Pippin, Sonny D'Agata, Peter Endyke, Mike Nahill, Dave Frasca, Rick Angus, Steve Bedrosian, John Kiessling, Gary Ruffen, Glenn Gallant, and Donald Kassilke; my son Liam and nieces and nephews Matt, Katie, Owen, Reese, Shane, Nick and Michaela; Father Paul O'Brien and Father Paul McManus of St. Patrick's church in Lawrence, Mass.; writers Paul Marion, David Robinson, Peggy Rambach, and Matt Miller; amiable gym rats Joe Ippolito, Jay Guzaj, Steve Fisichelli, Lisa Rosenberg, Chris Sideri, Chris and Tanya Pierce, Sue Viscosi, Keira Lyons, and Jason and Stephanie Massa, all helped me with this book. Of course, I wouldn't have this point of view if not for my siblings Jodie, Jill, Jamie and Patrick; their spouses, Deanna "G", Sparky and Berries, and my late parents, Jim and Lois. As Thomas Hardy said to Robert Graves, "I have usually found that what my mother said was right."

Jay Atkinson is a novelist, short story writer, essayist, critic, investigative journalist, and itinerant amateur athlete from Methuen, Mass. He is the author of two novels, a story collection, and three narrative nonfiction books. Atkinson's latest book is PARADISE ROAD: JACK KEROUAC'S LOST HIGHWAY AND MY SEARCH FOR AMERICA (John Wiley & Sons, 2010) His book, ICE TIME, was a *Publisher's Weekly* notable book of the year in 2001, and LEGENDS OF WINTER HILL was on the *Boston Globe* bestseller list for 7 straight weeks in 2005. A former two-sport college athlete, Atkinson has competed in rugby for three decades and continues to play in exotic locales with the Vandals Rugby Club out of Los Angeles.